*Women, Work, and Sexual Politics
in Eighteenth-Century England*

Women, Work, and Sexual Politics in Eighteenth-Century England

Bridget Hill

Basil Blackwell

First published 1989

Basil Blackwell Ltd
108 Cowley Road, Oxford, OX4 1JF, UK

Basil Blackwell Inc.
432 Park Avenue South, Suite 1503
New York, NY 10016, USA

British Library Cataloguing in Publication Data
A CIP catalogue record for this book is available from the British Library

Library of Congress Cataloging-in-Publication Data
Hill, Bridget.
Women and work in eighteenth-century England/Bridget Hill.
p.   cm.
Includes index.
ISBN 0-631-15461-2
1. Women—Employment—England—History—18th century. 2. Home labor—England—History—18th century. 3. Women in agriculture—England—History—18th century. 4. Women—England—Social conditions. I. Title. II. Title: Women and work in 18th-century England.
HD6136.H55   1989
331.410942—dc19   88-34690
CIP

Typeset in 11 on 12 pt Sabon
by Setrite Typesetters Ltd
Printed in Great Britain by Camelot Press Ltd., Southampton

Contents

Preface   vii

1   Introduction: Pinchbeck and After   1

2   The Social Context   9

3   Women's Work in the Family Economy   24

4   The Undermining of the Family Economy   47

5   Female Servants in Husbandry   69

6   Female Apprenticeship   85

7   Housework   103

8   Domestic Service   125

9   Ignored, Unrecorded, and Invisible: Some Occupations of Women   148

10   The Economics of Courtship and Marriage   174

11   Clarity and Obscurity in the Law Relating to Wives, Property, and Marriage   196

12   Spinsters and Spinsterhood   221

13   Widows   240

14   Conclusion   259

Index   268

v

Preface

When I started this book I was aware that women's history in the eighteenth and early nineteenth century owed much to Ivy Pinchbeck. But as I proceeded the greater became my consciousness of the size of that debt. She was a pioneer in women's history and her achievement remains remarkable. It is against her work that must be measured the contributions of the last half century to our knowledge and understanding of eighteenth-century working women. My debt to her is immense. She was not only a historian of women but a social historian. It is a sad irony that such a distinction can be made. Since Ivy Pinchbeck wrote, eighteenth-century social history has moved on, leaving women's history increasingly separated from it and distinct. This book is an attempt to bring them together.

The inclusion of 'England' in the title is intended as a broad indication of the main focus of the study and it has not been interpreted as excluding the experiences of women in Wales, Scotland, and Ireland when they make useful points of similarity or contrast.

I have drawn extensively on the work of others but in particular on that of Ann Kussmaul, Caroline Davidson, and Keith Snell. Among the many who have been generous with references and their own carefully collected material are Maxine Berg, Mary Prior, Anjie Rosga, Susan Staves, Eric Richards, and Keith Wrightson. I owe those who participated in lively seminars in the universities of Auckland, Sydney, Melbourne, Canberra, Perth, Adelaide, the City University in New York, Rutgers, St Louis, Georgetown, Maryland, and in the Folger Library, my grateful thanks for fruitful and stimulating discussions, and above all to my own seminar in the New

School, New York. I benefited greatly from a rigorous weekend tutorial with Penelope Corfield. I am grateful to Marcus Rediker for bombarding me with searching questions, and uncomfortably probing areas of uncertainty. To Barry Reay I acknowledge a very special debt for giving so generously of his time to reading much of the book and being so encouraging. His thoughtful and stimulating comments were always helpful, and his suggestions fruitful. To Dinah Hill I owe thanks for her technical expertise. To my husband, as always, I owe more than words can convey.

B.H.

1

Introduction: Pinchbeck and After

> In 1930, when *Women Workers and the Industrial Revolution* was first
> published, such a historical project was unprecedented: social history and
> women's history owe Ivy Pinchbeck a great debt.
>
> Kerry Hamilton, Foreword to Virago's 1981 edition of Ivy Pinchbeck's
> *Women Workers and the Industrial Revolution, 1750–1850*

When Ivy Pinchbeck's *Women Workers and the Industrial Revolution, 1750–1850* was first published in 1930, very little was known of the part played by women in the Industrial Revolution, and even less in the pre-industrial period. If, as she claimed, it was 'often assumed that the woman worker was produced by the Industrial Revolution' (ibid., p. 1),[1] with the advent of the factory and the mill, such a view is no longer tenable. Throughout her study, the point is constantly being driven home that women in the eighteenth century, single or married, worked – and worked hard. Long before the impact of industrialization it was taken for granted that women by their labour made a valuable contribution to the subsistence of their families. In many cases that contribution covered their own and their children's maintenance.

The fact that today any investigation of women's work in the eighteenth century must start with a study that is now over half a century old, and that covers a period ending in the middle of the nineteenth century, is a tribute to the continuing importance of that study and a comment on the paucity of the work that has followed it. It is a book that requires constant rereading. Information and comment are so concentrated that it is all too easy to miss points. There is always something new to be found on going back to it, and whenever you believe you have come up with a new idea, it is worth checking whether Pinchbeck got there first. The sheer volume of primary source material through which she worked carefully and methodically is immensely impressive, and indeed daunting, to those

---

[1] Page references in parentheses refer to the Virago (1981) edition of Pinchbeck.

who have come after her. Her bibliography remains valuable for any student of eighteenth- and early nineteenth-century working women.

One earlier study of working women demands mention here. Alice Clark's *Working Life of Women in the Seventeenth Century* (1919) is mainly concerned with the seventeenth century, it is true, but much of it anticipates, and relates closely to, the later century. Clark and Pinchbeck remain by far the best entry into a study of eighteenth-century women. Another product of that remarkable group of women historians that emerged in the period following the First World War was Dorothy George. Her *London Life in the Eighteenth Century* (1925), while not solely concerned with women, contains a great deal about London women and their occupations, about female servants and apprentices.

What has been written about eighteenth-century working women since Pinchbeck wrote?[2] There have been several general surveys of eighteenth-century agriculture which, while not primarily concerned with women, contain some useful references.[3] In 1930 very little was known about service in husbandry, and almost nothing about the role women played within it. Understandably the section of the book Pinchbeck devoted to the subject is brief. The studies of Ann Kussmaul, *Servants in Husbandry in Early Modern England* (1981), and 'The ambiguous mobility of farm servants', *Economic History Review*, 342 (1981), while not confined to female servants, shed light on their work, the terms and conditions of their engagement, and their mobility, and revealed the importance of service in the education and training of the young. On the decline of service there is K. D. M. Snell, *Annals of the Labouring Poor* (1985), chapter 2.

Pinchbeck was not unaware of great regional differences in the nature and extent of women's employment in agriculture. She saw a divide between employment opportunities in the north and the south. But it was not a theme she developed. Keith Snell's article 'Agricultural seasonal unemployment, the standard of living and women's work in the south and east, 1690–1860', *Economic History Review*, 34 (1983), extended and updated in his more recent *Annals of the Labouring Poor*, chapter 1, has shown how in the south and

---

[2] Of value as a general bibliographical review is Olwen Hufton's 'Survey articles: women in history. 1: Early modern Europe', *Past and Present*, 101 (1983).

[3] Dealing with the earlier part of the century is R. W. Malcolmson, *Life and Labour in England, 1700–1780* (1981): Joan Thirsk (ed.), *The Agrarian History of England and Wales*, vol. v: *1640–1750*, pts. 1 and 2 (1984 and 1985). On the later period there is E. L. Jones (ed.), *Agriculture and the Industrial Revolution* (1978); Pamela Horn, *The Rural World: Social Change in the English Countryside* (1980).

east the seasonal pattern of employment between men and women diverged. With this divergence a much clearer sexual division of labour emerged in agricultural tasks, leaving women with fewer opportunities for agricultural employment and restricting them to the less prestigious and worst paid of agricultural work. A subsequent volume planned by Snell on the north will make possible a direct comparison between the experience of women in the north and south.

Only briefly mentioned by Pinchbeck was the effect of changing agricultural technology on women's employment and the sexual division of labour. Michael Roberts, in 'Sickles and scythes: women's work and men's work at harvest time' (*History Workshop Journal*, no. 7 (1979)), has looked at the relationship between women's exclusion from the work of reaping and the substitution of the scythe for the sickle in the south. On the nineteenth century, Eve Hostettler's 'Gourlay Steell and the sexual division of labour', *History Workshop Journal*, no. 4 (1977) is an interesting sequel.[4]

Since Pinchbeck wrote there has been no study of textile manufacturing in the eighteenth century which focuses specifically on women workers, although several works on textile manufacturing have been published.[5] Nor with the exception of Maxine Berg's *The Age of Manufactures, 1700–1820* (1985), particularly chapter 6, has there been any comprehensive study of women workers in domestic industry, and most notably in those where female labour was predominant – lace-making, straw-plaiting, and the manufacture of buttons and gloves. There have been two articles of seminal importance, notably Eric Richards's 'Women in the British economy since about 1700', *History*, 59/197 (1974), and N. McKendrick's 'Home demand and economic growth: a new view of women and children in the Industrial Revolution', in *Historical Perspectives: Studies in*

[4] On women's experience in Swedish and Western European agriculture see Bengt Ankarloo, 'Agriculture and women's work: directions of change in the West, 1700–1900', *Journal of Family History*, 4/2 (1979).

[5] Reference is made to women workers in: A. P. Wadsworth and J. de Lacy Mann, *The Cotton Trade and Industrial Lancashire, 1600–1780* (1931); E. P. Thompson, *The Making of the English Working Class* (1963); F. Collier, *The Family Economy of the Working Classes in the Cotton Industry, 1784–1833*, Chetham Society, vol. xii, 3rd ser. (1965); H. Heaton, *The Yorkshire Woollen and Worsted Industries from the Earliest Times up to the Industrial Revolution*, 2nd edn (1965); M. M. Edwards, *The Growth of the British Cotton Trade, 1780–1815* (1967); D. Bythell, *The Handloom Weavers* (1969); J. de Lacy Mann, *The Cloth Industry in the West of England from 1640 to 1880* (1971); K. Ponting, *Essays in Textile History* (1973); D. T. Jenkins and K. G. Ponting, *The British Wool Textile Industry, 1770–1914* (1982). For studies of framework knitting see W. G. Hoskins, *The Midland Peasant* (1957); J. D. Chambers, *Nottinghamshire in the Eighteenth Century* (1966).

English Thought and Society in Honour of J. H. Plumb, edited by N. McKendrick (1974). There are also two collections of essays on early modern England which contain interesting discussions of women's work.[6]

Pinchbeck amassed a formidable body of information. With few of her facts can one quarrel; it is the conclusions she drew that call for some reassessment. My aim in writing this book is to try and provide students of eighteenth-century working women with a synthesis of work done since Pinchbeck wrote and to examine some of those areas of women's work on which she did not concentrate, themes which she broached but had no space to develop. When she wrote, knowledge of the social history of the eighteenth century was limited. If in the last sixty years there has been little added to our knowledge of working women, we do know far more about the changing eighteenth-century social context. Chapter 2 attempts to summarize some of the main work that has changed our understanding.

The working women on whom Pinchbeck's study focused were almost always seen against the background of one particular occupation or employment. But everything we now know of working women in the eighteenth century suggests how often they were involved in more than one occupation. Pinchbeck was not unaware of this aspect of women's work. She drew attention to how often a household combined work in agriculture with work in a local industry. The household was the most important unit of production, and encompassed an economy in which by far the greater part of the work of women was carried out. Because that economy was experiencing development, we need to be aware of the changing role women were called ŏn to play within it. Most pertinent here is the work of Louise Tilly and Joan Scott, 'Women's work and the family in nineteenth-century Europe', *Comparative Studies in Society and History*, 17 (1975), and their *Women, Work and Family* (1978).[7] The working role of women in the family economy,

[6] Lindsey Charles and Lorna Duffin (eds), *Women and Work in Pre-Industrial England* (1985); two contributions are particularly thought provoking: Michael Roberts, 'Words they are women, and deeds they are men: images of work and gender in early modern England', and Chris Middleton, 'Women's labour and the transition to pre-industrial capitalism'. For a useful case study of women's work in the urban economy in early modern England see Mary Prior (ed.), *Women in English Society 1500–1800* (1985), ch. 3.

[7] There are a number of demographic studies of the household which make reference to women: Peter Laslett, *The World We Have Lost* (1971); Peter Laslett and Richard Wall (eds), *Household and Family in Past Time* (1972); Peter Laslett, *The World We Have Lost Further Explored* (1983), esp. ch. 10; Lloyd Bonfield, Richard M. Smith, and Keith Wrightson (eds), *The World We Have Gained* (1986).

the changes it underwent in the course of the century, and the consequences for women's work are the subject of chapters 3 and 4.

Pinchbeck only briefly made reference to female service in husbandry, but together with apprenticeship it provided opportunities for the training of women and is the theme of chapter 5. The whole area of female apprenticeship in the eighteenth century is one curiously disregarded by historians. O. J. Dunlop and R. D. Denman's *English Apprenticeship and Child Labour: A History* (1912), on which Pinchbeck drew, still remains the standard authority. Despite a number of useful county and town studies of apprenticeship, there has been little on female apprenticeship. By far the best and most comprehensive recent study is in Keith Snell's *Annals of the Labouring Poor* (1985), where a chapter is devoted to the apprenticeship of women. I take up this theme in chapter 6.

Although Pinchbeck acknowledged housework as a responsibility of women over and above their involvement in agriculture and industry and saw home-making as perhaps their most important role, she did not devote much space to it. Social historians with few exceptions have taken housework for granted as part of women's role, without ever enquiring how it influenced the evaluation of the other work they performed. Until recently no serious historical study had been made of it. Since the publication of Caroline Davidson's *A Woman's Work is Never Done: A History of Housework 1650–1980* (1982), this is no longer true.[8] What housework meant in the eighteenth century is considered in chapter 7.

Another group of women workers omitted from Pinchbeck's survey is domestic servants. The reason she gave for excluding them was that her concern was with those 'women's activities' that were 'definitely affected by the industrial and economic reorganisations of the time' (p. 4). Whether or not female domestic service is really to be seen as unaffected by industrialization, it constituted by far and away the most important occupation for women after agriculture. Although its importance is generally recognized, little work has been done on it. The most authoritative work on domestic service remains Jean J. Hecht, *The Domestic Service Class in Eighteenth-Century England* (1956).[9] Also of importance is Theresa

---

[8] There is also C. Hole, *English Home Life, 1500–1800* (1947); Rosamund Bayne-Powell, *Housekeeping in the Eighteenth Century* (1956); and Ann Oakley, *The Sociology of Housework* (1974).

[9] There is a general survey in the Historical Association pamphlet by Dorothy Marshall on 'The English domestic servant in history' (1949). On female domestic service there is D. M. Stuart, *The English Abigail* (1946), which is mainly concerned with the nineteenth century.

McBride's *The Domestic Revolution: The Modernisation of House-hold Service in England and France, 1820–1920* (1976), which raises points that are as relevant to the eighteenth as to the nineteenth century. Cissie Fairchild's *Domestic Enemies: Servants and their Masters in Old Regime France* (1984), is a stimulating study and has relevance to our own experience. Female domestic service is discussed in chapter 8.

While a great deal – even most – of women's work in the eighteenth century was within their own households, there was also work that was not. Attention has mainly been focused on women's work in textile manufacture and other domestic industries, at the expense of ignoring the wide range of other employments in which women worked. Much of this work was not full-time. A great deal of it was combined with other work, or seasonal. Often it was work on which few commented and that failed to be recorded in the early nineteenth-century censuses. It is these ignored, unrecorded, or invisible occupations of women which are considered in chapter 9.

Pinchbeck saw clearly both how changes in agriculture and domestic industry could transform the nature and extent of women's work and how those same changes were contributing to the undermining of the family economy. That economy had an importance that went far beyond economics or productive work opportunities for women. Relations between the sexes, the degree to which patriarchal power within that unit was oppressive, the nature of courtship, attitudes to, and age at, marriage – all these were influenced by the nature of the family economy and the work contribution each member was able to make to it. So when that economy began to disintegrate, more was involved than a change in the nature of women's work, or where, or even for whom, they worked. In chapter 10 we look at the economics of courtship and marriage, how labouring women regarded marriage, the importance of the contribution they made to the setting up of a separate household, and of the role played by their work skills in maintaining its independence.

Marriage deprived a woman of any legal existence. How far was the law relevant to labouring women, and what, if any, were the consequences for them of the law relating to property in marriage? Many women in the eighteenth century never went through any legal marriage ceremony. Those who did were often deserted, or sometimes sold. Were the customary alternatives to an unacceptable and costly marriage and divorce law to which the labouring population resorted of equal advantage to women and men? These questions are the subject of chapter 11.

Although there has been a great deal written about courtship and marriage in the eighteenth century, there is remarkably little on the plebeian experience.[10] There is J. R. Gillis, *For Better, For Worse* (1985), a general survey which covers marriage practice from the sixteenth century to the present day, and his 'Married but not churched: plebeian sexual relations and marital nonconformity in eighteenth-century Britain' in *'Tis Nature's Fault*, edited by Robert Purks Maccubbin (1987).[11] On the practice of wife-sale there is Samuel Pyeatt Menefee's *Wives for Sale* (1981).[12]

Closely related to apprenticeship and the ability of women to set up independently in business is the work role of the widow and the unmarried and never-to-be-married woman. If the law entitled *feme sole* to rights of trading and property-owning denied to wives, how far were those rights actually used by them? If there were possibilities open to spinsters and widows of some means, what prospects faced those without? At the end of the seventeenth and beginning of the eighteenth centuries, we now know that something like a crisis occurred with regard to marriage, with far more women remaining unmarried than earlier. Yet very little is heard of them. Widowhood also was a far more frequent experience in eighteenth-century England than later. Both widows and spinsters are often found heading households, yet despite their importance they remain shadowy figures. On both widows and spinsters there is Richard Wall's 'Women alone in English Society', *Annales de démographie historique* (1981), 303–17. There is the special issue of the *Journal of Family History* (vol. 9, no. 4, 1984) devoted to 'Spinsterhood' with a valuable contribution from Professor Olwen Hufton. On widows there is Barbara J. Todd's, 'The re-marrying widow: a stereotype reconsidered', in *Women in English Society, 1500–1800* (1985), edited

[10] A useful survey but by no means focused on the eighteenth century is R. B. Outhwaite (ed.), *Marriage and Society: Studies in the Social History of Marriage* (1981). Although again more on the seventeenth than the eighteenth century there is a wealth of ideas to be found in Martin Ingram, 'The reform of popular culture?', in Barry Reay (ed.), *Popular Culture in Seventeenth-Century England* (1985), and in J. A. Sharpe, 'Plebeian marriage in Stuart England', *Royal Historical Society Transactions*, 5th ser. 36 (1986). There is also R. M. Smith, 'Marriage Processes in the English Past: Some Continuities', in Bonfield *et al.* (eds), *The World We Have Gained*. More general works on marriage include Edward Shorter, *The Making of the Modern Family* (1975); Lawrence Stone, *The Family, Sex and Marriage in England, 1500–1800* (1977); Peter Laslett, *Family Life and Illicit Love in Earlier Generations* (1977).

[11] See also his 'Peasant, plebeian and proletarian marriage in Britain, 1600–1900', in David Levine (ed.), *Proletarianization and Family History* (1984).

[12] On wife-sale there is also E. P. Thompson. 'Folklore, anthropology and social history', *The Indian Historical Review*, 3/2 (1977).

by Mary Prior.[13] Spinsters and widows are the subjects of chapters 12 and 13.

Finally, in the light of work done in the last fifty years, we return to Pinchbeck to reconsider her conclusions. The study concludes by asking how far our increased understanding of working women in the eighteenth century demands some rethinking in the debates which are currently concerning social historians.

There are many areas of women's history in the eighteenth century that I am conscious of omitting. Women's work in domestic industries would make another book, and one that needs to be written. I have not talked specifically of women in towns, although some of the occupations with which I deal in chapter 9 are those of urban women. A serious omission is the work of women in bearing and rearing children. It is a big subject and one on which recently there has been a lot of work done. I should have liked to have given much more space to prostitution in the eighteenth century, a theme on which very little has been published. But something had to be left out, and these topics were sacrificed.

[13] Particularly stimulating but on an earlier period is Vivien Brodsky Elliott, 'Single women in the London marriage market: age, status and mobility, 1598–1619', in Outhwaite (ed.), *Marriage and Society*; and her 'Widows in late Elizabethan London: remarriage, economic opportunity and family orientations', in Bonfield *et al.* (eds), *The World We Have Gained*. On a neglected aspect of single women's experience in the nineteenth century there is A. James Hammerton, *Emigrant Gentlewomen: Genteel Poverty and Female Emigration, 1830–1914* (1979).

2

The Social Context

Suddenly, almost like a thunderbolt from a clear sky, were ushered in the storm and stress of the Industrial Revolution.

C. Beard, *The Industrial Revolution*

Like most dramatic concepts, that of 'industrial revolution' in conveying a major truth, exaggerates the suddenness and completeness of actual happenings.

John Rule, *The Labouring Classes in Early Industrial England, 1750–1850*

When Ivy Pinchbeck's book was published in 1930, there was little discussion, let alone debate, on eighteenth-century social history. The full impact of Clapham's challenge to what he called the 'legends' created by some historians, most notably the Hammonds, had not been felt.[1] The historiographical 'standard of living debate' still lay ahead. This did not prevent what were seen as the main landmarks of the period from being clearly defined. The very title of her book, for example, suggests that Pinchbeck entertained few doubts about whether an 'industrial revolution' ever occurred. In this certainty she was not alone. It was shared by most historians of the period, and as elaborated in school textbooks provided generations of children with their understanding of what the eighteenth century meant. The Industrial Revolution dominated the scene. To Pinchbeck it signalled 'the separation of home and workshop' as 'one industry after another was taken from the home by invention and the development of large-scale industry'. It was 'to establish a new order of things'. In common with most other social historians of the time, she saw the Agrarian Revolution — an indispensable accompaniment to the revolution in industry — as almost coincident

[1] See J. H. Clapham, *An Economic History of Modern Britain*, 3 vols (1926–38), vol. i, Preface.

9

with it and covering the years 1750–1820. In 1750 England remained 'an agricultural country' where 'the old type of rural organisation persisted with its open field farms and common lands'; in the following seventy years, agriculture became 'a capitalistic trade aimed at increased production to supply the new market in the growing industrial towns'. Before 1750 farming had been for subsistence and 'to supply the needs of the immediate community'; after 1750 large farms and the landless labourer replaced a 'rural organisation which had existed for centuries'. The 'old village organisation . . . was broken up'.[2] The two revolutions combined to create a new class of landless labourers wholly dependent on wage-earning. So Pinchbeck was in no doubt about the eighteenth-century context in which women workers were to be seen and the nature of the changes which were to transform their working lives.

Alas, almost all such certainties about the period have been severely shaken if not demolished in the last half-century. What has replaced them is no single new orthodoxy but a number of often widely disparate interpretations. What broadly defined trends are discernible? The first changes associated with an 'Agricultural Revolution', it is now agreed, occurred well before the middle of the eighteenth century. Many would see them as originating in the sixteenth century but developing very slowly until the second half of the following century. Even then their impact was gradual, affecting different areas of the country at different times, and revealing very uneven rates of development. But between 1650 and 1750, agricultural practice and techniques were transformed. When population began to grow rapidly, the potential for feeding it was already created. Some agrarian historians have resisted the use of the term 'revolution' as inappropriate to describe such change, while conceding that if there ever was a revolutionary phase it had occurred before the eighteenth century, in the period of the Commonwealth and Restoration.[3] What is clear is that agricultural production and productivity increased steadily in the eighteenth century. It has been suggested that the percentage increase in total output was 'approximately double that of the two preceding centuries'.[4] According to N. F. Crafts, in the period 1710–1800 total agricultural output must have risen by 80 per cent. The period of greatest growth was

---

[2] Ivy Pinchbeck, *Women Workers and the Industrial Revolution* [1930], (1981). pp. 4, 7.

[3] Roderick Floud and Donald McCloskey, (eds), *The Economic History of Britain since 1700*, 2 vols (1981), vol. i: *1700–1860*, p. 85.

[4] E. L. Jones, 'Agriculture 1700–1780', in Floud and McCloskey (eds), *The Economic History of Britain since 1700*, p. 68.

from 1710 to 1740, during which period England became a substantial exporter of food. Over the whole ninety years he sees output as increasing on average at 0.7 per cent per annum while the labour force was growing at an annual rate of 0.13 per cent.[5] Yet Pinchbeck's dating of the agrarian revolution retains some validity, for it was only under the stimulus of the rapid population growth of the second half of the eighteenth century that agricultural change, and particularly the process of enclosure, accelerated. The effect on the labouring population, and more particularly on women, was the creation of a vast body of people cut off from any access to land and wholly dependent for subsistence on selling its labour to others.

In many ways, the 'Industrial Revolution' has fared even worse. As with the 'Agricultural Revolution', queries have been raised about the semantics of the label. Were the changes going on between the mid-eighteenth and mid-nineteenth century sufficiently fundamental or rapid to warrant the term 'revolution'? Can a 'revolution' take so long? And what exactly does 'industrial' signify here – one industry, one branch of industry, or the whole of manufacturing industry, both domestic and factory? If ever it was a term intended to define technological innovation leading to the rapid mechanization of industry and its factory organization, it will no longer do. We now know that outside cotton, mechanization came very slowly indeed, and that for a considerable period of the nineteenth century, domestic handicraft industry in small units based on home or workshop persisted alongside the factories and mills. But if much industry remained in the home, a whole host of technical innovations were transforming its nature. The increasing sophistication of spinning technology, for example, was a process that took place largely within domestic industry. The same is true of changes in weaving following the introduction of the flying shuttle. Many of these innovations in domestic industry were minor, but the cumulative effect was considerable. If we are to continue to use the term 'Industrial Revolution', it must embrace such domestic industry, for it was here that a great deal of industrial expansion occurred. It bears out the claim that 'the obvious way of industrial expansion in the eighteenth century was not to construct factories, but to extend the so-called domestic system'.[6] Factory organization up to the

[5] E. A. Wrigley, 'The transformation of traditional society', in his *People, Cities, and Wealth* (1987), p. 171 n. 18; N. C. R. Crafts, 'The eighteenth century: a survey', in Floud and McCloskey (eds), *The Economic History of Britain since 1700*, tables 1.1 and 1.2, pp. 2, 3.
[6] E. J. Hobsbawm, *The Age of Revolution* [1962], (1969), p. 36.

middle of the nineteenth century only really applied to textiles, and cotton in particular. Even in 1851, 'the majority of those employed in manufacturing ... still did not work in factories'.[7] So as Eric Hobsbawm has emphasized, to contrast the eighteenth and nineteenth centuries by comparing cottage industry with factory industry is mistaken. For the first stage of the Industrial Revolution 'was not one which *replaced* domestic workers by factory workers, except in a very few trades ... On the contrary: it multiplied them.'[8]

Then the Industrial Revolution can no longer be interpreted as purely an industrial phenomenon. The fact that the term arose out of a concern with the social consequences tended to be temporarily forgotten by some historians in the backlash reaction of the 1930s, and 1940s to, among others, J. L. and Barbara Hammond. In the hands of the economists and economic historians of the 1950s, the Industrial Revolution became the whole process by which economic growth accelerated. Attention was focused on rates of growth and investment. Rostow equated the Industrial Revolution with a 'take-off into self-sustained growth', which occurred round about 1780.[9] More recently, economic historians have sought to quantify all evidence of such economic growth, with the result that the turning-point has moved backwards to the 1740s. Apart from the unreliability of eighteenth-century statistical sources which make possible considerable margins of error, the emphasis on quantification has the additional drawback that it has been largely those areas capable of quantification which have been studied.

The whole process of industrialization went on much longer than historians originally thought. Pinchbeck believed that 'England was not really industrialised until about the middle of the nineteenth century.'[10] Clapham went further, claiming that in 1850 the process of industrialization was 'not half over' in England'.[11] There are those who think the process only ended in this century, and some who believe that even today it remains incomplete. On the other hand, while there is still far more attention paid to the period 1780–1830 (recently the 1820s have been increasingly favoured by some historians as another important turning point), many would date the changes which first signalled the coming of the Industrial

[7] John Rule, *The Labouring Classes in Early Modern England, 1750–1850* (1986), p. 8.
[8] E. J. Hobsbawm, *Labouring Men* (1964), p. 116.
[9] W. W. Rostow. 'The take-off into self-sustained growth', *Economic Journal*, 66 (1956), pp. 25–48.
[10] Pinchbeck, *Women Workers*, p. 5.
[11] Clapham, *An Economic History of Modern Britain*, vol. ii, p. 22.

Revolution in the seventeenth century. A further thing historians have learnt is how impossible it is to generalize about the whole country. In the late nineteenth century, there were still areas almost untouched by industrialization: in others the process was well nigh completed a century earlier.

Recognition of just how long drawn out was the process has led some historians to reject the use of the term 'Industrial Revolution' as no longer appropriate. Some have gone further, claiming that the whole notion of an Industrial Revolution is a myth.[12] But the reaction of other historians to the searching scrutiny to which the label has been subjected has been to seek to define more exactly of what the revolution consisted. Peter Mathias, for example, has redefined it as 'a fundamental redeployment of resources away from agriculture'.[13] In that redeployment the whole way of life of the great majority of the population, women as well as men, changed. It was indeed 'a great upheaval', in ways that do not easily lend themselves to any measurement.[14] If this was true of the majority of the population, for women, as we shall see, it had a special significance. The whole notion of 'industrial revolution' has been broadened to embrace changes in agriculture, transport, trade, population, and urbanization. In consequence the concept has become much more complex.

One conclusion that has steadily gained ground is how singularly inappropriate the term 'pre-industrial' is for the economy before the first impact of 'industrialization', when there was in fact a great deal of industry. Indeed, one would have to go a very long way back to find a time when 'pre-industrial' meant a period before industry came on the scene. A great deal of recent work has been focused on the period immediately preceding factory industrialization in an attempt to define its nature, and its relationship to what came before and after. The term 'proto-industrialization' was coined in 1972 to describe 'pre-industrial industry'.[15] More recently it has been described as 'early and therefore uncentralized and unmechanised industry as in the countryside of ... Lancashire in the eighteenth century'.[16] It was a 'first phase which preceded and

---

[12] Michael Fores, 'The myth of a British industrial revolution', *History*, 66 (1981), pp. 181–98.

[13] Peter Mathias, *The First Industrial Revolution, 1700–1914* [1969], (1983), p. 2.

[14] M. W. Flinn, *The Origins of the Industrial Revolution* (1966), p. 1.

[15] F. Mendels, 'Proto-industrialization: the first phase of the industrialization process', *Journal of Economic History*, 32 (1972), 241–62 (p. 241).

[16] Floud and McCloskey (eds), *The Economic History of Britain since 1700*, Glossary, p. 316.

prepared industrialization proper'.[17] Hans Medick described it as 'industrialization before the factory system'. Characterizing this phase, it was held, was the 'close association between household production based on the family economy on the one hand, and the capitalist organisation of trade, putting-out and marketing of the product on the other'.[18] The products of this last phase of domestic industry, even before changing technology, mechanization, and the factory system removed industry from the home, no longer served local but national and international markets.

The ancestry of industrialization proper is primarily traceable through the domestic system as it operated in rural areas, not from the industrial workshops of urban industry. Historians concerned to explain the conditions in which rural handicraft industry emerged have linked it to the growth of population, the decline of the small landowner, and the increasing presence of a 'numerous, under-employed class of small peasants and landless rural dwellers' in need of supplementing their income. These provided 'unlimited supplies of labour' and 'created the conditions for the penetration of industrial production into the countryside'.[19] But such ideas are not new. Long before the term proto-industrialization was mooted, Joan Thirsk had suggested that the 'location of handicrafts' was 'probably not haphazard but associated with certain types of farming and social organisation', and had stressed its relationship to pastoral and upland areas characterized by poor soils and a precarious agriculture. But the rise of some of the domestic industries – pillow lace and straw-plaiting, for example – cannot be thus explained.[20]

The concept of proto-industrialization no longer commands the attention it initially attracted, although its assumptions still lie behind much of the debate on the contribution of increased fertility to the growth of population and its relationship to a declining age of marriage. There are still historians in Europe, the United States, and Third World countries who continue to pay it more than lip service. But a growing number of critics have found it a less than useful concept and concluded that the proto-industrial model is fundamen-

---

[17] Mendels, 'Proto-industrialization', p. 241.

[18] Hans Medick, 'The proto-industrial family economy', *Social History* (1976), pp. 291–315 (p. 296). Medick quotes C. and R. Tilly, 'Agenda for European economic history in the 1970s', *Journal of Economic History*, 31 (1971), p. 186.

[19] Medick, 'The proto-industrial family economy', pp. 296, 297.

[20] Joan Thirsk, 'Industries in the countryside', in her *The Rural Economy of England* (1984), p. 232; G. F. R. Spencely, 'The English pillow lace industry 1845–80: a rural industry in competition with machinery', *Business History*, 70 (1970).

tally flawed.[21] It ignores the building, mining, and metal industries — surely of crucial importance in the transition to industrialization. Moreover, the recognized proto-industrial model sometimes failed to develop into full industrialization: in the Wiltshire cloth industry, industrialization never happened. The domestic industry simply declined and disappeared. Domestic industry immediately before industrialization was far more diverse in its organization and structure than any model can suggest, and there was no one road followed to factory production. The wool textile industry of the West Riding is a case in point.[22] One thing that the whole proto-industrial debate has assured is a much closer study of domestic industry in different manufactures, in different places at different times. Although proto-industrialists have been vague in locating the process of proto-industrialization, the eighteenth century, when domestic industry was centred mainly in the household, and often combined with agriculture, must have been crucial. Within such domestic industry, we know women played a central role. Yet so far that role has been almost neglected by historians. Such neglect is all the more extraordinary when one looks at some of the claims made for proto-industrialization; Hans Medick, for example, argued that far from enforcing a stricter sexual division of labour such as is usually associated with industrialization proper, 'proto-industrialisation brought the man back to the household', and that there was less sexual division of household tasks than earlier. It 'even led to reversal of roles' and a reorientation of 'gender differences'.[23] Provocative claims, yet few have attempted to challenge them.

Recently it has been suggested that it is not just the importance of factory manufacture that has been exaggerated in the period of industrialization. The majority of those living in the countryside but 'no longer able to find work on the land' did not turn, as is often assumed, 'principally to industrial employment as a means of support, whether in the new form of the factory or in the older form of domestic industry', but to the traditional trades and services — that

[21] D. C. Coleman, 'Proto-industrialization: a concept too many', *Economic History Review*, 2nd ser. 36/3 (1983); Pat Hudson, 'Proto-industrialization: the case of the West Riding', *History Workshop Journal*, no. 12 (1981); R. Houston and K. D. M. Snell, 'Proto-industrialization? Cottage industry, social change, and industrial revolution', *Historical Journal*, 27/2 (1984).

[22] Hudson, 'Proto-industrialization: the case of the West Riding'.

[23] Medick, 'The Proto-industrial family economy', pp. 311–12; John Gillis, *For Better, For Worse* (1985), p. 119.

of butcher, baker, carpenter, mason — all of which 'depended on a local' rather than national or international market. Even as late as 1831, it is estimated, 'adult male employment in manufacturing constituted only 10% of total adult male employment, whereas retail trade and handicraft comprises 32%'.[24] It would be fascinating to have a similar analysis of the employments women entered when unable to find work in agriculture.

Social and economic historians of the eighteenth century have been under a considerable disadvantage as compared with their colleagues working on the nineteenth century for they lack the official statistics of the first censuses of population, occupational censuses, and the official evidence in the many government reports. It has made their attempts to establish definite trends or degrees of change difficult. Often such attempts have met with frank scepticism. If all eighteenth-century historians have suffered from this draw-back, historians of women, particularly labouring women, have been particularly hampered. Many contemporary writers never mentioned labouring women or failed to distinguish them from men. Terms such as 'labourers', 'servants', and 'apprentices' hide many women — but how many? It is easy to assume that they are all male. A belief that female domestic servants outnumbered male well before the end of the eighteenth century cannot be proved. The evidence of those unreliable contemporaries like Hanway and Colquhoun is no sub-stitute, we are told, for official counting. Proof of change requires quantification.

One dominant new influence in social history has been demography. Pinchbeck had very little to say about population except that during the period she covered it was increasing, and that towns were growing in size and number. It is generally agreed that England at the beginning of the eighteenth century was rural and relatively empty. Most people lived in small hamlets or villages. With the exception of London, towns were few and small. The population of England in 1701 has been estimated at 5.058 million, as compared with 8.664 million a century later.[25] This ties in well with Gregory King's estimate for England and Wales in 1688 of 5.5 million.[26] In the course of the century population grew, but unevenly. In the

[24] E. A. Wrigley, 'Men on the land and men in the countryside', in Bonfield *et al.* (eds), *The World We Have Gained* (1986), pp. 296, 303, 297.
[25] E. A. Wrigley and R. Schofield, *The Population History of England, 1541–1870: A Reconstruction* (1981), pp. 208–9.
[26] Gregory King, *Natural and Political Observations and Conclusions upon the State of England* [1696], ed. George E. Barnett (1936), p. 21.

early decades growth was 'relatively modest'.[27] Only from about 1740 did the rate of increase accelerate and continue to do so until, in the last thirty years of the century it increased by over two million, or more than 34 per cent.

The following century the population of England and Wales very nearly quadrupled. This massive increase in population, it is thought, had its origins in the eighteenth century. What is not agreed is how and why this increase came about. The demographers' debate on the eighteenth century continues. It hinges on the relative importance of a decline in mortality as against a rise in fertility. Nobody would now question that mortality rates fell, particularly in the second half of the century: better standards of hygiene, greater medical expertise, an improved water supply, the decline of the plague – all these contributed to that fall. But important as the decline of mortality was, it cannot alone have accounted for the increase in population. Some other, more important, factor must have been involved, and that other factor was fertility. It was not that the fertility rate within marriage significantly altered, or that illegitimate births dramatically increased, but that because women married earlier, their years of greatest fertility were lengthened. The age of women at first marriage, it is estimated, fell by something like three years between the end of the seventeenth and the beginning of the nineteenth century.[28]

By the beginning of the nineteenth century, one in seven of the population is estimated to have lived in towns with a population of over 50,000, and of these, three-quarters were in London. In contrast, at the beginning of the eighteenth century, apart from London, no town had exceeded 30,000 in population.[29] In the second half of the century, population was increasing all over the country, but there was a marked shift northwards towards the new industrial counties – Staffordshire and Warwickshire, the West Riding of Yorkshire and, above all, Lancashire. The growth in some of the towns of the north and the Midlands was phenomenal. Manchester, for example, grew from a mere 9,000 to 102,000 – over ten-fold – in the course of the century. Birmingham, with a population of over 15,000 when the century began, ended with 70,000. In the last

---

[27] E. A. Wrigley, 'The growth of population in eighteenth-century England: a conundrum resolved', *Past and Present*, no. 98 (Feb. 1983), p. 127.

[28] Wrigley and Schofield, *Population History*, p. 256; but see the whole discussion, pp. 228–57.

[29] Floud and McCloskey (eds), *The Economic History of Britain since 1700*, p. 106; Wrigley, *People, Cities and Wealth*, table 7.1, p. 160.

forty years it doubled. The same rapid increase was repeated in the case of Liverpool, Leeds, and Sheffield.[30]

The population in towns grew more rapidly than the population in the country as a whole. Partly this was the consequence of the number migrating to towns in the eighteenth century, partly it was the result of a fall in the urban death rate, but, it is argued, it was probably also the result of a higher birth rate resulting from a lower age structure as towns attracted 'disproportionate numbers of young adult migrants to their ranks'.[31] Among those migrants, women were very prominent. Most towns in the eighteenth century contained 'a majority of women'. This hindered women's chances of marriage.[32] Many of them were destined to become unmarried domestic servants, some for life.

There has been a tendency to equate 'Industrial Revolution' with 'urbanization'. If urbanization has hitherto been seen largely as the consequence of industrialization, urban historians have been at pains to persuade us that it played a far more positive role in promoting industrial change. In considering the degree of urbanization, of course, much depends on how a town is defined. Urban historians now tend to favour a population of 2,500 as marking the point at which a community becomes a town. The lower the threshold, the greater the degree of urbanization appears. By such a definition the urban population grew from 18.7 per cent in 1700 to 30 per cent in 1801. But communities of 2,500 are very small, and it is questionable whether they exhibited the characteristics that urban historians claim for them. Were they all, for example, 'based on a non-agrarian economic function' and had they all 'a distinctive social and cultural identity'?[33] It would be difficult to prove. No longer does Professor Jones's cautionary comment that 'above 5,000 people there is less doubt that we are dealing with something urban' seem to have much influence.[34] The growth of urban history in the last thirty years has meant that towns have come in for close study. However small a minority the urban population was in the eighteenth century, it is argued, urbanization is not merely a question of numbers, and the urban minority exerted an influence out of all proportion to its size.

[30] J. D. Chambers, *Population, Economy and Society in Pre-industrial England* (1972), p. 23; W. G. Hoskins, *The Making of the English Landscape* (1970), p. 221.
[31] Penelope Corfield, *The Impact of English Towns, 1700–1800* (1982), p. 107.
[32] Ibid., p. 64.
[33] Ibid., pp. 6, 7.
[34] E. Jones, *Towns and Cities* (1966), p. 5.

As the present-day concern over the growing divide between north and south makes clear, there has been a partial return to the pre-industrial contrast between the most highly populated and econ-omically richest south-east and the poor, backward, and sparsely populated north. By the end of the eighteenth century that relation-ship had been reversed. It was the north that saw the first impact of industrialization, that maintained the highest standard of living, and that probably experienced the greatest population increases.

London was by far the biggest urban concentration, with a popu-lation rising from 575,000 in 1700 to 900,000 a century later.[35] If it still dwarfed any other town, by the end of the century it no longer exerted the economic dominance over the rest of the country that it had enjoyed earlier, and its rate of growth had been overtaken by that of the new industrial towns. London throughout the century remained an important manufacturing town, the centre for a number of new industries and a wide variety of crafts, but in the course of the century many of those industries migrated into the countryside in search of cheap labour. If by the beginning of the nineteenth century three-quarters of the urban population of England lived in London, one should not forget that, as Malcolmson has so pertinently reminded us, this still meant that five out of six of the population never saw London.[36]

Throughout the century, the majority of the English population lived in the countryside − in 1700, according to Wrigley, 83 per cent, although by the end of the century, the proportion had fallen to 72 per cent. This involved no decline in the total agricultural labour force but a slowing down of the rate of its increase in relation to non-agricultural employment. Even as late as the middle of the nineteenth century the population was fairly evenly divided between country and town, where a town is defined by Wrigley as a community numbering more than 5,000. Most of this predominantly rural population thus lived and worked in small communities.[37]

At the beginning of the century well over half of the population was employed in agriculture. By the end that proportion had fallen. Patrick Colquhoun, on the basis of the 1801 census of population figures and the pauper returns of 1803, estimated in 1806 that there were still 3,310,000 working in agriculture comprising 'farmers',

[35] E. A. Wrigley, 'London's importance, 1650−1750', *Past and Present*, no. 37 (1967), p. 44.
[36] R. W. Malcolmson, *Life and Labour in England, 1700−1780* (1981), p. 20.
[37] Wrigley, *People, Cities and Wealth*, table 7.4, p. 170.

'freeholders', and 'labouring people in husbandry', but excluding cottagers.[38] This would suggest that about 38 per cent were
still engaged in agriculture. A recent estimate of the proportion of
the population engaged in agriculture differs little from that of
Colquhoun, arriving at the figure of 36 per cent, or a little more
than a third.[39] Such figures would seem to indicate that even by the
end of our period, agriculture constituted by far the most important
individual occupation. However, 'the paucity of reliable data
on occupations and social labels before the censuses of the mid-
nineteenth century' has led to new efforts to revise ideas hitherto
held of England's occupational structure in the eighteenth century.[40]
Up to now such ideas have relied on contemporary estimates
made by, among others, Gregory King, Joseph Massie, and Patrick
Colquhoun, but studies making use of burial registers and local
listings of population have recently attempted to revise these notions.
The results suggest that England and Wales may have been far more
industrial and commercial by the end of the seventeenth century
than King recognized. Such a claim may well prove true, but the
estimates produced so far, as the authors readily admit, are subject
to very wide margins of error and are 'little more than guesses'.[41]
Any confidence in them is badly shaken by the revelation that they
virtually exclude women's work as the sources used quote only
male occupations, and that they are based on the assumption – a
very dangerous one to make of the eighteenth century – that one
individual practised one occupation, and only one.[42]

There is one other area on which demographers have focused in
the last twenty years: the household, and particularly its structure.
Historians used to assume that 'the domestic group was universally
larger and more complex than it is today'. In pre-industrial Europe
the 'extended' or 'multiple' family was thought to be the predominant
model. It was normal, it was assumed, to find added to the conjugal
family unit, 'one or more relations other than offspring, the whole
group living together on its own or with servants', or even multiple
family households where 'two or more conjugal units connected by
kinship or by marriage with their respective children lived together

[38] Patrick Colquhoun, *A Treatise on Indigence* (1806), pp. 23–4.
[39] Wrigley, *People, Cities, and Wealth*, table 7.4, p. 170.
[40] P. H. Lindert, 'English occupations, 1670–1811', *Journal of Economic History*, 40 (1980), p. 686.
[41] Ibid., p. 701, quoting P. Deane and W. A. Cole, *British Economic Growth, 1688–1959* (1969), p. 142.
[42] See David Levine, 'Industrialization and the proletarian family in England', *Past and Present*, no. 107 (1985), p. 172.

under one roof'. In fact historians had got the past wrong. We now know that far from industrialization leading to any decrease in household size, the latter remained largely unchanged. Mean household size altered little from 'the late sixteenth to the first decade of the twentieth century', remaining fairly constant, Peter Laslett estimated, at 4.75.[43] The nuclear 'family' − a man, his wife, their unmarried children, and often servants of one kind or another − appears to have been the predominant form over the whole pre-industrial period. Only in 1891 did the size of the domestic group in England and Wales begin to fall, mainly because of a decline in fertility, and to fall continuously down to the present time. Within that statistical average, households varied in both size and character. What this mean household size meant in practice between 1754 and 1821, for example, was that 'nearly two fifths of the population' lived in households 'of 3, 4 or 5. But over half were members of groups consisting of six or more.'[44] One thing is certain: in many of these households there was living-in hired labour. Richard Wall has estimated that the proportion of households with servants in the period 1574−1821 was 28.5 per cent, and that they figured in nearly a quarter of the households of tradesmen and craftsmen. Sometimes even the households of labourers had servants.[45]

The methodology of demographers − the use of selective parish registers in the technique of family reconstitution, for example, or the use of a combination of parish registers and household listings as the basis for estimating household size and structure − has provided historians with new information. It has been useful, but it is recognized to have its limitations. It is not just that the very nature of the source material makes possible serious error, but, as Miranda Chaytor has emphasized in looking at an earlier period, it suggests a far more static and unchanging institution than the household was in practice.[46] In the attempt to define the structure of households, the lives and interrelationships of the human beings of which they consisted have tended to be forgotten. So if the simple nuclear family was the most common domestic group in eighteenth-century England, it is essential to avoid too rigid a view of it. Keith

[43] Peter Laslett and Richard Wall (eds), *Household and Family in Past Time* (1972), pp. 5, 29, 562, 139. Laslett emphasizes that his figure for mean household size is not to be used as a universal multiplier.

[44] Laslett, *The World We Have Lost Further Explored* (1983), p. 95.

[45] Laslett and Wall (eds), *Household and Family in Past Time*, pp. 152−3.

[46] Miranda Chaytor, 'Household and kinship: Ryton in the late sixteenth and early seventeenth centuries', *History Workshop Journal*, no. 10 (1980), p. 33.

Wrightson has stressed how 'it was characterised by its flexibility and adaptability'.[47]

Inevitably this concentration on the nature of the household initiated a reassessment of its importance as a unit of production. The idea of the 'family' or 'household' economy is not a recent invention, but in recent years it has become the focus of debate. Richard Wall, among others, has suggested that the meaning of 'family' and 'household' have subtly changed over the centuries.[48] The virtual synonymity of the two words in pre-industrial England is no longer the case. The word 'family' today suggests the exclusion of those not part of the biological family — servants in husbandry and apprentices, for example — who in pre-industrial times were almost as much members of the 'family' as the children of their masters and mistresses. Some historians have taken one or other of these words to describe not just the institution but the economy based on it, although not all are agreed about the nature of that economy. While all subscribe to the belief that the household as an economic unit changed, there is no agreement as to what caused that change; how it affected, altered, or undermined the household as an economic unit; and from what time such change is to be dated. The result is some rather conflicting claims and terminology: the 'household economy', the 'family economy', the 'family wage economy' and the 'family—household system'.[49] For some the transformation was wholly the consequence of industrialization; others see it beginning much earlier, with greater commercialization of agriculture, and continuing over a long period, with industrialization merely accelerating a long-established trend.

Anyone concerned with working women in the eighteenth century cannot ignore the household and the economy, whatever one chooses to call it, that was based on it. For here was focused the work of the vast majority of women (as well as men) in the eighteenth century. What happened to that economic and demographic unit, at whatever time, profoundly affected the work opportunities of women, the nature of women's work, and the conditions under which it was performed. Not all women's work in the eighteenth century was in the household, but a great deal of it was. And from what we know

[47] Keith Wrightson, 'Household and kinship in sixteenth-century England', *History Workshop Journal*, no. 12 (1981), p. 154.

[48] Laslett and Wall (eds), *Household and Family in Past Time*, p. 159.

[49] For a discussion of the problem see Maxine Berg, 'Women's work, mechanisation and the early phases of industrialisation in England', in Patrick Joyce (ed.), *The Historical Meanings of Work* (1987), pp. 64–7.

of the predominantly rural population and of the continuing importance of agriculture, the livelihood of a large number of households
throughout the century was based — at least in part — on agriculture.

What proportion of the population in the eighteenth century were
women? 'Slightly over half the nation', we are told.[50] The 1801
census confirmed the existence of a surplus of women, and there are
reasons for thinking it may have existed for some time. By 1851,
365,159 more women than men are recorded in the census figures.
On the basis of the hearth tax returns of the 1670s, Professor
Malcolmson has estimated that three-quarters of the population
were labouring men and women, but that as the source conceals
those who were servants living in households, the true figure was
nearer 80 per cent.[51] Accordingly, it seems reasonable to assume
that labouring women formed a significant group within the population. Is it then unreasonable to assume that the experience of this
half of the labouring population is an important consideration in
the areas of present-day debate and controversy on the eighteenth
century? If the age of women at first marriage played a vital role in
population increase, then the reasons for women marrying earlier
are as crucial, if not more so, as the reasons for men marrying
earlier. Where increased fertility is concerned, women surely played
a central role! In the debate on the consequences of enclosure and
the erosion of common rights, the experience of women, and more
particularly wives of smallholders and cottagers, has so far played
little part; yet for them it represented as great a loss as for men. In
the claims that are made about the effects of industrialization on the
labouring population women surely deserve to be considered. In the
debate on the standard of living women's experience has been
virtually ignored. If ideas about the eighteenth-century occupational
structure need revising, can it be done without including women? If
the experience of women is not readily accessible to quantification
and measurement, is it a sufficient reason for leaving them out? As
the work of a majority of women in the eighteenth century was in
the household, it is with the household that we must begin.

[50] Roy Porter, *English Society in the Eighteenth Century* (1982), p. 35.
[51] R. W. Malcolmson, *Life and Labour in England, 1700–1780* (1981), pp. 18–19.

3

Women's Work in the Family Economy

The interdependence of work and residence, of household labour needs, subsistence requirements, and family relationships constituted the 'family economy'

Louise Tilly and Joan Scott, *Women, Work and Family*

The natural economy of the working classes was a family economy dependent upon the efforts of each individual member and one in which the role of both partners was equally crucial.

Olwen Hufton, 'Women in the Family Economy in Eighteenth-Century France'

Whatever the variations in the constitution of households, wherever they formed the most basic unit of production in the eighteenth century there were certain shared characteristics. Firstly, home and workplace normally coincided for some or all members of that household. Secondly, within this unit work was directed towards the subsistence and maintenance of its members. Thirdly, although the members of the household contributed to its maintenance either in the form of goods or of money, the economy was not consistently motivated by any idea of maximizing profit any more than of maximizing production. Indeed, its values cannot easily be defined in terms of money or output.[1] If it aimed at achieving a level of self-sufficiency, that level varied greatly between households; but what many had in common was a measure of economic independence.

In her work on the seventeenth century, Alice Clark attempted to distinguish between the different kinds of productive work performed by a woman in the household. The contrast she made was between 'the extent of her production for domestic purposes as opposed to

---

[1] See Stephen Gudeman's comparison of corporation 'profit' and household 'surplus' in 'Remainders on the margin, profits in the core', *International Symposium on Democratizing Economics*, Institute of Advanced Studies, University of Sao Paolo (1988); E. P. Thompson, 'Time, work-discipline, and industrial capitalism', *Past and Present*, no. 38 (1967).

industrial and professional purposes'. The term 'industrial' was used in its broadest sense to embrace work in agriculture – and much of women's productive work in the eighteenth century was agricultural. But the point that Alice Clark was making is important: we need to make the distinction between work done by women that contributed solely to the household and that done for sale or exchange. It is the distinction between work that has 'use value' and that which has 'exchange value'. She went on to define three kinds of household production. The first is production directed only at the members of the household, where nothing is sold or exchanged. The second type, while still partly or even largely directed towards the maintenance of the household, produces a surplus which is either sold or exchanged. The money made from marketing such products goes towards the upkeep of the household. In this type of production, the ownership of the raw materials and the tools rests with the members of the household. The third type is where production is no longer controlled by the household alone (even if usually it remains located within the home), but is controlled by agents operating on behalf of capitalist merchants who own the capital involved and provide the raw material. The producers receive payment in the form of wages, the productive effort of each member of the household being rewarded by an individual wage even though it goes towards the maintenance of the whole family. This system of production is sometimes referred to as the 'putting-out system'. In a final stage, the identity of work place and home is broken, and the productive process is removed to a workshop or factory. Many households in the eighteenth century failed to conform to any one of these types, although some did. I have avoided using Alice Clark's terms – 'domestic', 'family', or 'capitalistic' – of household production, not only because some of these labels have other meanings today, but because they suggest too rigid a classification often belied by the facts.[2]

It is doubtful whether production in any eighteenth-century household remained solely for use. Then problems of definition arise when members of the household begin to move out of the home, when their productive effort is focused elsewhere – on someone else's farm, or in some master craftsman's workshop. If the exit from the household of some members is seen as undermining the family economy, at what stage do we recognize that a fundamental and irreversible change has taken place? The question can never be

[2] Alice Clark, *Working Life of Women in the Seventeenth Century* (1982), pp. 4, 6–8.

answered satisfactorily, for households so often seem to occupy a position somewhere between the types of production distinguished. Nevertheless it is important to be clear about what factors we recognize as contributing to undermining the family economy. However long the period in which the household is seen as defining a distinct and viable economy, it cannot be regardless of the degree to which production is retained within the home, or the extent to which production is controlled by members of that household. Above all, it must take account of the independence which a measure of self-sufficiency ensured to its members.

Even if the average family in the eighteenth century was nuclear, we must avoid too rigid a view of it for there were certainly cases of extended or multiple family households. Among all the households in Cardington in 1782, for example, just short of 7 per cent were those of extended families.[3] Mary Leadbeater's father, Richard Shackleton, was an English schoolmaster in Ireland. In 1726 he had married Elizabeth Fuller and had four children. He was left a widower when his wife died at the age of 28, but he soon remarried Elizabeth Carleton. His household centred on the school at which he was headmaster, where fifty to sixty boys boarded. There was a housekeeper, Elizabeth Haughton, a near relation of Richard's first wife, who was a widow left in poor financial circumstances. She brought with her into the household two children. There was also a steward, an old retainer, and a group, of unstated size, of 'inferior servants'.[4] It was an unusually complex household. More common was a household like that of Henry Coward, ironmonger and grocer, to whom William Stout was apprenticed. In 1684 it consisted of Henry, his wife, apprentices, and 'two made [maid] servants, one to wate upon her mistress, who minded little but her own ease and apetite, and the children, who were nursed out to suck. And the other servant [was put] to the kitchenwork, which made the housekeeping chargeable.'[5] But what these examples suggest is the great variety of households despite the average size. It is impossible to point to a representative eighteenth-century household because households were never static but constantly changing and developing.

[3] David Baker, *The Inhabitants of Cardington in 1782*, Bedfordshire Historical Record Society, vol. lii (1973), p. 22.

[4] *The Leadbeater Papers: A Selection from the MSS and Correspondence of Mary Leadbeater*, 2 vols (1862), vol. i, pp. 37, 41–2.

[5] *The Autobiography of William Stout of Lancaster 1665–1752*, ed. J. D. Marshall (1967), p. 76.

Members died, others were born, members moved out, others re-placed them, so that over a very short period of time the whole constitution and method of working of a household could be totally transformed. Wives were left widows, and they or their sons assumed the role of head of the household. Unmarried daughters left orphans were rendered homeless and forced to seek a livelihood in the world. Female servants in husbandry came and went regularly. Daughters left home to marry or become servants in the households of others.

One of the difficulties in analysing women's role in the eighteenth-century household in Britain is the lack of the sort of evidence — police records, records of ecclesiastical courts, a still vital folklore, and the continuance of the family economy — used by those con-cerned with the household in France. In England there is evidence available about households, but only rarely those of the labouring class. So while we have evidence of the working role of wives of farmers with moderately sized farms, there is little or none of individual wives of smallholders and cottagers. But if anyone is doubtful of the role of women within the family economy, they should take a look at how it continues to function in parts of rural France and in many other parts of Europe.

In the first half of the eighteenth century by far the majority of households were rural, and the great majority were dependent at least in part on the cultivation of land. Very few of the labouring classes owned more than ten acres of land, and many owned none. The unit of production for these classes therefore was usually small. In whatever role they are found, outside the upper classes, it was taken for granted that women worked. 'Female labour', as one historian has put it, 'was universal ... it was normal for women to share in the heaviest manual work.'[6] It was indeed often essential for the bare subsistence of the household. The fact that a great deal of that work was done in the home and passed unnoticed does not make it any less work, and hard work at that. Women's work covered not merely active participation in the farm, trade, craft, or shop of their husbands, or work in a different and often subsidiary occupation, but all that the term 'housework' involved in the eight-eenth century, as well as bearing and rearing children.

To appreciate the role women played in the household we need to

[6] Eric Richards, 'Women in the British economy since about 1700: an interpretation', *History*, 59/197 (1974), p. 339.

look more closely at some examples. Mary Hardy (1733—1808) was the daughter of a prominent Norfolk farmer. In 1765 she married William Hardy, a young tenant farmer from the locality, who rented a small farm and maltings at Coltishall, and in the neighbouring parish of Horstead. In the eight years that followed their marriage she gave birth to three children — two boys and a girl. In 1780 William Hardy bought a house, brewery, and fifty acres of land in Letheringsett. There they moved and settled. Mary Hardy was an intelligent and methodical woman and she played a central role in the management of the farm and in brewing. Mary 'by her upbringing knew all about farming and country ways and customs. Nothing escaped her.' She recorded in her diary the work done every day on the farm and how she, her husband, their servants, workmen, and hired labourers occupied their time. Her daily entries are brief but to the point: 'Brew'd. Killed 4 piggs,' 'sowd 3 sacks of Barly,' 'stick'd some pease in Garden ... Began to make cheese.' Even when she recorded 'Mr Oaks put his stock into my turnips', or the terse 'Mother-in-law went away has been here 51 weeks', there is no further comment. Her life was an active one, and she had no time to note anything but the bare facts of day-to-day existence.[7] Nevertheless her diary offers one of the few descriptions by a woman of a working household.

Exactly how many female living-in servants the household possessed is difficult to judge from her diary, but at different times there are references to the hiring of a 'Mrs Baker as housekeeper', of an 'Ann Waller' who 'came as Cook and dairymaid', and of Jane Rece, Sarah Jeckel, Ellen Mason, Ann Claxton who 'came as upper maid', Amy Green, Sarah Clark, Susan Ward, Eliz. Coo, Pleasance Gidney, Hannah Boone, Sarah Goodman, and Hannah Dagliss, among others — all of whom at one time or another were living-in servants. They came and went frequently, and Mary Hardy was not unusual in this rapid turnover of servants.[8] Her entry for 29 November 1773 reads: 'Men cleansd and maids washed', but who exactly were the men, whether living-in servants or hired day labourers, is not made clear. The household seems always to have had a boy living in, and at least on one occasion Mary was responsible for his hiring. The diary has regular references to a gardener, and on occasions to two. Several day-labourers were employed.

---

[7] *Mary Hardy's Diary*, with an Introduction by B. Cozens-Hardy, Norfolk Record Society, vol. xxxvii (1968), pp. 1, 2, 5, 6, 15, 6, 34.

[8] Ibid., pp. 131, 31, 45, 42, 60, 71, 73, 79, 109, 95.

Indeed, the impression is that there were far more working for the family than living-in servants. On 25 April 1774 she noted 'a new Labourer at work this afternoon'. In March 1777 she roasted a swan for dinner and recorded 'all our men dined here'. Among labourers working on the farm, several women are mentioned: Betty and Goody Freary, for example, T. Jex's wife, and 'our Molly' come to gather in the barley harvest. Other women assisted the maids with the washing: Goody Tompson, Greves, Gidney and Ram, Elizabeth Bullock, S. Boyce, Elizabeth Loades, Susan Lamb, and a C. Milegan. Often it seems these women were wives of their regular farm labourers. There are references to a Christmas Day dinner given to all their 'labourers and familys amounting to between 60 and 70 our own family included'. The work for women in providing such a dinner can be imagined from the amount of food that was prepared: '32 lbs. mutton, 16 lbs. pork, 16 lbs. beef, 2 st. flour, about 12½ [presumably also lbs.] plumbs, 5 lbs. suet, about 20 pints Milk'. At hay-time and harvest the household hired additional labour. Sometimes, as with Joseph Blumfield, Mary was responsible for the hiring. In September 1775, she refers to 'three companys of harvest men here'. They were boarded for the period of the harvest. In 1806, not long before her death and when she was already ill, she recorded how a 'Mr. Forby came with his sister to stay with me as an assistant in the Harvest time.'[9]

Mary took an active part in the work of the farm. She sowed barley, helped with the hay and corn harvest, ground malt for brewing, and supervised the loading and unloading of the wherry they bought in 1776 which plied backwards and forwards from Yarmouth. When the subtenant left their inn at Horstead Serjeant in 1776, for two months she helped run it. She had responsibility for the pigs, poultry, and, at least in part, the dairy. It was she who made cheese. She looked after the vegetable garden. She hired her female (and sometimes her male) servants and supervised their work. In 1776 the Hardy family also took on lodgers, a Mr and Mrs Ansell, not only housing them but sharing their dinner table with them. There were always people coming to the farm to buy hay, to survey their land, to buy farmyard muck, and to kill their rats. They ate with the family and often stayed the night. A Mr Christmas, anxious to learn the brewing trade, came to stay for a few days in 1780. In 1786 he returned as their regular maltster. The new tenants of their

[9] Ibid., pp. 5, 6, 23, 15, 34, 9, 31, 45, 51, 70, 109, 125, 130, 103, 125, 97, 113, 15, 16, 122.

inn at Horstead Serjeant lodged with them. In 1787 a Mr Scott
came from Yarmouth to learn the art of brewing; a year later, a
miller, Robert Starling, came to live with them. When in 1784 they
had a new water mill built, the thirty workmen plus six others
concerned 'supt' with the family. In 1790 they employed a new
clerk, Mr Wright, who lived with them. Two years later he was
replaced by a Mr Dexter. In 1800 an apprentice clerk, Henry
Raven, left them after living with them more than seven years. The
house was clearly a large one, and its upkeep must have made
constant demands on her time. Shortly after they moved in, carpenters and bricklayers followed and were regularly employed over
the next six years. Yet Mary Hardy still had time to devote to her
children and to her friends and neighbours. She also had the leisure
to make regular visits to the theatre and to public lectures; to take
holidays in London, Lancashire, and Yorkshire; to be meticulous in
her attendance at church, and, on occasion, to sample visiting
Methodist preachers and attend Quaker meetings. Her diary covers
thirty-five years, and she never missed a daily entry except when she
was ill.[10] This farming household was not unusual in combining
agriculture with another occupation. That Mary Hardy was not only
closely involved in the running of the farm and brewery but contributed a great deal of work to their successful management should
not surprise us. She was only doing what most farmers took for
granted of their wives.

In agriculture there were areas of farm work which traditionally
had always been the monopoly of women: all the work involved in
the dairy — the milking, the cheese and butter-making — the poultry
and the pigs, the vegetable garden and the orchard. Almost always
the preparation for, and attendance at, the local market was the
women's work. The day began early: a farmer's wife would be up
soon after five o'clock, ready, as Howitt recalled, 'to see that the
calves are properly fed, and to bargain with the butcher for the fat
ones; to feed her geese, turkeys, guinea-fowls, and barn-door fowls;
to see after the collection of eggs; how the milk is going on in the
dairy, the cream churning, and moulding the butter for sale'. On
larger farms, the work of the farmer's wife could be as much
supervisory as practical. Many had the responsibility for training
and organizing the day's work of a large body of living-in servants
of both sexes. Households of twenty were common, and large farms
could have far more. Farmers' wives had their housing and feeding

---

[10] Ibid., pp. 20–1, 38, 60, 22, 62, 66, 51, 72, 80, 109.

to arrange, and, in the case of the women servants, the direction of their work within the house, the dairy, and often elsewhere on the farm. It was not unusual to give day labourers partial board, so at midday the household might be considerably expanded. It was the wife of the farmer who got the female servants up in the morning 'to light fires, sweep the hearth, and get to milking, cheese-making, churning'.[11] When they were not working outside on the farm, it was the farmer's wife who directed their spinning and the making of clothes for the family. Many wives seem to have been in control of the finances of the farm, and to have kept the accounts.

The wife of the farmer usually took charge of the whole work of the dairy. 'The management or immediate superintendence of a large dairy especially one of which cheese is the principal object, is not a light concern,' as one author put it, 'it requires much thought, and much labour ... This arduous department is generally undertaken by the mistress of the dairy; especially on middle-sized and small farms.'[12] On larger farms, depending on the number of their cows, several dairymaids might be employed besides the mistress of the household. Dairy work involved long hours and the lifting of heavy weights. A 'famous Dairy-woman' in the early years of the century 'used to make her Butter in balls of Thirty or Forty pounds Weight'. In one 'great Dairy', twenty-two gallons of cream went into the churn from which 'with the Labour of a Lusty Man and Maid' butter was produced.[13] But this was nothing as compared with the heavy work involved in making cheese. In large dairies in Cheshire, for example, cheeses could weigh 'upwards of 140 lbs.'[14] Cheddar cheeses might weigh up to 100 lbs. One can see why William Marshall, observing the dairywomen of north Wiltshire, thought cheese-making 'too great a Labour for any woman'.[15] The cheese of Wiltshire dairywomen had a high reputation and it 'generally sold, retail, at a penny, and often twopence per pound, more than good cheese in common'. Wiltshire dairymaids were acknowledged as the best, and, as Twamley wrote, 'regularly bred to it from their childhood, it being almost the sole employ of the farm'. On some of the larger farms of Cheshire, Gloucestershire, and Wiltshire, by the end of the century men were being taken on as assistants, 'the weight of a large Cheshire Cheese, being too great to be wrought by a woman'.[16]

[11] William Howitt, *The Rural Life of England* (1840), pp. 109, 108.
[12] William Marshall, *Rural Economy of Gloucestershire*, 2 vols (1789), vol. i, pp. 263–5.
[13] J. Laurence, *New System of Agriculture* (1726), p. 136.
[14] H. Holland, *General View of the Agriculture of Cheshire* (1808), p. 282.
[15] W. Marshall, *Gloucestershire*, vol ii, p. 156.

But this was exceptional, and well into the nineteenth century, 'the labour of turning and cleaning cheese' was 'performed almost universally by women'.[17]

It seems to have been generally agreed that about ten to twelve cows to one milker was the average. When a farmer was questioned about how many cows a very good dairymaid could milk in an hour, the answer he gave was six, but he went on to add that he 'thought his wife could milk as far and with as much strength as anybody could', and 'she could once have milked eight, but she was not able, though of but a middle age, to do so now'.[18] Two milkings a day were common, but some dairies had three!

It was not just such physically heavy and time-consuming work that burdened farmers' wives. As we have seen, the responsibility for farm servants who lived in was theirs the whole year round. At harvest with the hiring of additional labour and, as in the case of the Hardy household, labour that was often temporarily housed, there was a great increase in the amount of food and drink that needed preparation, and, at least at midday, carrying into the fields. On some farms, one servant-maid was employed to do nothing else. In early September 1775, Mary Hardy recorded that she had gone into Norwich and 'bought a tea urn cost £1.1.0 and a tray 10/—'. The explanation followed: 'Three companys of harvest men here.'[19]

The day-to-day running of the household of even a middling-sized farm the whole year through meant careful planning and organization. The Hardy farm was moderately large and the family enjoyed comfortable if not luxurious circumstances. The smaller the farm or holding of land, the more crucial the contribution made by the wife. The family of William Stout came from comparatively prosperous yeomen stock, but when William's father settled on his estate it was small — not more than 12 acres. Stout described the work of his mother at the end of the seventeenth century. She was, he wrote, 'not only fully imployed in housewifry but in dressing their corn for the market, and also in the feilds in hay and corn harvests, along with our father and servants'. Both his father and his mother were 'very industrious'. It was rare for smallholders to

[16] J. Twamley, *Dairying Exemplified or the Business of Cheese-making* (1787), pp. 23–4, 20.

[17] Holland, *Cheshire*, p. 282; for an account of the time spent by farmers' wives in the dairy see Arthur Young, *A Six Week's Tour through the Southern Counties of England and Wales* (1772), pp. 57–8.

[18] Edward Lisle, *Observations in Husbandry* (1757), p. 298.

[19] *Mary Hardy's Diary*, p. 16.

be able to afford the cost of hired labour, so they were all the more dependent on the members of the family. At certain times of the year every hand available was needed. Even in the relatively prosperous Stout family, the children were 'taken off the schools, especially in the spring and summer season, plowtime, turfe time, hay time and harvest, in looking after the sheep, helping at plough, goeing to the moss with carts, making hay and shearing in harvest'.[20] Some cottagers owned or rented sufficient strips in the common fields to rank alongside of small farmers. An anonymous writer of 1767 tells us that 'there are some in almost every parish who have houses and little parcels of land in the field with a right of common for a cow or three or four sheep, by the assistance of which the profits of a little trade or their daily labour they procure a very competent living'.[21] 'Who does not know', wrote Howitt, 'what sums are made by cottagers and small occupiers, of the produce of their gardens and orchards, by carefully looking after it, and some one of the family bringing it to market, and standing with it themselves.'[22] It was usually the woman who cultivated the garden, and who was the 'someone' who took any surplus produce to market to sell. Some cottagers were their own masters for most of the year, only becoming wage-earners in hay-time and harvest. Others with little or no land were permanent wage-labourers, and they would leave to the care of their wives the cultivation of whatever small plot of land or garden they possessed, as well as the care of any livestock. This was 'the best situation for a labourer', a writer in 1796 explained, for 'the rest of the business is done by his wife, and his labour is not interrupted'.[23] Indeed, it was often *only* because of the role of the wives that a measure of self-sufficiency, and therefore of independence, was enjoyed.

Women's contribution involved work of many different kinds, both waged and unwaged, both in the home and outside of it. Whatever the small area of land possessed it was usually they who undertook the sowing, the weeding and hoeing, and usually the harvesting of crops. Even the wife of a cottager or squatter with no land at all could, by her cultivation of the cottage garden, provide

[20] *Autobiography of William Stout*, pp. 68, 70.
[21] Stephen Addington, *An Inquiry into the Reasons For and Against Enclosing Open Fields* (1772), p. 33; and see David Davies, *The Case of Labourers in Husbandry* (1795), p. 56.
[22] Howitt, *Rural Life of England*, p. 105.
[23] *Annals of Agriculture*, 26 (1796), p. 235; and see *A Political Enquiry into the Consequences of Enclosing Waste Lands* (1785), pp. 44, 46.

vegetables and other produce that helped achieve a measure of self-sufficiency. Within the home she cooked, baked and brewed. She did the housework and looked after her children. Sometimes with her children she would spin to provide yarn for the weaving of cloth, and by this means could clothe the entire family. The practice noted by Eden at the end of the century as confined to the north of England had earlier been almost universal: 'Almost every article of dress worn by farmers, mechanics, and labourers, is manufactured at home, shoes and hats excepted.' 'The linen thread is spun from the lint', he continues, 'and the yarn from the wool, and sent to the weaver's and dyer's: so that almost every family has its web of linen clothes annually, and often one of woollen also, which is either dyed for coats, or made into flannel, etc.'[24]

At hay-time and harvest the wives of agricultural labourers would help on local farms. It was taken for granted that everyone in the countryside left whatever they worked at to help bring in the harvest, but even with the extra labour of women, local resources were often insufficient and had to be supplemented from outside. In the 1730s, the poet Stephen Duck (1705–56) published his poem 'The Thresher's Labour', an account of the hardness of the day-to-day work of the agricultural labourer. The only two tasks in agriculture at which women were employed in his area of Wiltshire, according to his account, were hay-making and gleaning after the corn harvest. He was anything but complimentary about the way the 'Throng of prattling Females' performed these tasks. It was only as 'good expecting wives', waiting for the return of their weary husbands at the end of the day, with the bacon ready and the dumplings in the pot, that women won any praise from him. Even that was grudgingly given, with Duck suggesting wives were impatient of their husbands dawdling on the way home.[25] A somewhat different picture is painted by Mary Collier in her response to Duck. After a day 'spent in throwing, turning, making hay', women returned home to start on the 'domestic toils':

> our House in order set;
> Bacon and Dumpling in the Pot we boil,
> Our beds we make, our Swine we feed the while.

---

[24] F. M. Eden, *The State of the Poor*, 3 vols (1797), vol. i, pp. 554–5; and see James Spershott, *Memoirs of Chichester*, Sussex Archaeological Collections, vol. xxix (1879), pp 222–3.
[25] Stephen Duck, *Poems on Several Occasions* (1736), pp. 15–25.

Nor, according to her, was it only at gleaning that women worked in the harvest. Women also reaped, cut peas, and

> always ready are
> In ev'ry Work to take our proper Share.[26]

The agricultural tasks on which women were employed varied from one area to another. In Yorkshire, Elizabeth Montagu, the bluestocking who turned farmer on the death of her husband, considered 'women as capable of assisting in agriculture as the men', but she only mentions employing them to weed corn, hoe turnips, and set potatoes.[27] Often women (and their children) took part in hop-picking and gathering of fruit and vegetables; these were all tasks for which they were paid day-rates, and rates always less than those of male labourers — generally about half. If there were areas of work in agriculture traditionally regarded as belonging to women, there were others in which no such clear demarcation of sexual roles appears to have been drawn. The smaller the farm or landholding, the less any sexual division of labour appears. There were tasks to be done, and someone had to do them. Women were engaged as much in work outside on the farm as in work in the house or dairy. Arthur Young tells of a smallholder from the north of England who spoke of 'the necessity of turning out his wife or daughter to drive the plough in the depth of winter'.[28] The work done by female pauper apprentices and servants in husbandry seems to have differed even less than that done by men. By the end of the century, the persistence of the practice of employing women in the same tasks as men was beginning to attract attention. A distinction was already clear between the tasks in agriculture on which women in the south and east were employed and those which they performed in the west and north. In 1793, a writer describing a tour of Wales commented on the absence of any sexual division of labour in agriculture. 'As for the difference of sex, it would hardly be perceived ... if it was not for the criterion of the breeches,' he wrote, 'for labour seems equally divided between men and women, and it's as common to meet a female driving the plough, as it is to see Taffy seated at the milk pail.'[29]

[26] Mary Collier, *The Woman's Labour: An Epistle to Mr. Stephen Duck; in Answer to His Late Poem, Called 'The Thresher's Labour'* (1739), pp. 8, 9, 11.

[27] Dr Doran, *A Lady of the Last Century (Mrs Elizabeth Montagu)* (1873), pp. 210–11.

[28] Arthur Young, *The Farmer's Magazine* (1801), p. 19.

[29] E. D. Clarke, *Tour through the South of England, Wales and Part of Ireland, Made during the Summer of 1791* (1793), p. 216; for an indignant comment on this situation see A. Pringle, *General View of the County of Westmorland* (1794), p. 265.

It may seem surprising that so many families with either very small landholdings or no land at all save that attached to their cottages managed to maintain their independence, albeit frugally. Without common rights many would not have survived; with them the viability of the family economy was increased. Even a landless family could still secure 'a major part of their livelihood from the land because of the wide prevalence of customary rights of usage'.[30] Alan Everitt has written of how 'important though the labourers' individual small holding was, the vital factor in his fortunes was his rights of common. Preeminent ... were his grazing rights on common pasture' which were 'often extensive'.[31] They provided the means for keeping cows, sheep, hogs, and other livestock. For the smallholding family, they were a very useful supplement to their own pasturage. For those with no land they could make all the difference. Such rights varied from area to area, often from village to village. On the commons proper, there was no limit to those who could make use of the rights of pasturing they provided. On the village's common fields, rights were sometimes limited to those who actually owned land in the village fields, but were sometimes enjoyed by all those who owned or rented a house or cottage in the village. Ivy Pinchbeck thought such rights 'one of the greatest advantages of the old system'. 'While the labourer was earning a money wage or cultivating his strips in the common field, the commons gave his wife an opportunity of contributing to the family maintenance.'[32] Exactly how much she contributed depended on the stock she owned and the amount of time she could give to exploiting common rights. But they did present her with the possibility of providing food for her family. In the early eighteenth century, although by no means universal, common rights persisted in several parts of the country, particularly where as yet enclosures had made little or no progress and in forest areas. In Atherstone, in South Warwickshire, for example, in 1730, 100 out of 160 cottagers were keeping up to two horses and two cows, which, we are told, were 'plentifully supplied with Grass'. The rights that arose from the working of the village's common fields were also of benefit. They afforded 'a certain Livelihood'.[33]

[30] J. M. Martin, 'Village traders and the emergence of a proletariat in South Warwickshire, 1750–1851', *Agricultural History Review*, 32 (1984), p. 179.

[31] Joan Thirsk (ed.), *The Agrarian History of England and Wales*, vol. iv: *1500–1640* (1967), p. 403.

[32] Ivy Pinchbeck, *Women Workers and the Industrial Revolution, 1750–1850* [1930], (1981), p. 22.

[33] Quoted Martin, 'Village traders', p. 183.

Common rights did not end with grazing. There was also the right to gather wood, furze, bracken, and ling. In Atherstone 'the right to gather fuel' could bring 'in an additional 6−8 shillings per week in its season'.[34] In the month of September, farmers were directed to 'employ Women and Children to gather Most [acorns and beechnuts] for feeding Hogs at home for it is a Food which will make the Fat of these Creatures firm'.[35] There was sometimes the right to cut peat. To such rights was added that of gathering wild fruits and berries that grew in the forest and on the commons. Joan Thirsk has talked of the 'privileges' that lay 'in the shrubs, woods, under-growth, stone-quarries, and gravel-pits of the common' and of their yield of rabbits and hares, pigeons and deer.[36] Often such rights provided a vital supplement to a family's subsistence.

There is evidence of abuse of such rights, particularly of the overstocking of the commons by sheep. At Nottingham, for example, on 9 July 1733, 'Ellen Walter of Redhill Widow was fined for oppressing the Commons belonging to Arnold by depasturing there 300 sheep and other cattle belonging to her altho' she had no common rights there.'[37] Often, as in this case, the abuse was not by the cottagers and landless but by farmers who used the commons as additional pasturage. There were accusations, usually from would-be employers of cottagers' labour, of the way in which common rights generated sloth, and complaints were on the increase in the second half of the century. For the lazy, common rights may have provided the basis for a precarious but relatively industry-free exist-ence. But for the vast majority they would seem rather to have provided an incentive to industry.

One other customary right in which women and children were those mainly involved was 'leasing' or gleaning − gathering corn left in the fields after harvest. Sometimes the wives and children of those that harvested the fields benefited, sometimes the families of the poor in the parish concerned. 'Gleaning', wrote William Marshall, 'ought, most undoubtedly, to be considered, as an exclusive privilege of children, cripples, and superannuated reapers.' But Marshall was one of those with little sympathy for gleaners, and anyway this was in Yorkshire where women were still employed as

---

[34] Ibid.

[35] R. Bradley, *The Country Gentleman and Farmer's Monthly Director*, 3rd edn (1727), p. 155.

[36] Thirsk (ed.), *Agrarian History of England and Wales*, vol. iv, p. 404.

[37] *Nottinghamshire: County Records of the Eighteenth Century*, ed. K. W. Meaby (1947), p. 167.

'reapers' and where, as Marshall goes on to add, 'a young healthy woman ... would be ashamed to be seen gleaning'.[38] The results of such gleaning were increasingly the object of scornful comment from the rich. 'How many days during the harvest are lost by the mother of a family and her children', wrote one such critic of the practice, 'in wandering about from field to field to glean what does not repay them the wear of their clothes in seeking.'[39] Yet Eden claimed of Rode in Northamptonshire that 'several families will gather as much wheat as will serve them for bread the whole year'.[40] 'In the harvest month,' another writer adds, 'if the wife is not about the time of her delivery, she will glean three or four bushels.'[41] As the writer went on to point out, this was the equivalent of a labourer's wages over several weeks. In Atherstone in 1730, it was claimed, gleaning 'secured 15 shillings to a family'.[42] In Gloucestershire the average earnings of a labourer's wife in 1787 were given as £2. 11s. 6d. for thirteen weeks' work in agriculture. Of this sum £1. 13s. 0d. was from gleaning 'or leasing six bushels at 5s. 6d. per bushel'.[43] Although there were areas where enclosure meant gleaning was no longer as accessible or as profitable as hitherto, there seems little doubt that where it still existed the right was worth all the effort that went into it.

In towns the household functioned much as it did in the country except that probably more of the women's time was spent at working alongside her husband at the craft or trade, or assisting in the shop, and less on what in the countryside came under the general label of household tasks. Urban households were generally far less self-sufficient than rural, and urban wives depended more on shops and markets. Time spent by rural women in tending vegetables, making clothes, and baking bread was spent by town wives in shopping. The urban wives 'spun for their weaver husbands, polished metal for cutlers, sewed buttonholes for tailors, and waxed shoes for shoemakers'.[44] As in rural households there was a rough sexual demarcation between tasks men and women performed, but the women were usually familiar with all the tasks of the trade and

---

[38] William Marshall, *The Rural Economy of the Midland Counties*, 2 vols (1790), vol. ii, p. 159.
[39] Thomas Ruggles, 'Picturesque farming', in *Annals of Agriculture*, ed. Arthur Young, 46 vols (1784–1815), vol. ix (1788), p. 14.
[40] Eden, *State of the Poor*, vol. ii, p. 547.
[41] *Annals of Agriculture*, vol. xxv (1796), p. 488.
[42] Martin, 'Village traders', p. 183.
[43] Davies, *The Case of Labourers in Husbandry*, p. 162.
[44] Louise Tilly and Joan Scott, *Women, Work and Family* (1978), p. 47.

capable of taking over any of them when the need arose. Sometimes there was little or no difference between the work done by husbands and wives.

To suggest a separation of agriculture and industry as between country and town dwellers is to misrepresent the nature of pre-industrial society. There was a great deal of manufacturing in rural households where agriculture remained either the main or an important component of the subsistence of its members. Alice Clark, on the other hand, drew attention to how many families of the gentry, professional men, and tradesmen living in small towns in the seventeenth century had enough land to have their own dairy, and often to employ their own dairymaid, as well as to grow sufficient garden produce for the consumption of the family.[45] Not for nothing did Bradley in 1727 stress that 'what may be had from a good Garden, I doubt not will be sufficient to save a large family a considerable Expence, and afford them likewise a great deal of satisfaction'.[46] About 1720, the household in the manse in Kirkmichael, a small town in Ayrshire, consisted 'of the minister and his wife ... sister Betty, and four boys and three girls ... three women servants, a serving-man, who slept over the byre, and a herd lassie'. The women worked in the house and the dairy, the serving-man had 'to look after the garden and the glebe, to plough, to reap, to thresh corn, and fodder the cattle'.[47] There is also evidence of families from both villages and towns with no regular involvement in agriculture going out to help bring in the harvest or to help in the annual hop-picking. 'In hay and harvest time', wrote an anonymous author in 1773, 'it is inconceivable what numbers of tradesmen and handicraftsmen flock into the country.'[48] There was a yearly exodus from London of small tradespeople to the Kent hopfields, and in the summer many labourers in towns were attracted into the country to help bring in the harvest. So the distinction between town and country was not a clear one.

In the first half of the eighteenth century, industry was wide-spread — as indeed it had been for much of the previous century if not before. Manufacturing industry had long been in existence, although almost always in small units of production. Characteristic of the eighteenth century was the way in which in many rural households manufacturing was combined with agriculture, and

[45] Clark, *Working Life of Women in the Seventeenth Century*, p. 43.
[46] Bradley, *The Country Gentleman*, p. xix.
[47] H. G. Graham, *Literary and Historical Essays* (1908), pp. 139–40, 143.
[48] Anon., *An Enquiry into the Present Price of Provisions* (1773), p. 50.

indeed with other occupations. Professor Malcolmson has suggested that 'regular, full-time employment at a single job was not the norm'.[49] If this was true of rural households, it was also true, although possibly to a lesser extent, of urban households. Already, and well before the opening of the century, there were regions where a combination of manufacturing and agriculture was carried on. Often these occupations were so closely integrated in the life of the household it was impossible to say which was the most important. Joan Thirsk has referred to such cases as examples of an economy of 'dual occupation'.[50] It was a pattern followed by many households particularly in South Lancashire and in the West Riding.

In South Lancashire, for example, some form of work in textiles was often carried on side by side with small-scale agriculture — frequently, stock-keeping and running a dairy. Samuel Bamford in 1844 was to recall the working life-style of such households. The description is worth quoting in full, for it gives a clear and detailed account of just how such a 'dual occupation' economy functioned and of the sexual division of labour as Bamford saw it.

> The farming was generally of that kind which was soonest and most easily performed, and it was done by the husband and other males of the family, whilst the wife and daughters and maidservants, if there were any of the latter, attended to the churning, cheese-making and household work, and when this was finished, they busied themselves in carding, slubbing, and spinning of wool or cotton, as well as in forming it into warps for the loom. The husband and sons would next, at times when the farm labour did not call them abroad, size [i.e. dress] the warp, dry it, and beam it in the loom, and either they or the females, whichever happened to be least otherwise employed would weave the warp down. A farmer would generally have three or four looms in his house, and thus, what with the farming, easily and leisurely though it was performed, what with the housework, and what with the carding, spinning, and weaving, there was ample employment for the family. If the rent was raised from the farm, so much the better; if not, the deficiency was made up from the manufacturing profits, and as the weaver was also the vendor, he had a pretty fair command of his own remuneration.

[49] R. W. Malcolmson, *Life and Labour in England, 1700–1780* (1981), p. 23.
[50] Joan Thirsk, 'Horn and thorn in Staffordshire: the economy of a pastoral county', *North Staffordshire Journal of Field Studies*, 9 (1969), p. 11.

There were farmers and cottagers round Rochdale and Bury whose households were also engaged in flannel manufacture. Bamford wrote of the great size of flannel looms that occupied 'a large chamber over a whole house'. These rooms 'were the working places of women employed in the carding, slubbing and spinning of wool'.[51] Aikin in 1795 talked of the area in the neighbourhood of Sephton where leasehold tenants predominated. They regarded themselves as 'better than the common small farmers, and are above going to service or day labour; in consequence of which the men betake themselves to some trade or business, and the women to spinning cotton, which causes their living and dressing better, and the consequent greater consumption of articles of provision and clothing'.[52] The combination of cotton-spinning and weaving with a small agricultural holding was common. The women undertook with their children all the work preparatory to the weaving, which was usually men's work, and managed the dairying. Such a wife was the mother of Samuel Crompton. The account of how Samuel was involved in the processes preparatory to spinning is well known. What is less familiar is that as a widow, Betty Crompton 'continued the somewhat masculine labour of farming' near Bolton, marketing her butter every week. The work she did in 'carding, spinning and weaving', we are told, 'occupied every leisure hour'.[53]

In the woollen manufacture of the West Riding there was the same combination of agriculture and manufacturing. Defoe, in passing through the area round Halifax in the 1720s, found 'the land is divided into small enclosures, that is to say, from two acres to six or seven acres each, seldom more; every three or four pieces of land had a house belonging to it'.[54] In the houses lived the small clothiers so representative of this area. Often they were modest employers using not only the labour of their wives and their children, but of journeymen who came to work for them from the surrounding cottages, leaving at home wives who were often also employed by the small clothier in spinning. Nearly all these small masters shared a dependence on agriculture. On the small acreage of land which they possessed they would keep a cow or two, poultry, and grow a small amount of corn and vegetables for the household.

The work of the wife of the small clothier was varied. Not only

[51] Samuel Bamford, *Dialect of South Lancashire* (1850), pp. iv–v, 27.

[52] J. Aikin, *A Description of the Country from Thirty to Forty Miles round Manchester* (1795), p. 326.

[53] Gilbert J. French. *The Life and Times of Samuel Crompton* (1868), pp. 16–17.

[54] Daniel Defoe, *A Tour through England and Wales*, vol. ii, p. 195.

would she be familiar with every process preliminary to and including the weaving of cloth, but often the work involved on the small holding of land or in the dairy was largely her responsibility. In many ways the training she was able to provide for her children was as good as an apprenticeship (although counting for less outside their own household), as it introduced them to every aspect of the trade which very likely would be their source of livelihood. When her husband was absent from home, whether collecting yarn from spinners, buying raw material, or selling the finished product, it was the wife who took charge of the work of journeymen and apprentices. A poem written about 1730 describes just what work was involved for the wife of a Yorkshire small master when he had to leave home to buy wool. The night before his departure, he tells all the members of the household what work they must do while he is away. When his wife cursorily is told, 'Mary — there's wool — take thee and dye it', she protests:

> So thou's setting me to wark.
> I think I'd more need mend thy sark [shirt].
> Prithee, who must sit at bobbin wheel,
> And ne'er a cake at tope of creel [the wooden frame hung near
>   the roof on which oatcakes were laid to dry]
> And me to bake and swing and blend
> And milk, and barns to school to send,
> And dumplings for the lads to mak,
> And yeast to seek, and syk as that;
> And washing up, morn, noon, and neet,
> And bowls to scald and milk to fleet,
> And barns to fetch again at neet

Her protest is much the same as that made by Mary Collier against Stephen Duck's scornful account of women's work. When the wife of the Yorkshire clothier is reminded by her husband that

> ... all things mun aside be laid,
>   When we want help about our trade

she accepts more willingly the responsibility:

> Why Bairn, we'll see what we can do,
> But we have both to wesh and brew,
> And shall want Malt, Hops, Soap, and Blue.

> And thou'll be most a week away,
> And I's hev t'wark folk to pay.

The most important thing was to keep the lads at their work, her husband responds. He will pay them when he returns. He gives her money and expects her to keep a careful account of her spending.[55]

This combination of manufacture and agriculture is found in the south of Yorkshire as well as in the West Midlands, among metal-workers of all kinds – in the cutlery trade of Sheffield, for example, and among nailers. David Hey has written of how households were occupied in nailing from March to August when they stopped to bring in the harvest. Apparently, dealers talked of the difficulties of getting nails at harvest time when nailers were gathering in the crops.[56] That this combination of occupations was often the basis of a degree of material prosperity is confirmed by the inventories of nailers who died in the period 1660 to 1710, leaving some possessions. If sometimes incomes from nailing were combined with those from 'lime-digging and coal-mining', they were 'more often than anything else from farming'.[57]

There were industries – mining, sugar-refining, and ship-building are examples – where no 'putting-out' stage was ever experienced, yet these too could be combined with agriculture. Richard Millward, for example, was a collier who lived near Shrewsbury. Around his house, and including the garden, there was not much more than an acre of land 'formerly taken', we are told, 'from Pully Common, since divided and inclosed'. Millward's family consisted of his wife and six children. 'The management of the ground', according to the account, 'is, in a great measure left to his wife Jane', although 'her husband always assists in digging after his hours of ordinary labour'. For thirteen years, 'chiefly by her own labour', the land had been cultivated. She had grown 'good crops' of wheat and potatoes she sold in Shrewsbury; indeed, her crops were 'of late fully equal, or rather superior, to the produce of the neighbouring farms, and with little or no expence'. She kept a pig, which provided some manure for the land, and she would go round scraping more from the roads.

[55] 'Poem descriptive of the manners of the clothiers, written about the year 1730', quoted Pinchbeck, *Women Workers and the Industrial Revolution*, p. 127; E. P. Thompson, *The Making of the English Working Class* (1968), pp. 300–1.

[56] David Hey, 'A dual economy in South Yorkshire', *Agricultural History Review*, 18 (1969), pp. 108–19.

[57] Marie B. Rowlands, *Masters and Men in the West Midlands Metalware Trades Before the Industrial Revolution* (1975), pp. 47–52.

In her garden she cultivated peas, beans, turnips and cabbages, some of which she also sold in Shrewsbury.[58]

Edward Thompson has written of how 'merely slips of garden' commonly provided a possibility of supplementary earnings in the eighteenth century.[59] However small, they provided a degree of independence. A household where such a partnership with agriculture existed, if at a very marginal level, is that of the lead-miner on whose dwelling Defoe had stumbled in his tour of Derbyshire. The first sign he had of any habitation was 'a little parcel of land hedg'd in, as if it was a garden, it was about twenty or thirty yards long, but not so much broad'. In it was a good crop of barley almost ready for harvesting. The wife of the lead-miner who owned this plot was the mother of five children – the eldest being 'about eight or ten years old'. Outside the 'large hollow cave' in which this family lived 'was a sow and pigs running about . . . and a little lean cow feeding upon a green place just before the door'. The inside of the cave revealed not only cleanliness and neatness, but on the shelves, 'tho' mean and ordinary', earthenware, as well as some pewter and brass. There was a side of bacon hanging in the chimney. The lead-miner on a good day could earn 5*d*. His wife told Defoe that 'when she was able to work she washed the oar [*sic*]' at which she could earn 3*d*. a day. Living in a cave was perhaps unusual, but the buffer against bad times that their smallholding and livestock provided was most certainly not. It is at the most basic level an example of a dual economy, but it is a case that fits uneasily into any attempts to categorize households too precisely.[60]

For many housewives, the family economy might seem to have had advantages. For much of their time they had control of the organization of their day and of how they allocated time between tasks; the wife could combine the tending of her children when young, and their training when older, with the demands of the household. When work was done outside the home and away from the workshop or farm, her children could usually accompany her, often playing their part in harvesting and gleaning, and the collection of fuel and rushes. Historians have argued that it was only when women left the household to work outside the home that they began to grow in confidence and to achieve any real independence.

[58] *Report of the Society for Bettering the Condition and Increasing the Comforts of the Poor*, 5 vols (1798–1808), vol. v, pp. 84–9.
[59] Thompson, *Making of the English Working Class*, p. 298.
[60] Defoe, *Tour*, vol. ii, pp. 161–3.

But wives must have been conscious of their role as contributors to the family budget, whether it was in the form of food — vegetables from the garden, milk, butter and cheese from her cows, eggs from her poultry, all of which were the result of her labours — or of clothes of her making from raw material of her gathering — either from growing a little flax or hemp, or from keeping a few sheep, or even, as Alice Clark suggested, from picking off the wool caught in the brambles in the countryside.[61] Fuel for both heating and cooking was often of her gathering from the commons and woods. When she made bread it could well be from the corn gathered at gleaning after the harvest. Her wages from the work she did at hay-time and harvest on neighbouring farms was a *money* contribution to the family budget, as was what she gained by selling her yarn at the local market, or what she was paid by the agent of the local clothier. Her earnings, like the products of her other labour, went into the pool of family or household resources. In France to the present day, wives of small peasant farmers refer always to *mes vaches* and *mes poulets*. They are their responsibility and they take an understandable pride in them. When they sell the milk, butter, cheese, eggs, or poultry, the money goes into their own pockets and provides them with a measure of financial independence.

It was an economy that put a premium on careful housewifery, the making the best use of every resource available. 'Almost every living thing in the parish,' writes Alan Everitt, 'however insignificant, could be turned to some good use by the frugal peasant-labourer or his wife.'[62] It was also a flexible economy. Production could be balanced against consumption by working harder or longer hours, by taking in another member of the family or a near relation to help. But when there was a need for another hand at harvest, or someone to replace an apprentice who was sick, or when a master weaver had exhausted his supply of yarn, it was the women who rallied to supply the need. It was they who filled the gaps. So women's labour was of necessity flexible, ranging over a great variety of skills and in consequence ill-defined. This very vagueness of delineation of women's work role — the way in which their work as mothers of children, as trainers of the young, as working assistants to their husbands on farms or in workshops, as seasonal hired labour at hay-time and harvest, as part-time spinners for the local

[61] Clark, *Working Life of Women*, p. 64.
[62] Thirsk (ed.), *Agrarian History of England and Wales*, vol. iv, p. 405; and on the importance of thrift see Gudeman, 'Remainders on the margin'.

master weaver merged together in this economy — was a source of weakness and of disadvantage to women. For merchant manufacturers in search of a plentiful, cheap, and unrestricted labour force, such women provided an ideal and convenient answer — and also a highly exploitable body of labour. Their very flexibility was used against them.

Yet before the undermining of the family economy had got far, the contribution that wives were enabled to make must have meant something approximating to a working partnership with their husbands. That it was not an equal partnership is true. Men remained the heads of households with children, servants, and apprentices, but also wives, subservient to them and owing them obedience. But even an approximation to a working partnership cannot but have affected the relationship between husband and wife. Writing of both rural and urban households among 'the lowest ranks' in eighteenth-century France, Olwen Hufton has claimed that 'no distinction is made between them about who is the boss, both are'.[63] Whether or not the same was true of England, the relationship between husbands and wives must have come nearer to achieving real equality than in the situation where making such a contribution to the maintenance of their household was no longer possible for women.

[63] Olwen Hufton, *The Poor in Eighteenth Century France, 1750–1789* (1974), p. 32.

4

The Undermining of the Family Economy

Good people give attention while I sing in praise
Of the happy situation we liv'd in former days;
When my father kept a farm, and my mother milk'd her cow
How happy we livd then to what we do now.
When my mother was a knitting, and my sister she would spin
And by their good industry they kept it neat and clean

> From '*The Farmer's Son*', Broadside ballad printed by John Pitts
> (1765–1844)

We cannot construct a satisfactory picture of the operation of the family economy and the impact of industrialisation on it unless we undertake a careful investigation of the perceptions of the actors involved. ... we must attempt to trace the range of meanings and values which were embodied in their behaviour.

> David Vincent, *Bread, Knowledge and Freedom*

The process of transformation and almost complete undermining of the family economy has extended over a long period of time, starting in the sixteenth century and, in areas of Ireland and Wales, still not completed today. All one can say with confidence is that the undermining had gone further in 1750 than 1700, and further still in 1800. In some areas transformation was rapid, in others extremely slow.

What this process meant for women's work is best revealed by comparing the working life of different women. For example, contrast the life of the wife of a small farmer, a smallholder, or even a cottager with access to land and common rights and that of a dispossessed agricultural labourer with no access to land and no rights of common. For the former, ownership of, or even only access to, land enabled her to contribute to a greater or lesser degree to the maintenance of the household; the latter could only

47

hope to contribute by becoming an agricultural worker herself on someone else's land, doing tasks no longer of her choosing and outside her control, or by finding some alternative employment to agriculture. In either case she became a wage-earner. Again, there was a difference between the work of the wife of a small master clothier in the West Riding, and the wife of his journeyman; for the latter, as indeed for all involved in the cloth industry in the South West and East, the work role was already restricted. If, unlike their husbands, their work remained in the household, the processes with which they were involved were few, becoming fewer, and carefully defined. If they still owned spinning wheels or jennies, they no longer owned the raw material and were no longer responsible for marketing the finished product. All control over the amount of work available and when it was available was dictated by the agents of capitalist clothiers. What do these contrasts add up to? How had the nature of the family economy changed?

It was not only that home and workplace no longer always coincided for all members of the family, although this was true. The woman's work remained in the home while the husband's was often outside it, so the household was no longer a productive unit as it was when all members of the household worked within it. Nor was it just a question of the ownership of the means of production, although this entered into it. We could further contrast the working life of the wife of the master clothier and the female framework-knitter who no longer owned even the frame with which she worked; it was more a question of the nature of the work available to women narrowing in scope (and presumably interest) and no longer being under their own control. It was also a matter of a woman's diminishing independence as her ability to contribute anything to her family's maintenance came to depend solely on the wages she could earn. It was a reduction, and finally, for many, an elimination of the margin of independent subsistence that was possessed by a household with access to land. 'The viability of a working man's household economy', Malcolmson has claimed, 'depended heavily on the degree to which his family could gain some sort of (often partial) living from the land.'[1] In the process of removing that possibility, any approximation to a working partnership between wife and husband tended to be eroded.

Many of the changes that undermined the family economy were

---

[1] R. W. Malcolmson, *Life and Labour in England, 1700–1780* (1981), p. 24.

in agriculture and pre-dated the process of industrialization. Engrossing and the consolidation of farms, the growth of capitalistic methods of farming — all had their effect. Many of these changes had begun before the time of parliamentary enclosure. 'It is probable', wrote Mingay, 'that in many cases enclosure merely reinforced, rather than initiated, an old tendency towards larger farm units and sharper social divisions.'[2] But with the speeding up of the enclosure movement in the eighteenth century, change accelerated. Enclosure was often followed by agricultural specialization, particularly in the corn-growing areas of south and east England. New methods of cultivation, new crops, new technology — all had the effect of changing the nature and extent of women's work in agriculture and of sharpening the sexual division of labour.

With the growth of a more capitalistic system of farming, the nature of marketing was to change from a mainly local to a national or regional orientation with the emergence of middlemen between farm and market. The continued and spectacular growth of the metropolis provided a vast and expanding market for foodstuffs. For the commercially minded farmer it gave promise of rich profits. But quite apart from the growth of London, the increase in the population of the country as a whole, the pressure of that population on food supplies and the consequent rise in prices, alongside of the failure of wages to keep pace with them after the mid-eighteenth century, were closely related to these changes. They led to the pauperization of a significant section of society, and the nature of the Poor Law administration that 'pauperization' called forth was an additional factor in the process of the undermining of the family economy.

If at one end of the social scale there was a significant increase in poverty, at the other was a growth in the ranks of those who, prospering from changed economic conditions, began to identify with middle-class aspirations to gentility. There were wives of large farmers who, prospering in conditions of a growing population and an expanded market for foodstuffs and raw materials, grew wealthier and emulated the life-style of the upper classes. They became aware of work as a class barrier cutting off those who laboured from those who did not. Aspirations to gentility influenced the outlook of both wives and husbands. For women, the increasingly sophisticated marketing arrangements for farm produce meant that no longer was

[2] G. E. Mingay, *Enclosure and the Small Farmer in the Age of the Industrial Revolution* (1968), p. 21.

the surplus production of the farm directed towards the local market. Now that farm produce was often taken away by middlemen to distant, unknown markets in London or some growing industrial town, the wife of the farmer might still go to market but no longer did she commonly attend with the purpose of disposing of surplus produce.

An anonymous author in 1786 made clear the link between the withdrawal of women's labour and the increasing size of farms at the cost of the smallholder when he wrote of 'the lands in their former state' being 'let to five times the number of tenants', and of how 'the farmers are reduced to one fourth of their number'. But 'they, very opulent' had sufficient to supply themselves and their families 'without any kind of business'. This was in sharp contrast to the experience of small farmers who 'were obliged to make money of everything they could sell', and so their wives 'used all their industry and care to raise all manner of poultry and eggs and to make the best of their dairies'.[3]

With the rise of prices of corn from the middle of the century, there was growing inducement for farmers to increase production. The consequent specialization of southern and eastern regions in corn production meant that many traditional work areas for women on the farm were eroded, particularly in the dairy and in butter- and cheese-making. In some places, farmers seem to have regarded such areas as troublesome diversions of labour from the main work of the farm. In other, more western areas and districts unsuited to corn, dairying continued to be essential to the farm's profits. But with their wives no longer willing to supervise the dairying, many farmers were reluctant to depend on hired labour alone and rented out their dairies or hired dairy-managers — almost always men — to take over the work. So control in what had always been an area of women's responsibility frequently passed into the hands of men. Where dairies were kept under the control of the household, the produce went more to supply the family than for market. The consequences of these changes for the local markets were great, and a reason for many of the labouring poor complaining at the end of the century of the shortage of farm products like milk and butter that earlier had been readily available.[4] The decline of service in husbandry, which we shall be examining later, was another major

---

[3] Anon., *Cursory Remarks on Enclosure ... by a Country Farmer* (1786), pp. 19–22.
[4] See e.g. J. S. Girdler, *Observations on the Pernicious Consequences of Forestalling, Regrating and Engrossing* (1800), p. 9.

responsibility removed from the wife of the farmer, and one which had ensured servants and their mistresses living and working close together in the household. So for a number of reasons, farmers' wives were distancing themselves from involvement in the work of the farm.

These changes were not confined to farming households. Some tradesmen and skilled artisans were also enjoying a far higher standard of living than formerly. As their trade expanded, more apprentices and journeymen were employed and the wife's involvement tended to decline. Finally, as business outgrew the workshop in the cottage or house, the wife became physically isolated from the place where the business was carried on. New ideas of gentility made some wives reluctant to participate in their husbands' trades. Defoe in the 1720s talked of women who 'marry a tradesman but scorn the trade'.[5] He was writing of London. Outside the metropolis this process cannot have gone very far by the time Defoe was writing, but it was to accelerate as the century progressed.

Many of the women concerned may have welcomed the release such changes brought from the heavy burden of farm work, the demands of the workshop, and the drudgery of housework. Yet the desire for freedom from such burdens was not the main motive behind this withdrawal from productive work. More important were the effects of the changes going on around them on their work role and new aspirations to gentility. When did a withdrawal of women from productive work begin? Alice Clark has suggested the process was already under way in the seventeenth century, if not earlier. She wrote of 'a tendency' among the wives of 'capitalistic farmers . . . to withdraw from the management of the business and devote themselves to pleasure'.[6] If her timing is right, the idea of lives wholly devoted to pleasure needs some qualification. Such a view echoes too uncritically the conservative reaction that their withdrawal called forth against any change — certainly any that took women out of their proper place in the kitchen, away from baking and preserving and brewing and making clothes for members of their families.[7] Thomas Day puts into the mouth of his Devon farmer a shrewd comment. His wife, unlike many mothers of daughters, believed in 'their milking, spinning and making themselves

---

[5] Daniel Defoe, *The Complete English Tradesman* (1726–7), from *The Novels and Miscellaneous Works of Daniel Defoe* (1840–1), vol. i, p. 216.

[6] Alice Clark, *Working Life of Women in the Seventeenth Century* [1919], (1982), p. 92.

[7] See *Gentleman's Magazine* (1801), pp. 587–8, for criticism of farmers' daughters.

useful', but, he went on, 'she would fain have them genteeel . . . all women are now mad about gentility, and, when once gentility begins there is an end of industry'.[8]

There was every reason for women feeling that much of this work was back-breaking and exhausting, but it was not just from the back-breaking work that some farmers' wives withdrew. There were those who also gave up the supervision of servants, the organization of the marketing of farm produce, and control of the financial management of the farm and the accounts. If such tasks were demanding and frequently laborious, they must also have exercised the women's intelligence, ingenuity, and good management and given them a real interest in the running of the farm, if not a participation that approximated to a business partnership. As Pinchbeck suggested, it must have 'tended to a development of independence and initiative'.[9] Had such labour been replaced by other interests, and an expansion of the educational and cultural horizons of such women, it could have represented an advance. But all too often, their newly won leisure was barren of interest. Their withdrawal came to mean not merely a retreat from active labour but a social contempt for labour, particularly manual labour, of any sort. Hence the desperate desire to separate themselves from those they saw as their social inferiors − those who needed to work in order to live. So this separation from work contributed to a polariz-ation of class differences, and an increasing consciousness of class. One consequence was that in order that the work of the household and dairy should continue to be done, domestic servants had to be hired. We shall be examining the role they played later.

Evidence suggests that change came about first in the south and east of the country. Only later was it to permeate the north so that a growing contrast in women's working experience was found between south and north. Elizabeth Montagu's comment on the contrast between women in the south and those of a Yorkshire farm where 'the farmer's wife spins her husband's shirts, and the daughters make butter and cheese at the hours our southern women work catgut and dress wire caps' supports such a thesis.[10]

For the wives of smallholders, cottagers, and squatters, the changes that led to some women withdrawing from productive labour almost certainly meant a decline in work opportunities, but for them there

[8] Thomas Day, *Sandford and Merton* (1786), p. 303.
[9] Pinchbeck, *Women Workers and the Industrial Revolution* [1930], (1981), p. 35.
[10] Dr Doran, *A Lady of the Last Century* (1873), p. 198.

was never the element of choice. So far, the effect of consolidation and growth in size of farms has been seen only as a problem for the men of the household who were now reduced to the status of wage-labourers hiring themselves to local farmers as opportunity arose. But this is only half the picture: for the women of such households, the changes had just as serious consequences, and moreover, what they lost was often crucial to the degree of independent subsistence enjoyed by their families — subsistence at however low a level.

Following the loss of their land, the wives of former smallholders — unless they had the possibility of alternative work in some cottage industry, and often even if they had — sought work as hired labour along with their husbands. What sounds like a pattern of work opportunity identical to that of their husbands was in practice very different. Common to both was the irregular and seasonal nature of such employment and the long periods of the year in which the chances of being hired by local farms were remote. After 1750, what increasingly differentiated female from male agricultural labour, at least in the south and east, was the changed nature of that employment and the very different female seasonal unemployment pattern. Up to this time, the pattern of unemployment for men and women was similar. The peak of unemployment was reached in winter, and the peak of employment in the harvest months. After the middle of the century, as we shall see, the pattern of women's labour began to diverge from that of men. For women it meant a trend towards highest employment in the spring, whereas men's employment was increasingly concentrated at harvest-time. The differing patterns of seasonal employment for women in agriculture reflected changes in the nature of the agricultural tasks available. The isolation of women's employment from that of men and its confinement to a period of low labour costs and low demand for labour resulted in the fall in female real wages from about 1760 and the tendency, at least for a period, for them to move in inverse correlation to those of men.[11] In the south-west of England and Wales, where pastoral farming continued, women's work in livestock, dairying, and hay-making continued, and no downward tendency in female money wages occurred.

Thus, with the specialization on corn production and the consequent decline of traditional areas of agriculture in which women's labour had predominated, the potential in the south and east for a wide participation of women in agricultural labour was in decline

[11] K. D. M. Snell, *Annals of the Labouring Poor* (1985), p. 37.

long before the process of industrialization got under way.[12] But how exactly did this specialization of the south and east affect the sexual division of labour in agriculture? In the first place, it is important to establish the area involved. It covered the counties of Cambridgeshire, Suffolk, Norfolk, Huntingdonshire, and Essex as well as Hertfordshire, Buckinghamshire, and Northamptonshire in the East Midlands, and extended as far south as Berkshire. In all these counties grain-growing predominated.[13] The trend for women's involvement in agriculture to move away from the summer tasks of hay-making and harvest towards springtime work started in the mid-eighteenth century but was confirmed and accentuated in the twenty years from the early 1790s. According to Snell, from the middle of the 1830s to about 1860 the shift was completed and a marked sexual specialization of agricultural work became clear.[14]

One point requires emphasizing. Women, whether from the countryside or the town, had always assisted in bringing in the harvest. For many women in the countryside it had been the only waged agricultural work in which they participated and which took them away from their own household. It had represented the best-paid work in agriculture. After the middle of the century, women in the south-east were involved in the less well paid and less prestigious areas of farm work. Many of the jobs were not new. In weeding and stone-gathering, hoeing and spreading manure, women had long been involved, but now such tasks figured more among women's activities. Spring weeding of corn was a result of the new importance given to keeping crops weed-free. In 1797 Eden writes of women at Gressinghall in Norfolk who 'for weeding corn are paid 6*d*. and 8*d*. a day'. In Swineshead in Lincolnshire, 'women receive 1*s*. or 1*s*. 2*d*. a day, for weeding corn'. At Alford in the same county, women 'for weeding corn, have 8*d*. or 10*d*. a day'.[15] William Marshall, writing of the agriculture of the Midlands, recommended the practice he found 'of employing a woman to follow the plough especially in fallowing, to pick up the root weeds exposed in the furrow, more particularly the Dock'.[16] Hoeing gained a new importance with the introduction of root crops like turnips, and for this women were paid at much the same rates as for hand-weeding. One extremely

---

[12] Ibid., p. 51.
[13] Ibid., p. 18.
[14] Ibid., p. 22.
[15] Sir F. M. Eden, *State of the Poor*, 3 vols (1797), vol. ii, pp. 470, 404, 390.
[16] William Marshall, *The Rural Economy of the Midland Counties*, 2 vols (1790), vol. i, p. 211 n.

arduous task, and one which had to be done by hand, was removing couch grass from among crops. In Surrey in 1775, Marshall reported that 'six women and one man were four hours in hand-picking half an acre'.[17] Removing stones from fields was another task at which chiefly women were employed. They were also employed in setting wheat, peas, and beans. 'One man and one young woman dibbled', Marshall wrote of the practice in Norfolk in 1781, 'while three women and three girls dropped.'[18] Provided bad weather did not intervene, this group of eight labourers could complete three-quarters of an acre in a day. Payment was ten shillings and sixpence an acre.[19] Outside these activities women found little employment in agriculture.

The trend was not confined to a greater sexual division of labour and a tendency for women's earnings to decline. It was a downward trend in the demand for women's labour. The change in women's work to spring tasks and away from involvement in harvest added up to less work. There was, as Keith Snell has suggested of the south and east of the country, 'a decline of women as a percentage of the total labour force' and 'a decline of their annual earning capacity'.[20] Nor was this trend only confined to counties in which there was specialization in corn production. The demand for labour of the more intensive, capitalistic farming was irregular, so that there were long periods when there was no demand for hired labour of either men or women. Then, in conditions of rising population and mounting prices, men's real wages began to fall from about 1780. So where the need to supplement inadequate male wages was growing, women's ability to make a significant contribution to the household budget was declining. Evidence of lack of work for women extending far beyond those counties specializing in corn production is abundant. Arthur Young lamented in 1771 that 'picking hops' was 'the only employment of women' in East Kent.[21] In South Wales, Eden found women who 'assist in harvesting, and in weeding and stone picking: their earnings are very inconsiderable. Employment for labourers' wives and children is much wanted.'[22]

---

[17] William Marshall, *Minutes of Agriculture on a Farm of 300 Acres of Various Soils near Croydon, Surrey* (1778), entry for 20 Apr. 1775.

[18] William Marshall, *The Rural Economy of Norfolk*, 2 vols (1787), vol. ii, p. 53; see also id., *The Rural Economy of Gloucestershire*, 2 vols (1796), vol. i, p. 140.

[19] Ibid.

[20] Snell, *Annals*, p. 63.

[21] Arthur Young, *The Farmer's Tour through the East of England*, 4 vols (1771), vol. iii, p. 48.

[22] Eden, *State of the Poor*, vol. iii, p. 898; vol. ii, pp. 398, 404.

In Gloucestershire a woman working in agriculture for a quarter of the year earned less than 4s. a week at bean and pea setting, fruit picking, hay-making, and gleaning.[23]

Changing agricultural technology may well have played a part in reinforcing the sexual division of tasks, at least in the south of the country and in some parts of the Midlands. In areas specializing in corn production there was a need to make the period in which costly additional harvest labour was taken on as short as possible. Farmers were also anxious to speed up the process of the harvest to take advantage of the best weather and the 'pre-harvest peak of prices'. The use of the scythe for 'mowing' corn enabled a much wider swathe to be cut. But the greater size and weight of the long-handled scythe over the much lighter, short-handled sickle made it a tool for the strong and the tall, and so effectively limited its use to men. Its disadvantages were that it was a less tidy cutter than the sickle and left behind more corn. With the increase in corn production, it was argued, this wasteage was less important than the speed with which the corn could be cut and the harvest gathered in. In his survey of harvest technology in the early modern period, Michael Roberts has found no evidence of women using scythes in mowing either grass or corn. The period in which the heavier tool was adopted in the south, he comments, coincides with the period in which the sexual division of labour becomes more pronounced — that is, the period following 1750. The area in which the scythe was introduced coincided with that in which the greatest change in the pattern of female agricultural employment occurred.[24]

Mowing may have been quicker than reaping, but it left behind far more subsidiary work. So when in the south of the country the scythe came to be used to mow wheat and rye, and so excluded women from the best-paid jobs available at harvest, it increased the subsidiary and less well-paid tasks — a familiar pattern in the effects of changing technology on women's work. So in the south and east, women from being the reapers became the followers and rakers of the harvest. Some writers specifically exclude women from any part in the reaping of corn. At Rode in Northamptonshire, 'women ... are never employed in reaping'.[25] In Houghton Regis in Bedfordshire, harvest work was 'entirely performed by men'.[26]

[23] David Davies, *The Case of Labourers in Husbandry* (1795), p. 162.

[24] Michael Roberts, 'Sickles and scythes: women's work at harvest time', *History Workshop Journal*, no. 7 (Spring 1979), pp. 3–28 (pp. 7, 20).

[25] Eden, *State of the Poor*, vol. ii, p. 544.

[26] Ibid., p. 4.

Even as far north as near Hull, Young found it was 'the custom to mow their wheat: they do it with a common scythe. . . . A woman follows every mower, to gather the corn and lay it in order for binding.' Yet it cannot have been a universal practice, for he goes on to suggest how 'women at the prospect of great wages clap their hands with cheerfulness and fly to the sickle'.[27] It makes the point of how reaping was the best-paid work in agriculture. It also emphasizes how reaping and mowing went on side by side.

But the scythe was only slowly adopted, and for some time its use was confined to certain areas. Even then its adoption was not consistent but depended on the availability of experienced mowers, and the weighing of the extra cost of such labour against its advantages. In some areas use of the scythe fluctuated, with a return to the sickle when there was a plentiful supply of cheap labour or when a shortage of male agricultural labour pushed up its price. For the nineteenth century, Eve Hostettler has shown how the fact that women's wages were generally half that of men influenced a farmer's decision on whether to use the sickle or scythe in harvest.[28] But it was not just a question of relative cost. 'With a sickle', it was said, 'a woman is as efficient a worker as a man.'[29] Throughout the first half of the nineteenth century in the north of England as well as in Scotland, reapers were quite as likely to be women as men. In areas where the scythe was not introduced, the division of labour between the sexes was not so clearly defined. Esther Boserup has shown how changes in the division of labour in agriculture in Africa and the Third World are closely related to farming technology and changes in population density. Where in more heavily populated areas the plough has been introduced, women are virtually excluded from agricultural work. This is true even in areas where formerly all the hoeing had been done by women.[30]

On the Shipcote Park Estates at Gateshead in the 1730s 'both hay and Corn harvests were largely dependent upon female labour'.[31] But even as late as 1797 in a survey of Northumberland's agriculture, it was reported that 'most of the corn is cut with sickles by women;

---

[27] Arthur Young, *A Six Months' Tour through the North of England*, 3 vols (1770), vol. i, pp. 111, 115.

[28] Eve Hostettier, 'Gourley Steell and the sexual division of labour', *History Workshop Journal*, no. 4 (1977), pp. 95–101 (p. 95).

[29] Henry Stephens, *The Book of the Farm* (1844), quoted Hostettler, 'Gourley Steell', pp. 95–6.

[30] Esther Boserup, *Women's Role in Economic Development* (1970), pp. 24, 33.

[31] Joan Thirsk (ed.), *The Agrarian History of England and Wales*, vol. v, pt. i. *1640–1750* (1984), p. 57.

seven of whom, with a man to bind after them, generally reap two acres a day'.[32] Northumberland farm wage-books of the middle of the century confirm that women were frequently responsible for reaping. Of Yorkshire practice in 1790, William Marshall wrote how 'all the wheat, generally speaking is reaped by women'.[33] Indeed, in the north of England it remained primarily women's work well into the nineteenth century. They were paid the same rates for the job as men, and sometimes even higher rates.

While as yet no comprehensive study of agricultural practice in the north has been made, contemporary evidence suggests that women there continued to do much the same work, and that no marked sexual division of labour revealed itself before the end of the century. So in 1796 in Northumberland, according to George Cully, 'our girls are all employed in agriculture, hoeing, hay-making and reaping, etc.'[34] It was not just the relative backwardness of agriculture in the north that accounts for this. Nor was it only the consequence of the bondage system operating in the north, and particularly in Northumberland. The demand for male labour from developing industries meant there was no excess supply of male agricultural labour. Indeed, as Paul Brassley has written of farming areas of Northumberland and Durham, 'a shortage of male labour was more likely than a surplus'.[35] Women were needed to do the same tasks they had always done. With alternative employment also available to women, it is likely that no decline in female real wages occurred nor any overall decline in the degree of participation of women in agriculture, at least until after the eighteenth century.

In Devon and Cornwall, where pastoral farming was predominant and the traditional areas of women's work in agriculture remained unchanged, there would seem to have been less decline in their participation. So 'women everywhere in the county', wrote the author of a survey of Cornwall in 1811, 'perform a large share of the rural labour, particularly the harvest work, weeding the corn, hoeing turnips, potatoes, etc., attending the threshing machines; by the latter business they have more employment in the winter than they formerly had'.[36] In Wales, women continued to do all 'the

[32] J. Bailey and G. Culley, *General View of the Agriculture of the County of Northumberland* (1797), p. 95.
[33] Marshall, *Rural Economy of the Midland Counties*, vol. ii, p. 159.
[34] Thirsk (ed.), *Agrarian History of England and Wales*, vol. v, pt. i, p. 57.
[35] Ibid.
[36] G. B. Worgan, *A General View of the Agriculture of the County of Cornwall* (1811), p. 159.

most arduous exertions and business of husbandry, and they are very commonly seen either driving the horses affixed to the plough, or leading those which draw the harrow'.[37]

What were the consequences for the male agricultural labourer of the diminished role of women? It is possible that it actually cushioned them from the full consequences of agricultural change, at least for a period. If women's involvement had not declined it is likely that men would have suffered more from unemployment and experienced an earlier decline in real wages. It is possible that the physical strength needed to wield the scythe was exaggerated in the interests of those anxious to exclude women from the better-paid and most prestigious of agricultural tasks. The use of the scythe achieved this on what appeared to be rational grounds. But there were other agricultural tasks which women continued to do which were just as physically demanding, if not as well paid. In those areas where the scythe was in use, periods of labour shortage could delay its extension. So behind changes in agricultural technology and their consequences for women, there lay the threat of unemployment for the male agricultural labourer and the need to reduce competition from women. It was not just from harvest work that women were excluded. Is it possible that employers of agricultural labour were prepared to ally themselves with male labour in the interests of confining women to the household and of keeping families' dependence on poor relief to a minimum? William Marshall, admittedly rather a misogynist, is vehement in his insistence in 1776 that 'if ever I employ women in future, in hay-time or harvest, it must be from a scarcity of men'.[38]

With the decline of smallholdings, two further developments contributed to the erosion of the already precarious family economy: the attempt to do away with cottages and the bit of land that almost invariably went with them, and thus the removal of the basis on which many were able to claim common rights; and the acceleration of the process of enclosure. Such common rights could prove as inconvenient to farmers anxious to consolidate their farms as were the tenants of smallholdings. Many writers in the second half of the century stressed the difference that a small amount of land could make to the labouring poor. Nathaniel Kent in 1775 had proposed that even the smallest cottage should have half an acre of land attached to it so that the inmates grow their own vegetables and fruit, and even keep a pig. For bigger cottages he proposed

[37] George Lipscombe, *Journey into South Wales in the Year 1799* (1802), pp. 111–12.
[38] William Marshall, *Minutes of Agriculture Made on a Farm*, entry for Sept. 1776.

that, besides the garden land, about three acres of pasture be added to enable the occupants to 'support a cow'.[39] Eden wrote of how he 'often observed that when the circumstances of a labouring family have enabled them to purchase a cow [and they would only have purchased one if they had available grazing for it], 'the good management of the wife had preserved them from the parish as long as the cow lasted'.[40] David Davies in 1795 lamented that so 'few cottages, comparatively, have now *any* land about them'. Davies had seen such parcels of land 'swallowed up' and even the cottages destroyed. The wives of such cottagers 'could formerly, when they wanted work abroad, employ themselves profitably at home; whereas now,' continued Davies, 'few of them are constantly employed, except in harvest'.[41] In 1795 in Farnham, Surrey, the wife of a labourer away in the militia assured her interrogator 'that she and six young children, and big of a seventh, none of whom can earn anything regularly, should have perished, if it had not been for the great assistance derived from her land, which she has, in her husband's absence, cultivated with her own hands, even to digging for sowing some rye and wheat'.[42] One can see why this slender basis of independence was resented by employers.[43]

In conditions of a decline in opportunities for day-labour in agriculture, the diminished payment of those tasks left for women, rising prices, the loss of their parcels of land, and often of their cottages, the ability of women to make any significant contribution to the household was lost. To accelerate all these developments came enclosure, or rather, for enclosure was not new, the acceleration of the process between 1760 and 1820. It came when the hold of many on a viable family economy was tenuous. It shut doors that had earlier still remained just ajar. If one considers what effect enclosure had on the ability of women to do productive work and thus contribute significantly to the household budget, it is difficult to avoid the conclusion that enclosure was wholly detrimental.

The Hammonds concluded that 'enclosure was fatal to three classes: the small farmer, the cottager, and the squatter'.[44] It is unfortunate that recent assessments of the Hammonds have concentrated almost exclusively on land ownership as it affected the first of

---

[39] Nathaniel Kent, *Hints to Gentlemen of Landed Property* (1775), p. 238.

[40] Eden, *State of the Poor*, vol. i, p. 628.

[41] Davies, *The Case of Labourers in Husbandry*, pp. 56–7.

[42] *Annals of Agriculture*, vol. xxxvi, pp. 588–9.

[43] For example see John Billingsley, *General View of the Agriculture of the County of Somerset* (1797), p. 52.

[44] J. L. and B. Hammond, *The Village Labourer, 1760–1832* [1911], (1987), p. 96.

the three classes at the cost of ignoring the general social consequences of enclosure. Attempts at a re-evaluation of the Hammonds have been based on land tax assessments; but the vast majority of those with whom the Hammonds were concerned were never rich enough to be assessed, so such attempts hardly meet the points the Hammonds were making. In any case there seem to be some serious reservations about the reliability of land tax assessments for these purposes among precisely those most anxious to discount the views of the Hammonds.

Recent attempts to review the orthodoxy that, far from enclosure leading to the disappearance of the smallholders, in many areas their numbers actually increased, have tended to concentrate on local studies. J. M. Neeson, for example, in her study of Northamptonshire, has underlined how the wrong questions have been posed of enclosure. The act of counting numbers of smallholders before and after enclosure conceals more important consequences than it reveals. When one looks at individual smallholders, the severity of the blow they suffered from enclosure becomes clearer for 'not only did they lose common right, but they lost land too'. Many sold up entirely, or sold most of their land. Many of those selling up, it is true, were replaced by other smallholders, but what is concealed is that the economy in which they now worked was an entirely different one. Enclosure had 'extinguished the old common right economy'.[45] Neeson's work underlines a point of importance in the standard of living debate: how dangerous it is for historians to be so intent on quantifying change that they ignore changes in those they are quantifying, and the qualitative gap that separates them.

If the extinguishing of the common-right economy dealt a severe blow at many individual smallholders, it was even more of a blow for their wives and families. The sexual division of labour that had already emerged as a result of changes in agriculture was to be increased by the effects of enclosure. Not only was the scope of women's work in agriculture reduced, but the amount of work available to women declined, and what remained was the least well paid work. It also made women totally dependent on wage-labour: no longer was part of their time spent working for their own families in the open fields of the village, or looking after their own

[45] J. M. Neeson, 'England: the disappearance of the small peasantry, revisited'. 1984 Paper based on 'Common Right and Enclosure in Eighteenth Century Northamptonshire', unpublished Ph.D. thesis, University of Warwick, 1978. See George Grantham and Carol Leonard (eds), *Agrarian Organizations during Industrialization: Europe, Russia, and America in the Nineteenth Century* (forthcoming).

sheep or cows grazing on the commons. At a time when their contribution was all-important to the continued existence of the family economy, opportunities for productive work were in decline. 'It was probably the case', writes Keith Snell of the early eighteenth century, 'that the decline then of both small tenants and owner— occupiers reduced the potential for a wide participation of women within the family economy.'[46] Enclosure and the erosion of common rights completed the process.

At a time when the cumulative effects of these changes in agriculture were being felt most, particularly by women, an additional factor was added to those already playing havoc with the viability of the family economy: the decline of some of the oldest handicraft and domestic industries and a marked change in the geographical distribution of others. Of course, not all were affected at the same time. Even in those industries where new technology first began to threaten home industry it was an uneven process, with some areas remaining almost unaffected for long after its first application. In some cases — framework-knitting is an example — the main changes were not to come until the nineteenth century. Nevertheless, many of those that survived after 1815 were in decline. Thus, though the woollen industry of the West Riding thrived in the eighteenth century, that of the West Country and East Anglia declined.

Domestic industry since the seventeenth century, and even before, had been an important source of employment for women. Indeed, historians have long emphasized how agricultural change from the seventeenth century contributed to the growth of a cheap and limitless supply of female and child labour for rural industry. The 'dual' or 'multi'-occupational nature of so many households in the eighteenth century was in large part a reaction to the growing difficulty of keeping the family economy going on agriculture alone. Of his family's resort to cotton manufacture, William Radcliffe explained how 'the principal estates being gone from the family, my father resorted to the common but never-failing resource for subsistence at that period, viz. — the loom for men, and the cards and hand-wheel for women and boys'.[47] Often the entry of women into some sort of domestic manufacturing had been essential to the continued subsistence of the household, a circumstance exploited from the beginning by employers. In 1782, in the village of Cardington in Bedfordshire, two-thirds of all the housewives were

[46] Snell, *Annals*, p. 62.
[47] William Radcliffe, *Origins of the New System of Manufacture* (1828), pp. 9–10.

employed in domestic industry – mainly in lace-making and spinning.[48]

Spinning had been an almost universal occupation of women, whether as a full-time or part-time employment. So long as it took the labour of several spinners to supply sufficient yarn to keep a male weaver fully occupied, spinning remained an occupation on which the wives or daughters of small farmers or cottagers could always depend to supplement the familial income. Wages were almost always low. They were to sink even lower, but the earnings that women (and children) gained often served to stave off pauperization and even to keep the family economy afloat.

In the cotton industry, the earliest technology – Hargreave's Spinning Jenny, patented in 1770 – at first did little to change the organization of spinning. It was used by both women and children, still within the home. For a brief time it enabled women spinners to earn much higher prices. Its limitation was that it produced thread only suitable for the weft. It was only with improvements in the jenny, and when finally it was harnessed to water power, that the new technology became a threat to the cottage industry. It resulted in removing not only cotton-spinning from the cottage, but also the preparatory processes of carding and roving. The increased sophistication of Crompton's mule completed the process. These changes in the cotton industry, unlike those in the woollen industry, occurred very rapidly. The highly localized nature of the industry and the rapidity with which the industry was growing, Pinchbeck has claimed, tended to reduce the ill effects for women. The fast absorption of male labour into the industry at significantly higher wages made it less essential for their wives to find alternative employment.[49] Behind such an argument there is the belief (shared by many in the early nineteenth century) that women's place was in the home. Those who suffered most from the decline of hand-spinning were older women, particularly widows, and unmarried women whose entire livelihood depended on their ability to spin. In a brief golden period when spinners could earn more than ever before, many were attracted into the industry; but once competition from the larger factory-based jennies developed, wages fell and unemployment grew.

The much slower mechanization and introduction of factories into the woollen industry might be interpreted as leading to fewer hardships. In fact the reverse was the case. Compared to cotton, the

[48] Malcolmson, *Life and Labour*, p. 58.
[49] Pinchbeck, *Women Workers and the Industrial Revolution*, p. 149.

industry was far more widespread not only as a full-time employment, but as a by-employment, and even as a very casual supplement to the family budget. Mechanization not only came slowly but its introduction came at very different periods in different areas, and hand-spinning persisted in some areas well into the nineteenth century. Again, there seems to be a line dividing the north from the south. In the north the introduction of machinery was rapid, and so great was the expansion of trade that mounting employment may have gone some way to counteract any feeling of hostility and any experience of hardship — at least for some women. Even if spinning wool became a factory-based industry, the spinning of worsted, where the jenny was little in use, was still left in the home. For the wives of small master clothiers, T. S. Ashton has argued, the development may even have had the temporary effect of consolidating the family economy, for now they were able to supply their husbands with all the yarn they needed and no longer were they dependent on spinners outside the household.[50] But where women were dependent on spinning alone, as was the case over much of the south, where no water-powered mills were erected in their village, where there was no compensatory expansion of other employment, women suffered. There was a great deal of distress in the south-east, particularly in rural areas. The strength of the protest against the jenny suggests that women in the south-east were desperately conscious of the absence of alternative employment. Wherever spinning had been the great stand-by of the rural poor there was a rise in poor rates as families were forced on the parish. Inside the earliest mills and factories, spinning, which had hitherto been almost exclusively an occupation of women, became work for men. The machines, it was said, demanded a strength and 'skill' beyond that of women. It is an interesting parallel to the argument about the scythe in harvesting. It meant a total reversal of the earlier sexual division of labour: in so far as women were employed, it was now under the supervision of men.

The main effect of mechanization on weaving lies outside the eighteenth century, but weaving had received a tremendous boost when spinning technology made for the production of a sufficiency of yarn. Wages rose. Weaving, although always primarily a man's trade, began to attract an increasing number of women towards the end of the century as hand-spinning declined. In 1808, half the total

---

[50] T. S. Ashton, *The Industrial Revolution* (1948), p. 58.

number of weavers were women and children. For a short period — Radcliffe thought it extended from 1780 to 1803 — women, exceptionally, could earn as much as men.[51] The French wars took many husbands as soldiers and sailors and, as a Wigan correspondent reported to the Home Office in 1799, 'if a man enlists his wife turns weaver . . . and I have heard many declare that they lived better since their husbands enlisted than before'.[52] It was a short-lived solution, for in the early nineteenth century the trade rapidly became overstocked and wages slumped; but in the period of expansion, master weavers became anxious to establish more control over outworkers, and from the 1780s they began to gather together their weavers in small workshops.[53] For many this signalled the end of work in the home.

It is often argued that the work opportunities women lost as a consequence of changes in agriculture and the decline of handicraft industry — hand-spinning and knitting, for example — were more than compensated for by the growth of factory employment and the expansion of other domestic industries. Factory employment in the eighteenth century meant cotton. How far were the cotton mills and factories of the north the employers of those women for whom work in agriculture or resort to hand-spinning was no longer possible? We need to recognize that the cotton mills and factories were confined to a relatively small area of the country — mainly Lancashire, Derbyshire, and Lanarkshire. We know that the increase in population in these new industrial towns outside the contribution made by natural increase was due to recruitment from the immediately surrounding area and not to long-distance migration. Of course exceptions can be found. There is the family of Philip Pedor, of Cranfield in Bedfordshire. He had earned 7s. a week as an agricultural labourer, his wife and daughters 5s. 10d. at lace-making, and their son 2s. 6d. as a ploughboy. At the end of the century they moved to Mellor, near Manchester. Their total earnings doubled to 30s. Pedor continued to work on the land, and his wife and children went into a factory. It is an exceptional case.[54] It was just not possible for most rural families to leave their homes and migrate to the towns. Even if they had wanted to, 'it would have been impossible for most

[51] Radcliffe, *Origins of the New System of Manufacture*, p. 63.
[52] Quoted Pinchbeck, *Women Workers and the Industrial Revolution*, p. 164.
[53] Edwards, *The Growth of the British Cotton Trade, 1780—1815* (1967), p. 9.
[54] Joyce Godber, *History of Bedfordshire, 1066—1888*, Bedfordshire County Council (1969), p. 421.

of the people who had worked in their own homes to become mill hands'.[55] In many families with husbands and wives working at more than one occupation, a move away from their home was made difficult if not impossible by a husband's employment in a local mine or on a local farm. But what suggests that in fact there was little continuity between the labour of the domestic and factory textile industry is the age of the majority of the factory labour force. In 1833, as Eric Richards has emphasized, there were 65,000 females and 60,000 males employed in the factories.[56] In both cases over half were under the age of fourteen, and only one-sixth of the females were married. Nor were most of these under-fourteens the sons and daughters of former domestic workers. Much of this child labour was apprenticed, and largely pauper apprentices at that.

Conveniently, it is argued, the smaller domestic industries — lace-making, straw hat and basket-making, the manufacture of gloves, and above all framework-stocking manufacture — emerged or expanded just as women's work in agriculture and the older handi-craft industries were in decline. How far did they provide an answer to shrinking opportunities for women's employment in the older handicraft industries? If they did, it was only in certain areas of the country. By the last quarter of the eighteenth century, for example, framework-knitting was firmly established in villages in Nottinghamshire, Derbyshire, and Leicestershire; lace-making had concentrated in certain areas of Bedfordshire, Buckinghamshire, and Northamptonshire; straw-plaiting occupied much the same area and extended into Hertfordshire. Glove-making was mainly located in three towns — Yeovil in Somerset, Woodstock in Oxfordshire, and Worcester. If in these areas women were offered some alternative employment to agriculture and the older domestic handicraft indus-tries, in many other areas of the country there was no such option.

Where lace-making or straw-plaiting were available, they served to postpone the final demise of the family economy. Lace-making in Bedford provided women, 'who otherwise', wrote Arthur Young, 'would have no employment at all', with work in their homes. Apart from a highly skilled minority, most of the lace-makers earned meagre wages. The average wage in 1770 seems to have been between 8*d.* and 10*d.* a day.[57] At the end of the century, when

[55] Frances Collier, *The Family Economy of the Working Class in the Cotton Industry, 1784—1833*, Chetham Society, 3rd. ser. vol. xii (1965), p. 3.

[56] Eric Richards, 'Women in the British economy since about 1700: an interpretation', *History*, 59/197 (1974), pp. 337—57 (p. 346).

[57] Young, *Six Months' Tour through the North of England*, vol. i, p. 26.

straw-hat manufacture was at its peak, a skilled plaiter could earn as much as a pound or more a week — but only at the height of the season. Average annual earnings were between £10 and £30.

Perhaps too late, the Poor Law authorities woke up to the consequences of change and of how the lack of occupations for women was augmenting Poor Rates. In the case of lace-making and straw-plaiting, one gets the impression that they were regarded by the Poor Law authorities as the last resort to prevent Poor Rates from increasing. How else is one to explain the desperate efforts to promote employment by the setting up of schools to teach lace-making and straw-plaiting to the children of the poor? At Little Gransden in Cambridgeshire and at other villages on the Essex and Bedfordshire border, for example, straw-plaiting was introduced in the 1790s.[58] A small wool factory established at Foulmire in the same period provided spinning work for women and children working at home. It 'dragged out a precarious existence' during the last decade of the century.[59]

That women ultimately lost out in employment opportunities in the final decades of the eighteenth century is difficult to prove, but if contemporary opinion is not to be entirely discounted, there is evidence that suggests this net loss for women. In Cambridgeshire by the end of the century there was little work in agriculture for women during the winter months; even in summer their average weekly earnings were only about 3s. Spinning was so badly paid it was no longer worth doing. 'The loss of textile by-employment', Hampson writes, 'was not accompanied by the growth of new industries in neighbouring towns.'[60] Of women in Swineshead, Lincolnshire, Eden found that 'in winter they have little or no employ, except in spinning jersey, or worsted, in which the earnings are so extremely low that scarcely one person in ten will apply to it'.[61] Arthur Young wrote of the area round Wentworth in Yorkshire how 'the poor women and children are much in want of employment; only a little spinning among them'. In Cleveland there was only 'spinning a little flax and worsted'. At Boynton 'three-fourths of the women and children were without employment'.[62] Writing in 1795, David Davies was in do doubt about the effect of lack of employment for women on familial income and the increase of

[58] E. M. Hampson, *Treatment of Poverty in Cambridge, 1597–1834* (1934), pp. 206–7.
[59] Ibid.
[60] Ibid., pp. 217, 218, 273.
[61] Eden, *State of the Poor*, vol. ii, p. 404.
[62] Young, *Six Months' Tour through the North of England*, vol. i, pp. 154, 348, 239–4.

those dependent on poor relief. The Society for the Bettering the Condition and Increasing the Comforts of the Poor commented on 'the *dead season* of the year, when there is general want of employment. It is at this period that most women and children consider themselves as laid up for the winter, and become a burden upon the father of the family, and in many cases upon the parish. The wife is no longer able to contribute her share towards the weekly expenses.'[63]

How far the unemployment or under-employment of women contributed to the lowering of the standard of living of a large section of the labouring class is a difficult question. We shall look at it later. But as a factor contributing to the undermining of the family economy, the decline of women's work in domestic industry represents the removal of what had been for some the final resort to maintain that economy. When it declined, for many the family economy was doomed.

[63] *Reports of the Society for Bettering the Condition and Increasing the Comforts of the Poor*, 5 vols (1798–1808), vol. iii, pt 1 (1801), pp. 76–7.

5

Female Servants in Husbandry

That so many women were at some time in their lives, productive farm servants is of importance, because women were to lose much of this productive role in agriculture as a result of the decline of farm service.

Ann Kussmaul, *Servants in Husbandry in Early Modern England*

'There is scarce any general Name of a *Calling*', wrote Richard Mayo at the end of the seventeenth century, 'that contains under it such different kinds of Persons, as this of a Servant.'[1] He had a point. The umbrella label disguised very different kinds of 'service': servants in husbandry, apprentices, domestic servants, and day-labourers were all covered by it. This chapter and the next are concerned with two of them – service in husbandry and apprenticeship – as they affected the training of girls and young women in the eighteenth century.

At the end of the seventeenth century, according to a 1692 poll tax sample where taxpayers were classified according to the type of occupation they were engaged in, the number of 'servants' and 'apprentices' in the City of London within the walls was as follows:

	Males	*Females*	*Total*	
Servants	721	971	1,768	(including 76 of undetermined sex)
Apprentices	164	9	176	(including 2 of undetermined sex and one journeyman)

Of the total of female 'servants', 246 were quite clearly domestic servants and 462 were as clearly not. The figures are only an indication, for in many cases (841 males and 456 females) the occupation of the taxpayer was not given. Yet they do show that

---

[1] Richard Mayo, *A Present for Servants* (1693), p. 1.

69

servants (including apprentices) constituted an important occupational group, at least in the metropolis.[2] Ann Kussmaul has estimated that in England in the early modern period, servants made up around 60 per cent of the population aged between 15 and 24.[3] If one sets this figure alongside the estimate of 63 per cent of the population under the age of 29 at the end of the seventeenth century, their importance is underlined.[4] In agriculture between a third and a half of hired labour was of this kind.[5]

Use of the same term for very different kinds of 'service' makes for problems of identification. Often it is difficult to determine to what kind of servant a contemporary source is referring, unless there is some detail included about living-in or conditions of hiring. This is particularly so with women as the line separating female domestic servants from female servants in husbandry is indistinct — if, indeed, a line can be said to exist. In many cases, writers refer to 'servants' without distinguishing their sex, so knowledge of female servants in husbandry remains slight. Further confusion arises from the practice of apprenticing parish children, both girls and boys, to farmers. The very title 'servant in husbandry' suggests agricultural work, mainly out of doors. The actual tasks allotted to women varied according to their age and skills. Apart from dairymaids there were women hired to look after the livestock, to drive the horses at the harrow or plough, to weed, to spread muck on the fields, to take charge of the poultry — in fact, to do most of the tasks involved on the farm, even the heaviest. When they were not employed out of doors, there was brewing, preparing for market, and sometimes the cleaning of the house and the cooking. When they were not otherwise engaged there was usually some spinning to fill up the time.

To distinguish female servants in husbandry from domestic servants, Adam Smith placed the emphasis on the 'productive' nature of the work of the former as against the 'non-productive' work of the latter.[6] But is this helpful when, particularly after the middle of the century, female servants in husbandry were also undertaking domestic work in the house and domestic servants were also performing 'productive' work on the farm and in the dairy? All that one can say with any certainty is that, like all servants, they were

---

[2] Peter Clark (ed.), *The Early Modern Town* (1976), p. 223.
[3] Ann Kussmaul, *Servants in Husbandry in Early Modern England* (1981), p. 3.
[4] John R. Gillis, *Youth and History* (1974), p. 11.
[5] Kussmaul, *Servants in Husbandry*, p. 4.
[6] Ibid.

'hired not to maintain a style of life, but a style of work, the household economy', and were engaged for a large part of their time in productive work on the farm. Within this economy, servants in husbandry played a vital role. It was they who enabled the achievement of a balance of production with consumption needs characteristic of that economy. It meant farmers were able to 'compose their household labour force independently of the number and skills of their children; their productive households could survive the death of any of its members'.[7] It was part of the flexible mechanism that made that economy so adjustable to changed circumstances.

How many female servants in husbandry were there? It is impossible to say with any degree of accuracy. It has been suggested that while there were more men than women, the sexes were more evenly balanced than in domestic service, or in apprenticeship. In 1770, Arthur Young attempted to estimate their number. He arrived at the figure of 222,996 menservants (excluding 111,498 boys) to 167,247 female.[8] This would suggest a ratio of female to male servants in husbandry of 3 : 4. By 1851, when service was already far gone in decline, females are recorded as constituting slightly less than a third of the total (213 males to 100 females).[9] The number of such servants in any one household varied. Occasionally, listings of local censuses of parish populations provide sufficient detail of members of households to be useful. Ann Kussmaul quotes the example of the household of Joseph Idle, a weaver/farmer. Besides Idle himself, the household contained his wife, described as housekeeper, and four others designated 'servants'. Two were women: Elizabeth Bowen, manager of dairy: and Betty Robinson, spoolswinder. Of the two menservants, one was described as 'husbandman' and the other as 'shepherd'. So one out of the three of Idle's servants in husbandry was a woman.[10] In fourteen listings of parish populations covering a period from 1695 to 1811, nearly half of the 181 farmers had no more than one female and one male servant in their households.[11] If women servants were rather less numerous than men, many women throughout the century must have spent some period in their youth as farm servants.

[7] Ibid., p. 3.

[8] Arthur Young, *A Six months' Tour through the North of England*, 4 vols (1770), vol. iv, p. 517.

[9] Kussmaul, *Servants in Husbandry*, p. 4.

[10] Ibid., p. 14.

[11] Ann Kussmaul, 'The ambiguous mobility of farm servants', *Economic History Review*, 342 (1981), pp. 222–35 (p. 226 n. 21).

Servants in husbandry lived in the farmhouse or nearby buildings, receiving board, lodging, and washing as part of their hiring. Such payment in kind, it has been suggested, made up about 80 per cent of the payment for their work.[12] Usually a farm would hire several servants of both sexes, the number depending on the size and nature of the farm. According to Blackstone's editor, they were 'frequently hired by the year, from Michaelmas'.[13] In the south and east this was the time at which the hiring fairs or statutes were held, but in the north they were usually held at Martinmas, and in the west and in pastoral areas it was more often Mayday. The period of service was clearly specified at the time of the hiring. Normally, at least early in the century, it was a year, but it could be, and as the century drew to its close often was, less. There was no written contract, although the verbal agreement was sometimes recorded. The hiring was often sealed by the payment of a token − the 'earnest', 'God's penny' or 'fastening penny'. Hiring statutes were held at local market or provincial towns where, before service began to decline, as many as 2,000 or 3,000 young people of both sexes would assemble in the statute yard to be hired. How many of these were women waiting to be hired as farm servants we cannot tell, for domestic servants were also present. Then there were many who moved between farm service and employment as servants to village and market-town tradesmen.[14]

In the south-west, some servants seem to have sought a hiring outside of any statute. William Marshall reported in 1796 on those who went from door to door in search of employment.[15] It suggests that there were servants particularly anxious to ensure their employment within a narrowly defined area. On the other hand, some farmers in need of female servants in husbandry were apparently prepared to go some distance to find the kind of servant they needed. William Ellis wrote in the 1740s of the farmers of Little Gaddesden, Hertfordshire, who went as far as the Aylesbury Statute 'because in Aylesbury Vale, there are great Dairies carried on, that employ considerable Numbers of these useful Females, who, if rightly chosen, commonly prove more hardy, more strong, and

---

[12] K. D. M. Snell, *Annals of the Labouring Poor* (1985), p. 86.
[13] Sir William Blackstone, *Commentaries on the Laws of England*, ed. George Sharswood (1894), bk i, p. 425 n. 5.
[14] Snell, *Annals*, p. 23.
[15] William Marshall, *The Rural Economy of the West of England*, 2 vols (1796), vol. i, p. 109; see also his *The Rural Economy of the Southern Counties*, 2 vols (1798), vol. i, p. 55.

more diligent than our Country Wenches, that are brought up more tenderly, and more unskilful in the Business of Husbandry'.[16]

The age at which girls left their families to enter other households was between 13 and 14, although it could be earlier. Many of them remained servants until marriage. Normally their exit from service was between the ages of 20 and 25, but often later. There were those who remained servants in husbandry for as long as 40 years. County agricultural societies sometimes awarded prizes for long service. In Devon in 1794, for example, the local society awarded prizes for servants of both sexes employed in husbandry 'to encourage diligence and industry'. Among the women receiving prizes was one who had served 46 years, another 40 years, and two more for 34 years.[17] But these were exceptional. Few remained servants after marriage, although there are some cases of hiring married couples. When in 1744 William Ellis was approached by a gentleman for help in obtaining a good ploughman, he recommended a married couple. 'The woman', he explained in his reply, 'becomes as necessary, almost as the man, particularly in the management of the dairy, as well as looking after the suckling of calves and house lambs, both in summer and winter.' What further recommended her, in Ellis's opinion, was that she was 'also so good a housewife, that she can perform several cures on horses, cows and sheep'.[18] It is an interesting example of how widely the work of a 'housewife' was interpreted.

As wages tended to be paid at the end of the year or period for which they had been hired, service represented an opportunity for saving. Not all saved equally. Some may not have saved at all. On his farm at Nantwich in the 1760s, Thomas Furber throughout the year gave advances on wages to his servants in husbandry. In some cases servants overdrew their wages, but provided it was not a large sum Furber was prepared to write it off. In 1769 he hired Martha for a year at a wage of £2. 7s. 6d. In the course of the year he advanced small sums to her, amounting in all to £1. 10s. The remainder of her wage Furber used (but whether on her instructions we are not told) to buy her 'shoes, "cloth for a shift", a handkerchief, a coat and a pair of stockings'. One other small item of 6d. was recorded as for a bottle of 'tincar of mor' [tincture of myrrh]. By the

---

[16] William Ellis, *The Modern Husbandman*, 4 vols (1743–4), entry for Oct. 1744 (vol. iv, p. 146).

[17] Ivy Pinchbeck, *Women Workers and the Industrial Revolution, 1750–1850* [1930] (1981), p. 17 n. 3.

[18] Ellis, *The Modern Husbandman*, vol. i, p. 121.

end of her term, what with withdrawals for pocket money, clothes and other small items, Martha's wages had been overdrawn by 2*s*. 1*d*. Furber apparently 'excused' Martha from repaying it.[19]

The differential between the wages of female and male servants was considerable. In an order fixing maximum wages made by justices at Nottingham in 1723, 'a Maid Servant aged twenty years' was to receive £2, and 'a Maid Servant aged sixteen and under twenty' £1. 10*s*. 0*d*., while a 'head man Servant aged about twenty' received £5.[20] In Gloucestershire, in 1732, the same wage was fixed for the 'Head Servant in Husbandry', while the 'Head Maid-Servant in Dairy, and Cook' received £2. 10*s*. 0*d*., and the 'Second Maid-Servant' £2. 0*s*. 0*d*.[21] In Kent the differential was even greater, and in the same year while the wage of the 'Head Ploughman, Waggoner, or Seedsman' was fixed at £8. 0*s*. 0*d*., the 'Best Woman-Servant' was to receive no more than £3. 0*s*. 0*d*. and the 'Second Sort' but £2. 0*s*. 0*d*.[22]

In Cheshire in the second half of the century, while the wages of a dairymaid on one of the large cheese farms could be as high as £5 a year, they could also be as low as £2. The latter figure was probably more representative. For example, Thomas Furber of Nantwich paid his menservants about £5. 5*s*. 0*d*. a year in 1767, but his women servants £1. 15*s*. 0*d*. or £2. 10*s*. 0*d*. − less than half.[23] In Spalding, Lincolnshire, between 1768 and 1785 the mean average female wage was £2. 15*s*. 0*d*., while that of men was £6. 5*s*. 0*d*.[24]

By the 1770s wages had increased; Arthur Young, in a survey extending from the north of England to the Thames valley, found the wages of dairymaids varying between about £2. 10*s*. and £6.[25] At the end of the century, Eden commented critically on the discrepancy between wages of male and female servants in husbandry in Cumberland. 'The wages of men servants in husbandry who are hired from half-year, are from 9 to 12 guineas a year,' he wrote, 'whilst women, who here do a large portion of the work of the farm, with difficulty get half as much. It is not easy to account for

---

[19] C. Stella Davies, *The Agricultural History of Cheshire, 1750−1850*, Chetham Society, 3rd ser., vol. x (1960), p. 80.
[20] *Nottinghamshire County Records of the Eighteenth Century*, ed. K. W. Meaby (1947), p. 232, dated 22 Apr. 1723.
[21] *Gentleman's Magazine*, May 1752, p. 771.
[22] Ibid.
[23] C. Stella Davies, *Agricultural History of Cheshire*, p. 80.
[24] Kussmaul, *Servants in Husbandry*, p. 37.
[25] Arthur Young, *A Six Months' Tour through the North of England*, 4 vols (1770), vol. iii, pp. 5, 8, 11, 13, 24.

so striking an inequality; and still less easy to justify it.'[26] Eden's figures are confirmed by Pringle, who four years earlier in his survey of Westmorland had claimed that 'in some farmers' families, where they are hard-worked, maid-servants receive £6 a year. Their ordinary wages in other families may be about £4. 10s. or, perhaps £5.'[27] But wages were higher in the north than the south. In his estimate of the total expenditure on service in husbandry in 1770, Arthur Young arrived at an average wage for male servants of £8. 9s. 9d. His figure for maidservants was £3. 9s. Boys received £3. 2s.[28] So female servants in husbandry rarely received more than half the male wage, and frequently less. Until they reached the age range in which wages were specified, they might receive nothing. Normally that age was from 10 to 20 for men, but from 12 to 16 for women.[29] Wages were graduated so that an adult wage was not normally paid until women reached their late teens. And not only were women's wages lower than those of men, but unlike them, they received very little increase with age.

In large farms the accommodation for servants might well be separate from that of the family. It has been suggested that by the end of the seventeenth century, 'every Kentish yeoman's house had a servants' chamber'.[30] But generally on small farms they shared the same table and slept in the same rooms as the members of the family. They seem to have been well fed, and there is no evidence of any discrepancy between the standard of life enjoyed by them and members of the family.

'The servant shall serve, and the master maintain him, throughout all the revolutions of the respective seasons; as well when there is work to be done, as when there is not.'[31] As Blackstone suggested, there must have been periods of bad weather when any outside work was impossible. Men may have profited from such confinement, but women seem to have been set to work indoors. Many job descriptions of female servants in husbandry wind up with a phrase such as 'and when she has done her worke she sits down to spin'.[32] Although female servants in husbandry were taken on to do work

[26] Sir F. M. Eden, *The State of the Poor*, 3 vols (1797), vol. ii, p. 47.
[27] A. Pringle, *General View of the County of Westmorland* (1794), p. 293.
[28] Young, *Six Months' Tour*, vol. iv, pp. 508–9.
[29] Kussmaul, *Servants in Husbandry*, p. 37.
[30] M. W. Barley, *The English Farmhouse and Cottage* (1961), p. 248.
[31] Blackstone, *Commentaries*, bk i, p. 425.
[32] *Purefoy Letters, 1735–1753*, ed G. Eland, 2 vols (1931), vol. i, p. 147.

on the farm, they nevertheless combined that work with tasks within the house.

While most servants in husbandry changed masters annually, there were some who changed far more frequently. Joseph Myett of Quainton (1783–1839), for example, worked in twelve different hirings between the age of thirteen and twenty.[33] But the normal contract was for a year, and was not renewed when the year ended. However, there were generally enough hirings for longer periods to ensure 'in most years, some continuity within the group of servants'. The mobility of most servants was in part a search for better wages and conditions. Rarely, it seems, was promotion won by staying in the same household. Servants moved to new places hoping for the opportunity of increasing their skills, so that at some future date they could command a higher wage. Some, no doubt, were anxious to escape from hard treatment from masters and mistresses, and moved in the hope of finding better. Many moved in search of new faces: most expected that a future marriage partner would be found in the period of service. Marriage could signal their exit from service, the setting up of a new household, and the beginning of life as independent adults. Alternatively, a change of master could enable them to move closer to home and the village community in which they had friends and relations, or to stay close to their chosen future spouse. If on the whole servants moved frequently, they did not move far. In the statute sessions at Spalding, Lincolnshire, between 1767 and 1785, there are records of 844 male and 722 female servants. The mean distance travelled by the female servants was less than eleven kilometres, for the men it was twelve.[34]

Service for both women and men was seen as a temporary and transitional period. Even if for some it turned out to be more permanent, most entered it assuming it would end. For a woman it tended to end with marriage and the formation of her own household. Her savings would contribute to determining when the couple could afford to marry and set up house. A very few remained in the same household for longer periods, sometimes for the entire period of their service. So Mr Thomas Baker, a rich farmer of Myddle, 'seldom changed his servants but when they married away, and then he sent them not away without a reward'. As a rare example of how

---

[33] *The Autobiography of Joseph Mayett of Quainton, 1783–1839*, Ann Kussmaul (ed.), Buckinghamshire Record Society, no. 23 (1986), p. xi.

[34] Kussmaul, 'The ambiguous mobility of farm servants', pp. 225, 228–9.

a few masters treated their servants it is notable that 'all this was thought to be done by the discretion of Mrs. Baker'.[35]

Service in husbandry was the family economy's Youth Training Scheme. It removed children from the parental home at the difficult age of adolescence. It was a means of training children for their future life. As William Fleetwood was to say it 'begets in them such an habitual Activity, as will in good time stand them in good stead, when they come to be at liberty, and at their own disposal.' As most women servants in husbandry were destined to marry, it was a way of equipping them for carrying out the many and varied tasks the women of the household undertook. 'All the care they take, and the Pains they are at', Fleetwood reminded them, 'are truly for their own Service at the last.'[36] But beyond a training for the future it provided an education in a much broader sense. There were some masters — in the eighteenth century a minority, one suspects — 'that do purposely allow them time, and see they spend it in Reading, and other Duties'.[37] Although they remained dependants, they were no longer dependent on their own families. They were usually living with a group of young people, and often with the children of the family. Such experience gave girls a chance of making new friends, meeting the other sex, and probably, opportunity for sexual experiment in their search for a marriage partner. 'Undue familiarity between Servants of different Sexes in a family', warned Richard Mayo, 'has had fatal and tragical Effects. How often has Opportunity and Privacy expos'd Men and Maids that live together to the Devil's Temptations.'[38]

Philip Aries has argued that in pre-industrial Europe there was no distinction made between early and late childhood, or between childhood and adult life. 'People', he writes, 'had no idea of what we call adolescence.'[39] But service in husbandry seems so peculiarly well fitted to cope with adolescence, it is difficult to believe it was not (at least in part) so intended. Writing of the age of entry to service at the age of puberty, Alan Macfarlane concludes: 'it is surely more than coincidence'.[40] If service represented a continuation of dependence, and full adulthood was only reached when that

---

[35] Richard Gough, *The History of Myddle* [1701–6], (1979), p. 89.
[36] William Fleetwood, *The Relative Duties of Parents and Children, Husbands and Wives, Masters and Servants* (1716), pp. 282, 284.
[37] Mayo, *A Present for Servants*, p. 70.
[38] Ibid., pp. 39–40.
[39] P. Aries, *Centuries of Childhood* (1962), p. 29.
[40] Alan Macfarlane, *The Family Life of Ralph Josselin, a Seventeenth Century Clergyman* (1970), p. 92.

dependence ended, it also meant a break with parental control. It removed the adolescent from the home and provided an opportunity to save sufficient to seek out a marriage partner without parental interference. One motive behind parents sending their children into service in husbandry, it has been suggested, was to lessen the psychological and economic blow involved in losing one or both parents.[41] From the parents' point of view, service represented a conscious distancing of themselves from their children, a loosening of ties. The nature of this transitional period was singular. It was a state of dependence, but the relationship between the head of the household and servants in husbandry was not that of superiors to inferiors. Servants in husbandry, Ann Kussmaul has written, 'did not understand themselves, and were not understood by early modern society, to be part of a labouring class, youthful proletarians'.[42] Originally there was little if any awareness of class difference between them and their masters. As a sixteenth-century writer on apprenticeship put it, 'few are born who are exempted from this fate, for every one, however rich he may be, sends away his children into the houses of others whilst he in return, receives those of strangers into his own'.[43] At first, servants in husbandry were recruited from every level of society. In the eighteenth century it was still common practice for small farmers to send their children into the households of others with the main motive of their acquiring useful training for the future. But with the growth in the size of farms and the decline of small farmers, the source of recruitment began to change. With the growth of a class of landless labourers, service came to be a source of support of daughters and sons whose parents were unable to maintain them at home. This change may well have contributed to the greater awareness of class between them and their masters and mistresses. It was expressed in the increasing separation between servants and the farmer's family, and a new and divisive relationship.

Many factors contributed to the decline in service in husbandry. We have seen something of the burden that the lodging, feeding, and supervision of servants imposed on the wives of farmers, a burden that many must have been anxious to discard once the opportunity arose. The effects of enclosure, growth in the size of

[41] Kussmaul, *Servants in Husbandry*, p. 75.
[42] Ibid., p. 9.
[43] C. A. Sneyd (trans.), *A Relation or rather a True Account of the Island of England ... about the year 1500*, by an Italian, Camden Society, vol. xxxviii (1847), pp. 24–5, quoted Macfarlane, *Family Life of Ralph Josselin*, p. 206.

farms, greater agricultural specialization, introduction of new crops and new methods of cultivation – all contributed to making the demand for hired labour more irregular and seasonal, and therefore more fitted to day-labour than living-in farm servants. Another factor, to which contemporaries attached importance, was the increased class consciousness of the prosperous farmers and their families. As we have seen, it led to a changed way of life in the farmhouse and a desire to separate members of the family from their servants. As a reason for no longer hiring living-in servants, several reported to the 1834 Poor Law Commission that since 'the improved condition of the farmers during the high price of agricultural produce, their families were unwilling to associate with labourers'.[44] Significantly, servants in husbandry had now become 'labourers'. A comment from Cobbett is suggestive of the increase in houseproud farmers' wives, whose homes were 'too neat for a dirty-shoed carter to be allowed into'.[45]

With prices rising, particularly those of foodstuffs, feeding hungry young people became more costly. So long as labour for hiring was in short supply and had to be recruited from parishes at a distance from the farm, it was economical to house it. But once labour was in abundant supply, and available locally, the need for living-in servants declined. As wages failed to keep pace with rising prices, it was more economical for the farmer to pay wages than to feed living-in servants. Middleton commented in 1807 on how expensive it was to feed servants who 'frequently consume more food than their masters'. The expense of boarding them and 'their rude manners', he wrote, had persuaded farmers to prefer paying them board wages, 'especially as this method lessens the trouble of the mistress and the female servant of the house'.[46] In the 1820s Cobbett summed up the change: 'Why do not farmers now *feed* and *lodge* their workpeople as they did formerly? Because they cannot keep them *upon so little* as they give them in wages. This is the real cause of the change.'[47] From about the 1750s, and more particularly in the south and east, farmers were increasingly reluctant to house servants in husbandry. Other methods were employed to avoid what was seen as the 'burden' of farm servants. While still hired for a year, they were paid weekly in order to avoid supporting them in

[44] Kussmaul, *Servants in Husbandry*, p. 128.
[45] Pinchbeck, *Women Workers and the Industrial Revolution*, p. 38.
[46] W. Hasbach, *A History of the English Agricultural Labourer*, trans. Ruth Kenyon (1920), p. 177 n. 2.
[47] William Cobbett, *Rural Rides*, 20 Oct. 1825.

times of sickness. One can see how quickly the system of living-in farm servants shaded into something indistinguishable from day-labour.

Contemporaries thought the decline of living-in arrangements was connected with the social aspirations of farmers' wives and daughters who 'esteem it a drudgery ... to provide suitable food for a number of workmen. The latter are consequently obliged to get their board and lodging where they can.'[48] There were hints of immoral goings-on among servants boarded in farmhouses, and in consequence that it was 'not pleasant having so many female servants and young men about'.[49] Curiously the same argument was used about the system of board wages where, according to Arthur Young, it was 'one material cause of an increased neglect of the Sabbath and looseness of morals; they are free from the master's eye, sleep where and with whom they please'.[50] But if the new social aspirations of the farmers and their wives contributed to the decline, it was not the most important factor.

Towards the end of the century, with growing unemployment and rising Poor Rates, parishes became increasingly sensitive about anything that threatened to increase the burden of rates. The laws of settlement had given parishes the responsibility of relieving only those with a legal settlement in that parish. From the middle of the eighteenth century these assumed a new urgency, and the means of acquiring a settlement became a heavy preoccupation of parish authorities. A settlement could be acquired in one of several ways, but that most affecting unmarried servants in husbandry was one year's legal service in the parish. Earlier in the century hiring for a full year was an assumed means of getting a settlement, although even then there were examples of masters' reluctance to incur the wrath of the parish authorities by hiring for a full year and thus giving settlement rights. Early in the eighteenth century, Ann Preece, a servant in husbandry in Herefordshire, was turned away by her master a few days before the year was completed. Her master told her 'she could not stay longer there, for it would not be safe for the parish for her to continue there'. When nevertheless she asked to be allowed to complete her full year's service, her master refused

---

[48] W. Davis, *Hints to Philanphropists* (1821), p. 97.
[49] *P. P. Report on Agriculture* (1833), V, p. 440.
[50] Arthur Young, *General View of the Agriculture of the County of Norfolk* (1804), p. 484.

to allow it, and 'her mistress paid her full wages without deductions'[51] − although by law no master could 'put away his servant, or servant leave his master ... without a quarter's warning; unless upon reasonable cause to be allowed by a justice of the peace'.[52] As far as women servants were concerned, pregnancy constituted 'reasonable cause', although employers were instructed not to turn away pregnant servants but to maintain them until one month after the birth of the child. In practice, employers commonly disregarded such instructions. At a settlement examination in 1758, Elizabeth King 'testified ... that she had been discharged from service in Cambridgeshire on grounds of her pregnancy'.[53] Only occasionally is the law found intervening and enforcing the instruction about their maintenance.

Servants were not always badly treated, but their situation made them particularly vulnerable to exploitation and abuse. Rarely was there any appeal to the courts. One such case occurred at Newark in 1755, when Mary Rawlin was hired for a year 'in the business of husbandry' by John Lightfoot, of North Collingham, at an annual wage of 37s. When her master discharged her without paying her the whole of her wages, she appealed to the justices at Nottingham. Lightfoot was found guilty and was 'ordered to pay 40s. into Court, half to be paid to Mary Rawlin'.[54]

Since each subsequent year of service cancelled the earlier right of settlement, the parish in which the servant last served normally became his or her permanent legal settlement. For women, however, there were complications, as automatically they lost their own settlement on marriage and acquired that of their husbands. Some parishes, in order to avoid any increased burden on the Poor Rates, fined any parishioner who gave settlement to a newcomer. The fine could be as much as £50. Many got round the problem by reducing the period of hiring to just less than a full year, as in the case of Ann Preece's master, or six months, three months, or even a shorter period. Service was in process of becoming indistinguishable from weekly hired labour. So poverty and the incidence of unemployment combined with the Law of Settlement did much to undermine the system of service in husbandry.

The tasks which the female servant was expected to undertake

---

[51] Snell, *Annals*, p. 77.
[52] Blackstone, *Commentaries*, bk i, p. 425.
[53] Kussmaul, *Servants in Husbandry*, p. 32 n. 10.
[54] *Notts: County Records*, p. 234.

had never been totally divorced from 'housework' and tasks carried on in the farmhouse. One problem for historians is that female servants in husbandry are rarely clearly distinguished from domestic servants. Both could be hired at the hiring fairs or statutes. In 1723, Judith Carpenter 'used to do all manner of work as a servant, as in all the time of Harvest she used to go every Day with the Tith Cart into the fields, and to rake after the Cart, and at other times used to do all the common business of the house, as looking after the Dairy, dressing fowls for market, and if the business of the house was done she used to spin'. Elsewhere she was said to have helped dress the children of the household and to have taken them to school, 'attending on them as a servant and carrying their victuals'.[55]

In 1737 Elizabeth Purefoy wrote to William Holloway, asking whether he knew 'of ever a faithful sober understanding girl to manage my Dairy and to help some other things in ye house that I shall set her about, particularly to help wash in washing time. I keep two maids besides, and she must go to market to make the best of my Dairy.' As an afterthought she added, 'pray don't let mee [*sic*] have any raw girl that don't well understand making butter and cheese'.[56] Elizabeth Purefoy may have been a particularly hard task-mistress, but she was not that exceptional. Masters and mistresses extracted as much work as possible from their servants in husbandry. Elizabeth Purefoy listed the work to be done by another maid. It included milking three or four cows, the entire work of the dairy, cooking, washing both the light and heavy wash, cleaning rooms, making beds, cleaning stairs, scouring all the iron and pewter ware. She added that 'there is very good time to do all this provided she is a servant, & when she has done her worke she sits down to spin'.[57]

This blurring of job descriptions of female servants in husbandry and domestic servants made it easy for the decline in service in husbandry to be obscured by the increase in domestic service. Often it was an almost imperceptible trend. Yet the difference between the two, like that between service in husbandry and day-labour, needs to be emphasized. It was not just a question of the work involved, which over the years became more and more work inside the house rather than out of doors on the farm, but a change in the relationship between masters and mistresses and their servants. Servants in husbandry were dependants. They were worked exceedingly hard,

[55] Norfolk Record Office DEP/60.
[56] *Purefoy Letters*, pp. 132–3.
[57] Ibid., p. 147.

but they were not subservient. As we have seen, and particularly on small farms, they often mixed freely with members of the family and especially with their children, and were treated as part of the family. They ate together, worked side by side, and often shared the same room if not the same bed. And just as they shared the hard work of the farm with other members of the household, they also shared the periods of recreation, celebrating together the local festivals and holidays.

Once servants in husbandry moved out of the farmhouse, there was a growing rift between employers and employed, a declining sense of responsibility on the part of masters and mistresses, less shared ground on which they could meet and understand one another. Even where a former female servant in husbandry returned to the house as a domestic servant it was no longer on the same terms. Servants had become inferiors who must be kept in their place. No longer was service a mutually satisfactory arrangement between small farmers for the training and education of their daughters. At the end of service there was still the likelihood of marriage, and still the possibility of setting up an independent household, but few expected to be masters and mistresses taking in servants in husbandry in their turn. 'The people who set out in life as servants in husbandry', wrote Ivy Pinchbeck, 'ultimately became the cottagers and squatters of the old, open village.'[58] The utmost a couple could expect at the end of their service was to be able to afford to rent a cottage with a plot of land attached to it and access to the commons. But even this was only possible so long as cottages were available, and commons and wasteland remained unenclosed. What was the point of saving when it could no longer provide a home and access to land? Why go into service when however much was saved there was no possibility of economic independence, and the only prospect was that of the life of a day-labourer? For women, the decline of farm service was one more factor contributing to the overall contraction in opportunities for productive work in agriculture. Earlier, as Hasbach explained, 'women of the lower classes would as a rule first go into farm service, and them marry some cottager or small farmer and occupy themselves on their own holding and in spinning, only going out by the day in harvest-time'.[59] It had been a pattern of life of many women. Service in husbandry had provided an excellent training for the future wives of small farmers or even of

[58] Pinchbeck, *Women Workers and the Industrial Revolution*, p. 19.
[59] Hasbach, *History of the English Agricultural Labourer*, p. 70.

cottagers with a small plot of land of their own, or at least access to land. But now the only work in agriculture that was left to women was day wage-labour — *when* it was available.

The decline of service in husbandry began around the middle of the century, but it did not disappear quickly. Decline was slow and affected different areas at very different periods. It started in the south and east, particularly in those areas of recently enclosed farms specializing in corn production. In the north and west, where on the whole small farms persisted longer, service remained — at least for a time. Where a labour shortage in agriculture continued, as in the industrial north, service in husbandry was to survive longest. Even these distinctions do not suggest just how uneven and gradual the decline was. In 1831, according to Snell, the agricultural labour force in the southern counties still comprised 15−38 per cent farm servants.[60]

What women lost when service declined was more than a training and more than a productive role in agriculture: they lost the chance of working together with young men. If there were some differences in the tasks they performed, there were a great many they shared. As service in husbandry merged with domestic service, there was a far more marked sexual division of labour. The experience of leaving home for a training shared with the opposite sex in a number of different households must have been a source of independence and self-reliance. It would be a long time before women had such an opportunity again.

[60] Snell, *Annals*, p. 84.

6

Female Apprenticeship

The involvement of women in the apprenticed trades ... is commonly omitted altogether ...

Keith Snell, *Annals of the Labouring Poor*

The other main source of vocational training for young women in the eighteenth century was apprenticeship. Apart from the printing and editing by local record societies of registers of apprentices, there has been very little on the subject since the publication in 1912 of *English Apprenticeship and Child Labour*, the work of O. J. Dunlop and D. Denman.[1] This most authoritative and comprehensive survey of apprenticeship includes a chapter entitled 'The Working Woman and the Girl Employee'. Since 1912, apart from useful occasional references in the work of the Hammonds, M. D. George, Dorothy Marshall, and Ivy Pinchbeck, there has been virtually nothing written on female apprenticeship.[2] Only with the appearance of Keith Snell's *Annals of the Labouring Poor* has the subject been reopened.[3]

One consequence of changes in industry was a growing restriction of the trades open to women. Increasingly, entry was confined to those regarded as traditionally 'women's trades' – millinery, mantua-making, and the work of seamstresses. Where both sexes continued to operate within a trade, the tasks done by each tended to become distinct and separate. On the whole, as in agriculture, women were left with the less well paid tasks. In nearly all cases there was a considerable differential between the wages of men and women,

---

[1] O. Jocelyn Dunlop and R. D. Denman, *English Apprenticeship and Child Labour: A History* (1912).

[2] J. L. and B. Hammond, *The Town Labourer* (1917); M. D. George, *London Life in the Eighteenth Century* (1925): id., *England in Transition* [1931], (1953); Dorothy Marshall, *The English Poor in the Eighteenth Century* (1926); Ivy Pinchbeck, *Women Workers and the Industrial Revolution 1750–1850* [1930], (1981).

[3] K. D. M. Snell, *Annals of the Labouring Poor* (1985), chs 5, 6.

with women's work consistently undervalued. Were such characteristics of women's work the consequence of lack of training, inadequate training, or of other factors? Such questions drive us back to
apprenticeship and to what, if anything, it meant to women in the
eighteenth century.

It has been assumed that, in a period when it is generally (but not
universally) agreed that the traditional, seven-year apprenticeship
was in decline, such apprenticeship as continued to exist was almost
exclusively male. Far more is known about male apprenticeship.
Records of guilds and corporations frequently omit to mention
women apprentices. So in the case of Coventry, the register of
apprentices covering the period 1781−1806 includes only men
indentured. This was not because there were no female apprentices
but because the completion of a man's apprenticeship had political
and social, as well as economic, consequences, that did not apply to
women. When a man completed his apprenticeship in Coventry he
qualified for freeman status, and thus for the parliamentary franchise.
It was therefore important that male apprenticeships should be
carefully recorded. This was not the case for women, and may
account for the far less complete records of female apprenticeships.[4]
In the General Register of Southampton Apprentices, women never
occur at all except as mistresses taking on their own apprentices. Of
these mistresses, by far the majority were widows.[5] This perhaps
explains why historians' work on apprenticeship records, such as
it is, has tended to focus on women as mistresses rather than as
apprentices or journeywomen. Female apprenticeship in the eighteenth century was indeed far rarer than male, but there is evidence
that it existed, and was far more widespread, and covered a far
broader range of trades than is usually acknowledged. Dunlop and
Denman recognized this as long ago as 1912, when they wrote: 'It
was not only in London that girls were apprenticed . . . both in the
country and provincial towns girls were bound to men in all kinds
of trades throughout the sixteenth, seventeenth, and eighteenth
centuries.'[6]

Apprenticeship in its objectives had much in common with service
in husbandry, but there were important differences. A premium was
payable on entering apprenticeship; the term was defined in advance,

[4] *Coventry Apprentices and Their Masters, 1781−1806*, ed. Joan Lane, Dugdale Society
Publications, vol. xxxiii (1983), p. ix.

[5] *A Calendar of Southampton Apprenticeship Registers, 1609−1740*, ed. A. J. Willis and
A. L. Merson, Southampton Record Society, vol. xii (1968), p. xxxiv.

[6] Dunlop and Denman, *English Apprenticeship*, p. 150.

and recorded in a more formal contractual agreement than was the case with service in husbandry. At the time of taking out indentures, all the conditions were written into the articles of agreement. Unlike servants in husbandry, who tended to move annually, or even more frequently, from one hiring to another, apprentices normally stayed with one master or mistress except in the case of death. When a master died, his apprentices were often transferred to his widow.

It was the parents of apprentices who decided to what trade their daughters and sons should be indentured, and often to what master or mistress they should apply. Like servants in husbandry they usually lived in the homes of their employers, were members of their household, and, at least in the intention of the Statute of Artificers of 1563, were regarded as belonging to the family. Normally apprenticeship began at the age of thirteen or fourteen. Apart from board and lodging, apprentices often received clothing, but normally no wages. The premium payable on entry varied according to the status of the trade, the reputation of the master or mistress, and, it would seem, on the conditions that parents wished to secure for their children. It could be as little as two pounds or as much as a few hundred pounds. Even a small premium could bar apprenticeship for the children of the poor, and for others, the size of the premium effectively restricted their choice of trades. The term of apprenticeship could vary from one or two years to as many as fourteen, fifteen, or even twenty. Most common, at least in the first half of the century, was seven years — the minimum laid down in the Statute of Artificers.

Side by side with this kind of apprenticeship where the premium was paid by the parents of the apprentices, there was a very different form: where the premium was paid by the parish authorities or charity. Originally the intention of the Act of 1601 had been a concern that children with no parents or with parents too poor to pay a premium should nevertheless be able to acquire a skill that would qualify them for earning their own living. But by the second half of the eighteenth century, if not before, one often important motive behind parish apprenticeship was to avoid such children becoming a threat to the Poor Rates. Hence the almost obsessive desire of some parishes to avoid any gaining a settlement and becoming a present or future liability. Under the Act of Settlement of 1691, the first forty days served gained the apprentices a settlement, so the object of parishes was to bind the parish child to a master or mistress of another parish and thus to ensure that at no future date would he or she become their liability.

Overseers of the poor were responsible for placing parish apprentices. Compulsion could be used to persuade families within the parish to take them in. Until the end of the century, all occupiers of property worth £10 per annum, and later £20, were liable to house parish apprentices. Under the Act of 1698 those refusing could be fined £10. A sum was paid to the master or mistress as premium, but it was commonly about half that payable for a regular apprenticeship, and insufficient to compensate a small farmer or tradesman for the burden of having to house and feed an inmate they did not welcome despite the potential additional labour he or she represented. In the south-west, where parish apprenticeship to husbandry was common, it was particularly resented by the many poverty-stricken small farmers who were forced to take them in.[7] But such resentment was by no means confined to the south-west. Under the Act of 1698 there was a right of appeal against taking such apprentices. In some areas, perhaps in consequence of the large number of appeals, a practice developed of parishes placing out the children for a few months at a time to a succession of different masters. So at Barnwell, Cambridgeshire, in 1748, Thomas Bidwell, a farmer, 'applied to be excused from taking as an apprentice the girl sent to him by the overseers'. Apparently the indenture was cancelled and the farmer was ordered to 'take the child to keep and provide for her two calendar months, persuant [sic] to the parish agreement for that purpose, and, so as his turn shall happen to be with other farmers of the parish'.[8] Parish apprenticeships, whether to agriculture or trades, were characterized by low premiums − normally about £5. The term of such apprenticeships was often longer than the usual, with apprentices beginning even as early as eight or nine and continuing until they reached the age of twenty-one or marriage.

Parish apprenticeship accounted for by far the greater number of female apprentices in the eighteenth century. In the southern counties (East Anglia, the East Midlands, Middlesex, Oxfordshire, and Hampshire), it is estimated that about a third were females. Of these, some 20 per cent were apprenticed to agriculture, and a slightly larger percentage to the clothing trades − seamstresses, weavers, spinners, tailors, mantua-makers, glovers, cordwainers, and cotton manufacturers. Nine per cent were apprenticed to trades concerned with food and drink, with apprenticeships to innholders,

[7] See Pinchbeck, *Women Workers and the Industrial Revolution*, p. 18.
[8] E. M. Hampson, *The Treatment of Poverty in Cambridgeshire, 1597−1834* (1934), p. 155.

publicans, and victuallers most prominent, followed by butchers, grocers, and bakers. This leaves about 47 per cent accounted for by other occupations. Included are bricklayers, blacksmiths, and brushmakers, but by far and away the greatest number were indentured to 'housewifery'.[9] Before we consider the full implications of apprenticeships to 'housewifery', we need to compare the experience of female parish apprentices with that of women apprenticed by their parents.

The records of parish apprentices, simply *because* they were bound out by the parish authorities, tend to be more complete, and there are far more of them than for those apprenticed by their parents. As we have seen there are reasons for thinking that records of apprentices for females were not so carefully kept as for males, but there is no doubt that the number of girls indentured by their families was far less than that indentured as parish apprentices. Many daughters and wives worked alongside their fathers or husbands but never served any apprenticeship. Parish apprentices either had no parents, or had parents incapable of instructing them in any trade. On the basis of the records available, the percentage of females among general apprentices never exceeded 10 per cent and was normally less than half that figure. In Bedfordshire, of those apprentices listed from 1711 to 1720 just over 4 per cent were women. In Warwickshire, apprentices indentured between 1710 and 1760 totalled 2,454, of whom 91, or just under 4 per cent, were females. Over the same period 215 female apprentices are recorded in Wiltshire, about 7.8 per cent of all the parish apprenticeships. In Sussex between 1710 and 1752 about 3.5 per cent of apprenticeships listed were women. In Surrey between 1711 and 1731, the 158 female apprenticeships recorded represent just over 5 per cent. The difference between the proportion of female to all parish apprentices is startling. What these small percentages reflect is just how inadequate apprenticeship records are as an indication of the number of women who practised a trade in some form or other.[10]

Both sets of records reveal the wide spread of trades to which

[9] Snell, *Annals*, pp. 279–82.
[10] *A List of Bedfordshire Apprentices, 1711–1720*, ed. Hilary Jenkinson, Bedfordshire Historical Record Society, vol. ix (1925); *Warwickshire Apprentices and their Masters, 1710–1760*, ed. K. J. Smith, Dugdale Society Publications, vol. xxix (1975) *Wiltshire Apprentices and their Masters, 1710–1760*, ed. Christabel Dale, Wiltshire Archaeological and Natural History Society, Records Branch, vol. xvii (1961); *Sussex Apprentices and Masters 1710–1752*, ed. P. Garraway Rice, Sussex Record Society, *vol. xxviii, (1924); Surrey Apprenticeships, 1711–1731*, ed. Hilary Jenkinson, Surrey Record Society, vol. x (1969).

women were apprenticed. Parents bound their daughters to trades later regarded as the monopoly of male labour. Again, apprenticeship to husbandry was common, although not accounting for as large as proportion as in the case of female parish apprentices. The distinction between parish and non-parish apprenticeships to husbandry is sometimes blurred, and it is often impossible to distinguish between them. Edith Gore in 1714 was apprenticed to Robert Huckle, a yeoman of Chalton in Bedfordshire. The premium paid was £20, and the term was to continue until she reached twenty-one years of age.[11] What kind of apprenticeship was this? It is just conceivable that she was a pauper apprentice − the wording of the term of the apprenticeship might suggest so, as does the fact that her father was dead − but the premium was far above that normally paid by parishes, and her father had been a yeoman. It seems more likely she was apprenticed by her surviving parent or relations. In Sussex there are several examples of girls apprenticed to husbandmen. In 1714 for example, Elizabeth Morris was apprenticed to Edward Hider of Fletching, husbandman 'to 21 years of age at a premium of £5'. In 1718 Elizabeth Taylor, daughter of James Taylor, was apprenticed to William Rose, a yeoman of Lewes, at a premium of £6 for a term of seven years.[12] Such female apprenticeships to husbandry are also to be found in the Warwickshire, Surrey, and Wiltshire records. In all these cases the masters are described as husbandmen. It is possible they represent smallholders who were unable to afford servants in husbandry but were prepared to house a single apprentice for a small premium to cover the cost of her board. What is clear is that service in husbandry was still seen by many parents as a desirable training for daughters, and one fitting them for their future role as the wives of smallholders or even of cottagers with a small plot of land and rights of common.

When the 1842 Commission on the Employment of Women in Agriculture reported, it concluded that the work done by female parish apprentices and adult women was little different from that of men. Both were involved in heavy manual work. In the counties of Wiltshire, Dorset, Devon, and Somerset, 'it appears to have been common practice, where apprenticeship prevailed ... to send girls into the fields with boys to work, no difference being made in their occupations'.[13] Dunlop and Denman are surely right in insisting

[11] *Bedfordshire Apprentices.*
[12] *Sussex Apprentices.*
[13] P. P. *Report on the Employment of Women and Children in Agriculture* (1843), xii, p. 27; see also ibid., pp. 105−6.

that 'the employment of girls and women was not limited by any opinion as to what was suitable and wholesome for them', at least until the end of century.[14] Charles Vancouver in 1808 passionately expressed his abhorrence at the work done by young female pauper apprentices to husbandry: 'What can a female child at the age of ten or twelve years be expected to perform with a mattock or shovel? Or how will she be able to poise, at the end of a dung-fork any reasonable weight, so as to lift it into dung-pots slung upon the horses' backs, for hacking out manure to distant parts of the farm?'[15] Vancouver called for greater control over the conditions of such apprenticeships. But women, young and old alike, had been doing the same kind of work throughout the eighteenth century – and earlier. What was new was the view expressed by Vancouver, that such work was unfeminine and therefore unsuitable for women. It was, as he put it, 'incompatible with the household and more domestic duties they ought early to be made acquainted with'.[16] Mary Rendalls, the wife of an Exeter farm labourer, a witness before the commission, gave an account of her work when she was an apprentice:

I got up as early as half-past two, three, four or five, to get cows in, feed them, milk them, and look after the pigs. I then had breakfast, and afterwards went into the fields. In the fields I used to drive the plough, pick stones, weed, pull turnips, when snow was lying about, sow corn, dig potatoes, hoe turnips, and reap. I did everything that boys did.[17]

We should note this evidence of lack of a clear sexual division of labour among apprentices to husbandry. The fact that they carried out tasks little differentiated from those done by men might be seen as making it less unlikely that other female apprentices practised the trades to which they were indentured. Often these included trades later the monopoly of male labour. In the course of the century the trend was towards more sharply defined female and male trades with less crossing of the frontiers separating them. But in the first half of the century there seems to have been less sexual division of

[14] Dunlop and Denman, *English Apprenticeship*, p. 147.
[15] Charles Vancouver, *General View of the Agriculture of the County of Devon* (1808), p. 360, as quoted by Pinchbeck, *Women Workers in the Industrial Revolution*, p. 18.
[16] Ibid.
[17] *Report on Women and Children in Agriculture* (1843), vol. xii, p. 112; and see Mary Puddicombe's testimony on p. 109.

labour between trades. Whether or not women's apprenticeship to the trades mentioned in the records led to their acquiring the skills of that trade, or whether, as some have suggested, whatever the nature of the trade to which they were indentured, by far the majority of women apprentices were used by their masters and mistresses in the work of 'housewifery', we shall need to examine later. If such a claim is justified, then any conclusion about the sexual division of labour between apprenticed trades, or the broad range of trades to which women were apprenticed, would be of little significance. But first we should consider to what trades women in the eighteenth century were apprenticed.

In a list of Bedfordshire apprentices covering the nine years 1711– 20, there are 23 female apprenticeships among a total of 429. Of these, the trades of 18 are recorded. A majority were to the traditional 'women's trades' – mantua-making, millinery, and that of the seamstress, but two, daughters of the gentry, were apprenticed to a linen draper and stationer at high premiums of £25 and £18 respectively – a reminder that apprenticeship was not confined to daughters of artisans or labourers. Two girls were apprenticed to agriculture, one to a spinster, one to a grocer, and, most interesting of all, one Mary Barr, to a blacksmith, at a premium of £4 for a term of three years.[18] Among Sussex apprenticeships in the period 1710–52, among 103 women more than half were in female trades. But there were other, less expected trades; three girls were apprenticed to brick-layers, three to carpenters, two to blacksmiths, one to a cooper, and one to a sawyer. Two were apprenticed to a watch-maker, but whether to watch-chain making, to gilding, or some other aspect of the trade is not clear. Watch-chain making, according to Campbell, required 'no great ingenuity', but the premium paid by the parents of Ann Withers to Isaac Guepin of Lewes in 1712 was £25 – suggesting a trade of some prestige – and the term of the apprenticeship was seven years. Six years later the same Guepin took as apprentice Mary Burell. This time the agreed term was five years and the premium has risen to £30.[19]

Among the guild trades, that of goldsmiths was one of the few still taking in female apprentices. Among the Sussex apprentices is the daughter of a surgeon, Mary Coppard, who was apprenticed to a goldsmith, 'Benjamin Westwood of St. Andrew's Holborn, goldsmith and Elizabeth his wife'.[20] The premium paid was £20 and the

[18] *Bedfordshire Apprentices.*
[19] *Sussex Apprentices.*
[20] Ibid.

term to be served seven years. The fact that the wife of Westwood is mentioned in the indentures suggests that she too may have practised the trade of goldsmith and had some share of the responsibility for training an apprentice. Whether she had ever served an apprenticeship herself we do not know, but the trade was one to which girls could be apprenticed and subsequently become mistresses in their own right. In 1747, for example, Ann Jaquin, having completed her apprenticeship, acquired the freedom of the Goldsmiths' Company. The following year she took on Elizabeth Bence as apprentice for a term of seven years at a premium of £30. Three years later a Mary Howard was apprenticed to Jane Hudson, Citizen and Goldsmith of London.[21] It is rare in Sussex apprenticeship lists to find an apprentice bound to both husband and wife, and difficult to avoid the conclusion that when the wife is included in the indentures it has some significance, and often indicates a wife's partnership with her husband in the trade. Where a wife practised a trade independently of that of her husband and took apprentices, they had to be bound to both husband and wife even though the husband did not practise the trade. In her study of Coventry apprentices in the last two decades of the eighteenth century, Joan Lane has remarked on the number of women listed as 'joint equal partners with their husbands'. In the early years of the nineteenth century there were Thomas and Lucy Ann Mercer, who together practised the trade of watch-case springers and liners; William and Hannah Howard, watch-case makers; Joseph and Elizabeth Salmon, watch gilders; Joseph and Sarah Vale, watch-pendant makers and clock cleaners. We also find Daniel and Hannah Butler, engine weavers, Jesse and William Johnson, grocers and tea dealers, and John and Rebecca Cheshire, bricklayers. There was even a father and daughter partnership: Edward Flack and Mary, his daughter, weavers.[22] There are cases of apprenticeship to the traditional women's trades where it is impossible to tell whether both husband and wife were involved or only the wife. So when Katherine Aldridge was apprenticed to the trade of mantua-maker she was indentured to 'John Edshaw of Midhurst, Suss., Sarah ux.'[23] It is yet another example of how easy it is to underestimate the number of women who practised a trade independently.

The wide variety of trades to which women were apprenticed in Bedfordshire and Sussex is also found in the lists of Surrey,

[21] Pinchbeck, *Women Workers*, p. 293, n. 2.
[22] *Coventry Apprentices.*
[23] *Sussex Apprentices.*

Warwickshire, and Wiltshire. In all three, about 50 per cent were to 'women's trades', but outside these there was a wide range. For example, thirty-eight trades figure in the Surrey female apprentice-ships, of which some — those of bricklayers, carpenters, blacksmiths, millers, pistol-makers, gunbarrel-forgers, skinners, iron-mongers, fishermen, spectacle-makers, barbers, and watermen — subsequently became 'male trades'.[24] One interesting detail of the Wiltshire lists covering the period 1710—60 is the large number of apprenticeships to mantua-makers — sixty-six in all. Of these, over 60 per cent were in the last ten years of the period.[25] It might suggest that by the second half of the century apprenticeships to women's trades in-creased at the expense of those to other trades, and that a much clearer sexual division of labour is found in trades where appren-ticeship persisted. What these lists also reveal is the hierarchy of trades to which women of very different social backgrounds were apprenticed. There were still guild trades to which women had some access — goldsmiths, pewterers, apothecaries, clock-makers, linen-drapers, and mercers. The Company of Clockmakers in 1715 had recognized and sanctioned the taking of female apprentices. Up to the middle of the century there were several examples of women bound to clockmakers. On 28 April 1715, 'Rebeckah Fisher was bound Apprentice to George Taylor and Lucy his wife for seven years from this day'; in 1730, Catherine Cext was apprenticed to 'James Hubert and Elizabeth his wife'. Both cases suggest husband and wife partnerships. There was also Elinor Mosely, apparently a single woman, taking Elizabeth Askell as apprentice in 1734.[26] Many widows took up the freedom of their husbands' guild and pursued the trade although they had never served an apprenticeship. In the records of the Pewterer's Company, Lucy Sellers in 1713—14 was bound 'as apprentice for seven years to Elizabeth Read, widow of Samuel Read'.[27] There is also evidence that when women were taken on as apprentices to these trades, it was assumed they would take up the freedom of the guild on the completion of the appren-ticeship. But the high premiums involved meant that only daughters of the well-to-do could have had access to them.

As we have seen, a large number of female apprentices entered the traditional women's trades. Throughout the eighteenth century

[24] *Surrey Apprentices.*
[25] *Wiltshire Apprentices.*
[26] S. E. Atkins, *Account of the Company of Clockmakers* (1881), p. 155.
[27] Charles Welch, *History of the Worshipful Company of Pewterers*, 2 vols (1902), vol. ii, p. 180.

the trades of milliners, mantua-makers, seamstresses, and stay-makers continued to carry some prestige. For aspiring parents of the middle class, these trades represented some possibility of social advancement for their daughters. When in 1751 Laurence Sterne was approached for advice about ways in which his sister Catharine could support herself, he replied 'that if she would set herself to learn the business of a mantua-maker, as soon as she could get insight enough into it, to make a gown and set up for herself', he and his wife would give her £30 'to begin the world and support her till business fill in'.[28] It is doubtful whether the £30 would have done much more than pay the premium on her apprenticeship, for premiums, while varying considerably, could be as high as £30 or even more. But as the author of *A General Description of All Trades* wrote in 1747, 'it is reckoned a genteel as well as profitable Employ, many of them living well and saving Money'. The prospects for those who could not afford to set up independently were not so rosy. 'Journey-women', we are told, 'have generally from 7 or 9s. a Week.'[29] They 'make Shift with great Sobriety and Economy to live upon their Allowance'.[30] The most prestigious of all the women's trades was that of the milliner. Premiums could be as much as £60 for a four-year term — the sum paid for the apprenticeship of Anne Rowe to John Keigwin of Covent Garden in 1745.[31] Such costly apprentice-ships were only within reach of daughters of gentlemen. Nor was it only in London that high premiums could be demanded.[32] But premiums could also be as low as £7 although such milliners were unlikely to be 'of the better sort'.[33] Milliners 'have vast profits on every article they deal in', Campbell tells us, "yet give but poor, mean wages to every person they employ under them'.[34] So here too prospects were limited unless parents could afford to set their daughters up in business once their apprenticeship ended.

There is some difference of opinion as to what capital was required. Campbell thought something between £100 and £1,000 was needed, as he put it, 'to set up genteelly'.[35] Others were more exact; £300 was thought to be sufficient, but 'a diligent, sober woman with a set

---

[28] *Letters of Laurence Sterne*, ed. Lewis P. Curtis (1935), pp. 37–8.

[29] *A General Description of All Trades* (1747), p. 134.

[30] R. Campbell, *The London Tradesman* (1747), p. 227.

[31] *Sussex Apprentices*.

[32] *Wiltshire Apprentices*.

[33] *A General Description of All Trades*, pp. 149–50.

[34] Campbell, *The London Tradesman*, p. 208.

[35] Ibid., p. 336.

of good Acquaintance, may do very well with £100'.[36] But even £100 was enough severely to restrict the number who could set up in business by themselves. Without such an option 'a good Shopwoman' was given '£20 a Year and her Board, and a quick Hand otherwise can earn 8 or 10s. a Week'.[37] Campbell thought she could earn five or six shillings at the most, 'out of which', as he reminds us, 'she is to find herself in Board and Lodging'.[38] Although many were apprenticed to these trades who never contemplated the possibility of setting up independently and becoming mistresses in their own right, there were always those anxious to enter them. In part this accounts for their becoming overstocked, and, in consequence, the payment of low wages to journeywomen. But by the end of the century it was these trades that continued to offer single women − or at least, those who had completed an apprenticeship and possessed some capital − the best chance to establish themselves as mistresses taking apprentices in their turn.

Earlier in the century, quite outside the prestigious guild trades and 'women's trades', there is evidence of single women pursuing a trade in their own right and taking on apprentices. In Wiltshire, for example, there was 'Mary Mills, wooden hat maker of Marlborough', to whom Sarah Andrews was apprenticed in 1716; and 'Elizabeth Hillier, glover of Upavon', to whom Mary Beare was apprenticed in 1719.[39] In Sussex in 1745, 'Mary Shuckforth, lacejoyner' took on Sarah Brown as apprentice.[40] In Warwickshire Susannah Murcott of St Andrews, Warwick, a fringe-maker, and Hannah Dowler of Birmingham, a clear-marcher, both took apprentices in the 1750s.[41] There were many others. Even at the end of the century it was not only widows who were found practising trades.

How was apprenticeship of daughters regarded by parents? What were seen as the main objectives? One intention of parents was that their daughters should acquire some skill, and preferably one that would lead to a measure of social advancement. This was certainly true of the more prestigious trades such as millinery and mantua-making. For some parents the object was achieved when their daughters were set up in business on their own account. But even where there was no possibility of attaining such independence, there

---

[36] *A General Description of All Trades*, pp. 149−50.
[37] Ibid.
[38] Campbell, *London Tradesman*, p. 208.
[39] *Wiltshire Apprentices*.
[40] *Sussex Apprentices*.
[41] *Warwickshire Apprentices*.

seems no reason for thinking that the learning of a saleable skill was not part of the parents' motive. Outside these prestigious trades with (on the whole) high premiums, there were related women's trades — embroidery, child coat-making, the trade of the seamstress and dress-maker — where normally premiums were lower. In the apprenticeship indentures of the early eighteenth century in Norwich, out of 113 women apprenticed, 90 were to such clothing trades,[42] trades to which the daughters of labouring parents sought entry with no hopes of rising higher than journeymen. It is not insignificant that the term 'journeywoman' was in common use in the eighteenth century.[43]

To suggest that learning some skill was part of the motive behind the apprenticeship of daughters is not to deny that for most daughters — and their parents — marriage was the ultimate goal. It was. But this only underlines the point made earlier; that for the lower classes, wives were assumed to be women who worked. Learning the skills of a trade could enable a woman to make a greater contribution to her family's maintenance. 'Many parents', it has been suggested, 'regarded skill in a trade as a good form of dowry.'[44] But if female apprenticeship was in part motivated by the desire for daughters to acquire a skill, it could be argued that the term served was in many instances an absurdly long one. Indeed it was, and this was equally the case for male apprentices. It suggests that learning a skill was not the only motive. However eroded the responsibilities of masters and mistresses were by the eighteenth century, originally, as in service in husbandry, they had the duty of imparting far more than the skill of a trade to apprentices. They had been responsible for their general upbringing and education, for their religious and moral training, and for preparing them for the roles they would be called on to play as adults. Such ideas lived on after any hope of general training and education had long ceased to be a reality.

So there was a desire for some kind of useful training to equip a daughter for her future role as a working wife, or, in the unhappy (and almost inconceivable) event of her remaining unmarried, to enable her to earn her own living. There was the possibility that such training would enable her to marry better, and the belief,

[42] Penelope Corfield, 'A provincial capital in the late seventeenth century: the case of Norwich', in Peter Clark (ed.), *The Early Modern Town* (1976), p. 252.

[43] Snell, *Annals*, p. 296.

[44] Dunlop and Denman, *English Apprenticeship*, p. 153.

however far from reality, that an apprentice received far more than mere training in a trade. All these motives played some part in parents' decision to seek a suitable apprenticeship for their daughter.

But what of the argument that whatever the trade to which girls were apprenticed, what they actually ended up doing was housework, so that they acquired no skill at a trade? Particularly was this the lot of female parish apprentices who, it is said in the case of those of Southampton in the seventeenth and eighteenth centuries, 'were not really intended to be taught a skilled craft in the same way as boy apprentices but simply to be taken off the town's hands and made to earn their keep as household servants'.[45] In his introduction to Warwickshire apprenticeships, K. J. Smith has written: 'we may suspect that most of the girls mentioned ... were entering domestic service, though only one of them is specifically recorded as being apprenticed to "housewifery" '.[46] Female apprentices to whatever trade, it is argued, were really domestic servants in disguise. Whether or not this claim is valid, it does suggest that many historians view 'housewifery' in the eighteenth century as inferior and unskilled work. Those taking on female apprentices destined to become unpaid domestic servants, it has been suggested, tried to conceal the fact. But as we have seen, for much of the century the term 'housewifery' in the very broad sense in which it was then used, 'embraced a wide range of skilled crafts'.[47]

Keith Snell has drawn attention to the loose way in which terms like 'housewifery' were used, commenting how terminological indiscrimination in indentures was common between 'servant', 'servant in husbandry', 'house servant', 'house servant in husbandry and housewifery', 'husbandry', 'husbandry and housewifery', 'good housewife or servant in husbandry', and 'housewifery'. He concludes that too much importance should not be given to the apparent preponderance of apprenticeships to 'housewifery' among parish children. We should not assume that 'housewifery' in the eighteenth century meant the equivalent of housework today.[48] So when in Wiltshire in 1729 we find the apprenticeship of 'Ann Chamberlin of Wilton to John Sparks of Dinton for hussefry' with a premium of three guineas; or when in the parish of St Clements, Oxford, in 1749, there is 'Mary Hall appt. to Mary Train of Holywell till 21 years in the "art of huswifery" '; or when in Warwickshire in 1759,

---

[45] *A Calendar of Southampton Apprenticeship Registers*, p. lii.
[46] *Warwickshire Apprentices*, Introd., p. xiv.
[47] *A Calendar of Southampton Apprenticeship Registers*, p. liii.
[48] Snell, *Annals*, p. 283 n. 30.

there is Elizabeth Stokes apprenticed to 'Henry Holloway of West Bromwich, Staffordshire, huswifery' for fourteen years with a premium of £2 – we should not necessarily assume that they were all doing the same thing.[49] Sometimes the wording of the indentures makes this clear. In 1701, Sarah Baisley of St Giles, Oxford, was apprenticed to 'George Belchingdon of Oxon dairyman' in 'Dairying & Good houswifry'; in Abingdon in 1780, Elizabeth Eaney was apprenticed to William Constable until the age of twenty-one in 'making up and spinning of mops and household work'.[50]

Whatever the changing nature of 'housework' in the course of the eighteenth century, parents continued to see domestic service as a respectable and useful occupation for their daughters, and, as we have seen, one where social betterment was possible. If parents wanted to apprentice their daughters to 'housewifery', they did so by openly indenturing them for learning those skills. There are several examples of such apprenticeships. Among the Sussex apprenticeship records, for example, we find Frances Langhurst who in 1728 was apprenticed to 'Mary Hollingsworth of Chichester, housewife' for eight years at a premium of £12; three years later there was Susannah Wingfield apprenticed to 'Mary Oliver of Hastings, Suss., housewife' for six years at a premium of £10.[51] These were high premiums for parents to pay unless they thought the skills their daughters were acquiring were of real value. As a future marriage partner a daughter trained in the skills of housewifery had definite attractions over one who lacked them. An apprenticeship could make all the difference to the level at which they entered the domestic service hierarchy. For most parents seeking an apprenticeship for their daughters, 'housewifery' was not seen as an ignominious occupation.

If by the end of the century the main motive behind parish apprenticeship was the removing of a financial liability, earlier it had aimed at providing pauper children with a means of supporting themselves in adulthood if necessary, but in any case of giving them a training that, as future wives, would enable them to make their contribution to the subsistence of their families. By the end of the century if this had ceased to be the prime consideration of parishes, it was still a closely related secondary object. The fact that these children were often orphans, or that they came from homes where

[49] *Wiltshire Apprentices*; MS DD Par. Oxford St Clements, c. 24, Oxfordshire Record Office; *Warwickshire Apprentices*.
[50] MS DD Par. Oxford St Giles, c. 24, Oxfordshire Record Office.
[51] *Sussex Apprentices*.

parents were unable to support them, made it unlikely they had any training in the main tasks associated with 'housewifery'. Many were ill prepared by their home experience for earning their living as domestic servants. A frequent complaint about domestic servants at the end of the century was that they lacked the training that mothers had given earlier to their daughters. So one of the aims of parishes was to train them either to enter domestic service or for the role of working wives. It was among female parish apprentices that indentures to housewifery figure so largely. According to a recent estimate, nearly 40 per cent of female parish apprentices in the southern counties were of this kind.[52] It represented a quite deliberate choice by parish authorities as the most likely training to fit the children to become economically independent. What is paradoxical in the light of the argument that most female apprentices ended up doing housework is that some parish authorities seem to have complained of the failure of some masters and mistresses to provide any training in the house! All too often, it was held, the latter, resentful of having to take parish apprentices, used them in the most menial and roughest work on the farm. As Mary Puddicombe reported to the 1843 commission, 'I worked more in the fields than in the house.'[53] But just because of the frequency with which these parish children were apprenticed to 'housewifery', there is reason for thinking that those apprenticed to any other trade were intended to be instructed in it and not another. So when in 1783 Mary King, aged eighteen, came up before the Winchester Settlement Examinations and reported that earlier she had been apprenticed to 'John Baverstock & Mary his wife' for a term of seven years 'to learn staymaking, starching, etc.', there is no reason for doubting that this was in fact the trade she was taught.[54]

Parish authorities no less than parents wanted their declared options acknowledged in the training given to apprentices. Unfortunately, all too often the speed with which the children were placed out and the lack of care to see that they were bound to suitable masters and mistresses defeated the object. Some parents were prepared to go to court over the failure to teach their daughters the trade for which they had been indentured, but these cases are of female apprentices who were not only used as domestic servants but were grossly exploited and often maltreated as well. Two cases

[52] Snell, *Annals*, pp. 279–82, table 6.1.
[53] *Report on Women and Children in Agriculture*, (1843), vol. xii, p. 109, quoted Pinchbeck, *Women Workers and the Industrial Revolution*, pp. 17–18.
[54] *Winchester Settlement Papers, 1667–1842*, compiled by Arthur J. Willis (1967), p. 53.

make the point. In Middlesex in 1715 Sarah Gibson was 'discharged from her apprenticeship to Joanna Worthington of St Andrew's Holborn, widow, mantua-maker, upon proof that the said Sarah instead of learning the trade of mantua-maker, had been employed in common household work, cleansing and washing lodgers' rooms and had been immoderately beaten and not allowed sufficient food'. In 1721 Mary Neale was similarly 'discharged from Elizabeth Prendergast mantua-maker who had set up a victualling house and obliged her said apprentice to draw drink and carry it abroad to customers, fetch in pots and scour them and to wait upon nine African recruits whom the said Elizabeth had taken into her house to bed and board'.[55] These cases suggest that female apprentices were particularly vulnerable to exploitation far beyond any possible interpretation of the conditions of apprenticeship. They also reveal that parents were concerned to get their money's worth: if they apprenticed their daughters as mantua-makers, they expected them to be taught that trade.

Many apprentices, both girls and boys, were frequently used by their mistresses for running errands and carrying out household tasks. But it is doubtful whether parents would have seen this as an infringement of the conditions of apprenticeship. Provided they were also taught the trade for which they had been apprenticed, such tasks were seen as part of the general training that apprenticeship involved – as important, perhaps, as the acquisition of the skills of the trade. If they were to be treated as members of the family, then they must expect to be used to do the household chores and errands.

Just as with service in husbandry, the decline of apprenticeship went through several stages: the reduction of the term served; the end of living-in and the boarding out of apprentices; the increased exploitation of apprenticed labour in an attempt to reduce labour costs and maximize profits; and the beginning of payment of wages to apprentices, in the effort to cut down the number of journeymen employed. By the end of the eighteenth century, in so far as apprenticeship survived it had often become something very different. Apprentices were sometimes indistinguishable from cheap wage-labour, and in consequence relations between employers and apprentices deteriorated. Then in the conditions of the late eighteenth century, the two systems of apprenticeship became increasingly, conflicting. Taking on low-premium parish or general apprentices

[55] Apprenticeship cases from *Middlesex Sessions Records*, from George, *London Life*, app. iv.

and ignoring the restrictions on the number of entrants to a trade led to an overstocking of many trades. Many completing an apprenticeship had no hope of becoming mistresses or masters in their own right, but even their expectation of employment as journeywomen or journeymen was increasingly frustrated. Why bother to serve an apprenticeship when it did little to guarantee employment at the end? Parish apprenticeship contributed to overstocking trades, and had a depressing effect on the wages of journeywomen and journeymen.

The parish apprenticeship records for the better-documented parishes of twelve counties, mainly covering East Anglia and the East Midlands, and excluding 'apprentices to husbandry, service . . . housewifery and collective indentures to lint and cotton manufacture', show a drop in the percentage of females from 27 per cent in the eighteenth to 17 per cent in the nineteenth century. Accompanying this fall was a sharp decline in the range of trades represented. By the latter century, female apprenticeship, in so far as it survived, was more clearly restricted to women's trades.[56]

Study of apprenticeship and service in husbandry reveals just how few women had either training. The records of both totally understate the work women performed, the training they receive, and the skills they acquired. The fact that women were in a minority among both apprentices and servants in husbandry is not an indication of how few skills they possessed. It is part of the invisibility of many women's productive work. Wives and daughters could work alongside their husbands and fathers, they could carry out the same tasks and exhibit the same skills, but never acquire any legally recognized training. It is true that widows who had never served an apprenticeship were able to carry on the trades of their husbands, and sometimes their daughters were also given entry into the trade. But for the vast majority of craftsmen with wives and daughters on hand as cheap labour, there was no point in apprenticing them. On small farms many daughters were never sent out to service in husbandry but were retained within the family home to help their mothers in the tasks on the farm and in the house and often to look after younger children. The consequence for many women was that they lost out on any systematic and recognized training, and in consequence their labour, and that of those who *had* been apprentices or servants in husbandry, was often undervalued.

[56] Snell, *Annals*, p. 283.

7

Housework

Housewives who do not work for money income, are not part of the labour force, as are not people who do not work, at all, such as small children.

The Economic History of Britain since 1700

... taking them in every class of life, the wives of England are by no means the least important of the workers.

The British Almanac, 1875

The housewife, we are told, is 'the person, other than a domestic servant who is responsible for most of the household duties (or for supervising a domestic servant who carries out those duties)'.[1] We might note in passing that this modern (1968) definition equates the work of housewives and domestic servants, their work roles being seen as virtually identical. Later we shall examine the implications of such a definition against the reality of eighteenth-century experience. According to which aspect of housework one wants to emphasize, it can be variously defined. If one sets out to stress its exploitative nature, one can view it as a 'woman's unpaid work role in the home'.[2] If one wants to show that such work is seen as exclusively *women's* work, then the absence of any parallel role for a 'househusband' might be stressed. If one wants to show that the role of a housewife is above all a dependent and inferior one, then she is to be seen as 'the wife of a householder'.[3] The role covers 'every activity required to maintain a home and meet the physical needs of its members (usually a family)'.[4] Questions must be asked

---

[1] Audrey Hunt, *A Survey of Women's Employment* (1968), quoted Ann Oakley, *Women's Work* (1976), p. 1.
[2] Oakley, *Women's Work*, p. ix.
[3] Ibid., p. 1.
[4] Caroline Davidson, *A History of Housework in the British Isles, 1650–1950* (1982), p. 1.

before any of these definitions can be accepted as valid for the eighteenth century. Was housework then defined as an important, if not the most important, aspect of women's role, and was it definable in such exclusively female terms?

First we should be clear what 'housework' excludes. While the close association between women and the home is directly related to their bearing and rearing of children, such child care is not part of 'housework'. Similarly, although the frontiers between cottage production and production for use in the family are often blurred, cottage industry is also excluded from 'housework'. Indeed, it excludes all production for the market even if, as so often happens, it is virtually impossible to separate it from production for home consumption. Directly one starts to look at the history of housework, one becomes aware of how its nature has changed and developed. It has involved very different activities in different periods. One has only to think of what the modern housewife regards as the essential tools and materials of housework to recognize that it was very different in the eighteenth century. Then, too, if 'housework' is the work done in the home, homes have changed — and were in process of changing rapidly in the late eighteenth and early nineteenth century. Those of the vast majority of the population in the eighteenth century were not two-storied, three-bedroomed, semi-detached houses equipped with kitchen, dining, and sitting rooms, bathroom, separate WC and downstairs cloakroom. Nor were they centrally heated or double-glazed. Most households were small, unheated, and ill lit, without water, gas, or electricity, lacking drainage or sanitation. Very many cottages of the labouring poor were without any privy well into the nineteenth century.[5] It is worth remembering that there were still many Oxfordshire villages long after the Second World War that had no piped water supply. Most cottages or houses were sparsely furnished, with walls, floors, and windows without covering. Carpets and wallpaper were only introduced at the end of the century, and even then only in the houses of the well-to-do. William Howitt, writing in the 1830s, found that in most parts of England, 'in the genuine country', where as yet aspirations to gentility had not permeated, there were still 'stone floors, and naked tables, and pewter plates, and straw bedding, and', he added, 'homely living in all conscience'.[6] The 'housework' involved in such houses as these was very different from what we understand by it today.

[5] M. W. Barley *The English Farmhouse and Cottage* (1961), p. 259.
[6] William Howitt, *The Rural Life of England* (1840), p. 100.

In the late eighteenth century, north of a line drawn from the Humber to the Dee, the only area where labourers' cottages normally consisted of two storeys, with house and parlour below and two chambers above, was the East Riding.[7] There were still many labouring families whose cottages consisted of only one room with no upstairs and no bedrooms. We have been so accustomed to think of the eighteenth century in terms of the great country houses of the wealthy that it comes as something of a shock to be reminded that such standards were representative of only a tiny minority. The vast majority lived in small cottages or shacks, or sometimes, as in the case of Defoe's lead-miner's family, in caves.[8]

In towns, and more particularly in London, crowded living conditions were the norm. Many lived as weekly tenants in furnished rooms. A large number of houses of the labouring population had a basement 'sunk entirely underground, for which reason it is damp, unwholesome and uncomfortable'.[9] Families of labourers were often found in lodgings. Even families of artisans frequently lived in one, or at best, two rented rooms. Archenholz remarked on how the poorer people of London strove to obtain a house for themselves rather than rent rooms because of the advantages of being a householder, but he added that 'it often happens that in such a house the whole furniture consists of a bed, a table, and a few chairs'.[10] Many had humbler aspirations. Francis Place, a journeyman leather-breeches maker, for example, started his married life with his wife Elizabeth in a single furnished room. By dint of careful saving they managed to buy 'a bedstead, a table, three or four chairs and some bedding'. This enabled them to rent an unfurnished room up two flights of stairs – and to halve their rent. In that one room Francis and Elizabeth lived and slept. In the same room their first child was born, fell ill, and died. Place remarked on the degradation that resulted from a woman 'having to eat and drink and cook and wash and iron and transact all her domestic concerns in the room in which her husband works'.[11] Shopkeepers and better-off artisans often chose to confine their living quarters to part of their houses. Their families would occupy the ground floor, or one or two rooms, in order that the rest of the house could be let. In such living

---

[7] Barley, *The English Farmhouse*, p. 266.

[8] Daniel Defoe, *A Tour through England and Wales*, 2 vols [1724–6], Everyman edn (1948), vol. ii, p. 161.

[9] Isaac Ware, *A Complete Body of Architecture* (1756), p. 354.

[10] J. W. Von Archenholz, *A Picture of England*, trans. from the French (1791), p. 265.

[11] *The Autobiography of Francis Place (1771–1854)*, ed. with an Introduction and notes (1972), pp. 111, 116.

conditions, housework was of necessity limited in extent, but nevertheless it posed almost insuperable problems for the housewife. Think, for example, of the difficulty of drying washing in one or two upstairs rooms where the inmates had no access to either garden or yard. 'We frequently went to bed', Place wrote 'with a wet or damp floor, and with the wet cloaths hanging up in the room'.[12]

In the late seventeenth and early eighteenth century, perhaps the most important change that was occurring in houses, and one that reflected the social distinctions of householders, was internal. How was the house divided inside? Was there still an open hearth with smoke escaping (or more often, not escaping) through a hole in the roof, or fire grates with carefully built chimneys that allowed the smoke to escape but also enabled the inmates to construct an upper floor and create new rooms from what had formerly been unused (and unusable) roof space? Was there now a parlour for the sole use of the family so that its members no longer lived and ate with the servants, if they had any, in the hall or kitchen? Such questions require answering, for if an important part of 'housework' is 'keeping a house in order',[13] then the size of the house and the number of its rooms and windows are all factors contributing to the work involved. The brushing of carpets, the washing of curtains and table linen, the polishing of furniture, brass, or silver – all tasks regarded in more recent times as of the essence of housework – assume the possession of carpets, curtains, furniture, brass, and silver. Yet in the eighteenth century, of these, the majority of households possessed only furniture, and of that only the bare necessities. So 'housework' in the more recent sense of the word was largely irrelevant to the experience of the overwhelming majority of households.

The floors of the houses and cottages of all except the upper classes in the early eighteenth century were mostly earthen, the damp earth being beaten down to form a hard and smooth surface. These, periodically, and particularly at festivals like May Day, were strewn with rushes or with sweet-smelling herbs.[14] They must have helped to make earth floors warmer, if not cleaner. This may be why they were used in churches. In the area round Preston in Lancashire rushes 'were strew'd once a year in ye pews of ye church'.[15] An alternative to earthen floors found in Lincolnshire

[12] Ibid., p. 138.
[13] Davidson, *History of Housework*, p. 1.
[14] Christina Hole, *English Home Life, 1500–1800* (1947), p. 98.
[15] John Loveday, *Diary of a Tour through Parts of England, Wales, Ireland and Scotland* (1890), p. 93.

and Nottinghamshire, as well as further south, were floors of lime or gypsum plaster. Some houses might have one or two rooms with brick floors — the hall or kitchen floor, for example, or where local bricks were unavailable, the floors might be stone-paved. But whether of brick, stone, or earth, such floors had in common the great disadvantage of being both damp and cold. As the century progressed, the fashionable alternative was wooden floors — both warmer and more proof against damp. Most average-sized farmhouses in the eighteenth century, it seems, on the ground floor had at least the parlour boarded, as well as the upstairs chambers. Rarely were the ceilings under such wooden floors of upstairs rooms plastered, so that dirt and dust fell through the floor boards into the rooms beneath.[16]

Earthen floors persisted in some areas well into the second half of the century, and only very slowly were they replaced by boards. In 1769, Elizabeth Shackleton, the mother of Mary Leadbeater, 'though she endured the demolition of her floor [that of the parlour], thought the washing of the boards of such a large room would be a job of too great magnitude; so she procured flags from Rosenallis for her parlour'. Fashion, however, ultimately prevailed, and 'as taste gained ground, even that room was submitted to timber flooring'.[17] What is interesting is that her reasons for opposing wood floors was the increased work involved in washing them. She had a point. Earthen, and indeed, stone-flagged floors almost certainly required far less cleaning than those of wood, which were often cleaned with sand. The Hampshire farmhouse of William Smith (1790—1858) had no carpets, and 'the oak floors were sprinkled with sand. . . . and if the sand was dry it kept the boards very clean; but damp sand was uncomfortable.'[18]

If one considers the bare essentials that a home must offer — shelter from the elements and a source of warmth, the means to cook food, the materials for providing a minimum of light, and the ability of inhabitants to keep themselves, their clothes, their cooking utensils and the house itself moderately (but only moderately) clean, the problems posed by eighteenth-century housework become clearer. What above all else strikes one is the amount of time, preparation, and energy, that went into the provision of even these bare necessities. Take, for example, the provision of water for cooking, drinking,

[16] Barley, *The English Farmhouse*, pp. 258, 263.
[17] *The Leadbeater Papers: A Selection from the MSS and Correspondence of Mary Leadbeater*, 2 vols (1862), vol. i, p. 72.
[18] George Sturt, *William Smith, Potter and Farmer; 1790—1858* (1978), pp. 157—8.

washing, and cleaning. Except for the houses of the very rich, a piped water supply was rare. There was no system of drainage, no sewerage, and, before 1770, no water closets. Water had to be drawn and carried from the water source. When eight-year-old Janet Greenfield went into service on a small farm in Sunderland in 1814, she was given the task — it was her first — of carrying leeks and potatoes down to the burn to be washed.[19] Local ponds, streams, and springs were commonly used by women for washing clothes and linen — a practice still to be found in many rural areas of Europe and beyond.[20]

Waterbutts for collecting water from the roofs of houses were common, but all too often they dried up in summer and on their own were inadequate to meet the needs of even a small family. Most rural dwellers had recourse to local wells and other sources for their needs. These might be at some considerable distance from the house. We do not need Charles Knight to tell us that 'to raise a bucket from the well' was 'very laborious', but we are apt to forget that this was only the beginning.[21] After the water was brought up it had to be carried to the house, which might well be at a distance of quarter of a mile or more. In towns access to water was made easier by the presence of pumps for bringing the water to the surface, or often some form of organized water supply, but sources were too few in relation to the population, and often water was in short supply. So in London, 'the Wives and Servant Girls of Mechanicks and Day-Labourers, who live in Courts and Alleys, where one Cock supplies the whole Neighbourhood with Water' were found on Sunday mornings at four o'clock, 'taking the Advantage before other People are up, to fill their Tubs and Pans, with a Sufficiency to serve them the ensuing seven days'.[22]

When Charles Knight asked 'an old woman in a country district, tottering under the weight of a bucket, which she was labouring to carry up a hill', how her family fared, she replied that as they could all work they could manage very well, but for one thing: the fetching of water. 'It was', she claimed, 'one person's labour to

[19] Janet Bathgate, *Aunt Janet's Legacy to Her Nieces* (1894), p. 65, quoted Davidson, *History of Housework*, p. 170.
[20] For practice in Glasgow and Belfast see *Memoirs of the Forty-Five First Years of the Life of James Lackington* (1794), p. 293; *Belfast News Letter* (1801), quoted Davidson, *History of Housework*, p. 11.
[21] Charles Knight, *The Working Man's Companion* (1831), pp. 79–80.
[22] *Low Life, or One Half of the World Knows Not How the Other Half Live* (1764), pp. 25–6.

fetch water from the spring.'[23] It is not insignificant that she left undetermined the sex of that 'one person'. Much later, Edwin Grey, writing of cottagers in a Hertfordshire village, thought that 'usually the labourers saw to it that the wife was always well supplied with water, drawing from the well and filling up the water pans each night, but, there were other men who left all for the wife to attend to'.[24] In London, so great was the labour involved in fetching water that 'many people obtained a living by carrying water'.[25] Even when water from a standpipe was available to urban dwellers, water carriers continued to do a good trade. It was said that 'old-fashioned people' were prejudiced in favour of water brought to the door, and that there was much sympathy with the cry of the water-carrier: 'Fresh and fair new River-water! None of your pipe sludge!'[26]

It has been estimated that in the south of England, the load of water carried by an adult woman was rarely less than a gallon, and averaged three. In some areas of both England and Scotland, women carried the water in 'skeels' or wooden tubs on their heads. They contained from three to six-and-a-half gallons, and were balanced on a pad of wool or straw.[27] But it was not only water that some women carried. Women in Wales, for example, wore 'a long piece of woollen cloth wrapped round the waist'. 'I have a hundred times', Catherine Hutton wrote of them, 'seen a woman carrying a pitcher of water on her head and a child or a loaf in this wrapper, and knitting as she walked along.'[28]

'Washing-up' posed its own problems. The very term suggests its origin in a period when water, if not hot water, came out of a tap at the sink. In the eighteenth century, the difficulty of procuring water, let alone hot water, meant that other cleaning agents were needed. Sand or granite powder was often employed for scouring cooking pots, and in the countryside, straw, wood ashes, or bran were used. A poem of 1755, written by Molly Leapor, a cook-maid poet, describes just how pewter plates were washed by a housewife at the time:

> . . . but now her dish-kettle began
> To boil and blubber with the foaming bran.

[23] Knight, *Working Man's Companion*, p. 80.
[24] Edwin Grey, *Cottage Life in a Herefordshire Village* (1935), p. 48.
[25] Knight, *Working Man's Companion*, p. 84.
[26] William Hone, *The Table Book* (1859), p. 733.
[27] Davidson, *History of Housework*, p. 14.
[28] *Reminiscences of a Gentlewoman of the Last Century: Letters of Catharine Hutton*, ed. Catherine Hutton Beale (1891), p. 52.

The greasy apron round her hips she ties
And to each plate the scalding clout applies.
The purging bath each glowing dish refines,
And once again the polish'd pewter shines.[29]

Bran was particularly effective in absorbing grease left on dishes, and it had an additional advantage in that it could afterwards be fed to the pigs. For many poor families the problem of 'washing-up' was simplified by the absence of all but the communal cooking pot or bowl — and this itself was rarely washed. But if the household had a dairy, or even if it possessed only one or two cows, a great deal of water was required for cleaning the milk pails 'washing the milk off with cold water, and brushing the chinks' before the pails were ready for scalding.[30]

Just what demands the washing of clothes imposed on a household is suggested by the infrequency of washdays. Dirty washing tended to be accumulated, sometimes for as long as two months. Many diarists, both men and women, thought washday an event of sufficient importance, as a rare and noteworthy occurrence, to comment on it. Mary Hardy, the wife of a Norfolk farmer, for example, regularly recorded the event. 'Oct. 18, Tues. Close foggy day, maids washed', or 'May 13, Mon. A showry day wind south — washed 3 weeks linen', or again, 'Oct. 5, Mon. ... Maids and Goody Tompson washed a fortnight's linen.'[31] In his diary William Jones, the Quaker weaver of Charlbury in Oxfordshire, faithfully notes the event by entering one word, 'Washing', often with no other entry for that day.[32] He had to do all the fetching and carrying of water for his invalid mother, so he may well have found washdays exhausting as well as time-consuming. Washing was clearly a household activity that made an impression on all members of the household. George Woodward, the East Hendred parson, used the dislocation occasioned by the extra washing as an excuse for discouraging a visit from his stepmother and her three daughters. 'The article of washing at home for so many', he wrote to her, 'we could not possibly undertake to do.' He dreaded 'the continual fuss and stir there would be with wet clothes, for what between the washing of our own family, and

[29] *Purefoy Letters, 1735–1753*, ed. G. Eland, 2 vols (1931), vol. ii, p. 280.
[30] Mary Leadbeater, *Cottage Dialogues among the Irish Peasantry*, 2 pts (1811, 1813), pt i, p. 26.
[31] *Mary Hardy's Diary*, with an Introduction by B. Cozens-Hardy, Norfolk Record Society, vol. xxxvii, (1968), entries for 18 Oct. 1774, 13 May 1782 and 5 Oct. 1778.
[32] M. Sturge Henderson, *Three Centuries in North Oxfordshire* (1902), p. 143.

hers too, which could not possibly be at the same time, the household would be continually full of this sort of business'.[33] His stepmother abandoned her visit.

But washing presented problems other than just the supply of water. Most households did not possess the means of heating water in sufficient quantitites for washing clothes. Large coppers under which fires could be lit existed, but only in richer households. Thus Mary Collier described her tasks on arriving at her employers in the early hours of the morning to do the washing: 'Water we pump, the Copper we must fill, / Or tend the fire'.[34] In other households the wife had to use the same iron boiling pots in which she cooked the family's meals. So, as Caroline Davidson has pointed out, it was cooking or washing — another explanation of why men in the household seem not to have welcomed washdays.[35]

Soap required hot water and was expensive because highly taxed. This was yet another reason why washdays tended to be infrequent. Most households used a mixture of soap and lye (water impregnated with wood or plant ashes). In the countryside many labouring households made their own lye, but when wood became more difficult to obtain they were forced to buy soap. Some farmers' wives made their own soap, but it was a laborious business. Purchasing soap was not cheap (nor was blue for whitening the linen), but in many labouring households the purchase of a small quantity of soap was a weekly necessity, as the lack of a change of clothes forced on them more frequent washdays than in richer households. Early on Sunday mornings, 'the Wives of poor Journeymen Mechanicks' could be seen in London 'getting up to buy a little Soap, and wash their Husbands a Shirt, Stock, Handkerchief, and Stockings, that they may appear in the Afternoon like *Christians*, though they live like *Brutes*'.[36]

Urine was widely used as a cleansing liquid. Samuel Bamford called it 'the great purifier' and told of how in his youth 'on the premises of every family might be found a tub, or a mug of a size sufficiently capacious to hold the whole product of this pungent liquid, and as a most precious cleanser, it was carefully collected and consigned to its appointed vessel, thence to be taken as wanted

---

[33] *A Parson in the Vale of White Horse*, ed Donald Gibson (1982), p. 44.
[34] Mary Collier, *The Woman's Labour: An Epistle to Mr. Stephen Duck, in Answer to His Late Poem, called 'The Thresher's Labour'* (1739), p. 16.
[35] Davidson, *History of Housework*, p. 48.
[36] *Low Life*, p. 33.

for use'. Apparently clothes, and particularly 'all the woollen things'
were not considered properly washed unless they had been thus
'thoroughly scoured' and 'afterwards washed and wrung out of
clean hot water'. But it was not just clothes that were washed in
urine, at least in Bamford's Lancashire, where 'both men and women,
girls and boys, made use of it to wash their persons'.[37] No wonder
there were complaints by foreigners that close-stools were but seldom
emptied.

One thing seems clear: the amount of water a family used had
little to do with what was desirable, or what might be considered as
necessary for reasons of health and hygiene. It depended on just
how much time could be spared — most often, but not exclusively,
by the women of the household — to fetch water. For many women
the amount of water they could afford to fetch each day imposed
limits on the extent and nature of other household tasks. It also
meant that personal cleanliness was often something a family could
ill afford.

Francis Place, looking back on the standards of cleanliness in his
youth in London and comparing them with those at the time he
was writing in 1824, thought that 'the increased cleanliness of the
people' was 'particularly striking'. Formerly 'women of all ranks wore
what were called full boned stays'. He commented, 'they were never
washed altho' worn day by day for years'. Elsewhere he wrote of
'petticoats of camblet' which were 'worn also day by day, until they
were rotten, and never were washed'. Nor was this surprising, given
the dirtiness of London, the inadequacy of supplies of water, and
the conditions in which many women did their washing. Place
talked of 'the women young and old ... washing on stools in the
street'.[38] Many housewives must have regarded water as an expensive
luxury. As late as 1842 when the *Report of the Sanitary Conditions
of the Labouring Population of Great Britain* was published, it
commented on 'the great extent to which the labouring classes are
subjected to privations, not only of water for the purposes of
ablution, house cleaning and sewerage, but of wholesome water for
drinking, and culinary purposes'.[39]

The ironing of clothes was confined to those possessing metal
irons that could be heated on a fire. But in so far as any attempt

[37] Samuel Bamford, *Dialect of South Lancashire, or Tim Bobbin's Tummus and Meary*
(1850), p. viii.
[38] Place, *Autobiography*, p. 51, note from Add. MSS. 27827 fo. 50; Add. MSS. 27827,
fo. 52, quoted Dorothy George, *London Life in the Eighteenth Century* (1966), p. 112.
[39] Davidson, *History of Housework*, p. 29.

was made to 'iron' clothes, most people used some kind of smoothing process using 'smoothing' stones or wooden rollers, or even their feet to trample linen into some degree of smoothness. Proper mangles were only used among the upper classes.[40] In her diary covering the period 1778—91, Elizabeth Brown, the wife of a Bedfordshire mealman, frequently mentioned ironing. We do not know what 'ironing' involved for her, but it seems to have occupied a great deal of time. 'Pretty fully employed in getting up linen' was her entry for 25 January 1779, and there are similar entries for 10 March and 16 June of that year. When she was not concerned with her own linen she was helping neighbours: 'went to assist Cousin A.B. at ironing this morning' or 'went to assist sister M.E. at ironing'.[41]

If provision of water for the household involved arduous work so did the collection of fuel for heating and cooking. The preparation, lighting, and tending of the fire, the cleaning of the hearth as well as the cooking that was done over it, were women's tasks. They assumed a supply of fuel. If it was often women — and children — who went out gathering wood and other fuel, it was not exclusively women, and men were frequently involved. In nineteenth-century French peasant households 'the main male activity', it is held, was 'to provide the wood'.[42] In England, in collecting wood from the forests and twigs from the hedgerow, in cutting peat, in collecting cow and horse dung for drying for fuel, women, as well as their families, went out into the surrounding countryside. Eighteenth-century 'housework' was not only work *in* the house. On the Isle of Portland, where horse and cow dung were the chief sources of fuel for the poor (as indeed was true of many areas of the country), a visitor observed 'an old woman hobbling after our horses in hopes of a little fuel from their excrement'.[43] In Scotland, cow dung was mixed with 'ye dross of Coals . . . rolling it up in balls, & drying it in ye Sun'.[44]

Wood was the most common fuel, but it became increasingly scarce as the century progressed, and in the absence of alternatives many labouring families were reduced to having their Sunday roast,

[40] Ibid., p. 155.

[41] *Diary of Elizabeth Brown of Ampthill, 1778—91*, ed. Joyce Godber, Bedfordshire Historical Record Society, vol. xl (1960).

[42] Martine Segalen, *Love and Power in the Peasant Family: Rural France in the Nineteenth Century* (1983), p. 94.

[43] E. D. Clarke, *Tour through the South of England, Wales, and Part of Ireland Made during the Summer of 1791* (1793), p. 47.

[44] Loveday, *Diary of a Tour*, p. 131.

and often their bread, cooked at the village bakery. Baking a week's supply of bread for a family was a considerable undertaking. Susannah, second wife of William Smith, farmer and potter, was fortunate in having the job done by her mother-in-law while her children were young, so 'the farmhouse was not encumbered with that industry'.[15] In the absence of other alternatives, many families resorted to taking wood wherever they found it and at whatever cost. Gilbert White held that so desperately short of fuel were many of the poor in 1768 that they gathered twigs dropped by nest-building rooks.[46] In the notebook in which William Hunt, a Wiltshire JP, recorded the cases that came before him in the 1740s, those convicted of wood-stealing and hedge-breaking predominate. Women were sometimes responsible, but just as often it was men who came before him.[47] For baking, the best fuel for heating the oven was furze. It made 'a very quick and brisk fire, as soon as 'tis cut'.[48] Gathering furze was most often undertaken by men and boys.

In cutting peat, another widely used fuel, there was a carefully worked out division of labour between men and women in the many tasks involved. Thus, the cutting of the peat was done by men but spreading out the turfs to dry was the work of women. A week later the heaping of the turfs into small piles, or 'footing', was also the work of women and children, and after a further ten days it was they who did the 'rickling' — stacking the turfs into even larger piles. The final stacking of the turfs, the 'clamping', was done by men. Finally, if the turfs were not carried by horse and cart to the home, it was often women who carried them on their backs where the men would restack them preparatory to burning.[49]

So in gathering fuel, the work involved for women was time consuming and often heavy. Moreover, the amount of time they could devote to collecting fuel had repercussions on their ability to heat the house, to cook, to dispose of rubbish — all tasks that were seen as the province of the housewife.

Most of the houses and cottages of the labouring poor in both town and country would have been dark most of the day as well as at night. Windows were few and usually small. For lighting, most

[45] Sturt, *William Smith*, p. 162.

[46] Lawrence Wright, *Home Fires Burning* (1964), p. 101.

[47] *The Justicing Notebook of William Hunt*, ed. Elizabeth Crittall, Wiltshire Record Society, vol. xxxvii (1982).

[48] R. Bradley, *The Country Gentleman and Farmers' Monthly Director*, 3rd edn (1727), p. 64.

[49] Davidson, *History of Housework*, p. 83.

households depended on rush lights, 'a small blinking taper made by stripping a rush, except one small stripe of the bark which holds the pith together, and dipping it in tallow'.[50] They had a short life and 'lasted only while anybody was undressing and getting into bed'.[51] Rushes required collecting, peeling, and drying in the open air before they were ready for dipping in hot fat. Gilbert White wrote of 'the careful wife of an industrious Hampshire labourer' who 'obtains all her fat for nothing, for she saves the scumming of her bacon pot for this use'.[52] The work involved in lighting homes of labouring families seems to have been a communal task in which men, women, and children all participated, but the actual gathering of rushes was a job for women and children.

Thus behind the tasks traditionally regarded as those of the housewife – cooking, baking, washing, and cleaning – lay a great deal of preparatory work. If the pressure of other work and time prevented that preparatory work from being adequate, those tasks could be seriously inhibited. In opposition to the status of housework in modern industrialized societies (and in their occupational censuses) as 'non-work' because economically unproductive, much of the 'housework' undertaken by women in the eighteenth century could be seen as just as productive as that of their husbands, whether farmers, smallholders, or labourers. The wife contributed fuel for heating, cooking, and lighting. She fetched water for cooking, washing, and cleaning as well as for drinking. Today, electricity, gas, or coal must be purchased, and a rapidly mounting water-rate makes water an expensive product: certainly the workers who today are responsible for producing such products do not regard themselves as 'unproductive'.

Of course, not all the work of a housewife in the eighteenth century was of this kind. Cleaning, washing, and mending were not 'productive' in this sense, but were tasks that serviced the household. Shorter's claim that in traditional French rural households in the eighteenth century 'relatively little cleaning as such went on' has relevance for the vast majority of English labouring households in the countryside. As he goes on to explain, roofs of thatch and floors of dirt meant that 'things were always dirty and little could be done to make them clean short of putting in flooring, rebuilding and plastering the walls and ceilings, keeping out the farm animals,

---

[50] Ibid., p. 103.
[51] Sturt, *William Smith*, p. 160.
[52] Gilbert White, *The Natural History of Selborne* (1789), p. 198.

separating the stable from the living quarters, and so forth'. For the majority of rural housewives in England as for traditional French peasant women, 'cleaning ... was not at all the floor-waxing, dusting, and cobweb-removing that consumes so much of the modern housewife's energies'.[53] Yet in the late eighteenth century, and even more in the nineteenth, this servicing part of housework loomed larger under the impact of cheaper coal, oil lamps, piped municipal water supplies. In particular, the increasing use of coal must have vastly increased the amount of cleaning in a house. When iron grates and kitchen ranges replaced open hearths, they required regular black-leading. Smoking chimneys seem to have been a perennial problem, and the smoke from coal fires would have produced new cleaning problems in the home. In the same way, as we have seen with the introduction of wood floors, quite small improvements in living standards could result in a great deal more cleaning work for the housewife. For those wealthy enough to be able to afford carpets, curtains, upholstered furniture, elaborate furnishings, ornaments of china and glass, pewter or silver, there had already come the realization that such evidence of affluence brought with it the need for a great deal more dusting, cleaning, and polishing. Take the kitchen of Sarah Fuller, described by Mary Leadbeater as 'unrivalled in cleanliness. The dresser shone with pewter bright as silver, and brass and copper-pots shining like gold', and how right was Mary Leadbeater in suspecting 'that some of these were kept chiefly for ornament'.[54]

A recent work by an American writer has claimed that so-called labour-saving devices relating to housework introduced in the eighteenth and nineteenth century saved little of women's labour.[55] This may be an exaggerated claim, but it is not so outlandish. For there was a great deal of new housework created by standards of genteel living introduced in the course of the eighteenth century. On his Hampshire farm in the early nineteenth century, William Smith talked of how housework involved 'hard scouring and scrubbing', but he went on, 'some of the distresses of modern housekeeping were avoided in that simple style of living. I have heard of no annual spring-cleaning, of no sweeping of chimneys; nor were there any grates to polish. But then, neither was there any coal.'[56]

[53] Edward Shorter, *The Making of the Modern Family* (1975), pp. 69, 70.
[54] *Leadbeater Papers*, vol. i, p. 51.
[55] Ruth Schwartz Cowan, *More Work for Mother: The Ironies of Household Technology from the Open Hearth to the Microwave* (1983).
[56] Sturt, *William Smith*, p. 158.

Whatever the truth of the claim that 'a large proportion' of women found cleaning a 'creative, satisfying and thoroughly moral activity, in which they took considerable pride', middle and upper class women seemed only too anxious to shift the work on to domestic servants.[57] Writing of the nineteenth century, Theresa McBride has commented on how 'the very slow increases in technology and the social services' affected middle-class housewives with new ideas of domestic comfort and cleanliness. 'The necessity to carry coal, shop daily for provisions, heat stoves, and keep themselves clean without the benefit of running water was solved at the expense of the servant class'. It was they who 'were used to take up the slack in the evolution of household technology'.[58]

The amount of cleaning in a house, as we have seen, varied according to its size, its standard of furnishing, and the cleaning materials available. For many households throughout the century, cleaning was confined to the hearth, floors, walls, and steps, and the few kitchen utensils they possessed. Some foreign visitors to England appear to have been impressed by the standards of cleanliness in which houses were kept. 'English women generally', wrote Pehr Kalm in 1748, 'have the character of keeping floors, steps, and such things very clean.' Their obsessive concern to keep their floors clean impressed him. 'They are not particularly pleased if anyone comes in with dirty shoes, and soils their clean floors, but he ought first to rub his shoes and feet very clean, if he would be at peace with them in other things.' He remarks on the habit of many women of wearing clogs over their shoes whenever they went out so that the dirt was not brought into the house. He was amazed at the multiplicity of mats inside houses, 'in the hall or passage, and afterwards at every door, though there were ever so many one within the other', and at the iron shoe-scrapers outside houses on which all were expected to remove dirt from their shoes.[59] Given the state of roads in the eighteenth century and the dirt and mud that accumulated on them, it must have been very difficult to keep floors clean without such provision. Another visitor to London in 1772 talked of how 'the plate, hearth-stones, moveables, apartments, doors, stairs, the very street-doors, their locks, and the large brass knockers, are every day washed, scoured or rubbed'. Mats or carpets he found

---

[57] Davidson, *History of Housework*, p. 134.
[58] Teresa McBride, *The Domestic Revolution* (1976), pp. 68–9.
[59] Pehr Kalm, *Account of His Visit to England on His Way to America in 1748*, trans. Joseph Lucas (1892), pp. 12–13.

'even in lodging houses'.[60] But this was in London, and standards
of furnishing were almost certainly higher there, more especially in
lodging houses, than elsewhere in the country.

Whitewash was widely used on walls, both inside and out, to give
at least the appearance of cleanliness. In the middle of the century,
John Wood found 'the Chimney Pieces, Hearths and Slabbs' in Bath
'were all of Free Stone, and they were daily cleaned with a particular
White-wash'.[61] Many housewives seem also to have seen it as
having hygienic properties. So Mary Leadbeater in her *Cottage
Dialogues* has a husband boasting of his wife's endeavours: 'Not a
spring of her life but my woman gave our cabin the good white-
washing, and oftener too, if there was any sickness among us.'[62] In
Wales the abundance of lime led to 'almost all the cottages' being
'white-washed on the outside, which gives them a neat appearance,
and the operation is so cheap that there is scarce a hut in the whole
country, which is not regularly brushed over once a month'.[63] Both
of these accounts were subsequent to Wesley's emphasis on 'Cleanliness being next to Godliness'. Keeping themselves and their dwell-
ings clean was seen as the moral duty of the poor. Whitewash was
a fitting symbol of the purity that lies only in outward appearances.
But if such standards of outward cleanliness were found in the
countryside, they do not seem to have existed universally. In an area
of London that foreigners were unlikely to have visited, Lambeth,
Francis Place described houses where 'the window frames and door
posts were perfectly black with soot and dirt, the rooms were
neither painted nor whitewashed for many years together; patches
of paper or a rag ... kept out the cold where the glass was
broken. No such thing as a curtain, unless it was a piece of old
garment, was to be seen at any window.'[64]

Contemporary accounts suggest that what mattered most, at least
to the authors, were appearances. The poor were less disturbing to
their social superiors if clean and neat. Hence the emphasis on the
neatness of labourers' cottages and their occupants. In 1784, another
foreigner visiting England insisted that the English only cleaned
where people would notice dirt, and that in some areas, particularly

[60] M. Grosley, *A Tour to London: Or New Observations on England and Its Inhabitants*,
2 vols (1772), vol. i, p. 73.
[61] Bernard Denvir, *The Eighteenth Century: Arts, Design and Society, 1689–1789* (1983),
p. 51.
[62] Leadbeater, *Cottage Dialogues*, pt ii, p. 201.
[63] Clarke, *Tour*, p. 203.
[64] Francis Place, Add. MSS 27827 fo. 52, quoted George, *London Life*, p. 112.

in kitchens, horrifyingly dirty conditions prevailed. Even worse, so it was held, were the standards of Scottish housewives, who swept 'large heaps of nastiness' into corners, or, in bedrooms, under the bed.[65] What is surprising is that many housewives persevered against shockingly dirty conditions outside their houses to impose some order and standard of cleanliness inside despite all the difficulties.

Although 'housework' properly speaking excludes work done other than for the use of the household, the distinction between it and work done for the market was often anything but clear. A farmer's wife or even a labourer's wife who owned one or two cows would provide her family with milk and possibly with butter and cheese. From her garden she would supply vegetables, from her orchard fruit. But when market day came round, any surplus of these products would be taken to market for sale. When a pig was slaughtered by a farmer or smallholder, it was not just his family that benefited, but his neighbours and anyone to whom he owed something in exchange for services and products they had supplied to him. Some of the pork meat might well be sold by the housewife at market or to her neighbours. In the same way, while many housewives spun yarn to be woven into cloth to supply their own families with clothes, on occasion some would be sold to neighbours. So, for example, in winter the womenfolk in a Scottish manse 'were engaged in making yarn and thread', and, we are told, 'it was not below the dignity of the women to sell their home-made wares e.g. to the laird's wife at Kilikie are sold 36 ells of yarn'.[66]

Such a distinction between production for the household and production for the market was not one that meant much to an eighteenth-century housewife, any more than the distinction between productive and non-productive was meaningful to her. The family economy was focused on the household. All work by members of the household, whether paid for or not, whether regarded as productive or not, was seen as contributing to that economy and influencing the life enjoyed by its members. Charles Knight made the point clearly when he wrote that 'all occupations, however apparently unproductive and trifling, are valuable, if they increase our pleasures, our comforts, and well-being'.[67] Just how wide could be the range of tasks performed by a wife of a Yorkshire clothier in

[65] Loveday, *Diary of a Tour*, p. 163.
[66] H. G. Graham, *Literary and Historical Essays* (1909), p. 144.
[67] Charles Knight, *History of the Middle and Working Classes* (1833), pp. 181–2.

the middle of the eighteenth century is suggested in the colloquial poem quoted by Pinchbeck (see pp. 42—3).[68]

The work of the wife of a smallholder was closely integrated with all other work in the family economy, and in this sense it was no different from that done by any other member. The same point has been made of the family economy as it operated in nineteenth- and twentieth-century rural France, and continues to operate in some parts. 'Preparing a meal, or giving the pigs their swill, all come under the household; men, women, children, servants and animals are all equal beneficiaries of this work.' Martine Segalen goes on to suggest how wrong historians of the household have been in seeing housework as a 'strictly defined category' of work, and has suggested that 'the classification of male—female work' needs careful re-examining.[69]

The 'housework' of the eighteenth-century housewife was often arduous, yet it was also varied. It took her into the woods and fields, or into the village or town. If the housewife of today is 'isolated in a way quite different from other workers', this was not so of her predecessor — at least for the greater part of the eighteenth century.[70] Peter Laslett is surely right in his claim that 'there was nothing to correspond to . . . the lonely lives of housekeeping wives which we now know only too well', and wrong in his later assertion that 'the only public appearance of women and children, almost their only expedition outside the circle of the family . . . was at service in Church', and sometimes at market, 'but otherwise they stayed at home'.[71] Adrian Wilson has drawn attention to the importance of certain focal points where women congregated — the well, the stream, the harvest fields — in providing opportunities for resistance to patriarchal power.[72]

In 1919 Alice Clark wrote that 'though it is now taken for granted that domestic work will be done by women, a considerable proportion of it in former days fell to the share of men'.[73] This was true not only of the seventeenth century, but also for much of the eighteenth century, at least where labouring people were concerned. Perhaps in France it was true that in the eighteenth century 'within

[68] Ivy Pinchbeck, *Women Workers and the Industrial Revolution, 1750—1850* [1930], (1981), p. 127.

[69] Segalen, *Love and Power*, p. 81.

[70] Oakley, *Women's Work*, p. 6.

[71] Peter Laslett, *The World We Have Lost Further Explored* (1983), pp. 11, 73.

[72] Adrian Wilson, 'Patriarchal power and women's resistance in early modern England', paper given at the University of Adelaide, 16 Mar. 1987.

[73] Alice Clark, *The Working Life of Women in the Seventeenth Century* (1982), p. 5.

the house, the men had virtually nothing to do — save perhaps, lighting the fire, in homes fortunate enough to have a baking oven', but not in England.[74] There was a sexual division of labour in many of the tasks involved in housework. Writers like Charles Varley were at pains to emphasize that division. 'The man's care', he wrote, 'should be over the land and out of door business', while the woman's was 'to mind the house, and teach the females to card, spin, knit, and such like, every one to their proper work as their age and sex requires.'[75] But in practice there was no such clear distinction. What David Davies observed in Aberdeenshire in 1795 — 'in the long winter evenings, the husband cobbles shoes, mends the family clothes, and attends the children while the wife spins' — could be found south of the border.[76] At the end of the century Richard Jones was a small boy living near Ruthin in Wales. He later wrote of how when faced by starvation after a disastrous harvest, his mother had the following conversation with his father:

> 'I'll make a bargain with thee; I'll see to food for us both and the children all winter, if thou, in addition to looking after the horse, the cattle and pigs, wilt do the churning, wash-up, make the beds and clean the house. I'll make the butter myself.' 'How wilt thou manage?' asked my father ... 'I will knit', said she, 'We have wool. If thou wilt card it, I'll spin.' The bargain was struck; my father did the housework in addition to the work on the farm and my mother knitted ... And so it was she kept us alive until the next harvest.[77]

Was this so exceptional an arrangement? We cannot be sure. Catherine Davidson draws attention to Nicholas Blundell's involvement in numerous household tasks: sharing with his wife the supervising of the servants, keeping the household accounts, feeding the pigs, preserving food, brewing, helping prepare for guests, and even dusting. He was 'an unusually assiduous husband', but such behaviour was not 'exceptional by seventeenth and eighteenth-century standards'.[78]

By the end of the century there was a perceptible change in the nature of housework and the position of the housewife, at least in

---

[74] Shorter, *Making of the Modern Family*, p. 70.
[75] Charles Varley, *A Treatise on Agriculture*, 2 vols (1766), vol. ii, p. 251.
[76] David Davies, *The Case of Labourers in Husbandry* (1795), p. 193.
[77] Davidson, *History of Housework*, p. 185.
[78] Ibid., p. 187.

the homes of prosperous tradesmen and better-off artisans. During
most of the eighteenth century that change was slow, but it started
to speed up in the second half. It began in London, and explains in
part the belief of foreign visitors that married women did not work.
As Dorothy George pointed out, London had reached a stage of
economic development — and for some, one should add, standards
of genteel living — 'where spinning, weaving, baking, brewing and
candle-making were no longer done by housewives', tasks that on
the continent it was assumed were part of their work.[79] But for
many labouring families, reliance on the baker to roast the Sunday
joint, or on shops for buying second-hand clothes, bread, and
candles, was not a question of choice but a necessity dictated by
lack of fuel and access to raw materials. Pehr Kalm, on his visit to
England in 1748, suggested that a change had already taken place
in some areas. He expressed amazement on entering farmers'
households to find 'when one enters a house and has seen the
women cooking, washing floors, plates and dishes, darning a stocking
or sewing a chemise, washing and starching linen clothes, he has in
fact seen all their household economy and all they do the whole of
God's long day, year out and year in'[80] — hardly 'no work'. But
Kalm, like most foreigner visitors, saw little of the labouring poor.

Thus it is clear that 'housework' in the eighteenth century meant
something rather different from what it means today or what it
came to mean in the nineteenth century. It was a term which
covered a much wider range of tasks than subsequently. Far more
of those tasks were 'productive' than later, when work servicing the
household became all important. For the majority of women,
housework in the eighteenth century was not confined to the house.
Some of the tasks were almost exclusively women's tasks; for others
the division of labour between the sexes was anything but rigid.
Tasks were shared out between members of the household of both
sexes. So when Hans Medick claims that proto-industry brought the
man back to the household, one's immediate response is to question
whether in the eighteenth century he had ever left it.[81] Curiously
the notes to the 1851 occupational census include the statement,
'the *Husband* as well as the *Housewife* in the British family performs
household duties' (emphasis in the original).[82] Despite this claim,

---

[79] M. Dorothy George, *London Life in the Eighteenth Century* (1966), p. 172.

[80] Pehr Kalm, *Account of His Visit to England*, p. 327.

[81] Hans Medick, 'The proto-industrial family economy', *Social History*, 1 (Oct. 1976),
p. 312.

[82] *Census of Great Britain, 1851*, Population tables ii, 'Ages, Civil Condition, Occupations,
and Birth Place of the People' (1854), vol. i, p. lxxxviii.

the trend was for that sexual division of labour increasingly to assert itself as the identity of home and place of work was broken, as the family economy was undermined, as housework became work confined more and more to the house, and as the nature of household tasks shifted away from the provision of the basic necessities of domestic life — food, fuel, water, and light — to meet the demands of increasing gentility. Changing household technology also played its part in making housework more and more exclusively 'women's work'.

The ideology of the independent working household in which women played an important role alongside of their husbands and other members of the household surely dates back to Puritanism, if not earlier. What was new in the eighteenth century, at least in the final decades, and in the early years of the nineteenth was that as the family economy was eroded and the household was no longer the focus of work within the family, women were left stranded in the home. Attempts to justify their retention there were based on what was held to be the moral duty of wives and mothers to devote themselves exclusively to home and family. The withdrawal of men from any involvement in housework has been explained more recently as the result of men being 'the main breadwinners, whether their wives worked or not, . . . it seemed only fair that they should be exempt from housework'.[83]

Social historians have not been forward in seeing the history of housework as an important field of research. But if one is to understand the way in which the notion that 'housework is women's work' influenced every attempt to train women for future work roles, and influenced the way in which their working identities, in whatever occupation, were seen and evaluated, one must start with what housework meant for women in the eighteenth century. Housework as women's work, I believe, led to a blurring of all definition of their working identities, whether as apprentices to a trade or as servants in husbandry. It was ever-present in the minds of those who saw women as a vital and underemployed potential work-force for rural industry. It was the basis for seeing women's work in that industry as merely a source of supplementary income, the main income-earner being the head of the household, and so a reason for paying them wages that were low, and always lower than male workers in the same trade.

Housework as women's work is also closely related to the recruitment of domestic servants in the second half of the century to

[83] Davidson, *History of Housework*, p. 188.

do the household tasks dictated by a newly acquired affluence of some households, and with it, a new gentility that found such tasks both distasteful and demeaning. As early as 1721, Defoe had Moll Flanders assuming that housework was the work done by servants, and that a gentlewoman was one who 'did not go to service, to do housework'.[84] The same point was made in a letter published in *The Lady's Magazine* in May 1771. The writer, 'the eldest daughter of a tradesman who had acquired a considerable fortune', and who had brought her up 'a gentlewoman', wrote that he 'would not suffer me to give myself the least trouble about his family affairs', so she remained 'entirely ignorant of everything belonging to that vulgar character a good housewife'. She had married a man 'much my inferior' who was 'so provokingly absurd as to expect me to look after his household matters'. She asks the readers whether as a gentlewoman she should pay any attention to the demands her family are making on her. The same attitude, much more common by the end of the century, is found in a novel by Charlotte Palmer of 1792. 'Men of Fortune like their wives to command respect,' a character says, 'and not to be like as if they had been ladies maids, or housekeepers! — I cannot say I should like to see my daughters pickling and preserving, and putting their hands into a pan of flour, and all that.'[85] What would he have thought of them scouring and scrubbing, black-leading, dusting, and polishing — all tasks that were embraced by 'housework' by the beginning of the nineteenth century?

[84] Lindsey Charles and Lorna Duffin (eds), *Women and Work in Pre-Industrial England* (1985), p. 123.
[85] Quoted R. P. Utter and G. B. Needham, *Pamela's Daughters* (1936), p. 26.

8

Domestic Service

Why this life of considerable hardship and not infrequent mistreatment should have continued to attract so many people into the ranks of servants, even after industrialisation provided alternative employments for some is an important and recurring question ...

Theresa McBride, *The Domestic Revolution*

In a period when the family economy was being steadily undermined, and in consequence the work of women in the household was in decline, when the work available to women in agriculture was diminishing, when many of the handicraft trades in which women for so long had played a central role were feeling the impact of mechanization and shrinking fast, the most important occupation for women, particularly unmarried women, was domestic service. It was no coincidence, I think, that the increasing importance of domestic service as an occupation for women was related closely to the decline of female service in husbandry and indeed, although far less significant, female apprenticeship. Female domestic service was not new in the eighteenth century, but there was a period when in its rural context it was very difficult to distinguish from female service in husbandry. Only slowly did it detach itself from service in husbandry and take on new and quite distinct characteristics. We need to be clear what those distinctions were. What exactly were the implications of its dominant role as an occupation for women in the period of industrialization? This is a question we shall consider later.

How certain are we of its growing importance as an occupation for women? How many female domestic servants were there? According to the 1851 occupational census there were 905,000 female domestic servants in Britain as compared with 134,000 males. In England and Wales alone, the figures were 783,543 females as compared to 124,595 males. Of these females, 40 per cent were under nineteen years of age, and 66 per cent under twenty-four.[1]

---

[1] *Census of Great Britain, 1851*, Population tables, ii, 'Ages, Civil Condition, Occupations, and Birth Place of the People' (1854), vol. i, p. cxli.

The census figures, in so far as they are reliable, indicate that domestic service represented far and away the most important occupation for women after agriculture. For how long had this been the case? Judging by subsequent occupational censuses the proportion of female to male domestics was increasing, so can we conclude that this trend was present earlier? In 1776 a tax was placed on all male domestic servants. It was extended to cover females in 1785. It could have been the source of some authoritative statistics, but unfortunately for the historian the tax was so often evaded as to be useless as an indication of numbers. Although there were no official occupational censuses in the eighteenth century, there were, at least in the last half of the century, some unofficial estimates of the number of domestic servants of both sexes. Contemporaries were of the opinion they were increasing. In 1767, Jonas Hanway thought that one in thirteen of the London population was a domestic; given the estimated population of London within the walls at the time, this would have meant 50,000 domestics in the metropolis alone. Later, in 1775, he was to increase this estimate to one in eight of the population, or 80,000 domestics.[2] In 1806 Patrick Colquhoun, the magistrate, estimated a total of 910,000 domestic servants in England and Wales, of whom 800,000 were female.[3]

Those who commented critically on the new and more luxury-loving way of life of prosperous tradesmen had no doubt that the demand for maids was on the increase. In 1795 an anonymous author wrote of the wives of London tradesmen who fifty years earlier had been satisfied with 'only one and, as an extraordinary thing, with two maid servants', implying that now they had far more.[4] Soame Jenyns talked of the shopkeeper 'who used to be well contented with one dish of meat, one fire, and one maid, has now two or three times as many of each'.[5] Whether or not Hanway's estimate was correct, he was right in thinking London represented by far the greatest concentration. But if more numerous in London and other towns than in the country because of greater concentration of population, the demand for domestic servants was not confined to towns. While the accepted explanation of this increase in the overall number of domestic servants is that it was the response to

[2] J. Jean Hecht, *The Domestic Service Class in Eighteenth Century England* (1956), p. 30.

[3] Patrick Colquhoun, *A Treatise on Indigence* (1806), p. 253.

[4] Anon., *Of Monopoly and the Reform of Manners* (1795), p. 3.

[5] Soame Jenyns, *Thoughts on the Causes and Consequences of the Present High Price of Provisions* (1767), pp. 12–13.

an increased demand that accompanied 'the accelerated growth of the middle class',[6] there are reasons for thinking that the nature of the work that increased demand represented favoured female rather than male servants. The different job descriptions that made up the hierarchy of domestic service indicate a close relationship between the changing nature of 'housework' and the increased demand for female domestics. Most of the new tasks associated with 'housework' towards the end of the eighteenth century are related to the middle-class wife's idea of domestic comfort.

Homes were more commodious, with separate chambers for the servants and the family. All family rooms had to have individual fireplaces, their own washstands with bowl and water-jug. There were new standards of furnishing – more furniture, curtains, carpets, hangings, pictures on the wall, brass and silver, ornaments. All these changes created new work, whether brushing, cleaning, washing, polishing, or dusting, the carrying of coal to upstairs rooms and laying of fires, supplying bedrooms with hot water in the morning and subsequent removal of slops. Add to these tasks a new emphasis on entertaining, often in lavish style, and it becomes very easy to see why more servants were necessary. But if men were employed as footmen, *valets de chambre*, and butlers, they were never employed as kitchen or scullery maids, maids of all work, housemaids – those lower strata of the domestic service hierarchy to whom the majority of these new tasks fell. By the time of the 1851 occupational census, the main categories of male servants were ostlers and other inn servants, grooms, coachmen, and gardeners.

The description of the work expected of a housemaid in 1796 makes its nature clear: 'to keep the whole house in a state of cleanliness, by carefully washing the rooms, stair cases, etc., cleaning the fire-grates, irons and hearths, dusting carpets, and rubbing the furniture, as well as the locks, knockers, glasses, chimney ornaments, picture frames, etc.'[7] A family wanting additional servants to perform these tasks would think twice before taking men as it would have cost the household far more. So changes in the living style of the middle class and indeed some of the artisan class created a demand for more servants, but the tasks for which they were required demanded women rather than men.

Although there is no conclusive evidence it seems likely that the supply of male domestic servants, particularly in the second half

[6] Hecht, *Domestic Service Class*, p. 1.
[7] Anon., *Every Woman Her Own Housekeeper*, 2 vols., 4th edn. (1796), vol. ii, p. 73.

of the eighteenth century, was not only less than that of females, but that it was in decline. By the time of the first occupational census the trend becomes clear. Between 1831 and 1861, while the number of female domestic servants recorded increased by 415,952, that of males showed an increase of only 30,267.[8] Caroline Davidson dates that decline from around 1780, and points out that one effect of the 1776 tax on male servants was effectively to prevent either male apprentices or male servants in husbandry from doing any housework.[9] Until then, as Alice Clark also made clear, they had often combined agricultural and domestic tasks.[10] There were far more alternative occupations open to men. John Fielding commented in the *London Chronicle* on how 'the infinite variety of professions, trades, and manufactures joined to the army navy and services, leave few men idle, unless from choice; whilst women have but few trades, and fewer manufactures to employ them. Hence it is, that the general resource of young women is to go to service.'[11] It is also possible that with the changing nature of the tasks servants were being called on to perform, men's interest in service declined. Did they begin to view it as 'women work', and, parallel to what was already occurring in agriculture and domestic industry, leave it to women as inferior and menial? Whatever the explanation, the 'feminization of domestic service' occurred. Theresa McBride dates the process from 1800, but evidence suggests that the trend began much earlier.[12] In France, the proportion of female domestic servants grew in the last decades of the *ancien régime*; by the mid-nineteenth century, domestic service was predominantly female. In France 'feminization' is seen as reflecting the trend towards the 'middle class overtaking the nobility as the chief employer of servants'.[13] In England, as we have seen, the process was closely linked with new middle class ideas of domestic comfort. The notion that such feminization was 'one way masters sought greater control' seems rather a large claim, and one almost impossible to prove.[14]

[8] *Report of the Census of England and Wales* (1861), p. 34.
[9] Caroline Davidson, *A History of Housework in the British Isles, 1650–1950* (1932), p. 180.
[10] Alice Clark, *Working Life of Women in the Seventeenth Century* (1982), p. 5.
[11] *London Chronicle* (1758), vol. iii, p. 327c.
[12] Theresa McBride, *The Domestic Revolution* (1976), p. 9.
[13] Cissie Fairchilds, *Domestic Enemies: Servants and Their Masters in Old Regime France* (1984), pp. 15–16.
[14] John R. Gillis, 'Servants, sexual relations and the risks of illegitimacy in London, 1801–1900', in Judith I. Newton, Mary P. Ryan, and Judith R. Walkowitz (eds), *Sex and Class in Women's History* (1982), p. 123.

· Demand for domestic servants increased with the growth of the middle class because one aspect of the desire to emulate their betters was a far greater awareness of class. Newly arrived members of the middle class both wanted to move closer to the nobility and gentry, indeed to become indistinguishable from them, and to distance themselves from the lower orders. Domestic servants provided one means of demonstrating wealth and social status; the number of domestic servants a family employed was a status symbol. In fact, the number of servants per household varied enormously; the London-based family of the fourth Duke of Bedford in 1753 employed forty. The well-to-do gentry might employ about seven. Mary Berry, for example, had three men and four female servants in 1796. But the vast majority of lesser gentry and those of the middle class of limited income rarely employed more than three or four, and many only one.[15]

From where were these female domestic servants recruited? 'The grand supply of servants', according to an article in the *Oxford Magazine* of 1771, 'comes from the country; and I believe more *women* from the north of England, than from any other quarter' (emphasis in original).[16] It was daughters of farmers who first met the increased demand. As an anonymous author of 1766 confirmed, 'small farmers were the people that used to stock the country with the best of servants'. The households of such small farmers 'were the nurseries for breeding up industrious and virtuous young men and women'.[17] But small farmers were declining in number, and the demand for servants must soon have outstripped that supply. The daughters of agricultural labourers joined those of small farmers, craftsmen, artisans, and shopkeepers as well as those of penurious clerics and even sometimes of 'decayed Merchants and Gentlemen' to swell the ranks of domestic servants.[18] With the decline of service in husbandry, daughters of farmers may first have looked for, and found, places in the country, but not for long. The disappearance of other sources of employment for girls in the countryside, the decline of the family economy where a daughter's labour could easily be usefully employed, meant pressure to move into towns where more places as domestic servants existed. The best place to hire a good maidservant in London, it was said, was at the inns at which the wagons from the country arrived. William Hogarth,

[15] Hecht, *Domestic Service Class*, pp. 5, 7.
[16] *Oxford Magazine* (1771), vol. vi, p. 82.
[17] *An Address to the P——t on Behalf of the Starving Multitude* (1766), p. 39.
[18] *British Journal*, 15–20 June 1723.

in *A Harlot's Progress*, showed the fate that awaited many a country girl arriving in London in search of a place: falling into the snares of a procuress. Contemporaries tell us that country girls were preferred by masters and mistresses, particularly those of London. In his visit to England in 1780, Archenholz was convinced it was 'the idea of the pleasures to be enjoyed in the capital' that brought so many country girls to London in search of places.[19] Others thought it was 'the prospect of high wages'. Both of these contributed to the flood of country girls arriving in London, but the main motive for their leaving their homes and their villages was that their families could not afford to support them at home and there were not enough places for them to fill in the countryside. In Myddle, Thomas Hayward's daughter Elizabeth 'was a comely good humoured young woman, but her father having no portion to give her she was constrained to betake herself to service'.[20]

One difficulty in studying female domestic servants is that nearly all that has been written of them is from the point of view of the master and mistress. There are numerous books of advice to servants on the qualifications necessary in a 'good' servant — the deference, loyalty, obedience, and proper humility that had to govern their relationship with their masters and mistresses. The interesting aspect of such writings is not what they tell us about the life of servants, which is negligible, but that such directives were thought necessary. It suggests that if masters complained of servants, servants had their grievances against masters; and there is some evidence that the domestic servant class was not always servile and submissive. Take the note written to the Revd Richard Lardner by one of his maidservants in 1745:

I see there is no such thing as pleasing you I think it is proper to speak to those who dress your victuals, and not to them as has nothing to do with it ... and though I can't please you, I don't doubt but I shall please other people very well, I never had the uneasiness anywhere, as I have had here, & I hope never shall again; for you are never easy let one do never so much for you ... I will not stay with you, to be found fault with for nothing. ... and I expect to be paid for the half year I have been without cloaths.[21]

[19] J. W. von Archenholz, *A Picture of England*, trans. from the French (1791), p. 191.
[20] Richard Gough, *The History of Myddle* [1701–6], (1979), p. 113.
[21] Hecht, *Domestic Service Class*, p. 78.

The majority of comments on servant-maids in diaries, journals, memoirs, and autobiographies give the impression that female domestic servants were a body of totally unscrupulous, inefficient, immoral, unreliable, and dishonest women. They rarely satisfied their employers. They regularly stole from them, were for ever getting pregnant, being dismissed, and moving on. 'The faults of Servants', one author claimed, 'are a general Theme of Complaint. Some Families have been ruined, others made uneasy, and great Sufferers by the Frauds and Falsehoods, Idleness and Obstinacy of their Servants.'[22] To arrive at the truth means constantly allowing for employers' prejudices, while granting that many servants were in a position to exploit their situation at the expense of their employers. Of course, the very complex nature of the relationship was not one making for harmony. The paradoxical situation of employer's dependence on employees they wanted to keep servile and submissive, the conflict between wishing to distance themselves from the lower orders while increasingly relying on them, made for resentments on both sides. George Woodward wrote in a letter to his uncle of a Mrs Croft who was having trouble with servants as 'a vexatious, though not uncommon case, particularly in and about London'. Domestic servants were 'an order of our species that we can't well do without; but there are but few of us', he claimed, 'who have not reason to complain of them'.[23] There were those like Richard Mayo who stressed the interdependence of employer and servant: 'as the Hands need the Head for Guidance and Direction, so does the Head need the Hands for Work and Service'.[24] But it was not quite as simple as that; another writer warned servants against the dangers of revealing their influence over their masters: 'if he regards his own, or his Master's Character, he will conceal his Influence as much as possible ... as that his Government may not appear'.[25]

Domestic service for women began young. If thirteen to fourteen was normal, girls often went to service earlier. In 1782 in Cardington, Sarah, the daughter of John White and his wife Ann, was a servant at Bedford at the age of twelve.[26] She was not exceptional. The

---

[22] *The Servants Calling* (1725), pp. 9–10.
[23] *A Parson in the Vale of White Horse*, ed. Donald Gibson (1982), p. 110, letter of 15 Apr. 1758.
[24] Richard Mayo, *A Present for Servants* (1693), pp. 5–6.
[25] *The Servants Calling*, p. 44.
[26] David Baker, *The Inhabitants of Cardington in 1782*, Bedfordshire Historical Record Society, vol. lii (1973), p. 104.

magistrate John Fielding wrote of 'girls of the labouring poor, from eleven years of age and upwards' who fell 'a sacrifice to the bawd'.[27] Richardson's Pamela was fifteen when her mistress died, and she had been with her 'for three or four years'.[28] For most girls, service ended when they married; this could be at any age but tended to be at least twenty-four. There were women who remained servants after their marriage, and those who remained servants and married later or even not at all. In the household of George Woodward of East Hendred, for example, there were two servants who in 1760, after working for Woodward for fourteen years, were married. Despite the fact that the wife, Sarah, was over forty she had three children by 1765, and both she and her husband continued to work in the same household.[29] Elizabeth Beech, a parish apprentice to William Wakeley of Myddle, 'proved a good servant and lived in that family above twenty years, and was married from thence'.[30] There are other examples of women, married and unmarried, who remained all their lives in one place, devoted to their employer and valued in their turn. But they were the exception, not the rule.

So far we have talked of female domestic service as though it was one occupation. In fact, it embraced a whole series of different occupations, each with its own particular job description, standard of pay and conditions, and status. In a society that was intensely aware of class distinctions and becoming more so, the domestic service hierarchy in the eighteenth century is a sort of microcosm of the society it served. The élite of female domestic servants were waiting women, ladies' maids, and companions. These were positions to be occupied only by those of genteel upbringing who had enjoyed 'a polite education'. Gradually descending the social scale there were housekeepers and cooks. All these comprised the 'upper servants'. In large households employing a number of servants, the upper servants' quarters were usually quite separate from those of other servants. Normally they ate separately. When a cook was hired by John Spencer she made it clear she knew her rights as an upper servant. 'She expected to dine in ye housekeeper's Room', she told him, 'as it was Always ye Custom where there was a second Table for ye cook to dine at it.' His housekeeper, too, asserted her rights. She had 'a very great objection' to sleeping 'with ye other Maids'. According to Nancy, Parson Woodforde's daughter, the

[27] *London Chronicle* (1758), vol. iii, p. 327*c*.
[28] *The Works of Samuel Richardson*, 19 vols. (1811), vol. i, p. 4.
[29] *A Parson in the Vale of the White Horse*, p. 23.
[30] Gough, *History of Myddle*, p. 158.

upper servants of the local squire kept the lower short of food in order to have more for themselves.[31] The lower servants were headed by chambermaids, followed closely by housemaids, kitchen-maids, and maids-of-all-work. Right at the bottom were scullery-maids. Reflecting the merging of the work of female servants in husbandry with that of female domestic servants, there were also dairymaids, although they became scarcer as time passed.

The wages of these different categories of female domestic servants varied so much that although it is in general true that the upper servants received more than the lower, there was nothing approaching a scale for a particular set of tasks. A lot seems to have depended on where in the country the hiring was made, although experience and the range of skills acquired also influenced the sum agreed. By the end of the century, most upper servants – ladies' maids, companions, and housekeepers – received annual wages of between £10 and £20. Cooks on the whole received less: between £7 and £15 a year. Yet as late as 1773, a wage of £5 was paid to Ann Maltby when she went to be cook for Abigail Gawthern's father in Nottingham.[32] She was no exception. Housemaids, scullery-maids, and maids-of-all-work earned wages that rarely exceeded £10 and were often much less. But the wages paid by individual mistresses and masters often seem illogical. In 1736, Mrs Purefoy paid her new housemaid Susannah Butler £4 a year. Seven years later she was seeking a new maid and outlined her duties in some detail. Mrs Purefoy wanted 'a thorough servant ... capable of seeing the sending in of 5 or 10 dishes of meat upon occasion'; she was also 'to wash the small Linnen & clean part of the house & make some beds'. For all this she was offered '£3 to £3. 10s.' The same year Mrs Purefoy sought a girl who was to combine the work of a milkmaid, a washerwoman (she was to do the heavy buck-wash), and a housemaid, and as well was to 'dresse victuals', look after 'a couple of Hogs & pluck fowls', and 'any other Thing she may be set about' for the princely sum of 40s. a year.[33] In June 1755 we find Thomas Turner, shop-keeper of East Hoathly, paying his servant Mary Martin 'in goods 30s. being in full 1 year's wages'. They were apparently due the previous March![34] But over the century the money wages of domestic

---

[31] Hecht, *Domestic Service Class*, pp. 35–6, 110.
[32] *The Diary of Abigail Gawthern of Nottingham, 1751–1810*, ed. Adrian Henstock, Thoroton Society Record Series, vol. xxxiii (1986), p. 29.
[33] *The Purefoy Letters, 1735–1753*, ed. G. Eland, 2 vols (1931), vol. i, pp. 127, 142, 145.
[34] *The Diary of Thomas Turner, 1754–1765*, ed. David Vaisey (1985), p. 9.

servants increased and in some cases doubled. While the number of those seeking positions as upper servants in wealthy families seems to have exceeded the demand for them, there was always a scarcity of those willing to fill lowlier positions in less affluent households. 'Maids of all work', said Fielding in 1758, 'are not sufficiently numerous to supply the wants of the families in town.'[35] Terms of service were agreed in advance. Normally an annual wage was specified, sometimes clothing, and very often tea or an allowance to buy tea. So in 1776 the Revd James Woodforde hired a servant maid and recorded in his diary, 'I am to give her per annum and tea twice a day – £5. 5. 0'.[36]

The hiring of servants could be done in a number of ways. Most important, as we have seen, were hiring fairs or statutes, where, alongside servants in husbandry, would-be cooks, housemaids, and kitchen-maids came in the hope of finding masters and mistresses. Defoe referred to them as 'Jade Fairs', and remarked on their decline as early as the 1720s.[37] But even at the end of the century there were still many held all over the country. William Hone recalled attending a statute at Studley in Warwickshire where 'the girls wishing to be hired were in a spot apart from the men and boys, and all stood not unlike cattle at a fair waiting for dealers. Some of them hold their hands before them, with one knee protruding, (like soldiers standing at ease,) and never spoke, save when catechised and examined by a master or mistress as to the work they've been accustomed to.'[38] Mistresses often hired servants at the statute fairs and hoped to keep them for the ensuing year. But when as frequently happened, servants left a place, some other method of hiring had to be found.

Often, friends or acquaintances were enlisted to help find a suitable servant or were asked to recommend one. The upper servant whom Woodforde hired in June 1776 'was well recommended to me by Mrs Howes', with whom 'she lived very lately'. Why was Mrs Howes prepared to part with her? 'She was turned away', we are told, for 'not getting up early enough'.[39] This did not dissuade

[35] *London Chronicle* (1758), vol. iii, p. 327c.
[36] *The Diary of a Country Parson: The Reverend James Woodforde, 1758–1802*, ed. John Beresford, 5 vols (1924–31), vol. i, pp. 182–3; and see pp. 271–2.
[37] Daniel Defoe, *A Tour through England and Wales*, 2 vols [1724–7], Everyman edn (1948), vol. ii, p. 31.
[38] William Hone, *The Table Book* (1859), pp. 174–5; see also ch. 11, pp. 219–20.
[39] *Diary of a Country Parson*, vol. i, pp. 182–3.

Woodforde from hiring her. 'You must enquire me a Housekeeper', wrote Hester Piozzi to Mrs Pennington in 1795, 'such as you know will suit us.'[40] Not always did the recommendations of friends turn out well. George Woodward had recommended to his friend George London the sister of his own much-loved and devoted servant, Joe Shepherd. By 1755 there were complaints about her to Woodward. He wrote back that he was 'sorry to hear that Molly Shepherd behaves so ill ... she was recommended to your service, as we thought it would be of advantage to her; but if she don't know how to behave, when she is well, she must look to the consequences herself, for we have nothing to say in her favour'.[41]

Sometimes tradesmen were asked to look out for a suitable candidate for a place. In March 1743, Mrs Purefoy wrote to John Whitmore, her shoemaker, asking him to enquire around for a suitable maidservant.[42] Sometimes, particularly where a household was known to be a good one where servants were well treated, servants would seek out places for themselves. So to Nicholas Blundell's home in Lancashire in 1704 came 'Elizabeth Johnson ... from Rightington to offer her Service to be my Cook', but adds Blundell, 'I think she will not be accepted on'. She was not, and next day he entered in his diary 'Elizabeth Johnson went hence.'[43] When in 1760 Thomas Wright eloped with his wife-to-be to Scotland, he stayed in an inn. One of the servant-girls offered to become their servant. She told them 'she could milk the cows, tend and clean them or other cattle, look after the dairy, and upon occasion, do any genteeler work'. As Wright added, 'I do believe if we had ventured to bring her, she would have made an excellent servant.'[44]

For Londoners it was easier. In addition to the staging inns at which country girls coming to the metropolis arrived, servants could be recruited at registry offices, where both girls in search of places and mistresses in search of maids could, for a fee, be provided for. From the middle of the century there were also statute halls where, just as at statute fairs in the countryside, would-be employers and servants were brought together. In 1774 one London newspaper

[40] Hester Piozzi, *The Intimate Letters of Hester Piozzi and Penelope Pennington, 1788–1821*, ed. Oswald G. Knapp (1914), pp. 132–3.

[41] *A Parson in the Vale of White Horse*, p. 77.

[42] *Purefoy Letters*, vol. i, p. 143; see also case of Susannah Butler, ibid., p. 127.

[43] *The Great Diurnal of Nicholas Blundell of Little Crosby, Lancashire*, ed. J. J. Bagley, Record Society of Lancashire and Cheshire, 3 vols. (1968, 1970, 1972), vol. i, *1702–1711*, p. 50.

[44] *Autobiography of Thomas Wright of Birkenshaw in County of York, 1736–1799*, ed. Thomas Wright (1846), p. 88.

referred to them as places 'where servants like cattle are viewed'.[45] Another method of hiring servants was by advertising in the local newspapers.[46]

Mrs Price in *Mansfield Park* talked of the 'shocking character' of servants in Portsmouth. 'It is quite a miracle', she explained, 'if one keeps them more than half a year: I have no hope of ever getting settled.'[47] The turnover of female domestic servants was remarkable. Mrs Purefoy went through thirty in ten years, but she was a hard taskmistress. The Revd James Woodforde was far more benevolent, yet he too went through a phenomenal number of servants. For what reasons did servants move? Although there were frequent complaints from masters and mistresses of servants constantly changing places, the impression is that often they were dismissed rather than moving from choice. In January 1779, Mary Hardy, the Norfolk farmer's wife, 'turned both the maids away for raking with Fellows and other misdemeanours'. In May 1797, she dismissed Hannah Dagliss, 'for leaving the back house door unbard for the chimney sweep and then was saucy'.[48] On 14 November 1776, Woodforde wrote in his diary of his servant, 'Molly made me very angry this morning, so angry that I gave her warning to go away at Christmas.' We never hear what she had done, but when Christmas came round and Molly went away he wrote, 'I should have been glad to have kept her as she is good tempered, but she never once asked to stay after I had given her notice, therefore I dismissed her.'[49]

Pregnancy was grounds for immediate dismissal. Mary Hardy hired Sarah Jeckell on 5 October 1782, but the following February she is found to be 'with child by old Richard Mayes', and dismissed.[50] When Woodforde's maid, Molly, 'declared herself with child' in November 1793, although the father was known to him, and was recognized to be an honest character who had declared his intention to marry Molly, she was dismissed. 'In her Situation,' he wrote in his diary, 'it is necessary for me to part with her as soon as possible.'[51] Even Parson Woodward was no exception in his treatment of pregnant servants. Yet it was more in sorrow than in anger

---

[45] *London Chronicle* (1774), vol. xxxvi, p. 46*b*; see also ch. 11 (below), pp. 219–20.
[46] See e.g. *Daily Advertiser*, no. 12534, 26, Feb. 1771.
[47] Jane Austen, *Mansfield Park* (1814), Adelphi edn, p. 435.
[48] *Mary Hardy's Diary*, Introd. B. Cozens-Hardy, Norfolk Record Society, vol. xxxvii, (1968), entries for 5 Jan. 1779, and 2 May 1797.
[49] *Diary of a Country Parson*, vol. i, pp. 190, 196.
[50] *Mary Hardy's Diary*, entry for 1 Feb. 1783.
[51] *Diary of a Country Parson*, vol. iv, p. 151.

that he wrote of his 'under maid, who came to us last Christmas, and a very good servant she was, we all liked her very much, as being an active, diligent and neat girl; and one that we thought was better disposed than ordinary'; but on discovering her pregnant, 'she was immediately discharged and advised to get herself married, as soon as she could' — advice which was unnecessary for she was intending to marry, and did so immediately.[52] 'The Cookmaid' hired by Mrs Purefoy in October 1740 was dismissed a year later, 'by reason she has had a Bastard'. The same fate was that of many of her servants.[53] Must we conclude that all female domestic servants in the eighteenth century were of dubious morality? Before we do so we should be aware of their vulnerability and of the risks they ran in many households. The sexual harassment of Richardson's Pamela by Mr B. is a fiction, but in real life there were numerous cases of servant maids seduced by their masters, their sons, or male servants of the households. John Gillis's claim for the nineteenth century that seduction of servants by their masters was rare is not true of the eighteenth.[54] Given the close quarters in which servants of both sexes and their masters lived, this is hardly surprising. Female servants were being warned constantly of the danger they were in from the men of their households. Thomas Broughton explained how 'whilst they are in service, they cannot avoid conversing with the men servants, and too frequently with such as are lewd and debauched'.[55] Certainly John Macdonald, a servant himself, suggests that liaisons with female servants were frequent and often ended disastrously for the girl.[56] But it was not only from male servants that the threat came. Thomas Turner in July 1757, in his capacity as Overseer of the Poor, went to investigate a rumour that Mary Hubbard, the servant of Thomas Osborne, was pregnant. For a long time she refused to name the father. Finally, a month after she had the child, she named him as her late master. Osborne agreed to pay the parish all expenses incurred in the birth.[57]

For a female servant, pregnancy meant far more than the immediate loss of a place, for without a character reference she was

---

[52] *A Parson in the Vale of White Horse*, pp. 82–3.

[53] *Purefoy Letters*, vol. i, pp. 139, 137–8.

[54] John Gillis, 'Servants', p. 132.

[55] Thomas Broughton, *Serious Advice and Warning to Servants* (1763), p. 20; see also advice of J. A. Stewart, *The Young Woman's Companion or Female Instructor* (1814), p. 619.

[56] *Memoirs of an Eighteenth-Century Footman: John Macdonald's Travels 1745–1779*, with an Introduction by John Beresford (1929), p. 41.

[57] *Diary of Thomas Turner*, pp. 104, 110, 120, 134, 135.

unlikely to get another. Moreover, if the child lived, she would be hampered in her ability to move freely in search of employment. Little wonder that of those women convicted of infanticide whose occupation was known, the majority were domestic servants, and there must have been many cases which never came to light. To be an unmarried mother in eighteenth-century England was of all plights the worst, and servants were peculiarly vulnerable. It was not just that they were working in close proximity to members of the family of the household and to fellow servants, but that the sleeping arrangements of servants were often little differentiated by sex, so that women were all too accessible to sexual advances.

Of course, female servants often left their places voluntarily in order to marry. Elizabeth Purefoy was exasperated when after weeks of looking she finally hired a cookmaid, and to confirm the hiring as was customary, 'gave her half a crown earnest'. The following day 'the cookmaid sent her earnest again & sais she is to be married'.[58] After the death of his sister Elin, for years his unpaid housekeeper, William Stout finally found a servant that suited him, but within three years he 'perceived' that she 'was inclined to marry and that [he] must look out for another servant'.[59] The trouble employers had in finding servants that suited them made them forget all too easily the devoted service they had received and blame them for leaving. Masters like Thomas Baker of Myddle were exceptional, it seems.[60]

The reason for many servants moving was in order to better themselves, either by moving to a place that gave them extra responsibility and an improved status in the domestic service hierarchy, or to extend the tasks they were capable of performing with an eye to future advancement. So James Woodforde's servant, Lizzy, on his recommendation, left her place in July 1784 to join the household of the local squire.[61] Jane Smith, cook to Nicholas Blundell, left his service in 1704 to become a dairymaid.[62] Sometimes the reason for moving on was incompatibility with masters or mistresses. In 1725, Claver Morris recorded in his diary that 'Betty Biggs ... having been told by Will Clark that I would allow no Sweet-hart to come to a Maid-Servant in my House, came to me & said, Though she

---

[58] *Purefoy Letters*, vol. i, p. 146.
[59] *The Autobiography of William Stout of Lancaster, 1665–1752*, ed. J. D. Marshall (1967).
[60] Gough, *History of Myddle*, p. 89.
[61] *Diary of a Country Parson*, vol. ii, p. 142.
[62] *The Great Diurnal of Nicholas Blundell*, vol. i, p. 61.

could very easily do the Work of my House ... she could not be settled in it.'[63] Mary Ann Ashford had already changed places twelve times by the time she reached thirty. Her reasons for moving on were various — the difficulty of living on her wages, frequent absences of her mistress who left her 'with very little to subsist on', inadequacy of the board provided ('very little meat, and the bread kept till it was mouldy') as well as to better her position.[64]

Frequently servants were accused of being incapable of doing the work for which they were hired. Elizabeth Purefoy not unexpectedly, was rarely satisfied. Of a dismissed cookmaid she commented that 'she neither could dresse victuals nor would learn'.[65] When Grosley visited London in 1772, his landlord complained to him of a Welsh girl 'who was just come out of the country, scarce understood a word of English, was capable of nothing but washing, scowering, and sweeping the rooms, and had no inclination to learn anything more'.[66] Long Meg, notorious heroine of the popular eighteenth-century chap-book, was born in Lancashire. 'At eighteen years old she came to London to get her a service.' Her mistress demanded what work she could do. 'She answered she had not been bred unto her needle, but to hard labour, as washing, brewing and baking, and could make a house clean.'[67] Her mistress was lucky, for the homes from which many female servants were recruited were no longer those of small farmers where daughters were trained by their mothers in housewifery and were already well accustomed to work on a farm or small holding. Many mothers, the wives of journeymen artisans and small craftsmen, particularly those in towns, had neither the time nor the kind of home where daughters could learn the skills expected by employers. Many when they started in service at twelve or even fifteen needed teaching the work they were employed to do. But only the rare mistress had the patience or the understanding to provide such training.

Accusations of theft by servants were frequent. There is no doubt that much pilfering occurred. 'It was encouraged in wealthy houses', J. M. Beattie writes, 'by the drudgery of the life, the lowness of the wages, and the abuse that was so frequently visited

[63] Hecht, *Domestic Service Class*, p. 127.

[64] *Life of a Licensed Victualler's Daughter, Written by Herself* (1844), p. 37.

[65] *Purefoy Letters*, vol. i, p. 140.

[66] P. J. Grosley, *A Tour to London: or New Observations on England and Its Inhabitants*, 2 vols (1772), vol. i, p. 75.

[67] 'The whole life and death of Long Meg of Westminster', from John Ashton, *Chapbooks of the Eighteenth Century* (1882), p. 327.

on servants, as well as by the extreme contrast between the lives of servants and masters and the ready availability of saleable goods.'[68] But it was not only in houses of the very rich that pilfering occurred. Timothy Burrell's servant, Sarah Creasy, was discharged in 1703 for 'taking vessels of strong beer out of the brewing, and hiding the same'.[69] William Ellis wrote of a 'Maid-servant, who was both a Drunkard and Thief, as well as possess'd of other Faults, insomuch that she would carry out Bread, Cheese and other Provisions, and give them away to a neighbouring Gin-seller, where she now and then got intoxicated'.[70] The only time the easygoing Revd William Cole became really angry with one of his servants was when, on returning home after an absence, he found that despite paying her 'handsome Board Wages in my Absence, the use of a Cow, Beer, Ale, Coals & Candles & other Things' she 'has not left me one Onyon or Potatoe, tho' there 3 bushells of the last & one of the former, when the Gardener brought them into the House for the Winter's use'.[71] Thomas Wright had a bad experience with servants after the death of his first wife. He had a housekeeper who 'carried out (whenever I was absent) to her father's and relations, meal, flour, butter, eggs, ribbons, small linnen, beer, and bottles of rum'. What made it particularly irritating was that this servant was 'the daughter of a near neighbour'.[72] The experience convinced Wright he must either be ruined or take a wife.

In many households the opportunities for petty pilfering were great. In Mary Leadbeater's *Cottage Dialogues*, there is one Rose who goes out charring. 'Many's the good bit I bring home and the fine ends of candles, and lumps of soap, and grease to dip my rushes, and sometimes a bit of tea and sugar,' she relates to her friend, 'Mrs Nesbitt knows nothing about it; but such things are no missed out of a big house, and I may as well get them as another.'[73] The opportunities for those living-in were even greater, and the temptation was particularly strong if they had needy families or relations living close at hand. Pilfering was a risky business, for from

[68] J. M. Beattie, 'The criminality of women in eighteenth-century England', *Journal of Social History*, vol. 8 (Summer 1975), p. 84.

[69] 'Extracts from the journal and account book of Timothy Burrell, Esq. barrister at law, 1683–1711', *Sussex Archaeological Collections*, vol. iii (1850), Extract dated 5 Apr. 1703.

[70] William Ellis, *The Country Housewife's Family Companion* (1750), p. iv.

[71] *The Blecheley Diary of the Rev. William Cole, 1765–1767*, Introd. Helen Waddell (1931), p. 11.

[72] *Autobiography of Thomas Wright of Birkenshaw in the Country of York, 1736–1797*, ed. Thomas Wright (1864), pp. 142, 143.

[73] Mary Leadbeater, *Cottage Dialogues among the Irish Peasantry* (1811), pt. i, p. 149.

1713 thefts of goods over 40s. in value were subject to capital punishment. Even stealing a loaf could lead to imprisonment and a whipping. Sometimes servants suspected of stealing were promised that no further action would be taken if they confessed and promised never to repeat the crime, but once they confessed they were brought to court anyway. In Surrey in 1738 a servant girl was tried for stealing half a guinea. She told the judge that her master had 'promised me that if I confessed . . . he would forgive me'. She was lucky in having several former employers who testified to her honesty and she was acquitted.[74] The frequency of pilfering was one reason that wives were advised to supervise their households carefully. Early in the century, Isaac Watts had written of the importance of educating daughters, whether rich or poor, in the affairs of the household, 'as to know when they are performed aright, that the servants may not usurp too much power, and impose on the ignorance of the mistress'.[75] William Ellis relates a case where a servant-maid imposed on the 'ignorance' of the master. A gentleman farmer 'confided in his chief Servant-maid to manage his Household Affairs; and as he kept a considerable Number of Cows, and made large Quantities of Butter for a *London* Market, he ordered this his Maid to make Cheese for the Servants of all skim Milk, and this she did when she could not help it, but when she had an Opportunity she threw into the skim Milk, the new Milk or Cream'. Ellis acknowledged that 'although she did this contrary to her Master's Order, yet in the main I think the Captain lost nothing by it, for when the Cheese was made with all skim Milk, the Servants gave much of it away to Dogs, and some they put into the Hog-tub, and otherwise wasted it'.[76]

For such disobedience and other misdemeanours, masters had the right to correct their servants. But according to William Fleetwood, they 'must not be over-rigorous in their Punishments, when Servants are faulty, but should inflict them with Deliberation, good Intention, and Compassion'.[77] The fact that the law did not extend this right to mistresses did not prevent them wielding it. One case that received no publicity but was related in some detail in the diary of the mistress concerned was that of a maid in the employ of Lady

[74] J. M. Beattie, 'Crime and the courts in Surrey, 1736–1753', in J. S. Cockburn (ed.), *Crime in England, 1550–1800* (1977), pp. 168–9.

[75] Isaac Watts, *The Improvement of the Mind* [1725], (1819), p. 346.

[76] Ellis, *Family Companion*, p. iv.

[77] William Fleetwood, *The Relative Duties of Parents and Children, Husbands and Wives, Masters and Servants* (1716), p. 323.

Francis Pennoyer at Bullingham Court in Hertfordshire in 1760. The maid had been caught speaking about some matter considered discreditable to the family. She was summoned to appear before her mistress who 'gave her choice either to be well whipped or leave the house'. The girl, who we are told 'hath but a poor home', chose the whipping. She was sent to 'fetch the rod', then made 'to kneel and ask my pardon. ... I bade her prepare and I whipped her well. The girl's flesh is plump and firm. ... she hath never been whipped before, she says (what can her mother and late lady have been about, I wonder!), and she cried a great deal.'[78] In March, 1776 a Mrs Burnell of Winkburn was brought before the Nottingham assizes 'for beating her maid servant'. Such was the reaction of the public 'she was hissed at going out of court'.[79] A different sort of ill-treatment, for which there was little redress, was that of mistresses who denied their servant-maids all training, in order to prevent them moving to new places. And ill-treatment could take even more subtle forms: Mary Ann Ashford found that at one of her places, 'it was the rule of the family I was in to go to a watering place on the continent in the summer — let the house, and discharge the servants'.[80]

Leaving aside those daughters who had no option but to enter service, what were seen as the advantages of domestic service? One major attraction, particularly towards the end of the century as prices were rising steeply, was that it included board and lodging. To poor parents this meant a great deal. One less mouth to feed eased the problem of maintaining an independent household. A girl lucky in her place might eat as well as the family, and enjoy a standard of life quite beyond the means of her own. In 1800, when Mary Ann Ashford worked for a family in Hoxton, she was 'well fed — living just the same as they did, and partaking of whatever they had'.[81] But whether or not she lived well, a girl going to domestic service was *fed*. Another advantage to which parents attached importance was that, unlike many occupations subject to the fluctuations of trade, domestic service, provided a girl could keep her place, meant continuous employment — and some security.

When both parents of Mary Ann Ashford died, her relations clubbed together 'to place me out genteelly'. Their choice for her was to become apprentice to a milliner, but an old friend of her

---

[78] Arthur Rackham Cleveland, *Women under English Law* (1896), pp. 214–15.
[79] *Diary of Abigail Gawthern*, p. 20.
[80] *Life of a Licensed Victualler's Daughter*, p. 53.
[81] Ibid., p. 23.

father advised against it, and thought she would be better off in service. Mary Ann was sceptical about her relations' 'desire for a genteel occupation for her', for as she said, 'Gentility without ability, was like a pudding without fat'. Her relations thought otherwise. After she had been a servant for some years, she found she had 'lost caste' with them. When she called on them 'if any one came in, I was requested to step into another room, and kept in the background, because I was a servant'.[82] The fact that many servants lost their places and were unemployed for periods between one household and another probably did not deter parents who, if they thought at all of the possibility, regarded it as something that happened to others' daughters, not their own. But the main reason for parents thinking domestic service a desirable occupation for daughters was the possibility of social betterment they believed it offered.

The story told of the people of Slough who regularly gathered to hear the blacksmith read aloud the most recent instalment of Richardson's *Pamela: Or Virtue Rewarded*, and who, on hearing that finally Mr B. had married her, rang the church bells, suggests how the possibility of social advancement motivated parents in choice of an occupation.[83] Saunders Welch wrote of the hope of parents who could not give their daughter a rich dowry, 'that she may mend her fortune by captivating some rich gudgeon, be qualified to wait upon a lady, or at least to be a chambermaid'.[84] Was such social advancement a reality outside fiction? As we have seen, it was possible for servants to ascend the hierarchy of service, although such cases were few. Nancy Bere was an exception. She emerged from the local poorhouse to work in the garden of the Hackman family in Lymington as a weeder. She then graduated to work inside the house as kitchen-maid. Finally she became lady's maid. Her ascent was confined to one household and was in no small part the result of her mistress giving her an education and training. Such mistresses were rare.[85]

A number of female servants seem to have married their masters. Indeed, to have served in a household where the wife died seems to have had definite advantages. Not unlike widows, who were forced to marry their apprentices in order to carry on their husbands'

[82] Ibid., pp. 20, 40.

[83] J. D. Chambers, *Population, Economy and Society in Pre-Industrial England* (1972), pp. 52–3.

[84] Saunders Welch, *A Proposal to Render Effectual a Plan to Remove the Nuisance of Common Prostitutes from the Streets* (1753), p. 4.

[85] Hecht, *Domestic Service Class*, pp. 183–4.

business, widowers found themselves unable to cope with the housekeeping and married their housekeepers or other of their own or neighbours' servants. Thomas Turner's second wife was Molly Hicks, the servant of one of the local justices of the peace. He admitted among the various motives for remarrying was that he had 'not anyone to trust the management of my affairs to that I can be assured in their management will be sustained no loss'.[86] Many servants married fellow servants, but only rarely did this mean social betterment. David Doyle, the servant of Mary Leadbeater's father, married Winifred Byrne, cook to Mary's brother. When they set up house together 'they were as poor as any of their neighbours', but gradually they were able to improve their circumstances, acquire a cow, and extend their house.[87] Occasionally the combined savings of a couple in service would enable them to set up as shopkeepers or keepers of an alehouse or public house. Quite exceptional was the case of Elizabeth Raffald who in 1763, after fifteen years as a housekeeper, married the gardener in her household and left service. They opened a confectionery shop in Manchester, ran a catering business, and managed a school for young ladies. Finally they took the Bull's Head Inn and for many years ran it as a profitable business.[88] But Elizabeth Raffald was a highly gifted woman. While still a publican she was to run a journal, compile a commercial directory of Manchester, and finally turn author of a book on English housekeeping. She and her husband succeeded in achieving real social advancement.

Rare as it was in reality, the myth of social betterment through service persisted. Just because of the close association with members of a superior social class, it was believed, something must surely rub off on the servants. The myth was unconsciously perpetuated by employers who, in order to demonstrate their own prestige and status, had their male servants in livery and their female servants so decked out in fine clothes that many complained it was impossible to distinguish servant from mistress.[89] Soame Jenyns explained that the pride of the upper classes led them 'to take the lowest of the people, and convert them . . . into the genteel personages we think proper should attend us'.[90] It was a curious irony that servants

---

[86] *Diary of Thomas Turner*, p. 319.
[87] *Leadbeater Papers*, 2 vols (1862) vol. i, pp. 194–5.
[88] Hecht, *Domestic Service Class*, p. 196.
[89] See Daniel Defoe, *The Great Law of Subordination Consider'd* (1724), pp. 14–15.
[90] *The Works of Soame Jenyns*, ed. C. N. Cole, 4 vols. (1790), vol. ii, p. 116.

were for ever being censored for 'a desire of appearing in a Habit above their Degree ... For being cloathed above their Equals, they think themselves equal to their Superiors, and begin to act accordingly'.[91] They are told to 'confine themselves to the Habit of their Degree'.[92] Some complained that the fault lay in the overgenerous wages paid to maidservants which enabled them 'to go in as good silks and as fine linen, as their mistresses; which', adds the author firmly, 'is not the condition of servants, whose wearing and living ought to be at a much greater distance'. It was getting above themselves that made them so 'saucy and negligent'. Lower wages and plain dressing would keep them 'in a state of humility, as servants ought to be kept'.[93] But the way in which maid servants dressed can only have been with the sanction of their employers, and indeed was often under their orders. It underlines their paradoxical position.

The truth was that, however well they dressed, the vast majority of female servants remained in the class from which they had come. Unlike servants in husbandry and some female apprentices, they would never themselves be mistresses employing their own servants. The point was made by one author of advice to maidservants on how to behave to apprentices in the same household. They were to be treated differently from fellow servants, for 'you must remember that they are servants only to become masters, and should therefore be treated not only with kindness but civility'.[94] Although domestic servants were called on to identify closely with their masters and mistresses, 'to consider what the Master would do himself, were he to act in Person, and to do the same',[95] they had to remain inferior and servile to the class they served. It was an impossible role.

In France in the seventeenth and eighteenth centuries, the relationship between servants and their masters was euphemistically referred to as one of 'domestic enemies'. It is a term that, as Cissie Fairchilds has written, 'with its suggestion of simultaneous closeness and distance, intimacy and enmity ... epitomized relationships between mistress and servant'.[96] It is a phrase not always inappropriate to domestic service in England in the eighteenth century.

The relationship between mistresses and maids was complicated

[91] Anon., *The Servants Calling* (1725), p. 21.
[92] Anon., *A Present for Servants* (1768), pp. 21–2.
[93] Anon., *The Laws Relating to Masters and Servants* (1755), p. 11 n.
[94] J. A. Stewart, *The Young Woman's Companion* (1814), p. 619.
[95] Anon., *The Servants Calling*, p. 29.
[96] Fairchilds, *Domestic Enemies*, p. xi.

by wives being closely identified with upper servants. In an anonymous work of 1721, the author talked of men who looked 'upon a wife but as an upper servant'.[97] There are many similar references. In discussing marriage and the sacrifice it involved for women, Daniel Defoe's Roxana saw a woman's entry into marriage as a capitulation 'to be, at best but an upper servant'.[98] Samuel Menefee has drawn attention to the similarity between the custom of wife-sale and the role played by female servants at hiring statutes.[99] Wives, children, and servants were all in the same category of those owing complete obedience to the head of the household. Some husbands denied their wives any control over servants, and made little distinction in their treatment of either. This cannot have endeared female servants to wives. Many husbands looked rather to their female domestics than to their wives for sexual satisfaction. What has been called 'the eroticism of inequality'[100] may in part explain the frequency with which masters are found seducing their dependent menials. It may explain the instant dismissal of servants found pregnant; mistresses must always have suspected that their husbands were responsible. In the novel *Millenium Hall*, Louisa Mancel, a beautiful girl of fifteen, finding herself in straitened circumstances, seeks a place as an upper servant. She takes advice, and is told that 'she must not expect, while her person continued such as it then was, that a married woman would receive her in any capacity that fixed her in the same house with her husband'.[101] All she could hope for was that some widow would offer her a place. It is hardly surprising that wives so often treated their female domestics badly, or that spinsters and widows were far more indulgent and generous mistresses. Within the hierarchy of domestic service, such ill-treatment by their mistresses, it has been suggested, was taken out on the lower by the upper servants, and on visiting tradesmen by both.

The role of domestic servant, if succesfully played, must have produced extremely complex and contradictory characters. Domestic service was a depersonalizing experience. It not only removed a servant from home and family and any known and sympathetic environment, both physical and cultural, but in the treatment they received from employers there was nothing to restore a sense of identity. There were cases of mistresses who with a preconceived

[97] *Reflections on Celibacy and Marriage* (1721), p. 2.
[98] Daniel Defoe, *Roxana* [1724], (1840–1), p. 157.
[99] S. P. Menefee, *Wives for Sale* (1981), p. 41; see also ch. 11 (below), pp. 219–20.
[100] Fairchilds, *Domestic Enemies* p. 166.
[101] Sarah Scott, *Millenium Hall* (1762), p. 66.

notion of what names were appropriate to servants, would even strip a servant of her own name and give her another. Servants were frequently dressed in clothes that bore no relationship to the background from which they came. When Pamela in Richardson's novel is contemplating abandoning her place to go home, she strips off all the clothes her mistress had given her and dresses herself in the garments of the rural poor. Many servants, it is suggested, must have developed serious inferiority complexes in relation to their employers. Desperately searching for a new personal identity some sought to imitate their employers and 'adopted and internalized their masters' [and mistresses'] ideals and values'.[102]

Most women who became domestic servants in the second half of the eighteenth century had no choice. For many country-born girls it was the one outlet, and an expanding one, open to them. The description of domestic service in early Victorian England as 'a form of disguised underemployment'[103] is surely right, but it applies just as much to the late eighteenth century. For if it had not been for the demand, and I believe it was an increasing demand, for female domestic servants, the loss of work opportunities for labouring women would have been even more devastating.

[102] Fairchilds, *Domestic Enemies*, p. 111; and see her whole chapter on 'The Psychology of Servanthood'.

[103] Eric Richards, 'Women in the British economy since about 1700: an interpretation', *History*, 59/197 (1974), p. 348.

9

Ignored, Unrecorded, and Invisible: Some Occupations of Women

LABOUR FORCE: All workers for money income. Housewives who do not work for money income, are not part of the labour force, as are not people who do not work at all, such as small children.

The Economic History of British since 1700

When Ivy Pinchbeck made her wry remark about the assumption of some historians that women workers were the creation of the Industrial Revolution, she was not merely emphasizing the ignorance of many social historians about women's work before industrialization.[1] She was drawing attention to the home-based nature of much of that work, and of how it was taken for granted. And if contemporaries rarely referred to it, perhaps it might be argued, modern historians can be forgiven for ignoring it. It was only when women's work moved out of the household, when women begin to enter cotton mills and factories in the first stage of industrialization, that they were seen to become 'workers' and no longer mere 'housewives'. In other words, women's 'work' was defined solely in terms appropriate to nineteenth-century industrialization. And, of course, defined in such terms, women in pre-industrial England, even in the proto-industrial stage, were not 'workers'. But when comparisons start to be made between women's situation before and after the impact of industrialization, and when historians, increasingly conscious of ignoring women's role in the standard-of-living debate, begin to assess what difference women might make to their analysis, such a restricted definition of work makes nonsense of the conclusions reached.

The trouble is that there are no official occupational censuses for the eighteenth century, although there are the unofficial contemporary

---

[1] Ivy Pinchbeck, *Women Workers and the Industrial Revolution, 1750–1850* [1930], (1981), p. 1.

148

estimates of Gregory King, Joseph Massie, and Patrick Colquhoun.[2] So for the most part, information about women's occupations in the eighteenth century has been deduced from the first occupational censuses of the nineteenth that distinguished between the occupations of men and women. Earlier no such distinction was made among those designated as 'occupied'. The 1841 census introduced a new procedure by which the name, age, sex, and occupation of each individual member of a household was recorded, but it was not until 1851 that the procedure was fully developed. Notwithstanding, these two censuses are the official basis for our knowledge of the occupational structure for a period that ended half a century earlier.

However defective as a source of information about women's work in the eighteenth century, these two censuses do suggest that some of the past assumptions about the effects of industrialization on women's work need reconsidering. After nearly three-quarters of a century, the impact of industrialization on women's gainful employment is revealing. It was not, after all, women employed in the cotton industry in all its different processes who dominated the scene but female domestic servants. Even if the women employed in all branches of textiles — wool, linen, and silk, as well as cotton, are included (the only area of industry where the employment of men and women was comparable) — the total falls very far short of those in domestic service. Moreover, those women employed in what were seen as traditionally 'women's trades' — mantua-makers, milliners, and seamstresses — far outnumbered those in the cotton industry. Recently it has been suggested that it was not only the nature of *women's* work which in the first half of the nineteenth century ran counter to assumptions about the effect of early industrialization. Looking at work for men in the countryside it had been assumed that if the size of the agricultural labour force increased only very slightly in the first half of the century, and far less than the population in the countryside was expanding, this surplus of men's labour was absorbed in industrial employment, either in domestic industry or in the new factories. What has now been revealed is that it was traditional trades — bakers, butchers, blacksmiths, and shoemakers, bricklayers, carpenters, and masons which

---

[2] Gregory King, *Natural and Political Observations upon the State of England* (1696); Joseph Massie, *A Computation of the Moneys that Have Been Exhorbitantly raised upon the People of Great Britain by the Sugar Planters, etc.* (1760); Patrick Colquhoun, *A Treatise on Indigence* (1806).

accounted, in absolute terms, for the increase in employment, and not manufacturing.[3]

In the occupations of women in Great Britain listed in 1851, another interesting detail is that, quite apart from those described as domestic servants, there were, it appears, 145,000 washerwomen and 55,000 charwomen.[4] Together they formed the fifth most important occupation for women. It is not quite the picture of women workers in early industrialized society that one has been led to expect. Whatever conclusion one may draw about the nature of the impact of industrialization on the lives of men and women in the early nineteenth century, 'the figures are still remarkable'.[5]

It has been suggested that as an indication of women's occupations in the nineteenth century these censuses are dangerously distorting. How much more distorting are they when used to indicate eighteenth-century women's occupations? Edward Higgs's criticism that a great many women who worked were excluded from the 'occupied' population is undeniable, but his concern extends beyond this to the numbers recorded as occupied in certain sectors. Notably, he questions whether female domestic service was indeed the largest occupation for women in the nineteenth century. Many of those recorded, he argues, were working without pay and were related to the head of the household, and others worked on farms or in shops.[6] But in the eighteenth century, as we have seen, domestic and farm service tended to merge, and the use of kin as servants was not uncommon and had a long history. But there are other reasons for thinking the importance of female domestic service in the period of industrialization cannot so easily be discounted. Esther Boserup, commenting on the large numbers of female domestic servants in Latin America, has written that 'it is a characteristic feature of countries at an intermediate stage of economic development for a large number of women to be engaged in paid housework'.[7] With little agricultural work left for women in the countryside, daughters are sent into the towns to become domestic servants. Lourdes Arizpe has revealed how women displaced from Mexican agriculture have moved into

[3] E. A. Wrigley, 'Men on the land and men in the countryside: employment in agriculture in early nineteenth-century England', in Bonfield *et al.* (eds), *The World We Have Gained* (1986).

[4] *Census of Great Britain, 1851* (1854) Population tables ii, 'Ages, Civil Condition, Occupations and Birth Place of the People,' vol. i, p. cxli.

[5] Peter Mathias, *The First Industrial Nation* (1983), p. 237.

[6] Edward Higgs, 'Women, occupations and work in the nineteenth-century censuses', *History Workshop Journal*, no. 23 (Spring 1987), pp. 59–80 (pp. 68–9).

[7] Esther Boserup, *Women's Role in Economic Development* (1970), p. 187.

Mexico City, where 64 per cent of working women are employed in the service sector, 74 per cent of them as domestic servants.[8] 'In general the whole domestic service sector grows with economic development', Esther Boserup writes, 'and, at the same time, tends to become more exclusively "feminine".'[9]

There are some intriguing details in the 1851 census: for example, the number of female teachers was more than double that of male. In the whole of Great Britain, 71,966 female teachers were recorded. Of these, over 40,000 were schoolmistresses, and more than half that number were governesses. Over 20,000 women were occupied as lodging-house keepers, as compared with less than 3,000 men. Excluding such shops as those of grocers and tallow-chandlers, there seem to have been rather more female shopkeepers than male and, if shopkeepers' wives are added in, considerably more. Over 11,000 women are listed as hawkers and pedlars, and this figure excludes nearly 5,000 female 'cow-keepers, Milksellers'.[10]

The criteria by which work performed by women was included in the occupational censuses did not remain constant, but one common factor throughout the earlier censuses was that it had to be 'gainful employment', that is to say it had to be waged work, and full-time. But, as we have seen earlier, much of women's work in the household in the eighteenth century was neither waged nor full-time. This does not mean that the work carried out by women was not often 'full-time' in the sense that they worked all day every day for long hours. But that work included a great variety of tasks, and even if the census had included as occupied all women who worked at all, there was still the problem of which of their occupations should be recorded. The 1851 census recognized the problem of dual occupations where men were concerned. 'The same person', it noted, 'is a member of parliament, a magistrate, a landed proprietor, and an occupier of land; in a lower circle, an innkeeper and a farmer; a maltster and a brewer; a fisherman in the season, a farmer or labourer in the rest of the year.' But the existence of exactly the same problem among women, where for example the wife of a smallholder could be dairywoman, agricultural labourer, or spinster as well as a housewife, was ignored. In 1851 the problem had been 'resolved' by instructing enumerators that 'a person following more

---

[8] Lourdes Arizpe, 'Women in the informal labour sector: the case of Mexico City', in Wellesley Committee (eds.), *Women and National Development: The Complexities of Change* (1977), p. 30.

[9] Boserup, *Women's Role in Economic Development*, p. 104.

[10] *Census of Great Britain 1851*, p. lxxxviii, ccxxv, lxxxix, cxlii, cxliv.

than one distinct trade' should list all *his* occupations in the 'order of importance'. In the classification, we are told, 'the first occupation was generally taken'.[11] The others were ignored. That this might lead to a very distorted idea of the occupational structure as far as men were concerned is clear. The failure to recognize the existence of the same problem among women meant that many were omitted from the records of the occupied. The instructions to enumerators in the censuses from 1841 to 1871, for example, made it clear that a great deal of the work performed by women in the home was excluded. One instruction read: 'The profession, etc., of wives, or of sons or daughters living with their husbands or parents, and assisting them, but not apprenticed or receiving wages, need not be set down.'[12] Apparently, some enumerators interpreted it by leaving the space against wives blank. The same definition of 'occupied' is found in many Third World countries today. In some Latin American countries, for instance, 'persons who for one reason or another did not earn or did not help other family members to earn a money income' are excluded from the recorded workforce.[13]

Nineteenth-century occupational tables, Edward Higgs has claimed, 'were constructed by men . . . who had certain assumptions about the position of women in society. In broad terms women tended to be defined as dependants, whatever their productive functions, whilst men were classified according to the nature of their labour.'[14] A more recent example of census procedures based on invalid assumptions comes from Southern India, where definitions date back to the Raj and are related to conditions found only in advanced Western countries. The officials responsible for the census were confronted by the category of 'cultivators'. They had some difficulty with it. Were household members who worked under the head of the household 'cultivators' or 'dependants'? The result of their dilemma was that 'hardly any women were classified in the census, although all the evidence was that many women perform as much farm work for their households as the men'.[15]

The 1851 census recognized that there were wives who assisted their husbands in the family business but received no payment.

[11] Ibid., p. lxxxii.

[12] Richard Lawton (ed.), *The Census and Social Structure* (1978), p. 172 and app. i, p. 7.

[13] Boserup, *Women's Role in Economic Development*, p. 81.

[14] Higgs, 'Women, occupations and work', p. 60.

[15] Polly Hill, 'The poor quality of official socio-economic statistics relating to the rural tropical world: with special reference to South India', *Modern Asian Studies*, 18/3(1984), pp. 507–8.

Some enumerators in the 1851 census listed as a separate occupation that of a 'shopkeeper's wife', a 'farmer's, grazier's wife' or an 'inn-keeper's wife', as well as the wives of shoemakers and butchers. There were only 31,000 women in Great Britain listed as shoe-makers, but three times that number recorded as 'shoemakers' wives'. Similarly while only 1,779 female butchers are listed, there are 26,000 'butchers' wives'. The reason for the inclusion of these wives was that 'they are generally engaged in the same business as their husbands'.[16] If this showed some recognition of women's involvement in family-based trades, it did not extend to all of them. And other women who assisted 'in family businesses on an informal basis, often without any formal payment'[17] — and who were not full-time — were ignored. When James Lackington opened his bookshop in London in 1774, he acknowledged that without his wife's help the business would not have thrived. She was, he wrote, 'immoderately fond of books', which proved 'a very fortunate circumstance for us both'. It 'made her delight to be in the shop, so that she soon became perfectly acquainted with every part of it'. When he had to be absent he could remain confident that his 'shop was well attended'.[18] She was in every sense a partner in the business, but if she had been recorded in any census it would have been as a 'housewife'. There is evidence that in the early eighteenth century, wives frequently were involved in the business of printing and publishing as well as book-selling. Many took over the running of the business on their husbands' death.[19] In the 1851 census, under the fifth class of female occupations, described as 'Persons engaged in the Domestic Offices, or Duties of Wives, Mothers, Mistresses of Families, Children, Relatives' are recorded over 2.5 million wives 'of no specified occupation'. Yet interestingly, this class is described as one which 'comprises large numbers of the population that have hitherto been held to have no occupation'. The census attempts to make amends when it refers to 'the wife, the mother, the mistress of an English family' who 'fills offices and discharges duties of no ordinary importance'. But of what these 'offices' and 'duties' consisted

[16] *Census of Population, 1851*, pp. lxxxviii–lxxxix; p. ccxxv n.

[17] Evelyn Bridge, 'Women's employment: problems of research', *Society for the Study of Labour History*, Bulletin no. 26 (1973), p. 5.

[18] *Memoirs of the Forty-five First Years of the Life of James Lackington* (1794), pp. 249, 326.

[19] See Margaret Hunt, 'Women and the London press: hawkers, bawlers and mercuries in the early Enlightenment', in special issue on 'Women and the Enlightenment' in *History*, 9 (1984); and James Sutherland, *The Restoration Newspaper and Its Development* (1986), ch. 6.

is made very clear. They were 'household works and processes' including 'the making and mending of apparel, washing, cooking, cleansing, nursing, teaching, and other offices'.[20]

There were other working women who can rarely have appeared in the occupational census, and even when some of the occupations in which they worked were listed, the totals almost certainly underestimated the number involved. Those women, for example, engaged in seasonal work of any kind often escaped the attention of the officers responsible for collecting census material. Keith Snell has drawn attention to how, in the case of the 1841 occupational census taken in the months of March and April, female agricultural employment in the west of the country would be underrecorded, for these were the months of greatest insecurity of employment for women there.[21] The particular date on which the census information was collected in a given area might well not coincide with the season when women were employed. Migrant women workers who moved south and east in search of the first hay or wheat harvest, women who crowded into the market-garden districts around London to pick fruit and vegetables — these almost certainly escaped the attention of the census. Then there were itinerant women workers: while there were over 11,000 hawkers and pedlars recorded in 1851, there must have been many more, particularly in the countryside, who evaded the requirement of obtaining a licence and were of no fixed abode. The greater number of those women workers unrecorded in census material were married women in part-time employment.

Because of the numerous changes made in the methods used in successive censuses, it is often difficult to make comparisons over time. One trend that emerges quite clearly from the occupational tables for the 1841, 1851, and 1861 censuses, however, is that the trades regarded as almost exclusively 'female' became increasingly important as outlets for women's labour. But even if the 1851 occupational census was an accurate record of the whole range and extent of women's work in that year, it is virtually impossible to make comparisons with earlier censuses and difficult to know whether the 1851 figures can be taken as an accurate indication of even the 'gainful labour' supply of the eighteenth century. There is some suggestion that it can. 'It is unlikely ... that the occupational distribution of the female labour force changed much', an economic

---

[20] *Census of Population, 1851*, pp. cxli, lxxxviii.
[21] Keith Snell, *Annals of the Labouring Poor* (1985), p. 57 n. 54.

historian has recently written, 'women had always made their chief contribution in the domestic service, textile and clothing sectors of the economy'.[22] It suggests a very static occupational structure for women over a long period, which is difficult to disprove. There are eighteenth-century sources that sometimes give information about women's occupations, such as local listings of inhabitants of a parish and burial registers, but all tend to suffer from unknown omissions and incomplete recordings. Often women are only identified by their marital status. 'Male clerks', P. H. Lindert has written, 'apparently considered this a more valid identification for a woman than her occupation.' Such an omission, he argues, produced 'the momentary anomaly that nobody made a living as a spinner of the yarn that employed so many male weavers'.[23] So attempts to re-create the occupational structure of women's work in the eighteenth century are difficult. They are, at best, subject to such margins of error as make any definitive conclusions unwise.

In addition to the four important areas of women's work so far considered here — in agriculture, in domestic industry, in domestic service, and as housewives — there are other areas that for one reason or another have attracted little attention so far from historians. The first is washerwomen. As Patricia Malcolmson has written of late nineteenth-century laundresses, the work of eighteenth-century washerwomen was 'too commonplace, too rough and too undramatic to attract much interest or public attention'.[24] It was hidden work, in the sense that much of it was done in the homes of the washerwomen, and when it was not, it was the work of women isolated from one another who entered into individual arrangements with their employers.

In the occupational census of 1851, the principal occupation groups in order of size were listed with the number of each sex employed. There were only two groups in which women alone were employed: washerwomen and charwomen. These had always been female occupations. The figure of 145,000 in the census covered only those employed full-time as washerwomen, yet in the eighteenth century many wives of labourers in London and elsewhere went out washing part-time. Wives of London journeymen, who worked at trades where women were never employed, would often take in

[22] Roderick Floud and Donald McCloskey (eds), *The Economic History of Britain since 1700*, vol. i: *1700–1860* (1981), p. 206.

[23] P. H. Lindert, 'English occupations, 1670–1811', *Journal of Economic History*, 60 (1980), p. 691.

[24] Patricia Malcolmson, *English Laundresses: A Social History, 1850–1930* (1986), p. 5.

washing. In the London Sessions Papers, an entry for April 1745 shows the wife of a hackney coachman who 'takes in washing'. In December 1758, the wife of a 'shagreen case-maker', in September 1767 the wife of a 'Sugar baker' likewise so described their occupation. In 1792 the occupation of the wife of a manservant is recorded as 'keeps a milk-cellar, takes in washing', and in 1794 the wife of a porter 'takes in washing, formerly had a milk-walk'.[25] But the demand for washerwomen was not confined to London or other towns, and the total number at any one time employed in washing for a wage must have been considerably larger than the figure recorded.

As we have seen, the absence of piped water made the task of washing clothes a difficult one. Either water had to be fetched to the house, or dirty clothes and linen taken to the water. This problem of providing sufficient water and of heating it made washdays infrequent occurrences. In 1742, William Stout's servant maid left him to get married. A bachelor, he decided he must either give up housekeeping or find another servant capable of housekeeping for him. He had living with him at the time the twenty-year old daughter of a niece, to whom he was giving some help in her education. 'Having knowledge of my way of living and having no parents living, I resolved to be served by her.' He recognized, it seems, the heavy demands made on a single servant by the household wash, and so agreed 'to get a woman each week or two to wash'.[26]

The stream of maids that passed through the hands of Elizabeth Purefoy were left in no doubt about the nature of their duties. 'Wee wash once a month', she told them, and to one, Betty How, she explained the household routine of washing: 'one day soap and another day ye Buck and you help iron and get up ye cloaths'. The 'buck-wash' was the heavy wash of coarser materials: 'buck' consisted of water made alkaline by impregnating it with the ashes of wood or plants. The duty of a future maid, Elizabeth Purefoy explained to her, was 'to help wash in washing time'. Some maidservants were told that their duty as far as washing was concerned was confined to 'the small Linnen', a much lighter task than that of the buck-wash. 'I should be glad of a young healthy girl', writes Elizabeth Purefoy at another time, 'to help her who can stand at the Buck-tubb'. Making the point of how often two women were needed to complete the wash, she wrote of another of her servants: 'she and

[25] Quoted M. Dorothy George, *London Life in the Eighteenth Century* [1925], (1966), app. vi.
[26] *The Autobiography of William Stout of Lancaster, 1665–1752*, ed. J. D. Marshall (1967), pp. 232–3.

the washerwoman wash the Buck'.[27] There are many examples of washerwomen hired to help the living-in maid servants with the wash. Indeed, in larger households this seems to have been a regular practice. Even the mistresses of smaller households, who sometimes employed no domestic servants, would hire washerwomen to help them.

If in fact William Stout washed every one or two weeks he was exceptional; most households washed far less frequently. In the 1770s and 1780s the wife of a prosperous Norfolk farmer, Mary Hardy, was washing every two, three, or four weeks. At the close of the century James Woodforde had a washday no more frequently than every five, but then, as he admitted, 'washing and ironing generally takes us four days'.[28]

The work involved long hours. A great quantity of water had to be heated before any washing could begin. 'Women Servants in large Families', the author of *Low Life* commented, had to be up very early 'lighting Fires under their Coppers'.[29] In some houses the water had first to be fetched. It is nowhere recorded how many rinses clothes and linen were given, but each involved replenishing the water. 'Perhaps there is not a class of people', wrote J. T. Smith, 'who work harder than those washer women who go out to assist servants in what is called a heavy wash; they may be seen in the winter-time shivering at the doors at three and four in the morning, and are seldom dismissed before ten at night.'[30] Mary Collier, the washerwoman poet, had first hand experience of early rising on winter mornings to go out washing for her living. She wrote:

> When to the House we come where we should go,
> How to get in, alas!, we do not know
> The Maid quite tir'd with Work the Day before,
> O'ercome with Sleep; we standing at the Door,
> Oppress'd with Cold, and often call in vain
> E're to our Work we can admittance gain.[31]

---

[27] *The Purefoy Letters, 1735–1753*, ed. G. Eland, 2 vols (1931), vol. i, p. 153, 132, 142, 145, 147.

[28] See *Autobiography of William Stout; Mary Hardy's Diary*, Introd. B. Cozens Hardy, Norfolk Record Society, vol. xxxvii, (1968); *Diary of a Country Parson: The Reverend James Woodforde, 1758–1802*, ed. John Beresford, 5 vols. (1924–31), vol. v, p. 198.

[29] *Low Life or One Half of the World Knows Not How the Other Half Live* (1764), p. 97.

[30] J. T. Smith, *The Cries of London* (1839), p. 81.

[31] Mary Collier, *The Woman's Labour: An Epistle to Mr. Stephen Duck, in Answer to His Late Poem, Called 'The Thresher's Labour'* (1739), p. 12.

Some writers suggest washerwomen arrived at their employers' houses the previous night in order to complete the wash by the end of the next day. The author of *Low Life* found them arriving for work at 1 a.m., but admitted that they often arrived much earlier.[32] In 1753, Ann Nichols, who washed for a masterbuilder at Hackney, arrived at the house at midnight. Surprisingly her master seems to have recognized good trade union principles, for he referred to her hours as 'what we call a day and a half's work'. One hopes he paid her accordingly. Another woman went every month to wash for an attorney. In giving evidence in connection with a robbery, she remarked 'I went that night a little before dark, time enough to have filled my tubs and copper.'[33]

The 1851 census shows that the majority of washerwomen recorded were between the ages of thirty and fifty-five, although a number of them went on well into their sixties. There is no reason for thinking it was different earlier. Mary Collier, for example, 'continued a Washerwoman till ... Sixty-Three Years of Age'.[34] She remained unmarried, but most washerwomen were married or, frequently, widowed. Often washerwomen are referred to as 'Dames'. George Sturt writing of the early nineteenth century noted that at Farnborough 'old widow women' were frequently 'called "Dame" this or that'.[35] The mother of Francis Place became a washerwoman at the age of sixty when her husband lost all his money in a state lottery. Although industrious, she was not used to 'the mere drudgery of household work to any considerable extent'. But 'without saying a word' to her husband, in case he made objections, 'she went into the neighbourhood she had left, told her tale to some of the housekeepers, and showed the necessity there was for her doing something by which to procure the means of maintaining her family, and requested them to give her their cloaths to wash which they did not usually wash at home, they all instantly complied with her request'. She washed in her own home, and 'she used to bring home large bundles of cloaths upon her head and take them back again in the same way'. Her days were long for 'often did she labour till twelve o'clock at night, and rise again at four in the morning to pursue her occupation'.[36] Later, when Place's mother-in-law was left a widow, she too took in washing; and by combining this with housing a few

---

[32] *Low Life*, p. 91.
[33] George, *London Life in the Eighteenth Century*, p. 207.
[34] Mary Collier, *Poems on Several Occasions* (1762), p. v.
[35] George Sturt, *William Smith, Potter and Farmer: 1790–1858* (1978), p. 116.
[36] *The Autobiography of Francis Place, 1771–1854*, ed. Mary Thale (1972), pp. 98–9.

lodgers, she was able 'to maintain herself and her younger daughter, and to save some money'.[37] Until they died in 1795, the parents of Mary Ann Ashford kept the City Arms. Mr and Mrs Long, with whom Mary Ann lived as a child, appear to have had no other means of support but Mrs Long's earnings. She 'had the whole of the washing from the City Arms'.[38] In Mary Wollstonecraft's unfinished novel, *The Wrongs of Woman*, Jemima is the victim of every unfortunate circumstance that can happen to a woman. At one stage of her life, desperate to regain her self-respect by the independence that earning her own living would bring her, she becomes a washerwoman. She describes her work of washing in people's houses as 'from one in the morning till eight at night', for which she earned 'eighteen or twenty pence a day'.[39]

Working such long hours, most of them standing and bending over the tub or copper, it is not surprising that many washerwomen were 'full of complaints of their coughs, asthmas, or pains in the stomach'. Washing was a demanding and gruelling task. 'This hard treatment', we are told, 'being endured for two shillings and sixpence a day.'[40] This sum may have been paid in London, but it was surely more than double that in the countryside. In 1760, the wife of shopkeeper Thomas Turner 'paid Mary Heath 18*d*. for two days washing'. Later Turner recorded how he 'paid Dame Akehurst 18*d*. for her two days' work'.[41] So the rate was about 9*d*. a day. On 31 May 1786, James Woodforde wrote in his diary 'To Norton's wife for washing my boy's shirts for a whole year ... 0. 10. 6.' It seems very little. She apparently 'grumbled about [it] not being enough and [was] rather discontented'. So Woodforde told her he would get someone else to do the washing in future and paid her an extra shilling.[42] Eden wrote of the washerwomen in Lincolnshire receiving 'from 6*d*. to 8*d*. a day'. On the other hand, a labourer's wife at Ellesmere in Shropshire who 'was formerly a laundry maid earns by washing 3*s*. a week, a sum that not one woman in 20 here, ever earns'.[43] It was slightly more than half what her husband earned, but a significant contribution to the family wage.

[37] Ibid., p. 105.

[38] *Life of a Licensed Victualler's Daughter Written by Herself* (1844), p. 12.

[39] Mary Wollstonecraft, 'The wrongs of woman (1798)', in James Kinsley and Gary Kelly (eds), *Mary and the Wrongs of Woman* (1980), p. 115.

[40] Smith, *Cries of London*, pp. 82, 81.

[41] *The Dairy of Thomas Turner, 1754–1765*, ed. David Vaisey (1985), pp. 208, 317.

[42] *Diary of a Country Parson*, vol. ii, p. 247.

[43] F. M. Eden, *The State of the Poor*, 3 vols (1797), vol. ii, pp. 398, 621.

For many poor women, a few days' washing plus a little spinning enabled them to make ends meet (if only just). Writing of the women at Spilsby in Lincolnshire, Eden wrote that they had 'very little employment at home', but how 'a few endeavour to get work in washing'.[14] For many poor women it was an occupation of last resort. It stood between them and going on the parish. In a list of 'Old and Decayed People — Poor and Widows' of Whickham parish in Durham for 1764, there are several examples of women supporting themselves (and sometimes their husbands, children, or parents) by washing. So the wife of 'John Usher old and not in his senses', who was 'about fifty', supported him 'by washing'. Jenny Parker, a widow, with three small children was 'a washerwoman and in great necessity'. Her earnings might have supported herself but not without difficulty her three children.[45] Early in the nineteenth century the Bath Society for the 'Suppression of Vagrants, the Relief of Distress and the Encouragement of Industry' kept 'a list . . . of washerwomen, charwomen, etc., wanting employment'.[46]

The author of *The Cries of London* talks of 'that description of people who go about to clean houses, either by washing the wainscot, scrubbing the floors, or brightening the pots and kettles'.[47] Although a much smaller group in the 1851 census (55,000 in Great Britain), the importance of charwomen is interesting. They related closely both to washerwomen and to that other vast group, female domestic servants. If most female domestic servants were unmarried, and left their employment on marriage, most washerwomen and charwomen were married or widowed. As with washerwomen, by far the majority of charwomen were over forty years of age. The biggest age concentration was among those over fifty. Charwomen and washerwomen together form an occupation group exclusive to women, and one that complements female domestic service. Indeed, it might be seen as an extension of domestic service, an occupation for married women, many of whom may have been living-in domestic servants before their marriage, who wanted to earn a living without becoming part of their employers' household. They were a 'great acquisition to single gentlemen'.[48]

---

[44] Ibid., p. 398.
[45] 'Lists of the "Old and Decayed People: Poor and Widows" in Whickham parish, 1764, Strathmore Papers D/ST 336/7, Durham County Record Office. I am indebted to Keith Wrightson for this reference.
[46] *Reports of the Society for Bettering the Condition and Increasing the Comforts of the Poor*, 5 vols. (1798–1808), vol. v (1806), p. 125.
[47] Smith, *Cries of London*, p. 82.
[48] Ibid.

So in the early stages of industrialization it was not manufacturing industry that loomed large as the employer of women but service occupations. Analysing middle-class expenditure in Victorian England, J. A. Banks has suggested that 'where there was a rise in income it was immediately followed by a disproportionately large increase in expenditure on washing and mangling'.[49] From what we know of the difficulties associated with washing days in the eighteenth century, many housewives would have welcomed the opportunity either to send out their washing or to employ women to come and help them or their servants on washdays. Patricia Malcolmson has talked of the increased importance attached to wearing well-laundered clothes in the second half of the nineteenth century as 'part of the paraphernalia of gentility'.[50] The link between increased standards of personal and domestic cleanliness and gentility is a close one. It was almost certainly present before the nineteenth century. So one major employment of women in the first stages of industrialization, if not of later stages, was the servicing of a new and more prosperous middle class.

The occupations of washerwomen and charwomen relate in another way. For Thomas Turner's washerwoman, Dame Akehurst, as for many other women, washing was only a part-time occupation. Elsewhere in Turner's diary we find her picking hops and being paid for it.[51] Many women combined the roles of washerwoman and charwoman. Mary Collier, for example, while described as a washerwoman, in fact went out charring. If the most important task in the households she visited was the washing, often, in addition, she was employed at cleaning pewter, brass and iron, pots, kettles, saucepans, and skillets, as well as brewing beer.[52] Sarah Tansley, the wife of the gardener of the Revd William Cole, carried out a variety of tasks for him: she helped to clean the house, took part in the washing and ironing, picked and sorted feathers, and even stood in for the cook when she was ill.[53] William Howitt, writing in 1838, described the ways in which wives of labourers could contribute to the maintenance of their families 'by taking in washing, helping in harvest fields, charring in more affluent peoples houses'.[54]

[49] J. A. Banks, *Prosperity and Parenthood: A Study of Family Planning among the Victorian Middle Classes* (1954), p. 63.

[50] Malcolmson, *English Laundresses*, p. 7.

[51] *Diary of Thomas Turner*, p. 303.

[52] Collier, *The Woman's Labour*, pp. 12–16.

[53] *The Blecheley Diary of the Rev. William Cole* [1765–7], Introd. Helen Waddell (1931), pp. 168, 176, 179, 211, 142, 145.

[54] William Howitt, *The Rural Life of England* (1840), p. 405.

The more the occupations of women in the eighteenth century are studied, the clearer becomes their involvement in a very wide range of employments. In some cases their omission from any eighteenth-century occupational records is understandable. So the failure to note the existence of at least one highwaywoman — she operated in Essex in the 1730s — might be excused.[55] But what of the body of female smugglers that George Lipscomb came across while making a journey in Cornwall, 'whose appearance was so grotesque and extraordinary, that I could not imagine, in what manner they had contrived to alter their natural shapes so completely'? On inquiry they freely acknowledged their occupation as 'smugglers of spirituous liquors'. The reason for their strange shape was that they conveyed the liquor from 'their Cutter to *Plymouth* by means of bladders fastened under their petticoats, and indeed, they were so heavily laden, that it was with great apparent difficulty they waddled along'. 'The principal annoyance to these *honest* traders', Lipscombe added, 'is their intercourse with drunken sailors.'[56]

Many women who, if they had been recorded in a census, would almost certainly have appeared as housewives and of no occupation, performed important working roles. Take local women physicians and surgeons, for example. In an anonymous pamphlet of 1739, Sophia discussed the role of women as physicians. 'Our sex seem born to teach and practice physic', she said, 'to restore health to the sick and preserve it to the well.'[57] Indeed, where no doctor was available, how important it was when sick to have a source of advice and remedies. Of Mary Leadbeater's aunt, Rachel Carleton, it was claimed that 'the country resorted to her for advice. She kept a large assortment of drugs, she distilled simples, she sold to those who could afford to pay, and dispensed gratis to those who could not.'[58] In the middle of the century William Ellis talked of how essential a 'Piece of good Housewifery' it was for those women who were able 'to distil Cordial Waters at home, to keep Balsam by them and to furnish their Closet with such Remedies as may relieve the necessitous poor people'. It was held that an 'old woman's receipt . . . has often been known to remove an inveterate distemper, which has baffled the researches of a college of graduates'.[59] Albinia

---

[55] *Gentleman's Magazine* (1735), p. 680.
[56] George Lipscombe, *A Journey into Cornwall* (1799), pp. 227–8.
[57] *Woman Not Inferior to Man*, By Sophia, A Person of Quality (1739), p. 41.
[58] *The Leadbeater Papers*, 2 vols (1862), vol. i, p. 60.
[59] William Ellis, *The Country Housewife's Family Companion* (1750), p. viii.

Woodward, the wife of the East Hendred parson, 'had some reputation in the housewifely arts, for patients came from three or four
miles around for her powders against agues'.[60] The poet and anti-
quary William Hall (1748–1825) finally settled in Marshland
in Norfolk where his wife Sukey 'practised phlebotomy and mid-
wifery'.[61] From Catherine Hutton we learn of Ellen Haythornthwaite,
a 'noted surgeon' who lived in the forest of Bowland in the 1780s.
For 'burns, scalds, fractured skulls, bruises, and all external wounds,
she will in a very little time, make a perfect cure, if they come to her
before they are mortified'. For more serious disorders such as
'asthmas, coughs, fevers', we are told, 'she will not prescribe a large
quantity of drugs, and yet effectually cure, if curable'.[62] Early in the
nineteenth century John Clare wrote of the village doctress

> ... one that owns
> The praise of half the village for her powers
> In curing every ill save broken bones
> With famous drinks & ointments made of flowers
> Sought for & gathered in propitious hours.[63]

Many of these women made their own potions and ointments
from herbs and plants. It was not uncommon for women to keep a
stock of these country remedies for the use of their families. In
towns, where it was not so easy for the housewife to gather them,
the work of the simpler came into its own. 'Women particularly in
some counties often constitute a greater part of the community' of
simplers. They are described as rising with the sun and collecting
their produce from 'the ditches and swampy ground' before trudging
'for fifteen miles to the London markets'. They collected 'water-
cresses, dandelions, scurvy-grass, nettles, bitter-sweet, cough grass,
feverfew, hedge mustard, Jack-by-the-hedge, or sauce-alone', and
sometimes snails and vipers, but 'of later years' these were 'little
called for'. These were sold to 'herb-shops in Covent Garden, Fleet
and Newgate Markets'. Simplers were in great demand and are
described as 'a most useful set of people' to whom 'the public are
much indebted as they supply our wants every day'.[64] As many

[60] *A Parson in the Vale of White Horse*, ed. Donald Gibson (1982), p. 25.
[61] William Hone, *The Table Book* (1859), p. 141.
[62] *Reminscences of a Gentlewoman of the last Century: Letters of Catherine Hutton*, ed.
Catherine Hutton Beale (1891), pp. 59–60.
[63] John Clare, *The Midsummer Cushion*, ed. Anne Tibble (1978), p. 143.
[64] Smith, *Cries of London*, pp. 77, 78.

seem to have slept rough in the countryside, it is doubtful whether any records based on households would have noted their existence.

An interesting group of migrant women workers was employed by the market gardens around London in the summer months. The explosion of the population of the metropolis had led to a greatly increased demand for fresh vegetables and fruit. Given their perishable nature and the slowness of transport, demand could only be satisfactorily met by increasing supplies locally. There seems to have been a remarkable growth of market-gardening: Battersea, Barnes, Chiswick, Fulham, Putney, Isleworth, Hammersmith, Brentford, and Twickenham, as well as many other districts round London, had extensive market gardens by the end of the eighteenth century. As early as 1727, Richard Bradley noted the great expansion of market-gardening around London, where there were 'about one hundred and ten thousand Acres cultivated for the same purpose'.[65] Pehr Kalm in 1748 remarked on the number of market gardens which lay 'on all sides round and close to London', and commented on how 'the land around Chelsea' was 'almost entirely devoted to nursery and vegetable gardens'.[66] In 1796 Daniel Lysons found 'above three hundred acres of land in the parish of Battersea', in Kensington 'about 230', 'about one hundred and fifty' in Barnes, the same number in Twickenham − the whole acreage devoted to market-gardening.[67] All were in areas close to the city and near the river − the means of transporting from the many stables the horse-dung essential for producing good crops.

Women had always been gardeners. Their meticulous skill as weeders had long been acknowledged. Parson Woodforde often employed women to weed his garden as did that most expert gardener, Gilbert White. By the second half of the eighteenth century, they were much in demand by farmers, as, in the words of Ivy Pinchbeck, 'English agriculture became characterised by its neatness'.[68] As early as 1747, in a survey of trades, market gardens are seen as employing 'labouring Men and Women too in their Grounds'.[69] But labour needs fluctuated. It was in the summer that they were greatest, and

[65] Richard Bradley, *The Country Housewife and Lady's Director*, 2 pts [1727 and 1732], Introd. Caroline Davidson (1980), pt i, p. 13.

[66] Pehr Kalm, *Account of His Visit to England on His Way to America in 1748*, trans. Joseph Lucas (1892), p. 27.

[67] Daniel Lysons, *The Environs of London*, 4 vols (1796), vol. i, p. 27; vol. iii, p. 170; vol. i, p. 541; vol. iii, p. 158.

[68] Ivy Pinchbeck, *Women Workers and the Industrial Revolution*, p. 61.

[69] *A General Description of All Trades* (1747), pp. 101−2.

local labour was probably inadequate to satisfy them. Market gardens were not alone in this need to employ vastly increased labour supplies for a limited period. The same problem faced many farmers in finding labour for hay-making and harvesting. It had always been a particular problem for hop-picking. The method of meeting this seasonal demand was to employ itinerant labour.

Such labour had been coming from Ireland since early in the century. Its influx into London was greatest round about the hay harvest. The demand for milk from the metropolis had led to the multiplication of small cow-keepers in the suburbs who cultivated hay intensively in order to supply their beasts with fodder, and the Irish seem to have provided the necessary labour for harvesting it. Before the hay harvest began, many Irish labourers arrived in London with their families 'having begged their way to town'.[70] They came for the summer season and in the autumn returned home with their earnings. It was not just from Ireland that such seasonal labour came but from Scotland and the north of England, from Wales, Shropshire, Staffordshire, and Wiltshire. 'There is nothing more common', wrote Charles Varley, 'than for labourers to go from the north of England and Ireland, reap the harvest in the south of England, and be at home soon enough for their own harvest'.[71] Much of this migrant labour was provided by domestic industry. Handloom weavers from the West Riding provided labour for the harvest in Lincolnshire, Nottinghamshire, and the vale of York. Stocking weavers from Leicestershire migrated to Cambridgeshire, and workers from the northern industrial towns moved to the Fens and East Riding to help with the harvest.[72] Of this migrant labour force, a large number were women. The work they performed was various. Apart from participating in the hay harvest, they weeded, they picked hops, they gathered vegetables and fruit, and then carried heavy loads of them from the market gardens on the outskirts of London to Covent Garden. Many went from one task to another, frequently moving from place to place, to earn all they could during the short season before once again taking to the road and returning home.

Pehr Kalm, on his visit to England in 1748, remarked on the influx of Irishmen at the beginning of May, and distinguished it

---

[70] George, *London Life in the Eighteenth Century*, p. 121.

[71] Charles Varley, *A Treatise on Agriculture*, 2 vols (1766), vol. i, p. 123.

[72] E. J. T. Collins, 'Migrant labour in British agriculture in the nineteenth century', *Economic History Review*, 29 (1976), pp. 38–59 (pp. 42–3).

from the migration southwards of the Welsh at the same time. The Irish settled 'north and east of London', the Welsh in Kent, but both 'earn their money . . . on this side of England'. But there was another difference; 'instead of only men coming as from Ireland, there come mostly only women and girls from Wales, all well, cleanly and very neatly clad'.[73] George Lipscombe, on the other hand, in his tour through South Wales at the end of the century, commented on how common it was for 'the Welsh peasantry to emigrate to the neighbouring counties, or even to proceed as far as the metropolis, in search of employment, in gardening and husbandry, early in the spring', but he thought it a male migration. He went out of his way to emphasize that the subsistence of the family did not rely on this migratory labour 'for the women, whom they leave at home, are extremely industrious'.[74] Whether or not women were part of the migrating labour depended on their circumstances and local employment possibilities. Elsewhere Lipscomb wrote of other Welshmen who 'with their wives and children, and all they had', journeyed 'towards Deptford, to procure employment in the dock-yard'.[75]

Thomas Baird in his survey of Middlesex, the main centre of market gardening close to London, commented on 'the great numbers of women' who were employed by market gardeners in the summer.[76] Middleton, also writing of Middlesex but later than Baird, found astonishing the 'number of women (mostly from North Wales) . . . employed by the farmers and gardeners round London, during every summer season, in weeding and making hay, in gathering green pease and beans, in picking fruits, and carrying strawberries and other tender fruit to market'.[77] Most of them, Baird thought, came from Shropshire and Staffordshire, 'from the neighbourhood of Shrewsbury and Dudley'.[78] Women working on the surface at Shropshire coal mines would often leave the pit in the spring, travel to London, and spend the summer months working for the market gardeners around London before returning home at the end of the season. They earned about 6s. a week in the summer months, exactly half the rate for men.[79] As Baird pointed out, it was a

[73] Kalm, *Account of His Visit to England*, pp. 82–3.
[74] George Lipscomb, *Journey into South Wales in the Year 1799* (1802), p. 102.
[75] Ibid., p. 101.
[76] Thomas Baird, *General View of the Agriculture of the County of Middlesex* (1793), p. 21.
[77] T. Middleton, *General View of the Agriculture of the County of Middlesex* (1807), pp. 497–8.
[78] Baird, *General View of the Agriculture of Middlesex*, p. 21.
[79] Pinchbeck, *Women Workers and the Industrial Revolution*, p. 254.

lower rate of pay than that paid to regular agricultural labourers and even to 'common gardeners'. The differential could only be explained, he believed, by the fact that 'their employment is more constant, more to be depended on, and perhaps less severe'. But the working day was long. In summer it began at five o'clock in the morning and did not end until seven in the evening, they had an hour off for breakfast and another at dinner.[80] The women travelled to London on foot, and lived 'at a very cheap rate' so that 'many of them' returned 'to their own country much richer than when they left it'.[81]

A vivid picture of the work of the fruit women of Isleworth is drawn by Lysons. Isleworth was noted for its crop of raspberries, where the gathering and carrying to market of the fruit was the work of women. Lysons thought they came from Shropshire and Wiltshire. Early in the morning a load (or twelve gallons, a gallon being equivalent to three pints) of fruit was gathered. Twelve women were employed, so each was responsible for gathering a gallon of raspberries for which she received a penny-halfpenny. One woman then carried the load, estimated to weigh between thirty and forty pounds, on her head from Isleworth to Covent Garden, a distance of ten miles, for which she was paid 3s. 6d. Lysons thought they could 'perform but one journey a day'.[82] But Phillips thought women carrying strawberries to Covent Garden made 'two turns'.[83] If, as Lysons believed, they could travel at five miles an hour, a journey to and from Covent Garden would take at least four hours, but often they seem to have found 'some conveyance back' — for which they had to pay. Women working in Hammersmith market gardens could perform three or four turns and received '8d. for each journey over and above their day's work'; at Kensington they were paid 'sixpence, and frequently go four times a day'.[84] Women at Ealing and Brentford, according to Eden, received only 6d. a journey to Covent Garden. He thought they could 'sometimes make two trips a day'.[85] Despite the confusion about the rates paid for carrying the fruit to market and the number of journeys the women could make in a day, daily earnings seem to have averaged between eight and nine shillings.

[80] Baird, *General View of the Agriculture of Middlesex*, p. 21.
[81] Lysons, *Environs of London*, vol. i, p. 27.
[82] Ibid., pp. 81–2.
[83] Sir R. Phillips, *A Morning Walk from London to Kew* (1817), p. 227.
[84] Lysons, *Environs of London*, vol. i, pp. 81–2; Phillips, *A Morning Walk*, p. 227.
[85] Eden, *State of the Poor*, vol. ii, p. 419.

In a rather sentimental account of strawberry pickers − mainly, he thought, from Shropshire and Wales − Sir Richard Phillips described how they lived 'hard, they sleep on straw in hovels and barns', they ate simply and in the course of the season of forty days could accumulate a sum of ten pounds. Their remuneration was 'unworthy of the opulent classes who derive enjoyment from their labour'. After the soft fruit season was over, the same women gathered and marketed vegetables for a further sixty days − but at lower wages. In all, Phillips reckoned, they returned home with little more than £15 from their summer labours. Such a sum contributed, he added, 'either to their humble comforts, or creates a small dowry towards a rustic establishment for life'.[86] It is an interesting comment, for it suggests that some of these women were single, and that the work enabled them to accumulate a dowry and marry. Apart from Pehr Kalm, most of those commenting on such work were writing at the end of the eighteenth century. It might suggest that this migration of female − and indeed male − labour was on the increase. Why was it necessary for them to leave their homes and travel such distances to find employment?

Recorded female hawkers and pedlars in Great Britain in 1851 numbered 11,000, and this excluded nearly 500 'Cowkeepers' and 'Millsellers' as well as 981 'hawkers' and 'vendors' of fruit and flowers.[87] Henry Mayhew thought the number recorded as hawkers, pedlars, or hucksters in the 1851 census was 'a gross understatement' as it covered only 'the permanent core of full-time hawkers and pedlars'.[88] Almost certainly underrecorded were street-hawkers. There were milk-women, fish-women, meat pie, apple dumpling, barley-broth, and sausage women. There were those who, as Pehr Kalm described them, 'walk or sit in the streets of London with baskets full of flowers, bound in small bunches ... which they offered to passers-by'. There were the 'old women with shoe-brushes, blacking, and such like, ready to clean shoes for anyone who may require their services'.[89] Those selling fish, fruit, victuals, 'almanacks, or other printed papers licensed by authority' were exempt from the need for a pedlar's license.[90] So were those selling their own produce. In London, street-hawking was one of the commonest occupations

---

[86] Phillips, *A Morning Walk*, pp. 228, 226−7, 228.
[87] *Census of Population, 1851*, p. cxlii.
[88] David Hey, *Packmen, Carriers, and Packhorse Roads* (1980), p. 204.
[89] Kalm, *Account of His Visit to England*, pp. 34, 62.
[90] Richard Burn, *The Justice of the Peace, and Parish Officer*, 3 vols (1762), vol. ii, p. 156.

and in it women predominated. There were goods that were a
virtual monopoly of female hawkers: fruit, flowers, vegetables, fish,
and milk. It was an occupation that attracted the very poorest. The
wives of Irish immigrants, for example, frequently took up street-
hawking, as did the wives of London day-labourers. According to
an account of 1811, milk-sellers were often women from Ireland or
Wales:

> The milk is conveyed from the cow-house, and sold, principally
> by robust Welsh girls and Irish women; and it is amazing to
> witness the fatigue these females undergo. . . . They arrive here
> in particular from different parts of the metropolis by 3 or 4
> o'clock in the morning laughing and singing to the music of
> their empty pails, with these, when filled, they return to town;
> and the weight they are thus accustomed to carry on their
> yokes for the distance of several miles, is sometimes from
> 100−130 lbs. [*sic*].[91]

With the increasing taste for fresh fruit and vegetables, street
hawkers provided an important outlet particularly in London. Their
cries varied according to their wares:, 'Delicate cowcumbers to
pickle', 'Crab, Crab, any Crab?', 'Ripe Speragas', or 'Milk: any
Milk above Maids, any Milk below?', 'Primroses, Primroses: four
Bunches a Penny Primroses'.[92] In Covent Garden market, fruit and
vegetables that remained unsold at the end of the day would be
sold off cheaply to hawkers, who then resold it in the streets either
from barrows or baskets. Not always was it the freshest or cleanest.
'It was but yesterday', observed Humphrey Clinker, 'that I saw a
dirty barrow-bunter in the street, cleansing her dusty fruit with her
own spittle; and who knows but some fine lady of St. James's parish
might admit into her delicate mouth those very cherries which had
been rolled and moistened between the filthy and perhaps ulcerated
chops of a St Giles huckster.'[93] The same process of buying up the
inferior produce left over at the markets was to be found among
fish-hawkers − the lowest of the low. Often they were near-beggars
who 'borrowed five shillings every morning at the ale house to buy

[91] P. J. Atkins, 'The retail milk trade in London *c.*1790−1914', *Economic History Review*, 33 (1980), pp. 522−37 (p. 523).

[92] *The London Cries, for the Amusement of all the Good Children throughout the World*, (1770), p. 29; *Cries of London* (1711), no pagination.

[93] Tobias Smollett, *The Expedition of Humphrey Clinker* (1775), quoted Dorothy Davis, *A History of Shopping* (1966), pp. 204−5.

them stock and paid it back with six pence interest every night, and never looked beyond this'.[94] It was not just fruit, vegetables, and fish but products of all kinds that were sold in this way: milk and matches, ribbons and laces, sausages and meat pies. There were even hawkers and pedlars of hair 'who go up and down the Country to buy up the Commodity, who generally dispose of it to . . . Hair-sellers'.[95] Street-hawking was also an occupation which attracted the better-off wives of artisans and day-labourers who had regular customers in a clearly defined area. Whether selling milk, fish, or their own home-made produce — meat and apple pies, sausages, or ginger bread — they could make a steady income from their trade. Apparently, a London milkwoman at the end of the seventeenth century 'sold on average sixteen pints of milk a week to each of her customers'.[96]

Margaret Spufford has shown how there is evidence of the growing number and importance of hawkers and pedlars in the last quarter of the seventeenth century.[97] More settled tradesmen and shopkeepers resented them and would have liked them suppressed. Their growing importance and successful trading put other ideas into the government's head. In 1696–7 they were taxed. Licensing of pedlars dates back to the sixteenth century, and Legislation was renewed at intervals. In 1696–7 an Act made it obligatory for 'every hawker, pedlar, petty chapman, or any other trading person going from town to town, or to other men's houses . . . to pay a duty of £4 a year'.[98] It was a fruitful source of revenue for the government. Nevertheless, many continued to trade without licences.

The activities of one female pedlar, Jane Broderick, came to light through a case coming before a JP in Morpeth. She had 'dureing most of her life travelled to and fro in severall parts of this kingdome to fairs and marketts and sold Inkle laces threads and other such wares'. Jane was remarkable in that she had a house in County Durham; the girl she worked with, Sarah, 'had no certain place of abode'. Little wonder that women pedlars are difficult to trace. They were highly mobile, wandering over considerable distances and journeying between markets and fairs. Often they were pedlars for only part of the year. Mary Rice was such a one. When in 1701 she was examined in Basingstoke she explained how before she was

[94] Davis, *History of Shopping*, p. 222.
[95] *A General Description of All Trades*, p. 116.
[96] Joan Thirsk, *The Rural Economy of England* (1984), p. 186.
[97] Margaret Spufford, *The Great Reclothing of Rural England* (1984), pp. 13–14.
[98] Burn, *The Justice of the Peace*, vol. ii, pp. 155.

married she had been a servant in Banbury. When she left her husband, she went to London where she worked at 'hay-making and weeding of gardens for gardners, and at gentlemen's houses some time of the year and at other times she used to buy books and ballads and sell them about the country going from place to place'. She seems to have had no permanent place of abode, for she described how 'sometimes she got her lodging in barns'. Would such a pedlar have had a licence? It seems unlikely. How easy for such women without any fixed home to escape any recording! Of course, not all women pedlars were such near vagrants as these. When the marriage of Joan Dant, a Quaker, was dissolved, she was left with little provision and became a pedlar. She had 'provided herself with with a well-selected assortment of Mercery, Hosiery and Haberdashery . . . and set off on her travels with her merchandise at her back'. When in 1714, aged 83, she made her will she had over £9,000 to dispose of.[99]

Hawkers and pedlars provided a useful service by selling a whole variety of consumer goods that were unobtainable in the countryside and the purchase of which would have necessitated, at the least, a visit to the nearest market town. Nicholas Blundell of Little Crosby, Lancashire, seems to have been regularly visited by them. Sometimes couples travelled together. So on 14 October 1702, 'John Steward & his wife came with their Packs to sell goods'. But ten years later she comes alone, for in April 1712 Blundell recorded how an 'Ailes Steward was here with her Pack & sold some goods to my Wife'. The same year he bought two lots of glasses from female pedlars. On 1 November 1720, 'Betty Thomas of . . . Liverpoole came hither to sell some Forraine goods'. A year later he buys china from 'a Woman as came from Preston'.[100] In the countryside many women, particularly married women, operated as 'badgers' travelling from farm to farm and buying up their surplus production of eggs, butter and cheese, chickens and corn to sell elsewhere. Sometimes they were on foot, sometimes they had packhorses. The experience recorded by Nicholas Blundell shows how any surplus of farm produce was often disposed of in this way. So in the month of January 1703 we find him recording how 'Huxter Women measured Apples in the Hall'. These were apples grown on the estate and

---

[99] Spufford, *The Great Reclothing*, pp. 24−5, 43, 46.
[100] *The Great Diurnal of Nicholas Blundell of Little Crosby, Lancashire*, ed. J. J. Bagley, Record Society of Lancashire and Cheshire, 3 vols. (1968, 1970, 1972), vol. i, p. 20; vol. ii, pp. 14, 33; vol. iii, pp. 26, 51.

stored. The women who bought them then travelled to Liverpool to hawk them on the streets. On 27 September 1725 he recorded that 'three women came from Liverpool to buy some Potatoes of me but we did not bargain'.[101] Many seem to have moved between town and country selling goods like meat and malt in the villages, buying up farmer's surpluses and returning to the town to sell them. Of life in a Hertfordshire village in the middle of the nineteenth century Edwin Grey was to write of how when coal supplies were deposited at local railway stations 'several people used to fetch a donkey or pony load . . . and hawk the coal round, selling it to the cottagers in small quantities'.[102] There was one other kind of hawking and peddling in which women played an active role: the sale of chap-books, newspapers, ballads, broadsheets, and pamphlets. Charles Knight wrote of Thomas Carter, a tailor born in 1792 who learnt to read using the Bible as textbook. When still very young he was befriended by an old woman who peddled cakes, sweets, and fruit, and also chap-books. Carter was given access to all the chap-books she had.[103] Archenholz, on a visit to London at the end of the century, noted the number of female hawkers and singers of ballads — often containing political comment. When bookselling and printing expanded into provincial towns, hawkers and peddlers played an important part in making reading matter accessible to the rural population.[104]

Washerwomen and charwomen, shopkeepers' wives, simplers and physicians, migrant harvesters and market garden labour, hawkers and pedlars — these are only some of the numerous occupations of women that have so far largely escaped attention. The reasons for their disregard are perhaps the unglamorous nature of the work involved, the fact that they were often part-time or seasonal occupations, the isolated and hidden nature of the work performed in their own houses or those of numerous individual employers, the great mobility of the labour, and also, perhaps, that they do not quite fit with historians' prejudices about the period of industrialization. What is remarkable is the number of women who moved casually in and out of occupations. Many within a year had two or more. Often they involved considerable mobility and travelling far from their homes. The very informality of the employment market

---

[101] Ibid., vol. i, p. 53; vol. iii, p. 167.
[102] Edwin Grey, *Cottage Life in a Hertfordshire Village* (1935), pp. 52–3.
[103] Charles Knight, *Memoirs of a Working Man* (1845), p. 20.
[104] J. W. von Archenholz, *A Picture of England*, trans. from the French (1791), p. 232.

for women defied careful recording. It suggests that in order to earn their living, many women could afford to miss no opportunity. They had to be prepared to move to where employment was offered. Some exploited to the full the harvesting season; others the surpluses of farm produce that went unmarketed; yet others the unsold produce at London markets, or the demand for cures that nature offered.

How does prostitution fit into this pattern of women's employment opportunities in the eighteenth century? Evidence suggests it was widespread – and increasing.[105] In 1806 Colquhoun remarked on its growth in provincial towns, particularly seaports and large manufacturing centres. London alone, it is thought, had over 10,000 prostitutes.[106] It might be seen as increasing with declining employment opportunities for women, underemployment, and low wages – all characteristic of the late eighteenth and early nineteenth century. What also appears to have characterized much of the growing prostitution was its part-time, seasonal nature. Acton talked of it as 'a transitory state, through which an untold number' passed. Many, he believed, returned 'sooner or later to a more regular course of life'.[107] Particularly vulnerable were domestic servants, dressmakers, milliners, tailors, seamstresses, lace and straw workers – all liable to periods of unemployment or underemployment. Many single women, particularly those with children to support, resorted to prostitution in the evenings to supplement their inadequate wages. For many women it was 'a rational choice', given the nature of the alternatives. Earnings were almost certainly higher than for most other female occupations. Many could earn in a day what they would otherwise take a week to earn. Is it to be seen, like domestic service, as 'a form of disguised under-employment' and one of 'the social consequences of the economic half-status that was women's lot'?[108] Before we can answer these questions, we need to know a lot more about prostitution in the eighteenth century.

[105] Among others, Saunders Welch, John Fielding, Jonas Hanway, Patrick Colquhoun, Samuel Johnson, and William Cobbett were of this view.

[106] Colquhoun, *A Treatise on Indigence*, p. 40.

[107] William Acton, *Prostitution, Considered in Its Moral, Social and Sanitary Aspects* (1857), pp. 73, 64.

[108] Eric Richards, 'Women in the British economy since about 1700: An Interpretation', *History*, 59/197 (1974), pp. 348, 341.

10

The Economics of Courtship and Marriage

Sukey, you shall be my wife
And I will tell you why:
I have got a little pig,
And you have got a sty;
I have got a dun cow,
And you can make good cheese;
Sukey, will you marry me?
Say Yes if you please.

The Oxford Nursery Rhyme Book

One thing all marriages in the eighteenth century had in common was close links with the economic circumstances of the couple concerned. This applies to the mercenary marriages of the upper class, which were often mere financial transactions, and to those 'prudent' marriages of the middle class summed up by the advice of Matthew Boulton: 'Don't marry for money, but marry where money is.' It also applies to servants in husbandry or domestic servants who agreed to marry once their joint savings were sufficient to buy a cottage, furnish it with the bare necessities, and even, perhaps, buy a cow or other livestock. It applies equally to the apprentice who on completion of his apprenticeship married a servant maid and set up as journeyman in a rented apartment of one or two rooms. In a back-handed way it is relevant to marriages arising from pressure exerted by parishes on the declared father of illegitimate children to marry the mother and remove the burden of mother and child from their Poor Rates. But if from this claim of a shared characteristic any idea of homogeneity of marriages is drawn, it would be wholly misleading. To talk about the institution of marriage in this period as though it were something monolithic that the majority of people experienced would be to distort the truth. As we shall see in chapter 11, marriage forms and practices were extremely diverse. A minority, it is thought, were church marriages.

So in talking of courtship and marriage in the eighteenth century it is the relationship between the two partners that needs emphasizing, not the particular form of marriage — regular, irregular, or common-law.

The economic circumstances in which marriages were concluded among the labouring class were different from those of their social superiors, and imposed distinct patterns on the nature of the married relationship. There is a mass of diaries, journals, memoirs, and autobiographies of both men and women of the middle class from which we can learn something of their motives for marriage, their hopes for, frustrations with, and disappointments in the marriage experience. Even so, often it is a one-sided account. It is not easy to get inside a marriage relationship and know how it was perceived by both spouses. But at least for marriage within the middle and upper classes there is no absence of material. When it comes to marriages of the labouring class, far less is known. Very few of the latter put pen to paper, or, if they did, thought to record their experience of courtship and marriage. Some use has been made of popular literature — ballads and songs, rhymes, and above all chapbooks, which were perhaps the most popular reading material accessible to the labouring class. It is impossible to prove that such literature reflects plebeian practice. If, as I believe, it does, it is weighted towards male plebeian practice and outlook, and 'the extent to which these coincide with female attitudes is at present uncertain'.[1]

One thing that emerges from such popular literature is just how far plebeian attitudes to courtship and marriage differed from those of the upper classes, and the contrasting notions of sexual morality that lie behind them. The contrast is apparent in the idea of what courtship meant. For the upper classes, where marriages were arranged between parents of the couple and their lawyers, there was little wooing. Indeed, often the couple concerned had barely met. So Henry Fielding's Sir Positive Trap, arguing that there was no need for courtship, admitted, 'I never saw my lady ... till an hour before our marriage. I made my addresses to her father, her father to his lawyer, the lawyer to my estate. ... the bargain was struck. ... What need have young people of addressing, or anything, till they come to undressing?'[2] Lady Sarah Pennington had never been in a

---

[1] J. A. Sharpe, 'Plebeian marriage in Stuart England: some evidence from popular literature', *Transactions of the Royal Historical Society*, 5th Ser. 36 (1986), pp. 69–90 (p. 72).
[2] Henry Fielding, *Love in Several Masques* (1728), II. vi.

room alone with her future husband until the marriage ceremony.[3]
There were some, like William Alexander, who acknowledged
that in such cases 'courtship, at least that kind of it which proceeds
from mutual inclination and affection is, among the great, nearly
annihilated'.[4]

A very different idea of courtship is suggested by the evidence,
scarce though it is, of the preliminaries to marriage among the
labouring population. William Jones, the Charlbury weaver and
Quaker, made several attempts at courtship before he found a girl
who would agree to marry him. On Monday 11 September 1791,
he woke up 'having a desire to have an help meet and companion'.
His choice was Hannah Wells, 'a sober virtues young woman'. He
went to her home and 'proposed to she to have she for an help meet
and companion if t'were agreeable to she and left it to Her solid
Consideration'. He saw her again eight days later and 'enquired ...
whether she had considered of that affair which I spoke to she of'.
But Hannah 'signified to me that she should not chuse to change her
situation'. William accepted her decision which 'satisfied' him, 'I
having left it to Her own freedom to do as she thought best'. Two
years later he courted his cousin Rebecca, but neither she nor her
mother would consent; William thought it best 'to say no more to
them about that particular' and took his 'kinde leave of them'.[5]

There can have been few women courted as was Elizabeth
Delamotte, sister to Charles Delamotte, the friend and companion
of Wesley, by the Methodist leader George Whitfield in 1740. To
her parents he sent a letter, which he wrote, 'comes like Abraham's
servant to Rebekah's relations, to know whether your daughter
Miss Elizabeth is a proper person to engage in such an undertaking;
and if so whether you will be pleased to give me leave to propose
marriage to her'. He added that they need not be afraid to send him
a refusal as he knew nothing of his own heart and was 'free from
that foolish passion which the world calls love'. Elizabeth, not
surprisingly, would not have him.[6]

At the beginning of the century, another Quaker, Samuel Bownas
(1676–1753), the son of a shoemaker, recorded his courtship of his

---

[3] Lady Sarah Pennington, *An Unfortunate Mother's Advice to Her Absent Daughters*
[1761], (1770), pp. 9–10.

[4] William Alexander, *The History of Women*, 2 vols (1779), vol. ii, p. 179.

[5] Journals and Notebooks of William Jones (1760–1838), MSS in the Library of the
Religious Society of Friends, Notebooks for 1790–1, and 1793, entries for 11 and 19 Sept.
1791, 27 May 1793.

[6] E. S. Turner, *A History of Courting* (1954), p. 114.

wife-to-be. As he was about to leave for a preaching mission in America, and so would have to delay marriage until his return, he was uncertain whether to propose or not. He admitted she 'had a strong hold' of his affections, he had already obtained the permission of her parents to 'lay it before their Daughter', and thinking it might be prudent to announce his engagement on his arrival in America so 'I might be freed from all Temptations or Offers of that kind', he made his intentions clear to her. While she was anxious to enter into an engagement, an uncle 'on whom she had some Dependence' intervened and insisted his niece was left at liberty 'that if any Thing offered in my Absence she might embrace it'. Bownas readily agreed, but the Uncle wanted him 'to stand bound'. Bownas would have accepted, but 'she objected' to her uncle's demand as it would be 'unreasonable, on her Part to desire such a Thing from me'.[7] They parted. Four years later he returned and married her.

One of the rare accounts of courtship written by a woman comes from Catherine Hutton, the daughter of the historian of Birmingham. In 1787 she went on a tour of Wales and stayed in a lodging house at Aberystwyth. She was singing one day with the window of her room open, unaware that anyone was listening. Someone in fact 'was listening and was caught'. Later 'this gentleman introduced himself by joining us on the shore, and begging to have the honour of carrying a large bundle of sea weed which I had in my hand'. After this he became their constant companion. Finally he proposed to her: 'he told me that he was only eight-and-forty, and that if I would marry him he would keep me a carriage'. But Catherine Hutton was not to be so easily won. 'I believe the gentleman is eight-and-fifty', she wrote, 'and I do not want a carriage, but I did want society, and I was well enough pleased with his till he made this proposal'. Luckily her stay was ending, for as she confessed 'if I were to stay here much longer his attentions would render the place insupportable'.[8] It is a remarkably modern-sounding incident, but then Catherine Hutton was an unusually enlightened woman. She was exceptional in having the leisure and independence to be courted in a way not open to many.

Mary Ann Ashford, who spent most of her life as a domestic servant, in between places went to stay with some friends of her

[7] *The Life and Travels of Samuel Bownas* (1756), p. 24.
[8] *Reminiscences of a Gentlewoman of the last century: Letters of Catherine Hutton*, ed. Catherine Hutton Beale (1891), pp. 51–2.

mother. While there, 'a young man, a jeweller, who visited them, sent me a very ardent love letter, and asked the person I was with to intercede with me for him, which they did'. She decided against accepting for as she said, 'there was something so effeminate about him ... that I would not hear of it'. Some time later she got a place with a family at Epsom where in a short time the son commenced courting her. Soon he proposed marriage, suggesting she should remain in her place 'for some time after'. Banns were called at Shoreditch Church. She began to have doubts about him when he took her walking in some lonely woods and decided 'never to go walking with him'. In the course of their acquaintance she started to detect his real character: 'I ... observed many symptoms of an envious and covetous temper — not towards myself ... but in his conduct to, and his opinions of, others; indeed, he seemed to me to wish nobody to prosper but himself.' As she had no property, once she 'became his wife, he might not use me well'. She broke with him and moved to another place. When at thirty and still a servant, she was approached by a local shoemaker, a widower, who asked her, she writes, 'if I had a mind to marry', for 'if I would have him, he would have me'. After thinking it over she agreed to marry him. It turned out well.[9]

In the diary of Thomas Turner, the shopkeeper, Molly Hicks, a servant who was to become his second wife, is first mentioned in March 1764 when she is recorded as drinking tea with him. A whole year elapsed before she was mentioned again but by this time, March 1765, she had become his 'favourite girl' to whom he had 'taken a great liking'. He began to see her every few days, riding over to pay his 'charmer, or intended wife or sweetheart or whatever other name may be more proper' a visit. He went to her home to drink tea with her and her family. On several occasions he sat up with her all night. She very soon became his 'intended wife'. They continued to meet frequently, and early in June they were taking 'serious walks together'. Before the end of the month they were married.[10]

In the chap-book *A York Dialogue*, Ned tells Harry of his courtship of a chambermaid which lasted 'a year or more'. His wife-to-be was at first 'very coy and huffish'. She told him 'she was not for

[9] *The Life of a Licensed Victualler's Daughter, Written by Herself* (1844), pp. 34, 45–7, 58.

[10] *The Diary of Thomas Turner, 1754–1765*, ed. David Vaisey (1985), pp. 288, 317, 318, 322.

marrying; she lived very well as she was'. But he continued to court her. She learns that Harry has a good trade and 'did mind it now very well', but how would he mind it if she consented to marry him? She expressed anxiety that his promises will not be honoured after marriage. 'You men always promise fair', she told him, 'before you are married, but when that job is over, you seldom or never perform that promise.' As Ned told his friend, 'I do assure you, Harry, that the servants, which we call chamber maids, stand as much upon their honour, as some of them will call it, in courting, than their mistress, ay, and more.'[11] So it was not only men who were 'prudent' in considering marriage. When Thomas Wright began 'to acquire a pretty large acquaintance among the fair sex', he noted ruefully that 'as I had made but little show in trade' and 'having indeed, but little spare money, I found myself objected to on this account'.[12]

Francis Place was first married in 1791 when he was nineteen and his wife was seventeen. 'I danced with her and fell desperately in love with her,' he wrote of their meeting, 'I therefore made it my business to see her again and again. I made enquiries about her and resolved to court her, at first I hardly knew on what terms, but in a little time for a wife.'[13] He described how 'having introduced her to my father and mother and they being pleased with her I laid before her my whole scheme of life and proposed that we should be married as soon as I was in a condition to earn as much money as would enable us to live'. She agreed 'to take her chance' with him and went out to service. Although so young, his wife, Place added, was 'as well qualified for a working man's wife as most young women several years older than she was, usually are'.[14]

Such examples make the point that, as William Alexander stressed in 1779, 'the poor are the only class who still retain the liberty of acting from inclination and from choice'.[15] All suggest that even where the economic circumstances of the couple are an important consideration determining *when* they could marry, marriage was not entered into by either party without careful thought, and often strong inclination. The suggestion that 'some women of middling

[11] *A York Dialogue between Ned and Harry* (1733), pp. 11, 5, 8, 9–10.
[12] *Autobiography of Thomas Wright of Birkenshaw in County of York, 1736–1797*, ed. Thomas Wright (1864), pp. 47–8.
[13] *The Autobiography of Francis Place (1771–1854)*, ed. Mary Thale (1972), p. 96.
[14] Ibid., pp. 100–1, 104–5.
[15] Alexander, *The History of Women*, vol. ii, p. 179.

rank, and the majority of females of the poorer classes, evidently enjoyed a good deal of freedom to seek out a potential mate' seems to have applied as much to the eighteenth century as to the seventeenth.[16]

Another very different aspect of courtship outside the upper classes was the role played by chastity. For many of the middle as well as upper classes, the virginity of the bride-to-be was an essential part of the marriage transaction. As Samuel Johnson made clear, 'confusion of progeny constitutes the essence of the crime', and where the inheritance of an estate was concerned a man needed to know that the children born to his wife were his own. It was on women's chastity, Johnson claimed that 'all the property in the world depends'.[17] Where there was no question of an inheritance, and little or no property was involved, the attitude to pre-marital chastity was far more tolerant. When in one of the earliest versions of the ballad, 'The Foggy Dew', discovered by the collector of songs and ballads, John Bell, at the beginning of the nineteenth century, the apprentice failed to make any headway in courting his master's daughter, he plotted with a neighbour to frighten the girl into his bed. The trick worked. Next morning, she at first goes through the motions of outrage and protest at the injury done her:

> You've taen from me my maidenhead, and I am quite undone
> You've taen from me my maidenhead, and brought my body
>   low

But the protest is not very serious, for she ends: 'But, kind sir, if you'll marry me, I will be your jo.' He does marry her, and, concludes the ballad 'she's proved to him a loving wife and joy of all his heart'.[18]

Not always was pre-marital sex entirely successful. When Thomas Wright courted Nancy Hopkinson, the daughter of a tanner, they were both very young. After the courtship had continued some time, they met, and as Wright recorded afterwards, 'on this occasion, though still very bashful, I went a step further than in my first amour, frequently presuming to give her a kiss'. Later he ventured to pay her a visit

---

[16] Barry Reay (ed.), *Popular Culture in Seventeenth-Century England* (1985), p. 135.

[17] J. Boswell, *Boswell's Life of Johnson* [1776], ed. G. B. Hill and L. F. Powell, 6 vols (1935–50), vol. ii, p. 55; vol. v, p. 208.

[18] From 'The bogle bo', a song quoted in A. L. Lloyd, *Folk Song in England* (1967), p. 233.

one night after the family was in bed. He 'passed part of the night with her ... but was terribly embarrassed to keep up the conversation, she not being a very talkative girl'. Wright was so disheartened by the experience that 'for fear of making myself appear ridiculous ... I never durst repeat my visit afterwards'.[19]

It was not just that pre-marital sex was, in some circumstances and among some sections of the population, tolerated; it was a widespread practice. According to one source, from 1540 to 1835 more than a sixth of all brides were pregnant — that is to say, baptisms were recorded within 8½ months of marriage. In the course of the eighteenth century, pre-nuptial pregnancy was to become the condition of 40 per cent of all brides. Records suggest it increased after about 1740.[20] In many areas the pregnancy of brides seems to have been assumed. John Rule has shown, for example, how in the mining community in Camborne in Cornwall in the period 1778—97, 45.2 per cent of first baptisms followed within 8½ months of marriage. Such a high level of pre-nuptial pregnancy 'probably depended on strong community sanctions against desertion'.[21] In 1836 Peter Gaskell thought pre-marital sex 'almost universal in the agricultural districts'.[22] In a pamphlet written in 1775, the Rev Mr Potter talked of pre-marital sex among the villagers he knew where 'the male and female often come together before marriage; and if the woman proves, as they term becoming pregnant, then the parties marry by a kind of law of honour and decency'.[23]

Toleration of pre-marital unchastity seems to have continued until the ideas of Victorian respectability reached down to the labouring class. As Francis Place was to write in the early nineteenth century of London tradesmen's daughters at the end of the eighteenth, 'want of chastity ... was common, but it was not by any means considered so disreputable ... as it is now'. 'Being unchaste did not necessarily imply that the girl was an abandoned person as she would be now and it was not therefore then as now an insurmountable obstacle to her being comfortably settled in the world.' Want of chastity in a girl 'was scarcely matter of reproach if in other

[19] *Autobiography of Thomas Wright*, pp. 35—6.
[20] P. E. H. Hair, 'Bridal pregnancy in rural England in Earlier Centuries', *Population Studies*, 20/2 (1966) pp. 239—40.
[21] John Rule, *The Labouring Classes in Early Industrial England, 1750—1850* (1986), pp. 197, 198.
[22] P. Gaskell, *Artisans and Machinery* (1836), quoted Rule, *The Labouring Classes*, p. 196.
[23] Quoted Jonas Hanway, *The Defects of Police the Cause of Immorality* (1775), p. 163.

respects they, as was generally the case, were decent in their general conduct.'[24] It is a view supported by the account of the courtship practices on the Isle of Portland, where a period of trial marriage was followed. 'When she becomes with child, she tells her mother; the mother tells her father; her father tells his father, and he tells his son, that it is then a proper time to be married.' If after a considerable period of courtship the woman failed to become pregnant, the couple concluded that they were not meant for each other and the courtship was ended. The reputation of the woman 'was no ways tarnished'. She was as free to find another suitor 'as if ... she remained an immaculate virgin'.[25] But, as Rule has suggested, the community had its sanctions, and when Smeatons' London workmen descended on the isle, got the local girls pregnant, and tried to escape back to London and avoid all responsibility, they were threatened with stoning. Apparently so great was the pressure on them to marry that only one case of bastardy occurred.[26]

Pregnancy often appears to have determined when a female servant in husbandry left service to marry.[27] It is difficult to know whether such pregnancy was the result of an understanding already reached that they would at some time in the future marry or whether it was the result of casual sex. Certainly, service in husbandry offered opportunity for sexual experiment. How far the opportunity was taken is more difficult to prove.

Some parents of sons may even have encouraged pre-marital sex with a view to getting a girl pregnant and securing her for marriage. A chap-book of 1775 relates a conversation between Maggy and Johnny as they are returning from market:

MAGGY: ... A man that's a mind to marry a woman he'll no make her a whore.

JOHNNY: It's a' true, Maggy, but fouks may do it yence ere they be married and no hae nae ill in their minds.

MAGGY: Aho, Johnny, many a ane has been beguil'd with yence, and do it yence ye may do it aye, what an' we get a bastard and hae to suffer for the foul act of fornication?

[24] *Autobiography of Francis Place*, pp. 81–2, 73.

[25] John Smeaton, *A Narrative of the Building and a Description of the Construction of the Eddystone Lighthouse with Stone* (1791), p. 65.

[26] Margaret Baker, *Discovering the Folklore and Customs of Love and Marriage* (1974), p. 19.

[27] Ann Kussmaul, *Servants in Husbandry in Early Modern England* (1981), p. 44.

JOHNNY: Ay, but mo mither says, if I dinna get thee wi' bairn I'll no get thee; so it's the surest way of wooing.[28]

Girls also could set out to get pregnant in order to secure a marriage partner. Where parents opposed a marriage, pregnancy was sometimes seen as a way of forcing their acceptance.

The wisdom of a girl testing the virility of her lover before she ventured on marriage was the theme of a broadside ballad, 'The Husband with no courage', in which a wife warns young girls to avoid her plight:

> Seven long years I've made his bed,
> And six of 'em I've lain agin him,
> And this morn I arose with my maidenhead
> That shows he's got no courage in him,
> O dear O, O dear O,
> That shows he's got no courage in him
> O dear O

A later verse cautions others:

> Come all pretty maids where'er you be
> Don't marry a man before you try him,
> Or else you'll sing a song like me.[29]

Evidence that the advice was taken, at least in some parts of the country is seen in the practice of 'bundling'. Although in detail the practice varied from region to region, and in some was not found at all, the essentials were that once a young couple had reached a certain stage in courtship, and with the full knowledge and connivance of the parents, they began to share the same bed. There is some suggestion that 'bundling' was the final of a series of stages of courtship. First there was a meeting of the couple, arranged by their friends, when there was love-making among the straw in the barn. It was followed — but only once a week, and in carefully prescribed hours, nine o'clock to midnight — by permitted love-making in front of the fire. Only then did a couple progress to 'bundling' proper. Of the practice followed in Caenarvonshire, Anglesea, and Merionethshire in Wales there is a nineteenth-century account which

[28] *A Dialogue of Courtship between Jockey and Maggy as they were coming from the Market, Giving Excellent Instructions How to Court a Young Girl* (1775), quoted Turner, *A History of Courting*, p. 110.
[29] Lloyd, *Folk Song in England*, p. 208.

tells how 'the lover generally comes under the shadow of night, and is taken, without any kind of reserve, to the bed of his mistress'. The author continues: 'here, as is generally understood, with part of his clothes on, he breathes his tender passion, and "tells her how true he loves"; and hence it is no uncommon thing for a son and heir to be born within two or three months after the marriage ceremony'.[30] Some parents were more anxious about the outcome than others. While there is general agreement that the woman had 'her petticoats on, and the man his breeches', some mothers provided a 'courting stocking' for their daughters, consisting of a tight-fitting body stocking that covered the girl from the waist downwards. Others, in parts of both England and Wales, as an extra precaution, placed a board down the middle of the bed.[31] Whether or not these devices were seriously meant to deter the couple's love-making, the frequency with which pregnancy resulted does not seem to have been greeted with anything but acceptance. In the great majority of cases, 'bundling' was followed by marriage. 'Nor does either sex', we are told, 'feel any impropriety in the practice.'[32]

Pre-marital pregnancy was not so tolerantly regarded among the middle class, and in the early nineteenth century, as Francis Place suggested, the rejection of the practice extended down the social scale to tradesmen and artisans. When in 1762 the wife of Thomas Davy, a shoemaker and close friend of Thomas Turner's, was delivered of a child six months after their marriage, Turner was appalled. 'Two people I should the least have suspected of being guilty of so indiscreet an act.'[33] As we saw earlier, the tolerance of George Woodward did not extend to his maid, Sarah, when in May 1756 she became pregnant although her young man had 'kept her company' for three years, and they had already agreed to marry the next Michaelmas — the end of the hiring term for many servants. 'Unfortunately', writes Woodword, they 'could not stay quite so long'.[34] For Defoe, pre-marital sex was the worst of crimes. 'For a man to make a whore of the very woman who he intends and really designs to make his wife', he wrote, 'defiles his own bed, pollutes his own seed, spreads bastardy in his own race, and shows a most vitiated appetite.'[35]

[30] Lady Auguste Hamilton, *Marriage Rites, Customs and Ceremonies* (1822), p. 171.
[31] Baker, *Discovering the Folklore*, p. 14.
[32] Hamilton, *Marriage Rites*, p. 172.
[33] *Diary of Thomas Turner*, p. 244.
[34] *A Parson in the Vale of White Horse*, ed. Donald Gibson (1982), p. 83.
[35] Daniel Defoe, *Conjugal Lewdness or Matrimonal Whoredom* (1727), pp. 65–6.

The lower classes, Lawrence Stone has argued, had always been 'freer to make their own choices than the children of the rich' and experienced less intervention by parents in the choice of a marriage partner, if only because parents 'had little or nothing to give or bequeath them'.[36] When a young couple decided to marry, there was a high possibility that both would be separated from their families. Given the average age of marriage it was also quite possible that their parents were already dead. Writing of arranged marriages among the eighteenth-century French peasantry, Olwen Hufton has argued 'one cannot perhaps in any society at any time arrange marriages for people of 26 to 28 who had laboured for twelve or more years on their own behalf'.[37] The point is applicable to English lower class marriages. As Martin Ingram has concluded of the seventeenth century, parental consent 'among the propertyless' was 'little more than a formality'.[38] The authority of parents among the labouring population seems to have rarely amounted to more than advice. Often such advice was disregarded. In the ballad, 'The Mother's Advice', by John Clare, it is clear that her boy Robin will not heed her:

> ... take your own trundle − I'll sit and content me
> To think that I've told ye the best in my power
> & do as ye please since theres nought to prevent ye
> But mind that ye dont pluck a weed for a flower.[39]

Hardwicke's Marriage Act (1753) made it obligatory for all girls under the age of twenty-one to have parental consent to their marriage. It may have had some effect in preventing rich heiresses from being carried off and married clandestinely, but it does not seem to have had much of a restraining influence on others. When in the 1760s, Thomas Wright met and fell in love with a Miss Birkenhead, who was then 'about eleven or twelve years old', he resolved to wait three years and then to try and 'obtain her for a wife'. Her parents disapproved, her father refused his consent, and the young couple eloped and were married in Scotland. Her parents never forgave them.[40]

On the other hand, daughters seem to have been more under

---

[36] Lawrence Stone, *The Family, Sex and Marriage in England, 1500−1800* (1977), p. 192.
[37] R. B. Outhwaite (ed.), *Marriage and Society* (1981), p. 199.
[38] Reay (ed.), *Popular Culture in Seventeenth-Century England*, p. 135.
[39] John Clare, *The Midsummer Cushion*, ed. Anne Tibble (1978), p. 298.
[40] *Autobiography of Thomas Wright*, pp. 69−70.

parental influence than sons. Mary Wollstonecraft was of this opinion and thought 'females ... too much under the dominion of their parents', and that all too often the 'slavish' submission to their parents 'prepared' them 'for the slavery of marriage'.[41] If this was true of the middle and upper classes, it was not so apparent where daughters of the labouring class were concerned. When the mother of Elizabeth Chadd opposed her daughter's marriage to Francis Place in the early 1790s she made her position clear. 'She told me', Place writes, 'that I should not have her daughter and forbid me the house — I told her I would have her daughter in spite of her, and would come to the house whenever I pleased.' Despite her threatening her daughter with 'all manner of things unless she gave up her acquaintance' with Place, the daughter 'resolutely refused compliance'. When finally threatened with a poker by her mother, Place decided to wait no longer and the marriage took place.[42]

Among the well-to-do, the dowry a father could offer on his daughter's marriage was all important. It determined the likely social status of the husband, the extent of his estate, the size and convenience of his residence, the scale of his equipage and servants. At the very beginning of the century, Mary Astell analysed the motives behind most upper-class marriages: 'What will she bring is the first enquiry? How many acres? Or how much ready coin?'[43] We do not have much evidence of how mercenary marriages were viewed by those lower in the social hierarchy. A wittily cynical poem by Molly Leapor, the cook-maid poet, entitled 'Stephon to Celia: A Modern Love-Letter', ends:

> You've wealth enough 'tis true, but yet
> You want a Friend to manage it.
> Now such a Friend you soon might have,
> By fixing on your humble Slave;
> Not that I mind a stately House,
> Or value Mony of a Louse;
> But your Five hundred Pounds a Year,
> I wou'd secure it for my Dear.[44]

There is the milkmaid of the traditional song who receives a

[41] Mary Wollstonecraft, *Vindication of the Rights of Woman* [1792], ed. Miriam Kramnick (1978), pp. 269–70.
[42] *Autobiography of Francis Place*, pp. 102–3.
[43] Mary Astell, *Some Reflections upon Marriage* [1700], (1706), p. 12.
[44] Molly Leapor, *Poems upon Several Occasions* (1748), p. 105.

proposal of marriage from a gentleman. When however he learns she is the daughter of a farmer, he asks what is her fortune. On her answering that her 'face' is her 'fortune', he withdraws his offer. 'Then I can't marry you, my pretty maid.' But she has the last word: 'Nobody asked you, sir, she said.'[45]

How far down the social scale did the system of dowries operate? In eighteenth-century France, according to Olwen Hufton, the ability of girls to accumulate a dowry by finding work as domestic servants or as farm *servantes* was a total preoccupation for daughters of most small peasantry. On it depended whether they could get themselves a husband and set up an independent household.[46] Was it the same in this country? Some evidence suggests it was. In 1742 Mary Baylif, a servant of William Stout's, at the age of thirty-one married John Marsden, a nailer twenty-three years of age. 'He had been a jurnaman three years but had not made any improvement,' Stout writes, 'but she had above fifty pounds, which he wanted as her friends cautioned.'[47] With her money he set himself up in trade and apparently prospered. Most women married younger and would not have accumulated so large a sum. William Howitt, describing the life of daughters of agricultural labourers in his youth, saw them at ten to twelve years of age going 'to nurse at the farm-houses', and 'a little older, they go to service'. They became 'dairymaids, or housemaids', and provided they did not go off to the towns to look for places, he saw them 'scrubbing and scouring, and lending a hand in the harvest-field, till they are married to some young fellow, who takes a cottage and sets up day-labourer'.[48] What Howitt failed to emphasize is that the girl would have contributed to their ability to marry and 'take a cottage'. What distinguishes the idea of the dowry among the labouring population is that it was a joint contribution to the marriage. But Howitt described a common pattern of marriage among the children of labouring people.

Girls tended to marry straight from service, often having accumulated earnings sufficient to make an important contribution to setting up house. When in 1785 it was argued that 'in the course of a few years service, a young man can scrape up £20 or £30', towards the cost of getting married and setting up house, the writer significantly

---

[45] *The Oxford Nursery Rhyme Book*, collected and edited by Iona Opie (1955), p. 175.

[46] Olwen Hufton, 'Women, work marriage in eighteenth-century France', in Outhwaite (ed.), *Marriage and Society*, pp. 186–203.

[47] *The Autobiography of William Stout of Lancaster, 1665–1752*, ed. J. D. Marshall (1967), p. 233.

[48] William Howitt, *The Rural Life of England* [1838], (1840), p. 112.

added that the young woman would be 'possessed with nearly an equal sum'.[49] In one of Mary Leadbeater's *Cottage Dialogues*, there was an exchange between Tim and Jem. 'You are past three and twenty', said Tim to Jem, 'and should be thinking of a wife.' Jem answered that he was thinking of marrying Rose but could not marry her immediately. 'What I mean to do', he confided to Tim, 'is to work every day that a man can stand out, to save all I can ... I believe Rose will endeavour to save too; and by the time we have as much as we think will turn to any account, and can take a bit of land, we intend to marry.'[50] Elizabeth, the first wife of Francis Place, was only seventeen when she was married and was in service. Place admitted that he 'had saved no money' up to the time he started to court Elizabeth seriously. But he 'now ceased to spend more than would suffice for a bare existence'. At the time he was foreman to a leather-breeches maker and if he had continued there, 'I should have saved', he wrote, 'nearly a pound a week'.[51] So the initial sum each partner could contribute played a vital part in determining when they set up house together. Reuben and Rachel in George Crabbe's poem, 'The Parish Register',

> ... though as fond as doves
> Were yet discreet and cautious in their loves;
> Nor would attend to Cupid's wild commands,
> Till cool reflection bade them join their hands:
> When both were poor, they thought it argued ill
> Of hasty love to make them poorer still;
> Year after year with savings long-laid by,
> They bought the future dwelling's full supply;

But Crabbe was not quite prepared to let them contribute equally:

> Her frugal fancy cull'd the smaller ware,
> The weightier purchase ask'd her Reuben's care:

Only finally did they pool resources:

> Together then their last year's gain they threw,
> And lo! an auction'd bed, with curtains neat and new.

[49] Anon., *A Political Enquiry into the Consequences of Enclosing Waste Lands* (1785), p. 44.

[50] Mary Leadbeater, *Cottage Dialogues among the Irish Peasantry* (1811), p. 46.

[51] *The Autobiography of Francis Place*, pp. 97–8.

Thus both, as prudence counsell'd, wisely stay'd
And cheerful then the calls of Love obey'd.[52]

The idea of a marriage portion — that is, of the wife-to-be making some contribution to the marriage stock — lay deep in the popular imagination. While rarely in the form of a traditional dowry, even the daughters of the poorest labourers made some contribution towards the new household. Yet even when a couple had saved diligently over a period, the sum accumulated might fall far short of enabling them to establish a separate household and equip it with basic essentials. It was here that in many areas the local community intervened to supplement the dowry that the girl brought with her. It is another example of local custom providing a support system for members of the community. It served to give young and needy couples a good start in their life together. Thus, a few days before or after the wedding took place, 'the parents of the parties' would have a 'bridewain' or 'bidding'.[53]

The exact nature of the occasion varied. In Yorkshire it was customary for a wagon on which the young woman sat working at a spinning-wheel (a significant acknowledgement of her future role) to take her to visit their friends. As the wagon passed through a village, gifts and furniture would be thrown up on to it.[54] In Cumberland the 'bridewain' was announced a 'short time after a match is entered into'. At the house of the bridegroom, 'the whole neighbourhood, for several miles round, assemble[d]'. They engaged in 'the various pastimes of the country'. The collection was discreetly arranged: 'a plate or bowl is fixed in a convenient place, where each of the company contributes in proportion to his inclination and ability, and according to the degree of respect the parties are held in'. 'A worthy couple' could benefit by between £50 and £100.[55] In some areas the contribution was more specifically made to the bride. So in Glamorganshire in Wales, long before the wedding took place, a post-marriage banquet was announced to which 'all, without limitation or distinction' were invited. The banquet was simple: plain and fruit bread, butter, 'cold and toasted cheese, with ale, some warmed and sweetened'. Once guests had eaten enough, 'a plate was set down, which went round, each person giving what

---

[52] From the poem 'The Parish Register' (1807) in *The Poetical Works of George Crabbe*, ed. A. J. and R. M. Carlyle (1914), pp. 66–7.

[53] Baker, *Discovering the Folklore*, p. 47.

[54] Ibid.

[55] William Hone, *The Table Book* (1859), p. 794.

they chose, from two to five shillings; this being done, the money was given to the bride'.[56] At this particular occasion £30 was given to her — by no means insignificant when her total savings from earnings as a domestic or farm servant might well fall short of £25.

Not always was the dowry a woman contributed a sum of money. One of the most popular chap-books was *The History of Two Brothers' Misfortunes, at and after their Marriage* (1777). When, the day after the marriage of Margery to Simple Simon, she urged him to go to work, the size of her dowry was her main argument. 'I have brought you a considerable fortune,' she told him, 'forty shillings in money and a good milch cow, four fat wethers and half a dozen ewes and lambs, likewise geese, hens, and turkeys; also a sow and pigs worth more than any of your crook back generation is able to give you.' She continued, 'do you think you shall lead as leud a life now as you did before you married; but if you do, then say my name is not Margery'. Margery was described as Simple Simon's 'Cruel Wife'. She at least was under no doubt that the union was a working one. 'Now I've got you in the bands of matrimony' she warns him, 'I will make you know what it is to be married; therefore to work, you rascal.'[57] The mother in John Clare's poem who advises her son Robin to marry Kitty Fell, a woman of forty, tells him:

> Neer let the abscence of beauty prevent ye
> That birdlime that catches charm-smitten men
> Shes horses & cows boy & money in plenty
> To make a face tempting at three score & ten

And she goes on, 'love without money brings winter for life'.[58] Parents, all this suggests, were often more anxious than their offspring to conclude 'prudent' marriages, particularly where daughters were concerned. The alternative might well involve the parents in greater expense.

In 1743 Eliza Haywood offered advice to servant-maids. 'Consider my dear girls', she wrote, 'that you have no portions, and endeavour to supply the deficiencies of fortune by mind. You cannot expect to marry in such a manner as neither of you shall have occasion to work, and none but a fool will take a wife whose bread must be

[56] Ibid., p. 792.
[57] *The History of Two Brothers' Misfortunes at and after Their Marriage* (1777), pp. 4–5.
[58] Clare, *The Midsummer Cushion*, p. 298.

earned solely by his labour and who will contribute nothing towards it herself.'[59] It is advice in accord with the assumption that all women of the labouring class worked, both before and after marriage. The assumption was that the wife would support herself and even her children too. It is advice that underlines the difference between the dowries of rich and poor. The only 'portion' servant maids could contribute to a marriage was their potential earning power. The small savings they could make during service might serve as an initial contribution to setting up a household, but it would not contribute to the household's ongoing subsistence and maintenance.

The potential contribution a woman could make as wife to the subsistence of the newly created household was what mattered most. Alice Clark quotes an early seventeenth-century wedding sermon which stressed the unimportance of the dowry in the choice of a wife: 'for the worst wives may have the best portions ... a good wife tho' she bring nothing in with her, yet, thro' her Wisdom and Diligence great things come in by her'. The sermon was directed at wives with the responsibility of managing large as well as small households, for it continues, 'she brings in with her hands, for, *She putteth her hands to the wheel*. ... If she be too high to stain her Hands with bodily labour, yet she bringeth in with her Eye, for, *She overseeth the Ways of her Household*' (enphasis in original).[60] The sermon might well have been preached in the eighteenth century.

In a chap-book of 1787, *The Young Coalman's Courtship to a Creel-wife's Daughter*, although the creel-wife describes her daughter as 'a muckle lazy useless jade', she admits she can 'work at husband work, card and spin, wash ladies rooms, and scour gentlemen's bonny things'. It proved enough for the coalman. As her portion, the creel-wife explains to him, her daughter 'has baith blankets and sheets, a covering an' twa cods, a cass-bed an bowster'.[61] Even if no other work is mentioned, importance is attached to the ability of the wife-to-be to perform household tasks. When in the popular ballad Billy Boy is questioned about the fitness of the lady he is courting to be a wife, he is asked 'Can she brew and can she bake?'[62]

Lawrence Stone has argued that 'for the rural or urban smallholder,

[59] Eliza Haywood, *A Present for a Servant Maid*, (1743), as quoted by M. Dorothy George, *London Life in the Eighteenth Century* (1966), p. 171.

[60] Robert Wilkinson, *Conjugal Duty* (1607), quoted Alice Clark, *Working Life of Women in the Seventeenth Century* [1919], (1982), pp. 39–40.

[61] *The Young Coalman's Courtship to a Creel-wife's Daughter* (1787), pp. 11–12, 14.

[62] *The Oxford Nursery Rhyme Book*, p. 189.

artisan, tradesman, shopkeeper or common labourer, a wife was an economic necessity'.[63] A small farmer or cottager relied on the labour of his wife, and often of his children, to survive. It was the same with urban tradesmen. In a popular chap-book of 1783, Ned told his unmarried friend Harry how he had wanted to persuade his wife-to-be that he must marry soon. 'For a man of my trade must have both journeymen and apprentices', he argued, 'therefore I cannot well be without a wife'.[64] We have already seen how widowers often expressed their inability to manage their households without a wife and tended to remarry quickly. So long as the family economy remained healthy, the role of the wife was indeed an essential one. The only exception was where increasing prosperity led wives of large farmers and substantial tradesmen and craftsmen to withdraw. But as we have seen, with the undermining of the family economy and with the growing restriction of employment opportunities for women in agriculture and in domestic industry, attitudes to marriage changed.

Eliza Haywood's advice was not only applicable to servants. As Politica bitterly explains in *The Levellers*, her fortune was inadequate to buy her a husband of her own class, but her education had not fitted her to be the wife of 'an honest tradesman'. If he was content with 'a portion of three hundred pounds' − the extent of hers − he 'has more occasion of a wife that understands cookery and house-wifery, than one that understands dancing, and singing, and making of sweetmeats'. Even 'an honest tradesman cannot keep a wife to look upon'.[65]

If for the majority of the population 'a wife was an economic necessity', there is also some truth in Stone's other claim that 'for a woman a husband was also an economic necessity'.[66] Indeed, one might surmise that far more women outside the upper classes would have remained unmarried but for the economic disadvantages of remaining single. But if this suggests that even the marriages of the labouring poor were frequently prudent, there was still room for affection and mutual respect.

Before marrying Molly Hicks, Thomas Turner entered in his diary his reasons for thinking she would make him a good wife. 'The girl is a very industrious, sober woman and seemingly endued

---

[63] Stone, *The Family, Sex and Marriage*, p. 54.
[64] *A York Dialogue*, p. 6.
[65] 'The Levellers: Dialogue Between Two Young Ladies Concerning Matrimony etc. (1703)', *The Harleian Miscellany*, 5 (1745), p. 416.
[66] Stone, *Family, Sex and Marriage*, p. 54.

with prudence and good nature, and seems to have a very serious and sedate turn of mind.' It is not insignificant that what he records first about her is that she is 'industrious'. It makes the point that outside the upper classes it was assumed that wives worked, and it was important to choose a good worker. Only after mentioning other desirable qualities in Molly, does Turner add that she 'may perhaps one time or other have some fortune'. It might suggest that mercenary considerations were not the most important in the choice of a wife among those outside the upper classes. Molly Hicks was no beauty. Turner describes her as 'plain', but she was 'clean', which as Turner goes on to add, 'is something more than at first sight it may appear to be towards happiness'. She was not well educated but had 'good sense and a seeming desire to improve her mind'. Turner acknowledged that she had 'always behaved' to him 'with the strictest honour and good manners, her behaviour being far from the affected formality of the prude, nor on the other hand anything of that foolish fondness too often found in the more light part of the sex'. Nobody could accuse Turner of rushing into a second marriage. But in his final choice of a wife there was both admiration and respect for the qualities she possessed. Six weeks after his marriage (it is perhaps significant that his diary ends there), he acknowledged how he was happy in his choice.[67]

So the ideal in the eighteenth century, as for the seventeenth century, seems to have been 'a union which combined *both* practical viability *and* strong affection'.[68] The married life of Samuel Bownas makes the point. Bownas writes of 'having very great Comfort and Satisfaction in my married State'. But he was constantly worried over 'how we should go on in the World'. His wife comforted him by saying 'if we get but little, we will spend less; and if we have a little out of our Getting, we shall do well enough, I am not at all fearful of it, neither would I have thee'.[69] Thomas Wright, after the death of his first wife, married again in 1781. He described his second wife as 'very young, but had got a tolerable education, had very good hands, was very ingenious, solid, and sensible'. He had, he wrote, 'an agreeable partner, whom I love and esteem ... I have got a house full of fine children, and straitened circumstances; and I had a thousand times rather choose this situation, than be bound for life to a person I could not love, though in the midst of affluence

---

[67] *Diary of Thomas Turner*, pp. 319, 323.
[68] Reay (ed.), *Popular Culture in Seventeenth Century England*, p. 136.
[69] *Life and Travels of Samuel Bownas*, pp. 111–12.

and worldly prosperity'.[70] When Mary Ann Ashford married a shoemaker, they pooled their meagre resources; she tells us, 'we acted fair and candid towards each other'. Her husband was older than her and already suffering from a painful complaint. Yet despite this, 'for the sake of his wife and children', he exerted himself as 'very few men would'. The best thing about their marriage was 'that my husband and I were thoroughly agreed in everything that was essential'.[71] When Defoe came across the wife of the Derbyshire lead miner who with her family lived in a cave, he asked whether she had a good husband. 'She smiled, and said, Yes, thanked God for it, and that she was very happy in that, for he worked very hard, and they wanted for nothing that he could do for them; and two or three times made mention of how contented they were.'[72]

Many labourers and their wives, with no land of their own, were wholly dependent on the wages they could earn. In the late nineteenth century George Sturt described such a couple. The wife, Lucy Bettesworth, had from childhood been accustomed to field labour so, Sturt wrote, marriage 'brought but little change of environment . . . she continued her field work'. Her life was one 'of crushing fatigue, of stinging hardship'. Their marriage was 'a kind of dogged comradeship . . . which commonly unites the labouring man and his wife; they are partners and equals running their impecunious affairs by mutual help'.[73] Many marriages among the labouring class in the eighteenth century must have been like this. Although a condition from which romantic love was excluded, it was not without affection, mutual dependence, and respect.

The assumption that women both before and after marriage invariably worked was by the end of the eighteenth century no longer valid. Changes in agriculture and industry were making it less possible for women to contribute significantly to the family budget. There was in consequence less 'economic sharing and mutual co-operation in work'.[74] An increasing physical separation of the work of men and women made rarer those marriages of 'dogged comradeship'. Keith Snell has drawn attention to the constantly recurring theme in Hardy's novels of 'a search for the conditions in which a

[70] *Autobiography of Thomas Wright*, pp. 147–8, 145.
[71] *The Life of a Licensed Victualler's Daughter*, pp. 62, 70, 71.
[72] Daniel Defoe, *A Tour through England and Wales*, 2 vols [1724–7], Everyman's edn (1948), vol. ii, p. 163.
[73] George Sturt, *Lucy Bettesworth*, 1913, pp. 13, 23, I have been unable to locate the source of the final words as quoted by John R. Gillis, *For Better, For Worse*, (1985), p. 114.
[74] Keith Snell, *Annals of the Labouring Poor* (1985), p. 308.

loving relationship could develop, and the consequent stress on the "falsity" of marriage where such co-operation in work was absent'.[75] When considering how the nature of the married relationship was affected by industrialization, it is an idea worth pondering.

[75] Ibid., p. 307.

11

Clarity and Obscurity in the Law Relating to Wives, Property, and Marriage

> Matrimony to a woman [is] worse than excommunication in depriving her of the benefit of the law.
>
> Widow Blackmore in Wycherley's play, *The Plain Dealer* (1677)

In the eighteenth century, the legal position of wives was clearly defined. 'By marriage', wrote Blackstone in 1753, 'the husband and wife are one person in law: that is, the very being, or legal existence of the woman is suspended during the marriage, or at least is incorporated and consolidated into that of the husband.'[1] So when a woman married, she was placed, along with underage children, 'in the same legal category as wards, lunatics, idiots and outlaws'.[2] By marriage a woman became a *feme covert*, that is to say 'under the protection and influence of her husband, her *baron* or lord'.[3] A 1732 treatise on the law as it affected wives added that 'their desires are subject to their husbands', for on good biblical authority, 'a Man shall forsake Father and Mother to stick to his Wife'.[4] A footnote by Edward Christian to the 1793 edition of Blackstone apologized for the use of the word 'baron' as 'it attributes to the husband not a very courteous superiority'.[5] But lest any reader should interpret it too lightly as an 'unmeaning technical phrase', he went on to explain that, in the eye of the law, 'if the baron kills his feme it is the same as if he had killed a stranger, or any other person, but if the feme kills her baron, it is regarded by the laws as

---

[1] Sir William Blackstone, *Commentaries on the Laws of England in Four Books* [1753] 4 vols (1793), vol. i, p. 441.
[2] Janelle Greenberg, 'The legal status of the English woman in early eighteenth-century common law and equity', *Studies in Eighteenth Century Culture*, 4 (1975), 171–181.
[3] Blackstone, *Commentaries*, vol. i, p. 441.
[4] *A Treatise of Feme Covert: or, The Lady's Law* (1732), Preface.
[5] Blackstone, *Commentaries*, vol. i, p. 445 n. 23.

a much more attrocious crime; as she not only breaks through the restraints of humanity and conjugal affection, but throws off all subjection to the authority of her husband'. The crime of a wife who killed her husband was 'a species of treason, and condemned her to the same punishment as if she had killed the King'.[6] Until 1790 that punishment was to be drawn to the place of execution, and there burned. For men the punishment for high treason was 'to be hanged, cut down alive, have the bowels taken out, and the body quartered'.[7] For every other species of treason the punishment was less severe for male offenders 'being only to be drawn and hanged by the neck till dead'. Blackstone's explanation for the different punishment given to women for the crime of high treason was that 'the decency due to the sex forbids the exposing and publicly mangling their bodies'. The mind boggles at the more 'decent' alternative, which as Blackstone so knowingly assures us, 'is to the full as terrible to sensation as the other'.[8] 'For several generations', we are told, 'it had become the invariable custom to delay the actual burning until after death had been produced by strangulation.'[9] After 1790 women were no longer burnt but 'drawn to the place of execution and there ... hanged by the neck till dead'.[10]

The main purpose of the law as far as it concerned wives was to define the property rights that must be surrendered by them on marriage. The personal property of the wife, Blackstone wrote, 'becomes absolutely her husband's which at his death he may leave entirely away from her'.[11] If the husband at the time of marriage had outstanding debts, they were a first charge on the personal property his wife brought him. It is true that the husband had responsibility for paying any of his wife's debts contracted before marriage. But it was not really such an equal arrangement for, as one writer explained, men had 'many Ways of concealing and misrepresenting their Circumstances which Women have not'.[12] Any personal property acquired by the wife during marriage, unless

[6] Ibid.
[7] Richard Burn, *The Justice of the Peace and Parish Officer*, 3 vols. (1762), vol. iii, p. 478.
[8] Blackstone, *Commentaries*, vol. iv, p. 92.
[9] Courtney Standhope Kennedy, *The Effects of Marriage on Property and the Wife's Legal Capacity* (1879), quoted R. Langley and R. Levy, *Wife Beating: The Silent Crisis* (1977), p. 49.
[10] Blackstone, *Commentaries*, vol. iv, p. 92 n. 10.
[11] Ibid., vol. i, p. 445 n. 23.
[12] *The Hardships of the English Law in Relation to Wives* (1735), p. 36.

it was specified that the 'gift was to her separate use', passed automatically into her husband's hands.[13] On her marriage the husband was entitled to the rent and any profits from land which she owned. If he had a child and outlived his wife, he retained such land, becoming a tenant for life. A character from Mary Wollstonecraft's novel *The Wrongs of Woman* was to comment; 'a wife being as much a man's property as his horse, or his ass, she has nothing she can call her own. He may use any means to get at what the law considers as his, the moment his wife is in possession of it.'[14] In consequence of this extinguishing of a woman's legal existence on marriage, no contract or covenant recognized by law could be concluded between husband and wife, for to do so would be for a husband 'to covenant with himself'.[15] If a wife was 'injured in her person or property' she was unable to bring any action for redress without her husband's agreement, and such action must be brought in his name as well as her own.[16] A wife could neither sue nor be sued.

The wife possessed no legal power in relation to her children but was entitled only to 'reverence and respect'; thus, this total control of a husband over his children, 'this empire', as Blackstone called it, could continue even after his death, 'for he may by his will appoint a guardian to his children'.[17]

The legal rights of the head of the household over children, apprentices, servants, and wives included that of 'moderate correction'. For 'as he was to answer for her misbehaviour the law thought it reasonable to intrust him with this power of restraining her by domestic chastisement'. This right, however, Blackstone assured his readers, 'was confined within reasonable bounds and the husband was prohibited from using any violence to his wife'.[18] Doubts were expressed about the legality of such chastisement after the Restoration. Sir Matthew Hale held that 'moderate correction' meant not a 'beating but only an admonition', but many jurists throughout the eighteenth century upheld the right of a husband to beat his wife provided he did not do it 'outrageously'.[19] Blackstone

[13] Greenberg, 'The legal status of the English woman', p. 174.

[14] Mary Wollstonecraft, *The Wrongs of Woman: Or, Maria, a Fragment*, from *Mary and the Wrongs of Woman*, ed. Gary Kelly (1980), p. 177.

[15] Blackstone, *Commentaries*, vol. i, p. 442.

[16] Ibid., pp. 442–3.

[17] Ibid., pp. 452–3.

[18] Ibid., p. 444.

[19] Langley and Levy, *Wife Beating*, p. 48.

was to admit that the legal questioning of the practice had not prevented wife-beating from continuing among 'the lower rank of people', and the courts continued 'to permit a husband to restrain a wife of her liberty, in case of any gross misbehaviour'.[20] But who but the husband was to determine that such a breach of good behaviour had been committed? And although the law forbidding husbands and wives to testify against each other was suspended in the event of the husband committing any offence against the person of his wife, who was to decide that the husband had committed such an offence? Against his repeated denials, and in the unlikely presence of any witnesses, a woman would have to be a strong character to persist in confronting her husband in a court. Not many women in the eighteenth century were prepared to make such a stand.

According to Daniel Defoe, who wanted local JPs to be empowered to punish the worst culprits, the practice of wife-beating was so common among the 'meaner sort of people, that to hear a woman cry murther now, scarce gives any alarm'.[21] Mary Rice, who had been a servant in Banbury, married a saddler. When he beat her she left him, went to London, and managed to earn a meagre living.[22] As late as 1777, an anonymous author still thought it of relevance to point out that 'a wife cannot recover damages for the beating of her husband, as she hath no separate interest in anything during her couverture'.[23] On the other hand, if someone other than her husband assaulted a married woman, her husband could sue for damages. 'If the Husband is thereby deprived of her Conversation', one anonymous author was to write, 'he alone may commence an Action of Trespass.'[24]

It was only in exceptional circumstances that wife-beating in the upper classes came to light. That it was confined to the lower classes seems doubtful. Among the poor who often lived in very close proximity to neighbours, wife-beating must have been far more difficult to conceal than among the upper classes. Early in the century a Mr Veezey was tried at the Old Bailey after his wife had committed suicide by throwing herself out of a window. The court found that he had confined his wife to a garret for some years 'without Fire, proper cloathing, or any of the Comforts of Life', and also that he had 'frequently Horse-whipt her'. Despite the proof of

---

[20] Blackstone, *Commentaries*, vol. i, p. 444.
[21] Daniel Defoe, *The Great Law of Subordination Consider'd* (1724), pp. 6–7.
[22] Margaret Spufford, *The Great Reclothing of Rural England* (1984), p. 43.
[23] Anon., *The Laws Respecting Women* (1777), p. 59.
[24] *A Treatise of Feme Covert*, p. 85

his guilt the husband was acquitted.[25] In an anonymous poem of 1739 urging Clarinda to remain single, she is reminded of some of the matrimonial habits of the husbands of her friends:

> Sly Charus bangs his Wife, and doth profess,
> 'Tis on mere Principles of Godliness.
> Cites Scripture-Texts to prove that Blows are good,
> To cure the vicious Sallies of the Blood;
> As necessary for his Wife as Food.[26]

Wife-beating among the labouring class, it is suggested, was often occasioned by hard times. At such times 'the failure of either spouse to live up to his or her prescribed duties', wrote John Gillis, 'might spark off violence', and he instanced a wife's failure to have a meal prepared and ready on the return of her husband at night.[27] When Francis Place was out of work for eight months in the early 1790s, his 'temper was bad'; far from giving his wife encouragement and support in such difficult times, he 'used at times to give way to passion and increase her ... misery'.[28] Not always was there this excuse. In a case that came before William Hunt in 1746, a warrant was issued against the husband, a yeoman, 'for assaulting, beating and abusing Jane Naish, his said wife, without giving him any sort of provocation'.[29] As a Bedfordshire justice wrote of a case of wife-beating in 1786 'the man seems to have a savage stupid idea that he may beat his wife as much as he pleases, provided he does not kill her'. The husband was sent to gaol.[30]

It is true that legal safeguards existed which, at least in theory, offered a woman 'more legal rights than are generally acknowledged'. For example, in equity, the body of law administered by the lord chancellor in the Court of Chancery, there lay the means of mitigating, to some extent, the disabilities women suffered under common law. By means of marriage settlements concluded before marriage, a woman could in theory retain 'to her own separate use and enjoyment' all or some control over her estate. Again, before marriage, she could, by conveying lands to trustees, retain the rents and

---

[25] *The Hardships of the English Law*, pp. 8–9.
[26] *Matrimony; or Good Advice to the Ladies to keep Single* (1739), p. 4.
[27] J. R. Gillis, *For Better, For Worse* (1986), p. 185.
[28] *The Autobiography of Francis Place, 1771–1854*, ed. Mary Thale (1972), p. 115.
[29] *The Justicing Notebook of William Hunt, 1744–1749*, ed. Elizabeth Crittall, Wiltshire Record Society, vol. xxxvii (1981), p. 55.
[30] *Bedfordshire County Records*, ed. W. J. Hardy and W. Page (1907), p. 59.

profits 'to her sole and separate use'.[31] Chancery could also confirm her right to retain to her separate use any bequest of personal estate received from a relative. But any woman who took advantage of such means to protect her interests would have needed a close familiarity with the law. 'If we reflect how extremely ignorant all young Women are as to points in Law, and how their Education and way of Life shuts them out from the knowledge of their true interest in almost all things,' wrote an anonymous author in 1735, 'we shall find that their Trust and Confidence in the Man they love, and Inability to make use of the Proper Means to guard against his Falsehood, leave few in a Condition to make use of that Precaution.'[32] In any case most women lacked the independent means to embark on legal procedures, which were usually highly expensive. Some women of the upper and middle classes may have managed to evade the Law's 'rigour by contracting themselves out of it'.[33] But very few women can have been in a position to take real advantage of such legal safeguards.

But how did the law relating to wives affect labouring women? As very few of them brought more than a bare minimum of personal property to the marriage, one might conclude that the law was largely irrelevant to their experience. At the end of the century, Eden claimed that the law that gave a husband the right to his wife's earnings, actually discouraged married women from working, and that this was 'one of the principal causes why they contribute so little to the fund which is to maintain a family'.[34] A little evidence exists to support such a claim. There is the case of the 'modest agreeable Gentlewoman' who married a tradesman who promptly exhausted their entire fortune and left his wife to join the army. She 'desired his permission to serve a Lady of Quality, by which Means she hoped to be able to provide for their two Children'. But, we are told, 'he refused it, unless he might have leave to visit her when he pleased; and the Wages which she should earn being his not hers, unless it was paid to him he might have sued the Person, who should entertain her'. The result was that 'this effectually barred the Doors against her as a Servant'.[35] But in this case virtual desertion of the wife complicated the issue. Without more evidence

---

[31] Greenberg, 'The legal status of the English woman', pp. 172, 176.
[32] *The Hardships of the English Law*, pp. 32–3.
[33] C. S. Kenny, *The History of the Law of England as to the Effects of Marriage on Property and on the Wife's Legal Capacity* (1879), p. 15.
[34] F. M. Eden, *The State of the Poor*, 3 vols (1797), vol. i, p. 625.
[35] *The Hardships of the English Law*, pp. 9–10.

it is difficult to decide whether Eden had a case, but he may well have arrived at his conclusion after seeing the increasing incidence of unemployment among women in the countryside at the end of the century. Whether that unemployment had anything to do with the state of the law relating to married women's earnings seems extremely doubtful. Eden went on to argue that the whole purpose of Female Friendly Societies, which multiplied towards the end of the century and enabled women to make provision for emergencies such as childbirth and the expenses of their lying-in periods, was jeopardized by this right of husbands.[36] Again, conclusive evidence is lacking. But if husband and wife separated, there is every reason for thinking the woman lost out as a result of the state of the law. So a landlady in a late eighteenth-century novel complained that after breaking with her husband he 'signed an execution on my very goods, bought with the money I worked so hard to get'.[37] In a similar position in real life, Charlotte Charke opened a shop but was obsessed by the fear that her husband 'had a right to make bold with anything that was mine'. She was, she said, 'horribly puzzled for the means of securing my effects from the power of my husband'.[38]

The legal rights of women in marriage may have been obscure in some particulars — the actual legal safeguards that existed by equity, for example — but in general they were carefully defined. As it was a law mainly concerned with property rights, it was more relevant to upper class wives than to those of the labouring classes. But if the legal rights of women in marriage were relatively clear, what actually constituted marriage was not. In the previous chapter I have talked of marriage as though it were a homogeneous state through which the vast majority of women passed. Nothing could be further from the truth. Marriage forms, and the possible alternatives to a church marriage, covered a wide variety of practices.

In the second half of the seventeenth century, for a number of reasons, church marriage seems to have fallen from favour. Throughout the first half of the eighteenth century, church marriage continued to be the exception rather than the rule. Marriage law, at least until Hardwicke's Act of 1753, was in such a confused and confusing state that many people were genuinely uncertain about the law and of what actually constituted a valid and indissoluble union.

---

[36] Eden, *State of the Poor*, vol. i, p. 630.
[37] Wollstonecraft, *The Wrongs of Woman*, p. 177.
[38] Charlotte Charke, *A Narrative of the Life of Mrs. Charlotte Charke* (1755), pp. 75–6.

The confusion had arisen as a result of 'three overlapping, occasionally hostile, but generally exclusive jurisdictions – the Church, the State and custom enforced by the local community'.[39] Church canons laid down the requirements of a regular and legally valid marriage. It must be the result of the free consent of both parties. 'A promise of Matrimony', said a treatise on Lady's Law of 1732, 'must be mutual'.[40] The age of consent was twelve for a girl and fourteen for a boy. There had to be no known legal impediments to the union, such as consanguinity. Notice of the ceremony had to be publicized well in advance by calling banns three times in the parish church or by obtaining an ecclesiastical licence. The wedding service had to be held between agreed times in one of the couple's local parish church and follow the service laid down in the Book of Common Prayer, and the marriage had to be recorded in the parish register before witnesses. Failure to observe any of these requirements made the marriage 'irregular' or 'clandestine', but so long as there had been free consent to the marriage by both partners and there were no impediments to that marriage, such unions were regarded by the church as valid and indissoluble.

Until 1640 the surveillance of the ecclesiastical authorities and the disciplining of those hauled before the church courts for infringement of canon law made such irregular unions subject to a degree of risk. Indeed, at least in theory, full civil rights could be withheld from an irregularly married couple until a properly solemnized ceremony had taken place. With the abolition of the church courts and the prerogative courts, the disciplining organs of church and state, such surveillance ceased. With the Marriage Act of 1653 and the introduction of civil marriage, the responsibility for the solemnization and recording of a marriage was placed firmly in the hands of magistrates and no longer of the clergy. The Restoration ended this experiment, but the church's control over marriage had been fundamentally undermined.

Meanwhile, common law was experiencing difficulties. In cases involving inheritance of property – questions of a widow's right to dower, for example – lawyers had to prove that a marriage had occurred. The most infallible proof was to demonstrate that a church wedding had been conducted by a member of the clergy and had been duly certified and recorded. But in the frequent absence of all of these, they settled for evidence only that a marriage

[39] G. R. Quaife, *Wanton Wenches and Wayward Wives* (1979), p. 38.
[40] *A Treatise of Feme Covert*, p. 27.

solemnized by a member of the clergy had been performed. Clandestine marriage — performed by a minister but often not in a church or chapel, not publicized either by banns or the obtaining of a licence — satisfied the requirements of common law. As one writer said, 'by calling attention to the lawless marriages, and stirring the question of their legality, the ecclesiastical chiefs had made the populace dangerously wise'. They had discovered 'that there was a considerable difference between the law of the Church and the law of the land'; whatever the canons required, 'a marriage might be solemnized at night, and in a secular building, and even without the assistance of a clergyman, and yet be as valid a union, for all civil purposes, as any wedding performed with banns or licence by half-a-dozen bishops in a cathedral'.[41]

We now know that 'Fleet' marriages, as clandestine marriages performed within the Fleet prison or its rules were known, accounted for between 200,000 and 300,000 marriages in London between 1694 and 1754 — and those were only the ones recorded.[42] A substantial number almost certainly were not. Just because the main opposition to such marriages came from the upper classes, it has sometimes been assumed that Fleet marriages were only resorted to by those of the upper class anxious to marry in haste to avoid parental obstruction, or in order to conclude a match between a wealthy heiress and her footman. In fact, those who resorted to such marriages were mainly the lower classes: it is estimated that over 6,000 took place in the Fleet in 1740 alone.[43] Such numbers suggest it was the method of marriage most favoured by the London labouring class. Many artisans as well as sailors home on short leave resorted to Fleet marriages. Some have gone further in claiming that 'regular marriage in the London of the first half of the eighteenth century was a minority practice'.[44] One nineteenth-century writer said that clandestine marriage was 'almost universal amongst the very poor, very general in the lower of the middle classes, frequent in the higher middle grades, and not uncommon amongst the rich and aristocratic'.[45] Nor were clandestine marriages confined to the Fleet or to London. All over the country there were places where

---

[41] John Cordy Jeaffreson, *Brides and Bridals*, 2 vols (1872), vol. ii, p. 130.

[42] Roger Lee Brown, 'The Rise and Fall of Fleet Marriages', in R. B. Outhwaite (ed.), *Marriage and Society* (1981), p. 117.

[43] Ibid., p. 123.

[44] R. B. Outhwaite (ed.), *Marriage and Society* (1981), p. 13.

[45] Jeaffreson, *Brides and Bridals*, vol. ii, p. 173.

such marriages were performed. It was not difficult to find clergymen anxious to supplement their inadequate livings in this way.

Then again, there were marriages which satisfied none of the requirements demanded by the church except that no kind of impediment existed and that both parties fully consented. Such marriages could result from a mere declaration of intent by the couple. A woman might find herself irrevocably committed to a marriage merely through rashly uttering the four words, 'I will marry thee'. As one writer warned 'the ecclesiastical law deems even bare encouragement, and particularly of behaviour towards a man, binding on the part of a woman'.[46] The nature of this betrothal (or spousals) varied between a declaration of present (*per verba de praesenti*) or future (*per verba de futuro*) intent. Where a promise was made in the present tense, the marriage was forthwith considered binding. Indeed, if there were witnesses to such a promise being made, it was extremely difficult to get out of it. There was, said Jeaffreson, 'no sinless alternative to marrying one another or remaining celibates so long as they both lived'.[47] A case of 'nonperformance of a marriage contract' came before the Norfolk County Sessions in 1764. It was brought by a young woman against a tradesman. 'After a fair and impartial trial', the newspaper report recorded, 'the defendant was cast in 300 guineas damages.'[48] If the espousal was a promise of future intent, it was enforceable only if consummated. But while by mutual consent an espousal could be terminated forthwith, it could prove difficult if either of the partners was reluctant to agree to the termination. Even if legally regarded as a future promise, 'great Regard is had to the Apprehension and Intentions of the Parties', insisted Salmon, 'for as it is the Consent only which makes the Marriage, and the Vulgar frequently confound the Tenses, and take the future for the present; where it plainly appears they meant present Marriage, it shall be so esteemed'.[49] So if for some people spousals were seen only as a preliminary to marriage, for others they constituted marriage itself and were far more important to them than any more formal wedding ceremony. Some couples considered a promise *de futuro* as a kind of legal

[46] *Considerations on the Causes of the Present Stagnation of Matrimony, etc.* (1772), p. 32.

[47] Jeaffreson, *Brides and Bridals*, vol. i, p. 85.

[48] *Selections from Norwich Newspapers, 1760–1790*, ed. E. A. Goodwyn (1972), p. 416.

[49] Thomas Salmon, *A Critical Essay Concerning Marriage* (1704), p. 182.

sanction to sexual intercourse. For them, whatever the law said, marriage had begun.

Under common law, women could not claim dower unless 'endowed at the church door'.[50] Indeed spousals were described as 'something less than marriage' for this reason, and because spousals 'failed to confer ... certain other rights pertaining to the fully married woman'.[51] As Salmon had said early in the century of those 'betroth'd' or 'espous'd', they were not 'so far Man and Wife, as to give either Party any Interest or Property in the other's Lands or Goods'.[52] 'For the property-owning classes — including some middling groups,' Martin Ingram has written, 'this was a powerful incentive in favour of church marriage.'[53] But it may also explain why many widows favoured a common law form of union. It gave them all the advantages of marriage without any threat to their property from their spouses. Other women who chose such a form of marriage might have to face the absence of 'dower' — of less importance perhaps to those whose husbands were without landed estates — but at least they retained any property they had on marriage.

There were a great variety of informal ceremonies which constituted spousals. The betrothal ceremony, or 'handfast', varied from region to region, but in many cases it was regarded as constituting as binding a union as any church marriage. In the south-west, Wales, and the borders of Scotland the mere joining of hands was sufficient. In parts of Wales, broomstick weddings — where the young couple by jumping over a broom placed aslant the door and avoiding touching it were considered as forthwith man and wife — persisted. In the late seventeenth century such common-law type marriages probably accounted for the majority.[54] Despite Hardwicke's Act of 1753 and the pressures that were being brought on poor couples to marry, such liaisons seem to have persisted well into the nineteenth century. From the early eighteenth century there was increasing pressure to reform the marriage law. Contemporaries were under no doubt that the move came from the upper classes. 'Not until the fashion of Fleet marriages began to spread upwards into fashionable society', it has been said, 'was there any active move for

[50] Barry Reay (ed.), *Popular Culture in Seventeenth Century England* (1985), p. 142.
[51] Jeaffreson, *Brides and Bridals*, vol. i, p. 63.
[52] Salmon, *A Critical Essay*, p. 180.
[53] Reay (ed.), *Popular Culture in Seventeenth-Century England*, p. 142.
[54] See for example Outhwaite (ed.), *Marriage and Society*, p. 12 and the chapter on Fleet marriages; John Gillis, 'Married but not churched: plebeian sexual relations and marital nonconformity in eighteenth-century Britain', Special Issue of *Eighteenth-Century Life*, 9/3 (1985), pp. 32–4; Samuel Menefee, *Wives for Sale* (1981), p. 8.

suppression.'[55] As a writer in the nineteenth century was to add, 'good society deemed the Fleet Weddings a sufficiently decent kind of matrimony for tradesfolk and fustian-wearing rabble'.[56] Charles Knight described the Act as 'brought in for the especial benefit of the titled classes, enabling them to close their order almost hermetically, against the approaches of any less privileged persons as wooers of their children'. It was 'a kind of new game law to prevent poaching on their preserves'.[57] In this objective the Act may have been successful. Parental consent was now needed before any girl under twenty-one could marry. Young heiresses could no longer be kidnapped from boarding schools and married off in haste. The Act made invalid any marriage not celebrated in the parish church by an ordained minister of the Church of England after the calling of banns on three successive Sundays or the obtaining of an expensive licence. As one critic of the Act wrote, 'the expense of being married will be so great that few of the lower class of people can afford it'.[58] Such marriages were to be duly witnessed and recorded. No wonder that Maria Brown's suitor thought mutual consent enough and that 'all the rest' was 'mere ceremony'. As he told her 'there are so many obstacles now to surmount and so many disagreeable steps to be taken, since the marriage-act had passed'.[59] So in its aim of doing away with all common-law and irregular marriage, and of what were seen as their evil consequences, almost certainly the Act was less successful.

Many were worried by the continuance of such practices. It is very difficult to disentangle the motives behind the attempts by individuals and charitable institutions to promote marriage. They may have been concerned as many of them claimed with what they saw as the threat to the population if the labouring poor – the source, it was argued of population increase – failed to marry and procreate. Blackstone was among those who criticized Hardwicke's Act for imposing 'restraints upon marriage, especially among the lower class' that were 'detrimental to the public, by hindering the increase of people'.[60] Many were concerned with the extent of pre-marital pregnancy. But what all the encouragements to marriage

[55] E. S. Turner, *History and Courting* (1954), p. 97.
[56] Jeaffreson, *Brides and Bridals*, vol. ii, p. 180.
[57] Turner, *History of Courting*, p. 97.
[58] Jeaffreson, *Brides and Bridals*, vol. ii, p. 185 n., quoting Alexander Keith.
[59] Anon., *Genuine Memoirs of the Celebrated Miss Maria Brown*, 2 vols (1766), vol. i, pp. 97–8.
[60] Blackstone, *Commentaries*, vol. i, p. 437.

insist on as a condition, is *church* marriage. 'Benevolent squires and Matrons' attempted to promote marriage among the labouring class by offering poor girls marriage portions. So in 1761, some ladies of Gloucester, announced a 'nuptial bounty' for poor girls of £5 on the occasion of their wedding (presumably, it had to be in church to qualify), and a further £5 a year later 'if she completed her first year of married life without losing her good reputation'.[61] Did her 'good reputation' include becoming pregnant, but not before nine and a half months after marriage? We are not told.

In 1772, John Perram's will included a bequest granting 'a marriage portion of £21 to any parishioner of All Saints Church, Newmarket, who announced six weeks before Easter their intentions of Marrying on the Thursday of Easter week'. Neither party was to be under twenty or over twenty-five, or to be 'worth more than £20'.[62] Between 1772 and 1837 the money was claimed only twenty times, which might suggest it was not just the cost that deterred many from church marriages. In a Norwich newspaper of 1780 there was a letter about a scheme proposed by a Mr P. as a consequence of his 'having observed with great concern, that many of the young women of his parish when they come to be married are already big with child, and wishing to put a stop to a practice offensive to decency and morality and often destructive to their own happiness'. His scheme was to promise 'every young woman of sober behaviour belonging to the Parish who shall hereafter be married in this Church, while under the age of twenty-five' certain financial encouragements on the birth of their first child 'if that shall happen nine months after the day of the marriage'. The encouragements consisted of '10s. for ye Christening Dinner and also a silver plate of 10s. value to be worn upon her breast every Sunday when she came to church with this inscription − "The Reward of Chastity".'[63] Alas, it is not recorded how many found such an offer irresistible.

'One of the reasons that they have for marrying secretly, as they generally do in England,' wrote Henri Misson, 'is, that thereby they avoid a great deal of expense and trouble.'[64] Such marriages avoided the cost of calling the banns, often that of a marriage licence, the

[61] Jeaffreson, *Brides and Bridals*, vol. ii, pp. 89–90.

[62] Margaret Baker, *Discovering the Folklore and Customs of Love and Marriage* (1974), p. 23.

[63] *Selections from Norwich Newspapers*, p. 24.

[64] Henri Misson, *Memoirs and Observations in His Travels over England*, trans. by Mr Ozell (1719), p. 351.

duty payable on it, and the whole charge of a ceremony and lavish entertainment that was the expected accompaniment of any public wedding. If the labouring class went through any form of marriage ceremony they chose the cheapest. Even where public weddings were the rule (as was the case in Wales, according to Catherine Hutton), the ceremony and the celebration was kept simple – and cheap. At a marriage at Llanbeblae, the parish church of Caernarvon, at the end of the century, a sailor was married to the daughter of a shoemaker. The actual ceremony cost four shillings. Catherine Hutton described how 'when the clergyman reached a certain part of the service, he stopped, and the sailor stepped forward' and put the money on his book. The parson 'gave one of them to his clerk and pocketed the other three'. The wedding party was held at a public house where 'all who came (and the more the better) dined, drank tea, and danced if they chose to do so'. Catherine Hutton explains how, far from such a celebration being 'ruinously expensive', it was 'just the reverse. Every guest pays a shilling, at least for dinner, and sixpence for tea, and many give more, even to half-crowns.' In this way a considerable sum was collected. If the father of the bride could afford it he paid the expense of the party and the sum collected was regarded as the bride's portion, but if not the bride paid the bill and kept the residue. It helped the young couple towards the cost of setting up house.[65]

Calling the banns was bitterly resented by many of the labouring class. It was, they thought, a way of keeping them under surveillance, and their marriages under control. 'To proclaim bans [*sic*] is a thing no body now cares to have done,' wrote Misson early in the century, 'Very few are willing to have their Affairs declar'd to all the world in a public Place, when for a Guinea they may do it Snug, and without Noise.'[66] Robert Nugent held in the House of Commons that proclamation of banns 'shocks the modesty of a young girl to have it proclaimed through the parish that she is going to be married'.[67] As Maria Brown's suitor claimed, 'it is only putting money in the priest's pocket, to publish three weeks before hand to all the parish, that on such a night a girl is to lose her virginity'.[68]

In the chap book, *A York Dialogue*, Ned tells how his wife-to-be, a chambermaid, had told him 'she was a gentlewoman born, and

---

[65] *Reminiscences of a Gentlewoman of the Last Century: Letters of Catherine Hutton*, ed. Catherine Hutton Beale (1891), p. 125.
[66] Misson, *Memoirs and Observations*, p. 183.
[67] Turner, *History of Courting*, p. 97.
[68] *Genuine Memoirs of the Celebrated Miss Maria Brown*, 2 vols (1766), pp. 97–8.

did not care to be asked in church: for she said, there was nobody asked in church but cook-maids and kitchen-maids'. 'So', Ned tells his friend, 'it cost me about twenty shillings for a licence.'[69] Sometimes, it seems banns were called without consulting the woman named. At Framlingham in Suffolk, this was the experience of Hannah Larter, 'the best housemaid in Suffolk . . . on the strength of a little innocent flirtation'. Reuben Gedney, 'a saucy, tippling ne'er-do-well instructed the parish clerk to have her asked in Church'. When the banns were called, she cried out 'I forbid the banns!', and on being asked what was her objection she answered: 'Because I am Hannah Larter, and Reuben Gedney is an impudent young man who has not so much as bordered [courted] with me.'[70]

Certainly the desire to avoid publicity was one reason why secret marriages were preferred. There was also the possibility that many of the labouring class realized that there were advantages in making it difficult to prove, or disprove, that a marriage had ever taken place. In secret marriages the couple concerned would withhold their surnames to make the marriage more difficult to trace. So in the Lincoln's Inn Register of Marriages for 1709 there is recorded the marriage of the 'first couple brought by one that keeps a chandlers shop backside Clem: They came from the City and went to Oxford.'[71]

If what constituted marriage in the eighteenth century was ill defined so that the entry into an indissoluble union could occur by 'mutual consent', almost without the woman being aware of it, legal exit for a woman from marriage was virtually impossible. Except by proving a marriage invalid, no divorce was possible. All that either spouse could obtain under canon law was a legal separation, a *mensa et thoro*, on the grounds that one partner was guilty of 'adultery, cruelty or heresy and apostasy'. After the Restoration, divorce was still not obtainable under ecclesiastical law but there was the possibility of divorce through a private Act of Parliament. That this means of exit from a marriage was conceived in anticipation of a husband wishing to divorce his wife rather than vice versa is clear. Early in the seventeenth century, Milton, in recommending divorce on the grounds of incompatibility, had spoken of marriage as 'the Solace and Delight of Man' and had argued that, for the husband, nothing could be worse than when 'the Blessing of

[69] *A York Dialogue*, p. 12.
[70] Jeaffreson, *Brides and Bridals*, vol. i, pp. 131–2.
[71] Ibid., vol. ii, p. 137n.

Matrimony' was changed into a 'drooping and disconsolate House-hold Captivity, without Refuge or Redemption'.[72] Similarly, early in the eighteenth century, Salmon had explained how for all the wariness with which marriages were entered into, 'it may yet befall a discreet Man to be mistaken in his Choice, the Soberest and best governed Men are least practised in these Affairs'.[73] There was no hint that a woman might also find herself mistaken in her choice.

The main purpose behind a divorce obtained by private Act of Parliament was the 'safe-guarding inheritance of property and family succession endangered by a *wife's* adultery' (my emphasis).[74] Indeed there seems to have been little expectation of a wife using the same process to obtain a divorce from her husband. For a husband the grounds necessary for securing a divorce were quite clear: the wife's adultery. How else was the descent of property to be secured? For a wife wishing to divorce her husband, the grounds were not only more complicated but there was no certain definition of what they included. Adultery by itself was not sufficient. To it had to be joined other grounds such as bigamy, rape, incest, or sodomy. To embark on the framing and passing of such an Act was an expensive and lengthy process. In 1850 the cost was said to be between £700 and £800.[75] It was thus a means of divorce for the wealthy and not for the poor. But it was also a means open to men rather than women: for most married women there was no way of obtaining a divorce. In a century and a half there were only four cases in which a private Act was passed at the instigation of a wife. Only in 1801 was a successful suit brought by a woman. In this situation, with no means of exit from marriages all too easily concluded, the only solution for the vast majority of the population was to take the law into their own hands, by desertion, bigamy, and wife sale. How did these affect women?

Wives were frequently deserted and left totally unprovided for. Take the mother of Francis Place, whose husband was both drunkard and gambler: she was twice deserted by him. The first time when 'he lost every thing he had in the world, even the furniture of his house', he went off, Place related, 'without the knowledge of my mother and she was turned into the Street'. He was absent for several months. Meanwhile she 'took a lodging and maintained

[72] Salmon, *A Critical Essay*, p. 123.
[73] Ibid., p. 127.
[74] O. R. McGregor, *Divorce in England* (1957), p. 11.
[75] Ibid., p. 17.

herself by needlework'. The second time he disappeared for a year. He gambled away the lease of his house so that she was left with one child to support, no home, and only a little furniture. Again, Place tells us, 'she was ... brought to great distress'.[76] There was little a wife could do in these circumstances except seek work to maintain herself. Not always was this possible. Take the case of William Burrage's desertion of his wife in 1756. From the moment he walked out, his wife was in a hopeless position. She was left with '6 poor helpless children (all small)' and was compelled to apply for relief immediately. Burrage, as Thomas Turner tells us, was not a bad man, even if in his action he had been 'unjust and imprudent'. He was 'a more than common industrious man and also one who did not spend his money, but readily and with cheerfulness shared it with his family'. So why had he left his wife? Turner's explanation is that cuts in his wages combined with rising prices had made it impossible for him to continue to support his family. Five years later he turned up in another parish and was apprehended and returned to his original parish. His wife, who had been maintained by the parish ever since his disappearance, had 'become a lunatic through grief'.[77] To judge by the lists of those in receipt of poor relief at the end of the century, the number of deserted wives appears to have increased as for many of the poor the margin of self-sufficiency was pared down. David Davies in 1795 talked of the effects of dependence on poor relief on some families. 'Sometimes the men', he wrote, 'from resentment at the hard usage they have met with are provoked to desert their families.' In the parishes of Barkham in Berkshire and St Austell, Cornwall, Davies wrote of two wives 'whose husband is run away, and six children', and, he adds, 'when the man ... is run away, we do not willingly allow the woman any parish relief, till the two eldest children are put out'.[78] Many deserted wives ended in the workhouse.

If it was also open to wives to desert their husbands, the law made it far more difficult, for she had no claim to any property. It was easy for a husband to disappear leaving no trace (particularly if he enlisted in the army or went to sea), but far more difficult for a wife with children. For just as she could claim no property, neither could she claim custody of her children. Moreover unless she acquired a legal separation, which was expensive, the husband could compel

---

[76] *Autobiography of Francis Place*, pp. 22, 23.
[77] Turner, *History of Courting*, pp. 67, 238.
[78] David Davies, *The Case of Labourers in Husbandry* (1795), pp. 26, 9, 143, 161.

her return. Richard Burn relates the case of a wife who had an affair with a Wiltshire gentleman referred to as Mr Nott. The affair continued for some time, the wife on several occasions going to Nott's house. Of her husband we are told 'it did not appear ... that he disliked her going and staying at Mr *Nott's*'. Indeed, in these circumstances they continued to live together. Later the affair appears to have ended. The wife left her husband and went to live in Marlborough, but, we are told, 'after leaving her husband's house, it did not appear that she ever saw Mr Nott, or lived in a lewd manner'. After some time had past, she sent an attorney to her husband asking him to take her back. The husband replied 'that if she came again, she should never sit at the upper end of his table, nor have the government of the children, but should live in a garret'. When the Attorney proposed that he made his wife an allowance he refused.[79] But when a husband deserted his wife there was nothing to prevent him coming back whenever he liked and resuming his role as head of the household.

Many marriages in the eighteenth century must have been bigamous: only the great difficulty of proving a bigamous relationship prevented there being far more examples in the courts. Women entered into bigamous marriages as well as men. In September 1719, 'Catherine Jones was indicted at the Old Bailey ... for marrying Constantine Boone during the life of her former husband, John Rowland.'[80] In 1737, also at the Old Bailey, there was a trial for bigamy where one witness, John Hall, testified that he had seen the defendant 'married at the Fleet to Robert Holmes'.[81] Wives of soldiers and sailors seem to have been particularly prone to making bigamous marriages. In 1725 there was the case of Jane, the wife of Henry Lawrence 'formerly a baker at Kensington'. After he had been married a year and a half he enlisted as a soldier and went abroad. Two years later his wife married a Mr Sweet. After four years of this marriage the first husband returned. Mr Sweet, we are told, 'left her to her first husband; if she please to goe and live with him'.[82] In 1737, when a sailor who had been away for three years returned home to his wife, 'he found her sitting by the fire with another Man, who said to the Woman, shew the Gentleman a

---

[79] Richard Burn, *The Justice of the Peace*, 3 vols (1762), vol. iii, p. 457.
[80] *The Newgate Calendar* (1774).
[81] Jeaffreson, *Brides and Bridals*, vol. ii, p. 141.
[82] *The Dairy of Thomas Naish*, ed. Doreen Slatter, Wiltshire Archaeological and Natural History Society, vol. xx (1964), p. 79.

Room. He thereupon ask'd her if she did not know him, and where she had got that Child, for there was one sitting upon her Knee; she reply'd, why dear Jack, I thought you were dead, and I'm married again.' The two husbands apparently came to an amicable arrangement by which the first husband claimed his wife when home on leave and when he went to sea the second husband resumed the position.[83] In the 1780s Eleanor French of Plymouth 'led a very bad life, and had a child in the absence of her husband about three years at sea, during which time she had credit, and he wrote her letters three or four times a year; and she hath married a second time ... to Richard Davis, mariner, under her assertion that the said John French was dead'.[84] But far more often it was men who contracted bigamous marriages, and bigamy did not by itself constitute sufficient grounds for a wife to divorce her husband.

The argument for a double standard as between a bigamous wife and a bigamous husband was that 'by such conduct in a husband nothing is committed that tends to bastardize the issue born in wedlock, that consequence arising entirely from the infidelity of the woman'. The law, it was explained, was not concerned with the relief of the individual, but with 'the great consequence it is of to the community, that all property should be transmitted to the heir lawfully begotten, with as little doubt and uncertainty as possible'.[85] It was only a short step to justifying polygamy for men but not polyandry for women. For 'the true Interest of Matrimony' did not require 'that the Man should confine himself as strictly as the Woman, for the Issue may be as well ascertained where the Man has two or more wives, but this cannot be, where a woman admits of more than one Man'. Whatever might be the motive behind a man being polygamous, 'it was an insatiable Lust only, that makes the Wife so averse to her Husband's taking another to his Bed'.[86]

Before the Hertfordshire Sessions in 1724, Francis Marionell was 'committed for marrying a second wife, the first being alive'.[87] But such cases were rare. In 1785 the father of Francis Place was involved in a case when 'a woman came to the overseers and claimed parish aid' as his wife, 'in consequence ... of a Fleet marriage some forty years previously'. Francis Place's father was advised by the parish 'to make a small weekly allowance for the

---

[83] Menefee, *Wives for Sale*, p. 61.
[84] Ibid., p. 17.
[85] Anon., *The Laws Respecting Women* (1777), p. 94.
[86] Salmon, *A Critical Essay*, p. 86.
[87] *Hertfordshire County Records*, ed. W. J. Hardy, 3 vols (1905), vol. ii, p. 58.

woman'. He refused to do so, saying 'she was no wife of his, nor ever had been'. All we know of him suggests he was guilty. Francis clearly thought so. A lengthy action was started in the ecclesiastical court, and finally he was excommunicated. The defence had cost him 'several hundreds of pounds', while all he had been asked to contribute to the maintenance of the woman was four shillings and sixpence a week.[88] When a Hampshire innkeeper, after a bigamous and financially advantageous marriage, was unexpectedly visited by the wife he had earlier reported dead, it was claimed in his defence that he had 'always till within these few weeks, allowed this unwelcome visitor a tolerable maintenance'.[89] It would be interesting to know how far a 'tolerable maintenance' exceeded four shillings and sixpence.

Remarriage in certain circumstances was legally permissible. 'If either a Husband or Wife, shall be beyond the Seas, or be absent in England, the space of Seven Years', it was asserted, then remarriage was possible.[90] In the case of a spouse being overseas, even if the other knew of their existence this made no difference to the right of remarriage, but if 'within this kingdom ... the remaining party' must have 'had no knowledge of the other's being alive within that time'.[91]

One customary alternative to divorce by private Act of Parliament for the labouring class was wife-sale. Recent research has produced many examples from the sixteenth to the nineteenth century. Recorded wife-sales increased at the end of the eighteenth and early nineteenth century, but whether this reflects an actual increase or merely that such sales were attracting greater publicity is uncertain. We now know of far more of them than earlier, of the form they most commonly followed, and of the circumstances in which the sale took place, its nature, and the consequences. But what still partly eludes historians is just why this particular form of ceremony was chosen. For historians of women there is a further problem: how did the wives concerned feel about their totally degrading role in such sales? Was it a customary alternative to legal divorce equally open to both sexes?

Most wife-sales were announced before the event, sometimes by advertisement in a local newspaper. They took place most commonly in markets at which a large potential audience could be

[88] *Autobiography of Francis Place*, p. 85.
[89] *Salisbury and Winchester Journal*, 27 July 1789, p. 3.
[90] *A Treatise of Feme Covert*, pp. 46–7.
[91] Blackstone, *Commentaries*, vol. iv, p. 164.

guaranteed. Almost invariably the wife to be sold was led into the market by a halter round her neck or tied to an arm. The sale took the form of an auction, the wife going to the highest bidder. Witnesses were essential to the procedure, and often some form of contract, duly witnessed, was drawn up after the sale. The sale as part of the commerce of a market was sometimes given further apparent validity by the payment of market tolls. Such are the bare bones of the custom, but attention to the detail was important and constituted in the minds of those participating part of the legitimation of the divorce process.

Sometimes wife-sale was the result of sudden impulse by a drunken husband. So in March 1766, a carpenter of Southwark in London sold his wife 'in a fit of conjugal indifference at the alehouse'. Not infrequently, as in this case, the sale was regretted at a later date. When the carpenter pressed his wife to return, she refused, and he hanged himself.[92] Sometimes a sale followed a domestic brawl. In June 1783, for example, a husband 'having a disagreement with his wife' sold her to a local farmer.[93] In some cases the husband seems to have been a wife-beater. In a few cases the sale appears to have been unpremeditated but to have come about as a result of a casual discussion entered into by the husband, the wife, and the purchaser. In by far the majority of cases, however, the motive seems to have been a genuine desire to bring a marriage to an end and to give the ending the legitimacy of divorce. There is no doubt that those that participated in wife-sales believed that the custom had a legal validity. Some of the newly formed couples eventually remarried, apparently confident that they were not committing bigamy. Others were more cautious and waited until the death of their former spouses. When legal advice was taken by a spouse contemplating wife-sale, it was often given in support of the custom as a legally valid means of divorce. This tolerant attitude towards the practice is supported by the rarity with which cases of wife-sale came before the courts of quarter sessions and, when they did, the mild sentences given.

What is significant is that the initiative, almost without exception, came from the husband. In many cases this is understandable as the adultery of the wife was a frequent, but by no means sole, cause of wife-sale. Already at the time of the sale she might be living with her lover. In 1804, a London shopkeeper returned home to find a stranger in bed with his wife. 'After some altercation on the subject

---

[92] *Annual Register*, 11 Mar. 1766, p. 75.
[93] Menefee, *Wives for Sale*, p. 73.

of this rencontre, the gallant proposed to purchase the wife, if she was offered for sale.' The husband agreed.[94] So in this instance the purchaser was pre-arranged and the ceremony was only a matter of form. Possibly, as Menefee suggests, it was a response to community pressure for some resolution of the situation. But not always was the purchaser pre-arranged. Often the wife faced a total stranger as her purchaser.

It has been argued that the consent of the wife to the sale was a necessary pre-condition, and was obtained 'in nearly every case'.[95] In the nineteenth century there were cases of wives opposing the practice, but none are recorded in the eighteenth. Yet when one thinks of the problem a woman faced in an unhappy marriage to a husband she loathed, what alternative was there? It must have seemed that any change would be for the better. How else was she to leave her husband? Without financial support, or the knowledge that she possessed a saleable skill, she abandoned a marriage at her risk. So if by far the majority of wives acquiesced in wife-sale, it does not necessarily mean they were unaware of the humiliation of the role they played. If a wife-sale was the only way to marry a lover, or to risk a better partner than the one she had, it was for many women the only course open to them. But if the wives concerned made little protest, by the end of the eighteenth century there is evidence of some hostility to the practice from the crowds that assembled to watch these events. When about 1777, a wife-sale was held in Carmarthenshire, for instance, we read how 'there was a great silence, and there was a feeling of uneasiness in the gathering', and some were heard to mutter 'that the entire sale was shameful and illegal'. In Dublin in 1756, a party of women intervened in a sale to 'rescue' the wife. The husband concerned was a porter. Those of his trade organized a mock trial. He was found guilty and punished by being placed in the stocks until early next morning.[96]

From the husband's point of view a wife-sale served a double purpose. It not only released him from a marriage with an unwanted wife, or a wife who had already abandoned him, but it freed him from any further financial responsibility for her, transferring the obligation to support her to her purchaser. Indeed, so important was this removal of future financial responsibility for the woman

---

[94] Ibid., p. 78.
[95] E. P. Thompson, 'Folklore, anthropology, and social history', *The Indian Historical Review*, 3/2 (1977), p. 252.
[96] Menefee, *Wives for Sale*, pp. 122, 124, 98.

that often a wife-sale was confirmed by a written contract in which the transfer of all financial responsibility to the purchaser was confirmed. A wife-sale in St Clements, London, in 1735 was followed by sending the 'common cryer' round the streets to announce that 'if any one hereafter should give any credit to the wife of the Alehouse keeper in Milford-lane, who was sold by her Husband on Saturday last for Ten Guineas; her Husband would not pay any Debts she should contract'.[97] In an advertisement placed in the *Ipswich Journal* in 1789 following the sale of his wife by one Samuel Balls, the same point was made: 'no person or persons to intrust her with my name ... for she is no longer my right'.[98] Wife-sales were often followed by a celebration in which husband, wife, and purchaser took part, and at which the husband 'often behaved with a generosity more humane than is encountered in today's divorce courts'.[99] Apart from the general relief of both husband and wife at the freedom from a marriage that had not worked, there was also some reason for the husband to behave generously. Henceforth he was free of any obligation to pay any debts she incurred.

Many customary alternatives to divorce were a reversal of common-law type marriage practices. A broomstick marriage could be negated, it was believed by both partners jumping backwards over the broom placed across the door in such a way as to avoid touching it. Those joined by handfasting ceremonies in Scotland and Ireland could reverse the process, local custom dictated, by turning their backs on each other and leaving the house through different doors. In Shropshire it was held that the return of the betrothal ring to the husband ended a marriage. It is not so easy to see to what common-law marriage practice wife-sale offered a reversal. It could be regarded perhaps as a logical extension of 'smock' marriages: when a woman was married only in her shift, her husband was taking her 'without worldly goods and would not be responsible for any debts she had contracted before marriage'.[100] But it seems more likely that it was seen as a reversal of the method by which marriages among the upper classes were concluded: wives (or husbands) had to be bought or bid for in an increasingly competitive market. So to dissolve a marriage it seemed rational to offer up a wife for sale at an auction. Attention has been drawn to the

[97] Ibid., p. 98.
[98] Ibid., pp. 97–8.
[99] Thompson, 'Folklore, anthropology, and social history', p. 252.
[100] Baker, *Discovering the Folklore*, p. 31.

many parallels between livestock/meat markets and wife-sales. Is it coincidence that butchers seem to have figured as both sellers and auctioneers? Sales took place in markets along exactly the same lines as livestock sales. The halter placed round the wife's neck was the equivalent of treating her, as one writer put it, 'as though she was a brood-mare, or a milch-cow'.[101] Very often the token given by the purchaser was a joint of meat. The wife was frequently sold by weight, just as were cattle — so much a pound.

It is no accident, I think, that both mercenary marriages and wife-sales were referred to as 'Smithfield bargains'. The connection between the two was made explicit by the *Morning Chronicle* in 1797, when it commented that 'modern marriages are so frequently and justly compared to Smithfield bargains, that a man who wishes to sell what he has bought, surely has a right to go back to the old market'.[102] The only problem here is that those of the upper classes who made Smithfield bargain marriages were not the people who made Smithfield bargain wife-sales. Hester Chapone, in the middle of the century, had talked of those marriages 'amongst people of quality of great fortune' as 'mere Smithfield bargains, so much ready money for so much land, and my daughter flung in into the bargain!'[103] In Henry Fielding's 'Love in Several Masques', Sir Positive Trap looked forward to a time 'when a man can carry off his daughter to market with the same lawful authority as any other of his cattle'.[104] But neither of them was talking of plebeian marriages. It may be then that we should see wife-sales as a plebeian take-off of upper class behaviour, a parodying of aristocratic practice. But if so, it was a joke at the expense of the wives.

Menefee has drawn attention to the parallel between hiring statutes, at which servants offered themselves for hire, and wife-sales. It makes for some interesting speculation on the relationship between wives (so often seen and treated as 'upper servants') and the servant class. Servants were paraded before prospective buyers who surveyed them much as they did livestock at a cattle markets. As some lines from a poem about a hiring fair at Henley, and which appeared in *Jackson's Oxford Journal* in 1827, described them:

> While ranks of village maidens, seeking place,
> On modest silence throng a distant space,

---

[101] Anon., *The Laws Respecting Women*, p. 55.
[102] Menefee, *Wives for Sale*, p. 151.
[103] Hester Chapone, *Posthumous Works*, 4 vols (1807), vol. ii, pp. 121–2.
[104] Henry Fielding, *Love in Several Masques* (1728), ii. vi.

And, like a show of cattle lent on hire,
Their points display to all who may desire.[105]

Just as law in the eighteenth century had little to offer labouring
women, customary alternatives to lawful marriage and divorce all
too often seem to have likewise favoured men at the expense of
women.

---

[105] Menefee, *Wives for Sale*, p. 169.

12

Spinsters and Spinsterhood

Damn me if I know any woman, young or old, that would *avoid* being married, if she could.

Sir Philip Baddely in Maria Edgeworth's novel Belinda

I believe in England many a poor girl goes up the hill with a companion she would little care for, if the state of a single woman were not here so peculiarly unprovided and helpless.

Mrs Reeves in The History of Sir Charles Grandison

Women without husbands in the eighteenth century deserve separate treatment for a number of reasons. Firstly their legal position set them apart from other women. Unlike wives they enjoyed a legal identity. As *feme sole* they had rights denied to married women. They could own property, and common law imposed no restrictions on their right to trade independently, although always subject to borough custom. How far are single women found using such rights in the eighteenth century? A legal identity was of some importance to women of property, but had it any meaning for women of the labouring class? Secondly, and particularly in the early eighteenth century, there were almost certainly more women remaining unmarried, as well as more widows, than in Victorian England. They constituted an important minority group. A remarkable number of them headed households. Their very preponderance demands attention. Then if women without husbands were in a sense an exclusive category, they were also an excluded one. In a period when women were 'understood either married or to be married',[1] when they were only regarded as fulfilling their destiny as wives or mothers, and when to be a 'maid' was essentially a temporary state passed through on the way to marriage, unmarried or husbandless women were an anomaly. Little wonder that such misfits could, on

---

[1] *The Lawes Resolutions of Womens Rights* (1632), p. 6.

occasion, focus all the malice, the hatred, and scorn that any non-conforming minority can attract to itself. If spinsters were the main sufferers they were not alone, and much of the same kind of malice was reserved for those left widows.

We know little about the incidence of spinsterhood before the first census of population in 1801 revealed a surplus of women over men. By 1851 there were more than a million unmarried women aged twenty-five and over in Britain, and with numbers apparently rising, attention was focused on the problem as never before. The question 'What shall we do with our Old Maids?' the problem presented by 'redundant' women, was a constant preoccupation.[2] If it was not confined to the middle classes, the very few employment opportunities suitable to unmarried women of genteel upbringing who needed to make a living may well have made their plight acute. Certainly they were better able to articulate the problem. The part played by middle class spinsters in the early women's suffrage movement, their responsibility for expanding employment opportunities and opening up higher education to women, their success in gaining some ground for women to enter the professions — all have long been recognized by feminist historians, and acknowledged in the work of Martha Vicinus, among others.[3]

Only recently have historians begun to suggest that spinsterhood may have presented problems, even greater problems, before the nineteenth century. On the incidence of spinsterhood in the seventeenth century, for example, there have been attempts to move beyond mere conjecture. In 1965 Lawrence Stone suggested how for the aristocracy there was a growing problem in marrying off daughters as the ratio between dowry (the sum paid by parents on their daughters' marriage), and jointure (the sum guaranteed to be paid to them in the event of their husbands' death) rose from about 5 : 1 in the middle of the sixteenth century to 8 or 10 : 1 by the end of the seventeenth, a level at which it was to remain in the early eighteenth century.[4] The same year a study of British ducal families supported Stone's conclusion. While in the period 1480–1679 only 6 per cent of ducal female offspring remained unmarried, by 1680–1729 the figure had risen to 17 per cent, or nearly tripled. Women of

[2] See e.g. Frances Power Cobbe, 'What shall we do with our old maids?', *Fraser's Magazine*, 66 (1862), pp. 594–610; W. R. Greg, 'Why are women redundant?' *National Review*, 15 (1862), pp. 434–60.

[3] Martha Vicinus, *Independent Women* (1985).

[4] Lawrence Stone, *The Crisis of the Aristocracy, 1558–1641* (1965), p. 645.

the aristocracy, it was argued, were far less prepared than men of the same class to marry their social inferiors, even though it might be to their financial advantage.[5]

The work of Wrigley and Schofield has attempted to broaden the social basis of the investigation. Estimates of the incidence of permanent celibacy in a community have been based on the relationship between the number of births in a given period of five years and the number of marriages occurring over the same period some twenty-five years later. The difference, it is argued, is made up by the number of deaths, the number of those migrating, and the number of those remaining celibate. Unfortunately this method of estimating celibacy makes no distinction between males and females. What the figures confirm, it is claimed, is the long-suspected relationship between late marriage and high levels of permanent celibacy. Average age at first marriage for women seems to have peaked in the period 1650–99 and remained high well into the eighteenth century. Only in the second half did the age of women at marriage begin to fall.[6]

On the experience of only twelve parishes (not a large sample), Wrigley and Schofield have concluded that the proportion of the total population never marrying rose steeply, reaching about 24 per cent among cohorts born at the turn of the sixteenth century and then falling steadily thereafter until rising even higher to 27 per cent of cohorts born in the mid-seventeenth century but marrying in the 1670s and 1680s. From this peak it fell steadily till the early eighteenth century, then more slowly and unevenly, to bottom in the 1740s. There was then a period of slow recovery until the 1780s, after which the proportion began to rise more steeply.[7] The figures, the authors readily admit, are subject to substantial margins of error. At the end of the seventeenth century, recorded marriages may well have born little relationship to the proportion of the population who went through some informal and irregular marriage ceremony, quite apart from those couples who, while effectively living as man and wife, went through none. Yet, granted a high margin of error, the figures suggest celibacy was at a high level at the end of the seventeenth and early in the eighteenth century. As

[5] T. H. Hollingsworth, 'A demographic study of the British ducal families', *Population Studies*, 11/1 (1957), p. 426; 'The Demography of the British Peerage', Supplement to *Population Studies*, 18/2 (1964), p. 27.

[6] E. A. Wrigley and R. Schofield, *The Population History of England, 1541–1871* (1982), pp. 257–8, 255.

[7] Ibid., p. 263.

male migration was always greater than female, and military service overseas was confined to men, the indications are that spinsterhood was becoming a sizeable problem. If the author of *Marriage Promoted* (1690) exaggerated the number remaining celibate when he talked of 'near one half of the People of England which die single', spinsterhood was far greater in its incidence than it was to become in Victorian times.[8]

Contemporary evidence, if not always in agreement about the size of the problem, supports the trend. In 1695 Gregory King estimated that there were 2.8 million women to 2.7 million men, but he took no account of the fact that under the age of sixteen the number of men exceeded that of women by 4,000, so that over the age of sixteen the surplus of women was higher. His explanation for the surplus was the greater vulnerability of men to the plague.[9]

Such national figures conceal great differences in the sex ratio between towns, between towns and country, and even between villages. We now know that in seeking a marriage partner few women or men looked far afield. Defoe commented on how the Cornish gentry rarely looked outside their own county for a wife, or the women for a husband. Sometimes choice of a marriage partner was confined to a town, or so Defoe wrote of Eltham in Kent where

> abundance of ladies of very good fortune dwell ... but t'is complained of that the youths of these families where those beauties grow, are so generally or almost universally bred abroad, either in Turkey, Italy or Spain, as merchants, or in the army or court as gentlemen; that for the ladies to live at Eltham, is, as it were, to live recluse and out of sight; since to be kept where the gentlemen do not come, is all one as to be kept where they cannot come.[10]

William Hutton, the Birmingham historian, believed there was a great contrast between the sex ratio in manufacturing towns and others. 'Those places where the manufactures flourish', he wrote in 1791, 'abound with males of the lower orders, so that we often behold a wife of sixteen; but Derby, having no internal commerce to retain her sons, they were diminished by emigration, or the

---

[8] Anon., *Marriage Promoted* (1690), p. 27.

[9] Gregory King, *Natural and Political Observations and Conclusions upon the State and Condition of England* [1696], ed. George Barnett (1836), p. 22.

[10] Daniel Defoe, *A Tour through England and Wales*, 2 vols [1724–6], Everyman edn (1948), vol. i, pp. 234, 100.

military service; and the girls were left longing for husbands'.[11] Unwillingness to marry beneath their class, thought Richard Pococke, accounted for the large number of spinsters in Preston. 'It is remarkable for old maids', he wrote in the 1750s, 'because these families will not ally with tradesmen, and have not sufficient fortunes for gentlemen.'[12]

In 1695, Gregory King estimated a sex ratio for London of 77, or 10 men to every 13 women. A more recent estimate based on a sample of 40 out of 97 parish returns for the Marriage Act enumeration of 1694 has produced a sex ratio of 87.[13] Such estimates suggest female migration to the metropolis may have been greater than for men. Almost certainly this continued to be the case throughout the eighteenth century and well into the nineteenth. The sex ratio tended to be lower in towns and higher in rural areas. In Lichfield in 1695, the sex ratio, according to King's figures was 83.3.[14] Here, remarkably, 31 per cent of all women in the fertile age group 25–44 were either spinsters or widows, and of these nearly half were spinsters between the age of 25 and 30. Over the age of 30 some 9 per cent of all women remained unmarried.[15]

The demographers' explanation for this rise in celibacy is that, like the age of first marriage, it tended to move in inverse correlation to the movement of real wages. Declining real wages, it is argued, tended to a postponement of marriage and to higher levels of permanent celibacy. 'When economic growth lagged behind population growth', Olwen Hufton explains, 'the result was more spinsters.'[16] How are 'spinsters' defined? Demographers have played safe. Wrigley and Schofield have measured celibacy in terms of those remaining unmarried between the ages of 40 and 44.[17] Others have preferred to relate it to the end of a woman's child-bearing years, and have selected the age of fifty. For the eighteenth century, by restricting the 'never married' to those over fifty, as Olwen

---

[11] William Hutton, *The History of Derby* (1791), p. 189.

[12] *The Travels through England of Dr. Richard Pococke*, ed. J. J. Cartwright, 2 vols, Camden Society (1888–9), vol. i, p. 12.

[13] Roger Thompson, *Women in Stuart England and America* (1974), pp. 31–2.

[14] Ibid., p. 34.

[15] D. V. Glass and D. E. C. Eversley (eds), *Population in History* (1965), p. 181, table 5; Lawrence Stone, 'Social mobility in England, 1500–1700', *Past and Present*, no. 33 (Aug. 1966), p. 41.

[16] Olwen Hufton, 'Women without men: widows and spinsters in Britain and France in the eighteenth century', *Journal of Family History*, 94 (1984), p. 357.

[17] Wrigley and Schofield, *Population History of England*, p. 260, table 7.28.

Hufton has commented, 'the work of the demographers can only understate the incidence of spinsterhood'.[18]

According to the values of eighteenth-century society, women who remained unmarried were social failures. Some of the responsibility rubbed off on their parents and families, so the obscurity in which the lives of so many spinsters is shrouded may in part be explained by an unwillingness to draw attention to their existence. Some families appear to have felt nothing but shame for their unmarried daughters. Few contemporary writers, whether in their diaries, autobiographies, or memoirs, seem to have considered them as worthy of comment. Among the inhabitants of the village of Myddle at the end of the seventeenth and the beginning of the eighteenth century, very few unmarried women are mentioned. Only twice are daughters directly referred to as 'unmarried', and one of these, Margaret the daughter of Arthur Noneley, is described as 'yet unmarried'. Only where there was something odd or exceptional about the women was their remaining unmarried worthy of remark. So Mary the daughter of Richard Gittins 'was a person of comely countenance but somewhat crooked of body. She was a modest and religious woman and died unmarried.' The only other instance was when she performed what was seen as an important role. The daughter of Richard Watkins, a London goldsmith, for example, 'was a modest and comely gentlewoman and was housekeeper to her uncle Thomas'.[19] There were advantages in having an unmarried niece as housekeeper as she would almost certainly be unpaid.

Spinsters remain shadowy figures who appear briefly, and often with no explanation, whenever a family crisis or problem arises. Of the unmarried woman of Victorian times who was without employment or independent means Janet Dunbar has written that 'she became the aunt, the nurse, the useful member of the family who had no responsibilities of her own, the person whom the others could call upon for help in any emergency'.[20] But it was a role they played long before the nineteenth century. Occasionally an unmarried woman emerges from obscurity and takes on a real identity. Elin was the sister of William Stout of Lancaster, whose autobiography covers the years 1665–1752. The daughter of a yeoman farmer, she was born in 1660. From an early age she suffered ill health, but this did not prevent her 'being early confined to wait on her brother,

---

[18] Hufton, 'Women without men', p. 357.
[19] Richard Gough, *The History of Myddle* (1979), pp. 96, 113, 51.
[20] Janet Dunbar, *The Early Victorian Woman* (1953), p. 22.

more than she was well able'. After her father died in 1679, William tells us, she was 'diligent in assisting my mother in her housewifry'. Apparently she had several offers of marriage 'but being always subject to the advice of her mother, was advised, considering her infermetys and ill state of health to remain single, knowing the care and exercises that always attended a married life and the hazerd of happiness in it'. She continued to look after the family house while her mother supervised the servants in the fields, dressed her corn, and went regularly to market. When, in 1688, William bought a shop, it was Elin who came to help him and 'was as ready in serving retaile customers as a young apprentice could have done'. After only three months in business, William fell ill. It was Elin who looked after both him and the shop. When his trade increased and he had need of more than assistance in the shop, it was Elin who became his housekeeper, which she did 'without a servant, but got one to wash and dress the house once a week and to brew upon occasion'. In the absence of her brother she continued to 'assist in the shop upon market days and assist the apprentice'. By 1709, their mother, now aged 79 and 'very infirme', had come to live with William, remaining there until her death in 1716. Elin looked after her. When William's brother Leonard was striving to bring up three sons and five daughters, it was to Elin's care that two of the children between the ages of two and five were given. Only two years later in 1721, William described his sister as 'growing weake' and 'become soe infirme that she could not inspect the apprentices as formerly'. Three years later she died.[21]

Catherine Hutton, the daughter of the historian of Birmingham, was born in 1756. She had several offers of marriage. When young she explained her declining them by asking 'How could I leave my mother?' When aged fifty and still receiving offers, she said 'How could I leave my father?' It is not an unfamiliar story, but Catherine Hutton was no ordinary woman. Largely by her own efforts she had educated herself. She had a lively and inquiring mind. In her travels with her father she missed very little and was to write fascinating accounts of the places they visited and the people they met. Only very occasionally in her letters can one detect a consciousness of the limitations of her spinster life. In 1792, when she was thirty-six, she wrote insisting that time did 'not hang heavy' on her hands. Her garden was occupying her time. 'There', she wrote,

[21] *Autobiography of William Stout of Lancaster, 1665–1752*, ed. J. D. Marshall (1967), pp. 68, 76, 87, 90, 105, 159, 178, 184, 185.

'I sow and plant and weed and water without end, and it does as well as anything else'. 'As well as anything else' is surely a revealing comment. Her father told her she would soon tire of gardening. She agreed, 'for man was not made solely for a garden nor woman either, but I hope I shall not tire of this till I have taken up some other employment'.[22] But Catherine Hutton was unusual. She had enlightened parents, she led a far more varied and interesting life than most single women of her class. She could write, and expressed herself with wit and vivacity. Above all else she was exceptional in not having to worry about earning her own living.

At the end of the century Priscilla Wakefield warned women to prepare themselves 'to sustain the unavoidable strokes of fortune'. She was thinking, it is true, of both spinsters and widows, but she went on to consider the prospects facing the unmarried woman who had reached an age when marriage was unlikely. For some the only prospect was to remain 'an inhabitant in her father's house' where her duty would be 'to enliven, to cheer, to amuse the latter moments of her parents' declining age'.[23] That she had in mind the daughters of the middle class is clear, for she omitted one other duty that faced most daughters who remained unmarried; that of contributing something to the subsistence of the household. Earlier, when within the majority of households the labour of every member was put to good use, it must have been easier to assimilate unmarried daughters, sisters, or sisters-in-law. Their contribution to the productive work of that household made them acceptable members. But when some wives withdrew from involvement in their husbands' business, whether on farm or in workshop, the addition to the household of an extra (and unwanted) female member with claims to being regarded as family but no longer in a position to make any working contribution was resented.

Mary Wollstonecraft, describing the lot of unmarried daughters left unprovided for by their parents, wrote of their dependence on 'the bounty of their brothers', and of how 'in this equivocal humiliating situation a docile female may remain some time with a tolerable degree of comfort.' But if and when the brother married, the situation was transformed. 'From being considered as the mistress of the family she is viewed with averted looks as an intruder, an unnecessary burden on the benevolence of the master of the house

---

[22] *Reminiscences of a Gentlewoman of the last Century: Letters of Catherine Hutton*, ed. Catherine Hutton Beale (1891), pp. 158, 111.

[23] Priscilla Wakefield, *Reflections on the Present Condition of the Female Sex* [1798], (1817), pp. 41–2, 43.

and his new partner.' In consequence, all too often she was 'thrown on the world', or on occasion 'sent as a great effect of generosity, or from some regard to propriety, with a small stipend, and an uncultivated mind, into joyless solitude'.[24] Earlier, in 1753, Jane Collier had compared the lot of the 'humble companion' taken in by prosperous families, and, as she added, 'under their protection', with that of servants. The servant 'receives wages, and the humble companion receives none; the servant is most part of the day out of your sight; the humble companion is always ready at hand to receive every cross word that rises in your mind'.[25] She was as much resented by the servants as despised by her mistress. 'Above the servants', Mary Wollstonecraft, who had experienced the situation, was to write, 'yet considered by them as a spy, and ever reminded of her inferiority when in conversation with the superiors.'[26] No wonder Thomas Gisborne in 1797 felt the need to make an impassioned appeal to mistresses for more humane treatment of female dependants.[27] For the majority of them, 'unable to work, and ashamed to beg', the life of the dependent spinster was grim.[28]

Economic dependence was far worse for single women than for wives. Wives who no longer participated in their husbands' business still retained their sexual function and could fulfil what was seen by many as their most important mission: to propagate the species.[29] But single women of the middle class were not merely deprived of their ability to work, but of any recognized usefulness in society. 'Surely nothing is more unprofitable', Robert Burton had written in the early seventeenth century, 'than that they die old maids, because they refuse to be used to that end for which they were only made'.[30] Such attitudes made women fearful of remaining unmarried, and led many to marry men they despised. It was not just the disgrace and the shame of failing to get a husband, but their denial by society of any identity. The virginity of spinsters was a wasted asset, yet there was surely more to the malice they attracted than that. They were also regarded as in some way a challenge to male authority, in particular the authority of husbands. The author of an

[24] Mary Wollstonecraft, *Vindication of the Rights of Woman* [1792], ed. Mirriam Kramnick (1978), pp. 157–8.
[25] Jane Collier, *The Art of Ingeniously Tormenting* (1753), pp. 42–3.
[26] Mary Wollstonecraft, *Thoughts on the Education of Daughters* (1787), pp. 69–71.
[27] Thomas Gisborne, *An Enquiry into the Duties of the Female Sex* [1797], (1798), pp. 291–3.
[28] Wollstonecraft, *Vindication*, p. 157.
[29] Anon., *Reflections on Celibacy and Marriage* (1721), p. 25.
[30] Robert Burton, *The Anatomy of Melancholy*, 2 vols. (1621), vol. ii, p. 49.

anonymous pamphlet of 1690 talked of men who remained single
as 'Disturbers of Government'.[31] In the same way, spinsters were
seen as a threat to a society that assumed all women would marry
and be subject to the control of their husbands. Aware of such
attitudes, it must have been very difficult for a woman to choose
to remain single. The only acceptable motive for spinsterhood, but
one which did not free the woman from scorn, was necessity. She
had wanted to marry but had failed to hook a husband. Those
remaining single were inadequate in some respect and therefore
failures. It was unthinkable that any woman could choose spinsterhood. William Hayley thought any woman who was not anxious to
enter the state of matrimony 'utterly devoid of tenderness and of
every amiable sensation'. He advised such a woman 'whenever she
has occasion to speak of the nuptial state, to . . . represent her own
exclusion from it, not as the effect of choice, arising from a cold
and irrational aversion to the state in general, but as the consequence
of . . . perverse incidents . . . as frequently perplex all the paths of
human life, and lead even the worthiest of beings into situations
very different from what they otherwise would have chosen'.[32]

In an article on female warriors, Dianne Dugaw has discussed the
use of disguise by women to enable them to enter into male-
dominated spheres, as, for example, soldiers and sailors. The motive
usually attributed by contemporaries to such actions on the part of
women was that they must have been in pursuit of a lover. I
wonder! On the same kind of assumption, all nuns are women
disappointed in love, all widows are lusting after every man that
crosses their path, all spinsters are women who desperately wanted
to marry but are unsuccessful in finding husbands. Such assertions
are suspect. Dugaw's is a fascinating theme that deserves further
probing. She quotes a late seventeenth-century London broadside
entitled 'The Female Warrior':

> Unto the wars she was inclin'd
> Being of courage bold,
> She always bore a stately mind.
> She scorn'd to be controul'd[33]

[31] Anon., *Marriage Promoted*, p. 44.

[32] William Hayley. *A Philosophical, Historical and Moral Essay on Old Maids*, 3 vols
(1785), vol. i, pp. 13–14.

[33] Dianne Dugaw. 'Balladry and female warriors: women, warfare and disguise in the
eighteenth century', *Eighteenth-Century Life*, n.s. 9/2 (1985), pp. 1–21 (p. 4).

As Defoe's Roxana explained to the suitor who was trying to persuade her into marriage, 'while a woman is single ... she is controlled by none because accountable to none, and is in subjection to none. ... while she is thus single she is her own person.'[34] And there were women who chose to remain single, and many more who, whether single from choice or necessity, lived both useful and fulfilled lives. There was Jane Barker, for example, who in her poetry extolled the single state:

> Ah lovely State how strange it is to see,
> What mad conceptions some have made of thee,
> As though thy being was all wretchedness
> Or foul deformity i' th' ugliest dress.[35]

We know most about those who were scholars or writers like Mary Astell Elizabeth Elstob, Elizabeth Carter, Catherine Talbot, Jane Collier, Sarah Fielding, Clara Reeve, Maria Edgeworth, and Jane Austen. If not all were financially independent, many were. Spinsterhood was a condition more easily accepted by women with a roof over their heads and either a saleable skill or an independent income. Roxana, we might note, 'wallowed in wealth'.[36] But what of those who lacked these advantages?

The stigma associated by some women of the middle class with work of any kind made difficult the lot of unmarried women of genteel upbringing but empty purses. The pity expressed by her friends for Elizabeth Elstob, the Anglo-Saxon scholar who throughout her life had to earn her own living, or the comment of Lady Mary Wortley Montagu on her cousin Sarah Fielding the novelist, that she was 'constrained by her circumstances to seek her bread by a method, I do not doubt she despises', make the point.[37] At the end of the century, Mary Wollstonecraft even suggested that middle-class women who were forced to earn their living were regarded much as prostitutes. As she was to ask, 'are not milliners and mantua-makers reckoned the next class?'[38]

Most fortunate were those single women who became mistresses of their own households. Normally it happened when their parents

---

[34] Daniel Defoe, *Roxana, or the Fortunate Mistress* [1724], (1840–1), p. 158.
[35] From the poem 'Virgin Life' in Jane Barker, *Poetical Recreations* (1688), pp. 12–13.
[36] Defoe, *Roxana*, p. 201.
[37] *Letters and Works of Lady Mary Wortley Montagu*, ed. Lord Wharncliffe, 3 vols (1837), vol. ii, p. 280.
[38] Wollstonecraft, *Vindication*, p. 157.

died. Widows may have outnumbered spinsters as heads of households but there were, none the less, many households headed by single women in the eighteenth century. The proportion increased with age, reaching a maximum at 75.[39] For others the death of parents often meant their removal from the parental household. Even if they were fortunate enough to inherit the house, they might well be unable to afford to live in it. An unmarried daughter of parents living in London or some other town might well be forced by her limited circumstances to abandon town life and search out some 'small country town to live in obscurity in order to . . . make her scanty income afford her a "genteel" living'.[40]

There are examples of single women of genteel background whose education in no way prepared them for earning their living facing up to their predicament by throwing themselves into productive work of a kind in which they had no experience. Eden in 1797 wrote of Sarah Spencer, the unmarried daughter of a Sussex gentleman, who on the death of her father was left just under £300. She took a farm, and with her sister, also unmarried, farmed for many years with much success.[41] Jane Barker took over 'the entire charge of her father's farm', where, we are told, 'she planned the work, hired the labourers, superintended the daily work that she had planned, paid the wages and kept the accounts'.[42] At the same time she continued to write novels and poetry. But Sarah Spencer and Jane Barker were scarcely representative of unmarried women. Jane Barker had a ready-made household and farm to take over; Sarah Spencer at least had enough of a fortune to buy a farm. For the great majority of women outside marriage, there was little possibility of creating an independent household.

It was fairly common to find unmarried women acting not only, as in the case of Elin Stout, as unpaid housekeepers to their bachelor brothers, but as servants to their own kith and kin. The upper ranks of the domestic service hierarchy offered one of the few openings available to those who needed to earn a roof over their heads but wished to remain acceptable to genteel society. But such acceptance was not guaranteed. In 1739 the *Gentleman's Magazine* placed the

---

[39] Richard Wall, 'Women alone in English society', *Annales de démographie historique* (1981), pp. 303–17 (p. 307).

[40] G. B. Needham, 'The old maid in the life and fiction of eighteenth-century England', Ph. D. thesis, University of California (1938).

[41] Sir F. M. Eden. *The State of the Poor*, 3 vols (1797), vol. i, p. 626n.

[42] G. E. and K. R. Fussell, *The English Countrywoman, 1500–1900* (1953), p. 108.

entire blame for unmarried and penniless daughters finding themselves in such a situation firmly on the parents, and the totally inadequate preparation for earning a living their education provided. Parents were urged to look beyond ornamental accomplishments and to apprentice their daughters at fifteen or sixteen to suitable 'genteel and easy' trades such as 'Linnen or Woollen Drapers, Haberdashers of Small Wares, Mercers, Glovers, Perfumers, Grocers, Confectioners, Retailers of Gold and Silver Lace, Buttons etc.'[43] In the first half of the century, if parents could overcome their prejudices against setting up their daughters in trade, there were still opportunities for providing them with a training that could be the basis for economic independence. But later the range of openings was to narrow and the cost of setting up independently in any trade to rise.

Even for daughters of labouring parents, in the early eighteenth century there had been a wide variety of trades to which they could be apprenticed, although apprenticeship to the commonest trade cost money. Parents had to weigh up the cost of keeping a daughter at home against the premium payable for an apprenticeship for a period during which she would be provided with board and lodging. As low a premium as five pounds might well represent 20 per cent of a family's annual earnings. So it was not an easy decision for parents to make, and the option was not open to all.

In Cardington, Bedfordshire, in 1782, all unmarried daughters over twenty years of age were either domestic servants or lived at home and worked as lace-makers or as nurses.[44] Richard Wall in his study of three communities – Lichfield (1695), Stoke (1701) and Corfe Castle (1790) – concluded that more unmarried women between the ages of fifteen and forty-four lived at home than were in service. In contrast, the majority of older unmarried women were either householders or lodgers, and in the case of Stoke and Corfe Castle, as many as half lived alone.[45] For younger daughters, much depended on what employment opportunities existed in the locality. In manufacturing areas, such as the lace-making area of Bedfordshire, so long as they remained in regular employment and lived at home, there was less of a problem of earning their keep.

Daughters tended to remain longer at home when their mothers were widows. Children of either sex stayed longer at home with

---

[43] *The Gentleman's Magazine*, 9 (1739).
[44] D. Baker. *The Inhabitants of Cardington in 1782*, Bedfordshire Historical Record Society, vol. iii (1973), pp. 101–2.
[45] Wall, 'Women alone in English society', pp. 310–12.

widows than with widowers, but more daughters than sons stayed at home when a family was headed by a widow. Olwen Hufton has suggested that daughters living with widowed mothers had a greater chance of never marrying. Particularly was this likely with widows of limited circumstances, where an additional earner in the house could make all the difference to their ability to maintain an independent subsistence. The widow might well try to keep the daughter at home 'beyond the usual age of marriage', and the daughter's need to contribute to the household meant she was less able to save something towards a dowry and so was more likely to remain a spinster.[46] In Cardington, in 1782, there lived Mary Watford, a lace-making widow of 62. Her two eldest children, Mary and Elizabeth, were 37 and 30 respectively, both unmarried and lace-makers. What happened to them when their mother died? There were two married sons, and it was unlikely that the two sisters would inherit the house.[47] In such circumstances daughters were left at the mercy of their brothers. Often they had neither money nor home to recommend them as wives or to enable them to establish a household of their own. As Richard Wall has expressed it, 'no familial role opens up to replace that of the daughter'.[48] The alternatives were either to become dependent on their brothers' charity or to fend for themselves by taking lodgings.

Many single women had no parental home to shield them from the problem of having to earn their subsistence. As rates of wages for women were fixed on the assumption that they were married and their earnings only supplementary to the main family earnings, they were always low: for many occupations, they were too low to support a woman living alone. If, as is claimed, spinsterhood grew with falling real wages, then the prospect for the unmarried woman was worsening as she strove to earn a living in increasingly adverse conditions. As mechanization began to invade hand-spinning and other traditional handicraft industries, rates of pay came under pressure. Eden in 1797 claimed that 'a woman in a good state of health, and not incumbered with a family can earn 2s. 6d. a week'. Earlier when the rate for spinning had been as much as 1s. or 1s. 2d. per pound, she could have earned 5s. or 6s. without difficulty. No wonder Eden saw 'the present dear times' as 'very severely felt by all families and even by single women who depend solely on

[46] Hufton, 'Women without men', p. 362.
[47] Baker, *Inhabitants of Cardington*, pp. 101–2.
[48] Wall, 'Women alone in English society', p. 312.

spinning for their support'.[49] Occasionally there were single women who refused to capitulate to mechanization and abandon hand-spinning. In the cotton industry, for example, Radcliffe described the effect of mechanization on the village of Mellor between 1770 and 1788. 'Hand wheels,' he wrote, 'with the exception of one establishment, were thrown into lumber rooms'. The exception was that in which four or five sisters combined the management of a small farm with a 'complete spinnery'. They insisted on their right to continue the trade despite all innovations. It was 'a right that had descended to them thro' their predecessors from the earliest period of time and till now had never been disputed'.[50] As late as 1822 they were still hand-spinning, apparently successfully. Such women had some advantage over individual hand-spinners isolated in their homes and unable to protest from any position of strength, but even so they were exceptional in achieving their object.

In the hand-knitting areas of Westmorland and in the Lancashire and Yorkshire dales, single women had little option but to go into service. Not always, however, was this possible. There might be little local demand for servants, or the need to look after an elderly parent or other family reasons might prevent a single woman travelling to London or some other town in search of a place. When this was the case she was left with little alternative but to resort to the parish. Where openings in domestic service were available, they provided by far the most important source of employment. This was recognized by local Poor Law officials anxious to rid themselves of the burden of unemployed unmarried women. Every effort was made to find them a place, preferably in another parish. Something akin to the attitude of many parishes to pauper children was adopted to single women. Some parishes, for instance, in their effort to rid themselves of the whole burden of supporting them, were prepared to pay something to a mistress-to-be towards the maintenance of women. According to Pinchbeck, it was a policy that resulted in a 'pauperizing of domestic service', for just as some farmers would employ pauper apprentices in husbandry, if they were available, to keep down their labour costs, so some mistresses began to refuse to engage any but pauper servants.[51]

[49] Eden, *State of the Poor*, vol. iii, p. 796.

[50] W. Radcliffe, *Origin of the New System of Manufacture Commonly Called Power Loom Weaving* (1828), pp. 61–2.

[51] Ivy Pinchbeck, *Women Workers and the Industrial Revolution 1750–1850* [1930], (1981), p. 80.

Domestic service had one great advantage over most other employment for single women: provided they did not lose their place, it gave them a roof over their head and board. Sometimes it provided them with clothes. These were vitally important considerations for the unmarried woman with no home of her own, or a home where parents could not support her. When Polly Ashford was left an orphan in 1801, her relations wanted her to enter an apprenticeship as a dress-maker or milliner, but on the advice of an old friend she became a domestic servant. Dress-making or millinery were 'all very well for those who had got a home and parents to shelter them when work is slack', but for many it was 'at times, a half-starved kind of life'.[52]

Vivien Brodsky Elliott sees the migration of daughters to London in the early seventeenth century as often coinciding with their fathers' death. They were then left without a home and were forced to move in search of alternative means of subsistence. Frequently they became domestic servants.[53] This remained true in the eighteenth century. Even for those who had homes, London possessed attractions. Not only was the demand for servants greater than elsewhere, but the wages paid were higher.

The number of single women who before enclosure owned or rented small plots of land is undoubtedly underestimated. But even without land, single women could still make a living by means of common rights. Tenants of cottages carrying rights of common could become small dairywomen, keeping one or two cows and some poultry and supplying the local population with milk, butter, and eggs. But when cottages were pulled down, their gardens engrossed and the commons enclosed, the ability of single women to make a living in agriculture was undermined. All that then remained for them in the countryside was occasional day-labour in the fields, in a few localities work in surviving cottage industries like lace-making, straw-plaiting, and framework-knitting, but for many only odd jobs — washing or charring. Mary Collier, poet and washwerwoman, was born in Midhurst, Sussex, of poor parents. When they died she moved to Petersfield in Hampshire, where she described her employment as 'Washing, Brewing and such labour'. She remained unmarried and continued to work until she had turned seventy.[54]

---

[52] *The Life of a Licensed Victualler's Daughter, Written by Herself* (1844), p. 20.

[53] R. B. Outhwaite (ed.), *Marriage and Society: Studies in the Social History of Marriage* (1981), p. 90.

[54] Mary Collier, *Poems on Several Occasions* (1762), p. iii.

She illustrates the problem facing single women in the countryside who, without any home, needed to earn a living. Even when they managed to find employment, old age must have presented a worrying prospect.

Single women seem to have made up a significant section of the migratory workers who moved in search of work at hay-time and harvest. Overseers of the poor, anxious to remove the threat of their becoming dependent on the parish rates, were sometimes prepared to subsidize such women's travelling expenses to areas offering employment. So a reference in the Hitchin Overseers' Account of 1730 reads, 'To Jane Gregory, to bear her charges into the hay country, 24s.'[55] Given the scale of allowances for single women, 24s. could represent as much as three months' relief.

What is astonishing is how many single women managed to survive on a mere pittance. Eden cites two sisters, both unmarried, who lived on 3s. 6d a week. One of the sisters was confined to her bed most of the year and received 1s. 6d. from the parish. The other had to devote much of her time to nursing her sister, but managed to spend some time spinning although this did not give her 'more than 2s. a week'. From this weekly sum they paid 6d. for lodging, leaving them 3s. on which to live.[56] Many were reduced to abysmal levels of frugality in their efforts to avoid dependence on parish support. Under the Old Poor Law the single woman fared even worse than the unmarried man. By the end of the century, rising Poor Rates had led to efforts to cut down the relief offered. Allowances for women, particularly after 1795, suffered. There was no incentive for single women to abandon their search for employment and rely on parish support. Where there was little employment, single women were regarded as the greatest threat to the poor rates. Where a system of allowances existed, those for single women without children were so small − often 1s. 6d. or 2s., and seldom more than 3s. − it would have been difficult to live on them. If a single woman could obtain employment, even at only 5d. or 6d. a day, it was preferable to depending on parish support. In some areas, most notably Essex, Hertfordshire, and Cambridgeshire, a

[55] Pinchbeck, *Women Workers and the Industrial Revolution*, p. 55 n.4: on methods used by parishes for subsidizing those liable to become wholly dependent on parish relief see K. D. M. Snell and J. Millar, 'Lone-parent families and the welfare state', *Continuity and Change*, 2/3 (1987), pp. 405, 421 nn. 22, 23; 422 n. 28.

[56] Eden, *State of the Poor*, vol. iii, pp. 798−9.

single woman who was able-bodied and not infirm was eligible for no allowance at all.[57]

By the end of the century, with declining employment opportunities in many areas, the only means for a woman to exist (short of moving to London or some other town) was by marriage, whether of a regular or irregular nature, or by prostitution. Of marriages of many female migrants to London in the early seventeenth century it has been suggested that 'given the difficulties and precariousness of life in London' at this period, it is impossible to 'ignore the importance of the economic dimension for women who had no families and no kin to fall back on'.[58] This same 'economic dimension' to marriage or some customary alternative loomed large in the closing years of the eighteenth century. The trend towards earlier marriages, argued by Wrigley and Schofield, may have been in part the result as prospects for the celibate worsened.

For the single woman facing unemployment and starvation, the best method of obtaining a husband was to become pregnant. It was, as Pinchbeck wrote, 'the single woman's only means of escape'.[59] Local Poor Law officials were so anxious to avoid giving settlement to a bastard they would do everything they could to marry off the pregnant woman, particularly if the father of the child proved to live in another parish. In this way the settlement of mother and child was transferred to that of the husband. The Reform Commissioners in 1833 invited parishes to suggest ways in which the law respecting bastardy should be changed. No doubt aware of this escape route for single women, the parishes of Foulmire and Histon in Cambridgeshire replied that 'the whole expense should fall upon the mother, if the woman knew there would be no provision for the child there would be fewer bastards'.[60] Even if no husband resulted, an illegitimate child entitled the mother to an increased allowance.[61] The increase in illegitimacy in the late eighteenth century could be

[57] Pinchbeck, *Women Workers and the Industrial Revolution*, p. 80; for single women's allowances in Buckinghamshire see *The Report of the Society for Bettering the Condition and Increasing the Comforts of the Poor*, vol. iii, pt 1 (1801), p. 147.

[58] *Marriage and Society*, p. 95.

[59] Pinchbeck, *Women Workers and the Industrial Revolution*, pp. 72, 80.

[60] E. M. Hampson, *Treatment of Poverty in Cambridge, 1597–1834* (1934), p. 176.

[61] According to Snell and Millar, 'Lone-parent families', pp. 397, 409, 407, between 1700 and 1850, of the 86 per cent of lone-parents dependent on poor relief who were women, 17.4 per cent were unmarried and between 1800 and 1834 the recipients of 'a very high level of parish support' estimated at 78 per cent of the average income of two-parent families from employment.

seen as a response to sheer economic necessity rather than any decline in moral standards.

If the woman charged a man with being the father of her child and he could be apprehended, he had either to pay for the maintenance of both mother and child, marry the woman, or be imprisoned. The 'forced' marriages that resulted rarely can have provided much happiness for either spouse. Very often the wives were later deserted. But the way in which the Poor Law was administered, in a period of unemployment and falling real wages for women, meant that single women were the main sufferers. That some pregnant women lied about the fathers of their children in an effort to secure adequate support is undeniable. Blackmail was often the only weapon women retained. 'It's hardly surprising', as E. M. Hampson has written of Cambridgeshire, 'that marriage at any price, or even illegitimate relations, seemed to some women the only solution to life'.[62]

In such circumstances it is difficult by the late eighteenth century to see choice of spinsterhood as a real option for daughters of the labouring class. In the first half of the century, provided they were in permanent employment and lived in the parental home or independently in a cottage with some access to land, they could have afforded to make such a choice. After the middle of the century, with enclosure, destruction of cottages and common rights, and the decline of handicraft industry, the possibility of choosing a single life was steadily eroded. How many marriages were then concluded in order to avoid the economic disadvantages of remaining single? It is impossible to say. How many women, all too aware of the difficulty of supporting themselves without a husband, thought any husband was better than none? The luxury of love can have played little part in such marriages.

[62] Hampson, *Treatment of Poverty*, p. 218.

13

Widows

PEACHUM: And had not you the common view of a gentlewoman in your marriage, Polly?

POLLY: I don't know what you mean, Sir.

PEACHUM: Of a jointure, and of being a widow.

POLLY: But I love him Sir: how then could I have thought of parting with him?

PEACHUM: Parting with him! Why, that is the whole scheme and intention of all Marriage-articles. The comfortable state of widowhood is the only hope that keeps up a wife's spirits. Where is the woman who would scruple to be a wife, if she had it in her power to be a widow whenever she pleas'd?

John Gay, *The Beggar's Opera* (1728)

One thing that emerges from any analysis of households in the early modern period is the large number headed by a single person rather than a married couple. In the period 1574–1821, it has been estimated, over a quarter of households were of this nature. Widows accounted for 12.9 per cent.[1] From the end of the seventeenth century the trend was towards more women – unmarried and widows – heading households, particularly in the 30 to 54 age group.[2] Widows always predominated. Behind such figures lies the frequency with which the premature death of a spouse could transform a household. For much of the eighteenth century, the duration of a first marriage among the labouring population was between seventeen and twenty years. The odds were against a couple surviving

[1] Peter Laslett and Richard Wall (eds), *Household and Family in Past Time* (1972), p. 147.
[2] Richard Wall, 'Women alone in English society, *Annales de démographie historique* (1981), pp. 303–317 (pp. 303, 305).

longer than a year or two after their children left home. There was very little chance of both of them living long enough to see their grandchildren. So, as Lawrence Stone has pointed out, 'less than half of the children who reached adulthood did so when both parents were alive'.[3]

Widows headed households far more often than widowers or single men. Why was this? One reason was that widows were less likely to remarry than widowers. According to Wrigley and Schofield, remarriages among both widows and widowers declined from the mid-sixteenth to the mid-nineteenth century.[4] The reason for this remains elusive. Greater longevity obviously played an important part, but by itself it is an inadequate explanation. From the experience of widows in Abingdon, Oxfordshire, in the period 1500–1800, Barbara Todd has produced some fascinating conclusions. While younger widows were more likely to remarry, it was the decline of remarriage among older widows that accounted for the trend. While before 1660 widows with young children were more likely to remarry than widows without, in the period 1660–1720, the remarrying widow tended to be childless. The wealth of a widow was far less of a consideration in determining whether or not she remarried than popular belief has suggested; those least likely to remarry were widows of artisans.[5] Another possible reason for the decline of remarriage among widows is its relation to changing sex ratios and a far greater incidence of celibacy. There was something like a crisis in marriage towards the end of the seventeenth and early eighteenth centuries when widows as well as single women may have found it more difficult to find husbands. There is some evidence of young unmarried women's resentment of widows in the competition for husbands.

The possibility of remarriage was greater for middle-class widows than for those of the labouring class. Yet even with youth and money, and no children to hamper her activities, a widow could still find it difficult to remarry. Moll Flander's first husband left her a widow with £1,200. Her two children by the marriage were taken off her hands by her parents-in-law. She was, by her own admission, 'still young and handsome ... and with a tolerable fortune in my pocket'. Yet for some time after the death of her first husband it

[3] Lawrence Stone, *The Family, Sex and Marriage* (1977), p. 60.

[4] E. A. Wrigley and R. S. Schofield, *The Population History of England, 1541–1871* (1981), pp. 258–9.

[5] Mary Prior (ed.), *Women in English Society, 1500–1800*, ch. 2.

proved insufficient to win her a second. As she said, while she never lacked admirers, she 'found not one fair proposal among them all'.[6]

On the other hand, there was considerable reluctance on the part of widowers, or indeed single men, to take on the management of a household without a housekeeper or a wife. Many found it impossible to cope alone. Sussex grocer Thomas Turner, for instance, referred to his wife shortly after her death in 1761 as 'one always found at home and everything serene and in order'. But the situation had changed; whenever he went home he found 'one or both servants out and everything noise and confusion'. Turner felt he could not manage on his own. He was convinced that to 'keep house with servants in the business I am situated in is not either agreeable to my natural inclination or advantageous to my interest'.[7] Two years later he married again, this time to a neighbour's servant. It was a familiar pattern. Who better to take over the management of a widower's household than one already experienced in the task? If a widower had young children, it was vital that he find a replacement mother as soon as possible. When Thomas Wright's first wife was dying in 1777, he wrote: 'We were at this time without a maid. I was left alone with the children. I hired a neighbour woman to do our occasional work, but as I was obliged to be often from home, and the children were little ones, I suffered much by her dishonesty.'[8] After a succession of housekeepers, most of them unsatisfactory, he remarried in 1781.

There are, on the other hand, many examples of a widow taking over their husband's farm, shop, or trade and managing the household successfully without remarrying. In 1679, when William Stout's father died, his mother was left with seven young children. She took on a farm manager and with his help ran the farm. William wrote of how 'she was employed in looking after her servants in the field and dressing her corn and going to market with the same as she usually did'.[9] We have seen how Samuel Crompton's widowed mother continued to run a farm, and to card, spin, and weave cotton.[10] It was not unusual for women to continue to run their farms on the death of their husbands where there was no son to

[6] Daniel Defoe, *Moll Flanders* [1721] (1924), pp. 46–7.

[7] *The Diary of Thomas Turner, 1754–1765*, ed. David Vaisey (1985), pp. 247, 265.

[8] *The Autobiography of Thomas Wright of Birkenshaw in the County of York 1786–1797*, ed. Thomas Wright (1864), p. 127.

[9] *The Autobiography of William Stout of Lancaster, 1665–1752*, ed. J. D. Marshall (1967), pp. 75, 76.

[10] Gilbert French, *The Life and Times of Samuel Crompton* (1868), pp. 16–17.

take over. Some took a lively interest in agricultural experiment and improvement, catching the attention, and winning the admiration, of writers like Arthur Young and William Marshall who, travelling from county to county, surveyed agricultural practice. In Stoke Poges in Buckinghamshire, for example, a Mrs Parker Sedding, a farmer of 'upwards of £400 a year' was 'universally allowed to be one of the best farmers'.[11]

In the early years of the century, Henry Casson, an innkeeper and chandler, died. He left behind a very confused will, but 'he made his wife Mary whole executor of it'. She was left in moderately comfortable circumstances. Her husband's estate amounted to £548, with houses and lands worth a further £700. Nevertheless the widow 'kept on the innkeeping and making candles and sope whilst she lived'.[12] Women played an important or even an expanding role as licensed victuallers after the Restoration. An increasing number, and by the end of the eighteenth century the great majority, were widows.[13] Many widows were in the publishing business. According to Olwen Hufton, 'about 50 per cent of publishing houses were run as family businesses in which the women worked, but 10 per cent were in the hands of women alone, usually widows'.[14] Nor was this new in the eighteenth century. Margaret Hunt has written of the 'centuries-old tradition of women taking over the supervision of printing, book-selling, book-binding or related businesses upon the death ... of male relatives'. The vast majority of these women were widows. The Stationers' Company gave widows of master printers the right to take over their husbands' apprentices and to take on new ones. It also made them eligible for a pension. Widows were particularly numerous in the occupation of 'mercury' − someone who bought newspapers wholesale from the printer and distributed them, either through a retail shop or via hawkers. Between 1701 and 1740, a period which saw a great increase in the number of English newspapers, a woman, and often a widow, is found 'as either publisher, printer, editor or major distributor' in over thirty of them. A century later women had virtually disappeared from all but the retail business.[15]

[11] *Report on the Society for Bettering the Condition of the Poor*, 5 vols (1798–1808), vol. v (1806), pp. 104–5.

[12] *Autobiography of William Stout*, p. 151.

[13] Peter Clark, *The English Alehouse: A Social History, 1200–1830* (1983), pp. 203, 285.

[14] Olwen Hufton, 'Women without men: widows and spinsters in Britain and France in the eighteenth century', *Journal of Family History*, 9/4 (1984), pp. 355–76 (p. 365n).

[15] Margaret Hunt, 'Women and the London press: hawkers, bawlers and mercuries in the early English enlightenment', in the special issue on 'Women and the Enlightenment' in *Women in History*, 9 (1982).

The death of a Mrs Higginson was recorded in the *Gentleman's Magazine* of 1731. She was described as 'a dealer in Timber'.[16] This was not a case of a recently widowed woman who had taken over her husband's business until she could find someone to manage it for her, for her husband had died in 1708. Elizabeth Montagu, the bluestocking, had always been closely involved in her husband's business, managing his colliery and keeping the accounts. When in 1775 he died, she took over both his farm and the collieries and managed both with success and obvious enjoyment.[17] In 1784, a Mrs Vicars ran a lead smeltery near Denbigh where '30 tons of lead were melted weekly'.[18] In 1783, Abigail Gawthern, the daughter of a Nottingham grocer, married her cousin, a white-lead manufacturer. Eight years later he died. His wife benefited both by the terms of the marriage settlement and by his will and inherited most of his property. Jointly with two of her husband's friends, Abigail was bequeathed the stock-in-trade of the leadworks and was given the option of either selling up her part or retaining it until their son came of age. She chose the latter course, and for sixteen years continued to run the leadworks, and was listed in the Nottingham trade directory as a 'white lead manufacturer'.[19] There is evidence of some widows functioning as money-lenders in rural society in order to put to the best use whatever wealth they had. The borrowers tended to be relatives, friends, or neighbours.[20] But women with money to lend can only have been a small minority.

Not always were widows anxious to continue their husband's trade left in circumstances that made it easy. Polly Ashford's grandparents kept the City Arms in Lombard Street, London. In 1776 her grandfather died from the shock of becoming overnight virtually penniless. Mrs Gaddener, the widow, was left with a heavy burden of debts. When a meeting of the creditors took place, they were prevailed on by one of the brewers concerned to allow the widow, who was known to be 'an honest as well as an industrious woman', to 'remain in the house for a year, to pay ready-money for what she wanted in, and see if, by instalments, she could pay off any of her late husband's debts'. Apparently 'she succeeded, and soon cleared herself'.[21]

---

[16] *The Gentleman's Magazine*, 1731, under Deaths recorded in April.
[17] Dr. Doran, *A Lady of the Last Century (Mrs. Elizabeth Montagu)* (1873), pp. 139–40.
[18] *The Torrington Diaries*, Introd. John Beresford, 3 vols (1934), vol i, p. 173.
[19] *The Diary of Abigail Gawthern of Nottingham, 1751–1810*, ed. Adrian Henstock, Thoroton Society Record Series, vol. xxxiii (1980), Introd., p. 15.
[20] B. A. Holderness, 'Widows in pre-industrial society: an essay upon their economic functions', in Richard M. Smith (ed.), *Land, Kinship and Life-Cycle* (1984), p. 428.
[21] *Life of a Licensed Victualler's Daughter, Written by Herself* (1844), pp. 8–9.

Even without financial problems, not all widows could assume responsibility for their husbands' business. When Thomas Wright (1736–97), of Birkenshaw in Yorkshire, was left an orphan at a very young age, he continued to live with his grandparents. His grandfather soon died, leaving his elderly widow 'very forlorn and exposed'. The family owned four mills and a farm. As Wright explained, 'the business of the mills was extensive and complicated, and required far more management and attention than she was capable of bestowing upon it'. Unable to manage alone, 'she was obliged to rely on the faithfulness of different persons to transact business for her'. The consequence was she was 'nearly stript of all her property'.[22] In the 1780s a widow of a London silk mercer was left with three children. She 'carried on the business as well as she could for some time', but being anxious to make a fortune, she gambled on the state lottery, lost everything, and 'took to drinking and died'.[23]

If sometimes a widow's difficulties in carrying on her husband's business were due to her age, there must have been many young widows of tradesmen who regretted having taken so little interest in the business during their husbands' lifetime. Defoe's warning to 'those ladies who stoop to marry men of business, and yet despise the business they are maintained by' was salutary, but in his lifetime there can have been relatively few wives who through total ignorance of it were prevented from running their husbands' business after their death. As the century progressed, one suspects, there must have been an increasing number. In part it was the price paid for aspirations to gentility entertained by some tradesmen's wives. Defoe may have exaggerated when, in comparing the situation in 1726–7 with that of earlier times, he claimed 'that where there is one widow that keeps on the trade now, after a husband's decease, there were ten, if not twenty, that did it then'.[24] The evidence points rather to the frequency with which widows assumed responsibility for running their husbands' businesses, and the efficiency and assurance with which they practised their trades. In Coventry, for example, widows are found in the period 1781–1806 following the trades of their

---

[22] *The Autobiography of Thomas Wright of Birkenshaw in the County of York, 1736–1797*, ed. Thomas Wright (1864), p. 127.

[23] *The Autobiography of Francis Place, 1771–1854*, ed. with an Introduction and Notes by Mary Thale (1972), p. 88.

[24] Daniel Defoe, *The Complete English Tradesman* (1726–7), from *The Novels and Miscellaneous Works of Daniel Defoe*, 2 vols. (1840–1), vol. i, pp. 216–17.

husbands as barbers, grocers, tallow-chandlers, bricklayers, cord-wainers, and even, in one instance, as a cutler and gunsmith.[25] In Sheffield in 1787, out of nine female scissors-makers, five were widows.[26] Yet even with a manageable business, widows were not always successful. In the first six months of 1731, the bankruptcies of half a dozen widows were recorded in the *Gentleman's Magazine*. They represented the trades of clothier, coffee-woman, vintner and inn holder, weaver/hosier and milliner.[27]

Widows taking over their husbands' business often enlisted the help of a journeyman but maintained overall management. Sometimes control of the trade lasted only as long as it took their sons to complete an apprenticeship. There are cases of sons' apprenticeships to their fathers being transferred on their fathers' death to their mothers. So in the case of our cutler and gunsmith, Mary Cutts of Coventry, her son Mark's apprenticeship was assigned to her on her husband's death. Within a few years he would have been in a position to take over the management of the business. In 1797, Charles Green was apprenticed to Samuel Greenway of Coventry, a ribbon-weaver. On Greenway's death he was assigned to the widow, Mary Greenway. Four years later she was still practising the trade, for we read of the brother of Charles starting his apprenticeship with her.[28] Rarely can these widow tradesmen have served an apprenticeship. It was enough that the husbands had practised the trade for seven years – the normal term of an apprenticeship – to give their wives the legal right to continue to do so, for they were regarded as having served the equivalent of an apprenticeship. Widows are often found taking up the freedom of their husbands' companies. Most guilds allowed widows of freemen admission with all the privileges that went with it, including the right to take apprentices. Katherine Eyre, widow of a member of the Company of Carpenters, in 1701 had a female apprentice bound to her for seven years. Four years later she took another girl as apprentice.[29]

There has been a tendency among historians in looking at appren-ticeship to assume that whenever a woman is found in a trade

[25] *Coventry Apprentices and their Masters*, ed. Joan Lane, The Dugdale Society Publications, vol. xxxiii (1983), p. xii.
[26] Penelope Corfield, 'Tinker, tailor, bleeder, grieve', *The Times Higher Education Supplement*, 13 Sept. 1985, p. 13.
[27] *The Gentleman's Magazine* (1731), Jan.–June.
[28] *Coventry Apprentices*.
[29] E. B. Jupp, *Historical Account of the Worshipful Company of Carpenters* (1887), pp. 543–4.

which later became the monopoly of men she must have been a widow. The implication is that only a widow who succeeded to her husband's business could have practised some of the 'masculine' trades which 'demanded physical skills that few women were likely to acquire'.[30] The assumption is that the widow's taking over the trade was only temporary until such time as she could either sell the business or find someone to run it for her. Female apprentices, it is suggested, even if entering such 'masculine' trades, rarely gained a training in them. This argument tends not only to underestimate the wide range of trades to which women were apprenticed in the early eighteenth century but also undervalues the real involvement and commitment of many widows to such trades. The way in which some publicized their intention of carrying on their husbands' business suggests they took their role seriously. So when in 1775 Sarah Baskerville, widow of the famous letter-founder and printer John Baskerville (1706–75), announced her intention of carrying on the business, she had weighed up all that was involved. Aware of just what demands on her each side of the trade would make, she had decided not to take on the printing side but to confine herself to the letter-founding 'in all its parts'. She would endeavour to do so 'with the same care and accuracy that was formerly observed by Mr Baskerville'. In 1779, the widow of a Newcastle watchmaker placed a notice in the local newspaper informing 'the friends of her late husband' that she would carry on his business 'having engaged able workmen therein', and hoped 'for the continuance of their favours'.[31] Of the five Sheffield widows practising the trade of scissors-maker in 1787, 'all had a public identification with the business, implying at least some level of involvement'.[32]

It seems to have been usual for wives of small clothiers, master weavers, and cloth-dressers to take over the business after the death of their husbands. Indeed, where a trade remained small, a widow could assume control with a minimum of assistance. In the case of the majority of retail shops, taverns, coffee-houses, and lodging-houses, a widow with the help of a son or daughter could carry on the business without relying on any outside aid. Sometimes, to ensure there were no difficulties when a son or daughter assumed control of the business, they were apprenticed to their mother.

---

[30] *Women in English Society*, p. 70.

[31] Ivy Pinchbeck, *Women Workers and the Industrial Revolution, 1750–1850* [1930], (1981), pp. 284, 285.

[32] Corfield, 'Tinker, tailor, bleeder, grieve'.

Among Oxford City apprenticeships in the eighteenth century, for example, there are several cases of sons apprenticed to their widowed mothers as bakers, butchers, grocers, and chandlers.[33]

Defoe had anticipated the gradual decline in the number of widows taking over their husbands' trades. If such women believed trade was vulgar and to be scorned, this was not the sole, or the most important, reason for their withdrawal from involvement in the trade of their husbands. Defoe had not overlooked the possibility that, as he put it, 'the difficulty often lies on the other side of the question, and the tradesman cares not to lay open his business to, or acquaint his wife with it'. It could be that the tradesman entertained ideas of 'making his wife a gentlewoman', and 'as to the business, she shall not stoop to touch it; he has apprentices and journeymen, and there is no need of it'.[34] Was the merchant Augustin Greenwood, who died in 1701 and of whom William Stout wrote, just such a case? Of his widow, Stout was to write that her husband 'had been so carefull and provident for her that she had little knowledge of his affairs or circumstances'. Her plight was made worse by the fact that the husband 'had no apprentice that knew anything of the management of the business'.[35] Defoe touched on the real reason why wives became less involved: businesses were growing in size, and wives were often left isolated in the home while the trade of her husband was transferred to bigger workshops that could house more workers. As their trades prospered, so more journeymen and apprentices were employed and there was less need for the wife's involvement. When such wives were widowed they were often far too ignorant of the trade to assume responsibility for it, and employing someone capable of running it was both expensive and fraught with dangers. Rather than depend on a stranger they did not know and could not trust, many widows abandoned the trade and sold up the business. Others married their husbands' journeyman or apprentice, balancing his youth against 'his past training ... in the same or related trade or craft as that of her late husband'.[36]

A widow by common law was entitled to dower. It was normally a third of her husband's estate, although it could be more, and was conditional on her not remarrying. If a husband had disposed of any freehold property since marriage without consulting his wife

---

[33] Oxford City Apprenticeship Lists, Oxfordshire Record Office.

[34] Defoe, *The Complete English Tradesman*, vol. I, p. 219.

[35] *Autobiography of William Stout*, pp. 132–3.

[36] Vivien Brodsky, 'Widows in late Elizabethan London: remarriage, economic opportunity and family orientations', in Bonfield *et al.* (eds.), *The World We Have Gained* (1986), p. 127.

and obtaining her agreement, in theory the widow was entitled to a third of it. But there were ways of circumventing the common-law requirement. A marriage settlement, agreed before marriage, by which the wife was assured an agreed jointure on widowhood was an effective bar to dower. 'Upon making such an estate in jointure to the wife before marriage', Blackstone wrote, 'she shall be for ever precluded from her dower.'[37] So in 1743, Henry Mitchell, a West Yorkshire landowner, drew up an agreement with Hannah, his wife-to-be, that in the event of his dying before her, 'she would be content with and desire no more than ten pounds a year out of my estate but would accept such ten pounds by the year in full of her thirds of dower'.[38] As is suggested here, the jointure a widow received was often less than she would have received from her rights of dower. On the other hand, an agreed jointure in a marriage settlement concluded before marriage might be some protection for a widow whose husband's land was entailed, and therefore excluded from his estate for the purposes of calculating her right to dower. In a novel by Clara Reeve, Mrs Darnford, the widow of a London tradesman, was left with no such protection. 'All that remained of his estate was entailed on the next male heir of the name; and the widow was left without any provision, and obliged to go out as governess to some young ladies.'[39] 'Despite separate property being secured to them,' Susan Staves writes, 'women were unwilling or unable even to hang on to it, being as contemporaries said "kissed or kicked", "bullied or coaxed" out of it by husbands who had physical or emotional power that rendered their wives' legal powers nugatory'.[40] If, however, the marriage settlement was drawn up after the marriage, the widow had the right to choose between taking either the jointure agreed in the settlement, or dower as provided by common law. She had this choice because as a wife at the time the marriage settlement was drawn up 'she was not capable of consenting to it during her couverture'.[41]

The choices facing a widow were often limited by the provisions of her husband's will. A husband could 'encumber his wife with the

---

[37] Sir William Blackstone, *Commentaries on the Law of England in Four Books* [1753] ed. Edward Christian (1793), vol. ii, p. 137.

[38] *Shore in Stansfield: A Pennine Weaving Community, 1660–1750.* Cornholm Branch of the Workers' Educational Association (1986), p. 52.

[39] Clara Reeve, *The School for Widows* (1791), pp. 8–9.

[40] Susan Staves, 'Pin money', *Studies in Eighteenth-Century Culture*, University of Wisconsin Press, 14 (1985), pp. 47–77 (pp. 49–50); and see her forthcoming *Our Fortunes Are in Your Possession: Married Women's Property, 1660–1833*, Harvard University Press.

[41] Blackstone, *Commentaries*, vol. ii, p. 138.

finding of sizeable portions and dowries for children at later ages, or he could alienate a shop and its equipment, the tools of the craft, and even pass on his apprentices to a son, mother or friend'.[42] But not always was it the state of the law which accounted for so many widows being near-destitute. Even those left with adequate provision were so conscious of the prior claims of children on their husband's estate, that many would part company with whatever they had legally acquired rather than feel they were prejudicing their children's future. Indeed it was a factor influencing whether or not they remarried, and − if they wanted to remarry − how long it was delayed. Many a widow was penalized by the conditions of her husband's will if she remarried for it might well cut across the interests of the children of the first marriage. Such interests needed to be protected. Widows could lose their home and its contents, their land, and even their right to reside in a son's household. These were important considerations for a widow contemplating marriage. How much would she lose by it? She would lose any legal identity on becoming again a *feme covert*, and unless of considerable wealth and fortunate in having a knowledge of the law, she could lose all control over the property that had been hers. There were, it is true, legal means of securing a widow's property against her new husband, but these were not available to the majority of widows. Was it for these reasons that many widows wishing to remarry chose a common-law type of union?

A widow left well provided for could look forward to an independent life free from both financial worries and 'that guardianship and control to which the sex are subject while virgins, and while wives'.[43] For some women, 'the comfortable state of widowhood', as Peachum described it, must have been 'the only hope that' kept 'up a wife's spirits'.[44] The newly widowed Mrs Strictland in the novel *School for Widows* by Clara Reeve described herself as 'banished from society for more than ten years'. She had been, she added, 'the slave and prisoner of a tyrant'. As a widow she felt 'as does the captive just delivered from his chains'.[45] But the widow left in comfortable circumstances was the exception, and few could opt for the independence of widowhood rather than remarriage. Often the third of her husband's estate to which she was entitled under common law

[42] Brodsky, 'Widows', p. 144.
[43] William Alexander, *The History of Women*, 2 vols. (1779), vol. ii, pp. 309−310.
[44] Gay, *The Beggar's Opera*, i. x.
[45] Reeve, *School for Widows*. pp. 7−8.

was insufficient to give her economic security. Jointures substantial enough to give financial independence were exceptional. In any case, marriage settlements outside the well-to-do were rare. Normally a widow had a family and sometimes a household to which she belonged. If her children were not yet of age, it depended to a large extent on her efforts whether that household could continue as a viable economic unit. Much would depend on the age of her children, and so for how long a period she had to fill the role of head of the household before one of them could take over. But for many women, widowhood meant at best a state of dependence. When John Fielden, the son of a family that combined farming and handloom weaving in the Pennines, died young in 1726, his entire personal estate amounted to only £19. 9s. 11d. By the time the costs of the funeral were met and the legacy to his cousin's widow of 'one cow and fifty shillings' duly paid, there can have been little more than £10 left. The Fieldens had had no children, and the house was left to 'my wife and heirs and assignees for ever'. At least the widow had a house of her own – or so it seemed. But at the end of the will there had been added a further instruction to his wife to allow Margaret, the sister of the dead man, and her husband, to occupy the house 'during the life of the said Mary' for a rent of £5 a year. By this addition, Mary was reduced 'from being economically independent to someone with a modest income and perhaps nowhere to live'. Her chances of remarrying were much reduced.[46]

When Bonham Hayes, a Kent farmer, died in 1720, he confided the care of his widow to his second son, Richard, to whom he had left his house and 220 acres of land. Bonham had felt it necessary to stipulate in his will 'that my loving wife shall have the use and benefit of the little parlour chamber and my little parlour below stairs ... and all the furniture in the same rooms during her natural life and her board gratis with my said son Richard Hayes'. All such provision was subject to her thinking it 'fit to take and accept the same'.[47] In fact, such provision for widows was a legal requirement. The substance of a deceased husband, as Blackstone explained, was what remained after 'deducting for the widow's apparel and the furniture of her bed-chamber'. Widows had a legal right to 'a room and board, and access to the communal fire, in the house of the eldest son'.[48] The fact that Bonham Hayes felt it necessary to

---

[46] *Shore in Stansfield*, p. 22.
[47] Ralph Arnold, *A Yeoman of Kent: An Account of Richard Hayes (1725–1790) of Cobham* (1949), p. 94.
[48] Blackstone, *Commentaries*, vol. ii, p. 518.

include such an instruction in his will might suggest that the law was not always regarded, or he might have felt that as Richard was not his eldest son he must spell out exactly the conditions his widow should enjoy.

When in 1680, the father of William Stout died, his mother was left 'sole executor of his personal estate, which was very considerable of goods and mony at interest' (*sic*), but the main part of his estate went to Josias, the eldest son, who was eighteen. His mother continued to run the household and manage the estate until such time as 'her own sones were capable to manage the same'. In fact, only in 1687 was Josias thought to have reached an age 'to manage for himself'. His mother acted as his housekeeper. At that time, William tells us, 'my mother, brothers and sister dwelt together in much concord and industry in managing their husbandry'. His mother, as well as housekeeping for them, continued to help 'in the husbandry in turf, hay and harvest time, and dressing corn in the winter'. Despite much encouragement from his mother to get married, Josias married only in 1709. By this time his mother was seventy, and the work of housekeeper had become too much for her. She suggested he get himself a servant to help in the housekeeping, but, we are told, he was 'not ... willing to keep house with a servant'. Understandably, by this date she was 'urgent on him to marry'. Finally he did so. His mother approved his choice, but after nearly thirty years of house-keeping for him it must have been difficult to hand over the responsi-bility to a young wife. She had 'thought to have some direction' in it, but her son's wife had other ideas.[49] Relations in the household seem to have grown strained, for in a year's time, Josias asked his brother William to take in their mother. Until her death she lived with William, who never married, and his sister Elin. In many ways, William Stout's mother was fortunate in her widowhood. There were no financial difficulties. She had a home, and for the first years of widowhood she continued to manage the household. Yet even in her case, not all her thirty-five years as a widow can have been easy. For by far the majority of widows of the labouring class there was little or no provision made by their husbands. Some were left with little more than their bed and bedding. 'Bed and bedding where and in which we are accustomed to lie together also with one chest' was how Abraham Fielden's will of 1754 provided for his wife.[50] Such provision was often only returning what she had brought to the

[49] *Autobiography of William Stout*, pp. 73, 75, 87, 131–2, 159.
[50] *Shore in Stansfield*, p. 31.

marriage as part of her dowry. How was such a widow to support herself?

Many widows, as well as unmarried women, managed to make a living by renting a cottage with common rights. Some widows were smallholders, renting or owning a strip or two in the common fields or a small plot of land. Nicholas Blundell in 1712 granted a tenancy to Elizabeth Swift, a widow. With Blundell's consent she was able to 'Erect & Build a Cottage upon the Waist not far from the Pound in Little Crosby & also inclose a Few Perches of Ground for a Garden Spot, which said Cottage & Ground', Blundell wrote in his tenants' book, 'she is to enjoy during her own Life & to doe yearly one day Reaping of Corne or pay in lew thereof sixpence'. Blundell was not unaware of the danger that such a widow or her offspring might present at some future date to the Poor Law authorities. 'She has no tenant's right,' he explained, 'but I shall allow it to her Children if she have any unless by so doing I may endanger bringing in a Famely of Beggars & in such a Case it may be more advisable to turne off her Children & give them some small Consideration.'[51] On their own, such widows were very vulnerable to the bullying of neighbours, if not worse. In 1753, for instance, Henry Purefoy wrote an angry letter to the Revd Mr Williams on behalf of his tenant, Widow Penell. The widow had complained that Williams had broken up 'her mounds' (banks of earth enclosing land), threatened 'to cutt her gates if she locks 'em', and insisted 'on having a horse way through her Grounds'. Purefoy wrote indignantly to Williams that 'there is no Horse way there & must desire you to desist & not come there, for the Woman is about to hayne [shut up from cattle in order to preserve for hay] her ground'. The same widow was summoned to appear before the church court at Buckingham shortly after her husband died and, despite Purefoy's intervention on her behalf, was fined a shilling. The widow had been left with five small children and a backlog of unpaid rent. The poor widow, Purefoy tells us, 'was not worth £5'. But all his compassion did not prevent his mother trying to extract the rent due from the widow. 'All her effects to the very bed she lies on were seized by my mother,' wrote Henry, 'and the Inventory came to but £3 odd shillings more than her rent.' 'Upon her freinds [sic] Importunity' Elizabeth Purefoy had allowed her to keep some of her stock to see if she could make a

---

[51] *The Great Diurnal of Nicholas Blundell of Little Crosby, Lancashire*, 3 vols. (1968, 1970, 1972), vol. iii, app. A.

living for herself and her children. 'Otherwise,' wrote Purefoy, ' 'tis impossible she should go on'.[52]

Almost certainly underestimated is the effect of engrossing of farms and enclosure on the widow or single woman with a small plot of land, more particularly if she was a tenant. Even if the woman had nothing more than a cottage and common rights she could still make a livelihood. Ironically, many Poor Law authorities recognized this. Aware, for example, of how ownership of a cow could be the means of a widow gaining a livelihood, they were sometimes prepared to contribute towards its purchase. In 1773, an entry in the Overseer's Accounts for the parish of Duffield reads: 'Widw. Webster toward a cow. 0. 12s. 0d.'[53] In the village of Tysoe in Warwickshire, a widow was given 4s. 'to take her to Birmingham to a place in service'.[54] A Suffolk woman widowed in 1779 had fourteen children under the age of fourteen. All that remained to her on her husband's death was 'two cows, with a very little furniture and clothing'. The Poor Law authorities offered to take the seven youngest children into the house of industry. The widow resisted the proposal, involving as it did the break-up of her family. Instead she asked that her landlord should 'continue her in the farm [14 acres of pasture land]', and guaranteed to maintain her family without relying on the parish. This was agreed, and the widow succeeded in supporting her family unaided until they were old enough to earn their own living. Nor was this at the expense of the landlord, we are told, for she continued 'to pay her rent regularly'.[55]

Without any access to land and with the erosion of common rights, what were poor widows in the countryside to do? The mother of William Smith, potter and farmer, was left a widow in 1801. William, the eldest of six children, had just begun at school. His schooling came to an abrupt halt after only three days, and he was sent out to work. The widow became a charwoman. She baked bread for sale, and when her son bought a cottage and established his pottery, she opened a shop in it while acting as housekeeper to him.[56] If a widow was fortunate enough to have a house, one way of making a living was as a lodging-house keeper. A remarkable

[52] *The Purefoy Letters, 1735–1753*, ed. G. Eland, 2 vols. (1931), vol. i, pp. 4, 26.

[53] Pinchbeck, *Women Workers and the Industrial Revolution*, p. 23.

[54] John Gillis, *For Better, For Worse* (1985), p. 113.

[55] *The Report of the Society for Bettering the Condition of the Poor* (1800), vol. ii, pp. 45–6.

[56] George Sturt, *William Smith Potter and Farmer: 1790–1858* [1919], (1974), pp. 55, 110–12.

number of widows are found as schoolteachers. If a widow could read and had a cottage in which she could house a few children, she could set up a dame school and eke out a meagre existence by charging parents a penny or a half-penny a day.[57]

Earnings as an agricultural labourer were insufficient to support a single woman. If she worked at hay-time and harvest and occasionally at other tasks, it was essential she had other employment for most of the year. Thomas Wright wrote of 'a poor woman who got her living by spinning hemp and line'. The growing of a little hemp or line was common, and many farmers set aside a corner of a field for the purpose. This particular woman travelled from 'house to house to enquire for work'. When a family employed her she was assured 'meat, and drink, and lodging (if she had occasion to sleep with them), for her work, and what they pleased to give her besides'.[58] Many widows, as we have seen, turned washerwomen, either going from household to household or taking in washing that was done in their homes. When the mother of Francis Place's first wife was widowed she was left 'in possession, as a tenant at will of a small house in Wilderness Lane White Friars. The House was meanly furnished', Place tells us, 'and mostly let out to Lodgers, this with taking in washing enabled her to maintain herself and her younger daughter, and to save some money'.[59] For such widows it was a makeshift existence. Take, for example, information that emerged about a widow at her settlement examination in Winchester in the 1780s; Elizabeth Dear, the widow of a wine-cooper who had died twenty-five years previously, had no children living. For some time after her husband's death she 'kept a shop'. What subsequently happened to the shop we are not told, but she was next 'hired to Alderman Smith ... to look after child'. After a few years she left this employer and went for the same purpose to the home of Richard Case where she stayed 'for 10 or 12 years'. The children grew up, but Case kept her on 'as a house servant with him at 4 gns per a.'[60] For widows with no children, domestic service offered the security of bed and board.

When her husband died in 1695, Widow Lovell, of Eastern Socon,

[57] See Victor E. Neuburg, *Popular Education in Eighteenth-century England* (1971); A. E. Dobbs, *Education and Social Movements* (1919); Margaret Spufford, *Small Books and Pleasant Histories* (1981).
[58] *Autobiography of Thomas Wright*, p. 132.
[59] *Autobiography of Francis Place*, p. 105.
[60] *Winchester Settlement Papers, 1667–1842*, compiled by Arthur J. Willis (1967), p. 28, and see the case of Barbara Hayes, p. 29.

Bedfordshire, had at first been able to scratch a living by boarding a young parish child at 1*s.* 6*d.* a week. But it was not enough, and on occasion she was forced to ask for help from the parish and for wood. At length in 1712, two years before her death, she was given a regular weekly allowance of 2*s.* 6*d.*[61] Much later in the century, Henrietta Edwards, a blacksmith's widow, who had been left after only four years of marriage with an infant son, managed to rent 'a tenement ... at £4 p.a. for a yr.' We are not told what work she found to support herself and her child, but it cannot have proved adequate. For the next three years she was 'hired by the County Hospital ... as a nurse at £7 p.a.'[62]

Parishes tried to avoid widows becoming dependent on relief. Like Widow Lovell some were given children to board. In straw-plaiting areas, bundles of straw were distributed to them, and sometimes hat-blocks on which straw hats could be moulded. Despite the decline of hand-spinning there were parishes which still thought it worthwhile to supply widows with spinning-wheels. There is the case recorded in Rugeley, Staffordshire, in February, 1784: 'A small wheel for Widow Atkin 7.0.'[63] Widows were employed, as was Henrietta Edwards, as parish nurses in the locality. In Aldenham, Hertfordshire, in 1783, 'a poor widow who had three children supported by the parish', was trained to act as midwife. She was 'sent ... for instruction, to the Lying-in Hospital in Store Street, near Tottenham Court Road'. When she returned she was 'so well instructed, as to exercise her calling in the parish ever since, without a single accident, or ever having to call in medical assistance'. Eventually she became independent of parish assistance, and attended, we are told, 'all the day labourers' wives at the stipulated price of half-a-crown'.[64] In 1776 Mary Hardy recorded how she 'went with children to Widow Ward's and had them innoculated for smallpox'.[65]

For other widows the struggle to avoid dependence on poor relief was less successful. At Eastern Socon in Bedfordshire, Widow Bleat was left with a young son and a cottage urgently in need of re-thatching. On several occasions the parish repaired it for her. In 1715 it was extensively rethatched. When Jane Bluck, a victim of smallpox, was brought back to the parish from Grafham, the widow

[61] Joyce Godber, *History of Bedfordshire, 1066–1888*, Bedfordshire County Council (1969), p. 366.
[62] *Winchester Settlement Papers*, pp. 28–9.
[63] Pinchbeck, *Women Workers and the Industrial Revolution*, p. 133.
[64] *Society for Bettering the Condition of the Poor*, vol. i, p. 91.
[65] *Mary Hardy's Diary*, p. 21.

was given the task of nursing her and was given 10s. a week for so doing. She also received from the parish 'bed, firing, bread, cheese and candles', as well as 3s. for houseroom. But Jane Bluck recovered and very soon after the parish recorded, 'Widow Bleat in need. 1s.'[66] In the lists of 'Old and Decayed People and Poor and Widows' of the parish of Whickham in Durham in 1764, there is evidence of many widows who managed to maintain themselves, if only just, by 'wealing' (removing stones and dirt from the coals at the surface of mines). So 'Phyllis Denham Wid.: about 80, maintained by her own labour which is wailing at the staiths, excessively poor'; or 'Betty Bainbridge, Wid.: with 4 chil. ye eldest about 12: she is a Wealer and miserably poor.'[67] There was great reluctance among widows to ask for relief from the parish. Many preferred independence at whatever cost, even near-starvation. Eden wrote of the widow Anne Hurst, who 'though bent with age and infirmities, and little able to work, excepting as a weeder in a gentleman's garden ... was too proud either to ask or receive any relief from her parish.' She lived on what she earned and a pound a year given her by some unknown benefactor.[68] Few had her good fortune in having a benefactor, and the lists of those receiving poor relief and the records of the inmates of workhouses bear witness to the number of widows whose efforts to survive alone failed.

For those left in comfortable circumstances, widowhood may have 'afforded unique opportunities for independence, economic self-sufficiency and a "social freedom" absent from the lives of both single and married women'.[69] There were such widows, but they represented a small minority. Legally women 'enjoyed their greatest rights out of coverture ... especially in widowhood'.[70] But the number of widows who could exercise those rights was strictly limited. Many who could failed to do so. Most widows enjoyed no security. Whether from the terms of their husbands' wills, or from their habit of relinquishing what they had to their children, the majority possessed little status and no independence. Often they were dependent on the continued tolerance of their children for a

[66] Godber, *History of Bedfordshire*, p. 366.

[67] List of the 'Old and Decayed People, and Poor and Widows', in Whickham Parish, 1764, Strathmore Papers D/ST 336/7, Durham County Record Office.

[68] Sir F. M. Eden. *The State of the Poor*, 3 vols (1797), vol. ii, p. 579.

[69] Brodsky, 'Widows', p. 123. Vivien Brodsky summarizes the view expressed by Richard Vann, 'Towards a new lifestyle: women in pre-industrial capitalism', in R. Bridenthal and C. Koonz (eds.), *Becoming Visible: Women in European History* (1977), p. 195.

[70] Richard M. Smith (ed.), *Land, Kinship and Life-Cycle*, p. 427.

home and support. Among the labouring class, widowhood was almost always a struggle for survival. As women alone, all widows were vulnerable. It is not surprising that often they drew together, sharing the same house or forming local networks of mutual help and support.[71] As lodging-house keepers, many widows were at least guaranteed company. Among middle-class widows there were those who became dependent on their maidservants to whom they showed far greater kindness and generosity than the majority of mistresses. Among even the most fortunate widows there was a tendency to seek out other female company. It suggests just how aware they were of their vulnerability. There was safety in numbers.

[71] See, for example, Vivien Brodsky on the existence of a poor widow subculture in late sixteenth-century London, in 'Widows', pp. 124, 150.

14

Conclusion

We have seen how, wherever there was the opportunity, the vast majority of women in the eighteenth century worked. They worked hard, for long hours, and often at heavy tasks. Much of the work was unwaged, a great deal of it was performed within the household. It embraced work in agriculture and domestic industry, in house-work, and in bearing and rearing children. Often their work was characterized by its multi-occupational nature. Nor was this characteristic found in women's work only in the household. What Olwen Hufton has described as 'an economy of expedients, multiple make-shifts which together permitted some kind of existence' was the context in which many single women worked, but it was not confined to them. Her 'straw plaiters who were hoers, weeders, and harvesters at stages of the year; salters of herring who were also kelpers and stocking knitters; silk workers who made fireworks in their spare time' were often married women.[1] Many women moved between occupations that were part-time or seasonal. It is one of the characteristics of women's work that defies recording and quantification.

In the first half of the century, women seem to have worked in a wide range of trades, some of them involving work that was later to become the monopoly of men. The grounds on which they were excluded from such trades were that the work was unsuitable, unfeminine, inclining to immoral habits because it required being in close proximity to men, or that it was physically too demanding. Very rarely is there evidence of open opposition to women working

[1] Olwen Hufton, 'Women without men: widows and spinsters in Britain and France in the eighteenth century', *Journal of Family History*, 8/4 (1984), pp. 355–76 (p. 363).

at certain tasks because they were competing with men, although when apprenticeship was already in decline, the efforts of some male craftsmen to enforce apprenticeship may well have been partly motivated by competition from unapprenticed female labour. In the course of the century, the range of occupations open to women tended to narrow. Side by side with the 'masculinization' of some tasks and trades went the feminization of others. By the end of the century, female blacksmiths, carpenters, bricklayers, and coopers were becoming rarities. On the other hand, domestic service was in process of being feminized and the importance of the so-called women's trades — milliners, mantua-makers, seamstresses, and dressmakers — was growing.

The same process can be seen in housework. While there had always been certain tasks normally undertaken only by women, there had been others where the men, and sometimes all members of the household, co-operated; there was no rigid sexual division of labour. But by the end of the eighteenth century, and more particularly in the early years of the nineteenth, what constituted 'housework' was to change, and become almost exclusively women's work. The Victorian ideology of women's place being in the home was not new, but when women's working lives tended more and more to be outside the home it took on a new meaning and strengthened the tendency for housework to become women's work. The feminization of domestic service was closely linked to this change in the nature of housework.

It was not merely a much clearer demarcation of working roles of women and men that was the consequence of eighteenth-century economic change. In the reorganization of agriculture and manufacturing, women on the whole were pushed toward what were called the less 'skilled' work and tasks. Whether in fact they were less 'skilled' is questionable. They were the more peripheral, preparatory, often arduous, and frequently boring tasks. But what above all else made them 'unskilled' was that they were almost all badly paid. In agriculture, particularly in the south-east, reorganization meant a concentration of women's labour in weeding and hoeing, stone-removing, dibbing wheat and potatoes, setting peas and beans, leading horses at the plough, and away from the better-paid work of reaping in hay-time and harvest. Changing harvest technology provided a useful rationale for such change. In textile manufacturing, after a brief period of high wages in the late 1770s, rates of pay tended to fall steadily where hand-spinning persisted. 'Thousands of women, when they can get work', petitioned the rioting cotton-spinners in 1780, 'must make a long day to card, spin and reel 5040 yards of cotton, and for this they have four-pence or five-pence and no more.'[2] No wonder that in Wiltshire, where hand-spinning 'had fallen into disuse', Eden found 'the Poor scarcely have the heart to earn the little that is obtained by it'.[3] If some former hand-spinners moved into weaving, it was not an option open to all, and in many agricultural areas there was nothing to compensate for the decline of hand-spinning.

Crucial is the question of how far the loss of women's opportunities for productive work that followed changes in agriculture and the decline of the older handicrafts was compensated for by increased employment opportunities in textile factories or in some of the smaller domestic industries like lace-making, straw-making, and glove-making. Pinchbeck was sceptical. 'If wage-earning occupations for women became more numerous', she wrote, 'their total contribution to productive work was not necessarily altered thereby.'[4] Eric Richards went further in claiming 'that the participation of women in the economy (though not necessarily as wage-labour *per se*) was substantially *greater* before the Industrial Revolution than during that process itself'.[5] Indeed, he claimed that it was still doubtful whether as late as 1974 they had fully recovered from the contraction of their economic role that accompanied industrialization. Of course, much depended on where women lived. But even when allowance is made for great regional diversity, the fact remains that there were many areas where no compensatory employment emerged. So in talking of how family earnings in South Warwickshire were undermined by women's loss of work in agriculture, J. M. Martin has written of how 'no work remained ... nor ... did any rural industry spring up in the Feldon to compensate for the loss'.[6] The same was true of many areas of the south and east. Those women in cotton factories in the eighteenth century were a small minority, mainly young girls who had no previous experience of the domestic textile industry. Significantly it was into the subsidiary processes they moved. No longer were the majority spinners. The spinning

[2] *The Case of the Poor Cotton Spinners* (1780), quoted Ivy Pinchbeck, *Women Workers and the Industrial Revolution, 1750–1850* [1930], (1981), p. 151.

[3] Sir F. M. Eden, *The State of the Poor*, 3 vols (1797), vol, iii, p. 796.

[4] Pinchbeck, *Women Workers and the Industrial Revolution*, p. 1.

[5] Eric Richards, 'Women in the British economy since about 1700: an interpretation', *History*, 59/1977 (1974), pp. 337–57 (p. 342).

[6] J. M. Martin, 'Village traders and the emergence of a proletariat in south Warwickshire', *Agricultural History Review*, 32 (1984), p. 186.

machinery, it was said, required greater strength and skill than women possessed.

The essence of the family economy was the measure of economic independence that access to land provided. It was therefore more a rural than an urban economy. In the eighteenth century, the ability to subsist without depending entirely on wages was steadily eroded. In the process of development of a more capitalist agriculture, growth in the size of farms, engrossing and enclosure, more agricultural specialization, many lost all hold on land. Many more lost common rights. If all the labouring poor benefited by such rights, it was often the women in the household who made greatest use of them and who were thus enabled to contribute to their families' livelihood. With the disappearance of such common rights, women may well have lost more than men, for common rights had often provided them with the opportunity for productive work.

With the disintegration of the family economy, by the end of the century more were forced to depend entirely on wage labour for their livelihood. The labour of men and women became competitive. While both worked in the home there had been no competition: there were tasks to be done, and somebody had to do them. If there was a division of labour in the family economy, there was no competition for jobs. Anything earned was for the entire family. But once both were dependent on wage labour, the recognized training a woman had received and the wages that in consequence she might be expected to command, should have worked to protect her. But the two main sources of training for women — apprenticeship and service in husbandry — were already far gone in decline. Those trades still open to female apprentices were becoming overstocked. The number of unapprenticed women seeking work at any price made apprenticeship of doubtful value. Completion of an apprenticeship was no guarantee of work. Employers now calculated carefully the financial advantages of employing cheap female labour against the increased burden on the poor rates of unemployed men. Whether or not men were conscious of it, the danger of competition for women was always lurking behind every reason produced for women's exclusion from tasks or trades. No one has closely analysed the motives behind the outcry against women's employment in factories and mines in the early nineteenth century, but the removal of female competition was not unrelated. There can be little doubt that women acted as a buffer protecting men from the unemployment and underemployment they would otherwise have suffered.

The training that service in husbandry gave women was largely irrelevant unless they were to set up in independent households with a farm or smallholding. When small farms, or even cottages, were difficult to find, the assumption that marriage meant the formation of a new independent household was no longer valid. Why bother to go to service when at the end of the day the most to be hoped for was irregular day-work as agricultural labour?

In the eighteenth century as strictly defined, there seems little doubt that women lost out as far as opportunities for work are concerned: the real argument is at what point in the nineteenth century employment opportunities for women began to expand, and how much they had to expand to make up for earlier loss. Such a conclusion is in no way contrary to anything Pinchbeck wrote. The 'changes of vital importance to women' introduced by the Industrial Revolution, she admitted had 'at first appeared to affect many women adversely. The family income was seriously depleted by the loss of their ... earnings, and ... lack of employment for married women had serious consequences.'[7] Unemployment or underemployment made women more dependent on their husbands. Once work took husband or wife, or both, away from the home, there could be no approximation to a working relationship between them. Women unable to make any contribution to the family budget must have lost self-confidence and self-respect. It would have been extraordinary if this failed to influence women's relations with their husbands. Far from industrialization meaning the emancipation of women, for many the first phase must have meant a greater servitude and conditions where they had no defence against the arbitrary wielding of patriarchal power. 'It mattered little how willing and anxious she was to work,' Pinchbeck wrote, 'she could no longer assist in the support of her family, nor could she maintain her own economic independence.'[8]

If this was the lot of married women they were not the worst sufferers. For those without husbands, whether spinsters, unmarried mothers, or widows, whose entire livelihood depended on their own exertions, the eighteenth century was a hard time. The lack of any acknowledgement of the problems facing single women was part of the failure to recognize that women had any existence outside marriage. To the difficulty of earning sufficient to support themselves was added resentment and scorn of their unmarried state.

Ivy Pinchbeck's researches led to some remarkable insights into

[7] Pinchbeck, *Women Workers and the Industrial Revolution*, p. 4.
[8] Ibid., p. 44.

women's experience of change in agriculture and industry. Curiously, while often her material points in one direction some of her conclusions seem to have been arrived at quite independently. For example, while acknowledging that lack of work for married women had serious consequences both for themselves and their families, writing in the 1920s when there was no turning back from industrialization, she was determined to salvage some good from it. If there had been suffering and distress, and if, as she admitted, 'a woman had little choice in the matter', lack of employment or under-employment 'resulted in greater leisure for women in the home ... relieved them from the drudgery and monotony ... that characterized much of the hand labour ... under the domestic system'.[9] If industrialization forced them to stay at home without work, then it was of benefit to their husbands and family. It is a view that can only be understood by looking at how the issue of motherhood and/or work outside the home, of the desirability of a balance between women's productive and reproductive labour, preoccupied women in the period after 1918.[10] Pinchbeck was not alone in sincerely believing that the role of motherhood and home-making for working-class wives was better than being an exploited wage-labourer in the conditions following 1918, when many of the gains won during the war were fast disappearing under the impact of unemployment and depression. Moreover, by fulfilling that role, 'the married woman makes an adequate economic contribution'.[11] More recently, and with less excuse, Sir Rhodes Boyson has claimed what a real advance the Industrial Revolution brought to women and their families 'because it introduced the first idea that men's wages should be sufficient to maintain a wife and family, and that women should make their contribution by looking after the home'.[12] Pinchbeck's final judgement on the effects of the Industrial Revolution on women is a cautious one: it 'has on the whole proved beneficial to women'.[13]

What women lost by the disintegration of the family economy involved much more than changes in their work opportunities and in the place that work was carried out. Reinforcing that economy

[9] Ibid., pp. 106, 4.

[10] See the introduction by Miranda Chaytor and Jane Lewis to Alice Clark, *Working Life of Women in the Seventeenth Century* (1982), particularly pp. xv–xxi; and the interesting comment on this attitude in K. D. M. Snell, *Annals of the Labouring Poor* (1985), p. 373.

[11] Pinchbeck, *Women Workers and the Industrial Revolution*, p. 313.

[12] Sir Rhodes Boyson, 'Industrialisation and the life of the Lancashire factory worker', in *The Long Debate on Poverty*, Institute of Economic Affairs (1972), p. 78, quoted Richards, 'Women in the British economy', p. 343.

[13] Pinchbeck, *Women Workers and the Industrial Revolution*, p. 4.

there was the network of common rights from which women stood to benefit most, there was the reciprocal arrangement between households for the training of daughters — and sons — and solving a household's changing demands for labour. Service in husbandry was also a useful preparation for marriage, providing both the training and the ability to save that was necessary for the setting up of a separate household. There was a reciprocal support system that seems to have operated between households by which help was provided from the community to a woman during her lying-in, or to a wife-to-be considered as having an inadequate dowry. When the family economy began to disintegrate, a whole way of life crumbled.

It has been called a 'thrift economy', and much of that thriftiness was practised by women making the best use of everything they had access to. Such thrift surely provided a source of great satisfaction to women. In the letters from emigrants to Canada and Australia of which Keith Snell has made such telling use, Philip Annett, a day-labourer of Corsley who emigrated to Canada wrote home in 1830 to his wife that 'here you can raise every thing of your own that you want to make use of in your family. You can make your own soap, candles, sugar, treacle, and vinegar, without paying any duty.' Similarly, Thomas Hunt, also formerly a day-labourer from Corsley, wrote home proudly that 'we make our own sugar, our own soap, candles, and bake good light bread'.[14] The psychological importance of having a bit of land of their own from which they could produce their vegetables and fruit cannot be overestimated, but even when they owned no land, access to the commons could still provide a measure of economic independence. 'The value of such an economy,' W. G. Hoskins has written, 'eked out though it had to be by a money-wage at certain times of the year, cannot be measured statistically and so is apt to be lost and forgotten, or at the best underestimated by the historian who allows himself to be carried away by large numbers.'[15] What is certain is that women were enabled to make a substantial contribution to the family budget. That this contribution does not lend itself to measurement may be inconvenient for the economic historian, but it alters not one whit the fact that such a contribution made a difference to the standard of living enjoyed.

If, as Eric Hobsbawm has written, 'early industrialization was a

[14] 'Wiltshire emigrants to Canada', *Quarterly Review*, 46 (1832), p. 367.
[15] W. G. Hoskins, *The Midland Peasant* (1957), p. 245.

catastrophe for the labouring poor',[16] it was the experience of women of the labouring poor as well as men. Yet that experience has hardly been considered. The virtual exclusion of women from the standard of living debate might be excused on the grounds that the vast majority of eighteenth-century women fit awkwardly into the nineteenth century concept of work — the basis on which its occu- pational censuses were compiled. That debate has been conduc- ted in terms that may be relevant to nineteenth-century work practice but are singularly irrelevant to everything we know of the eighteenth. The unpaid nature of much of the work of women, its part-time, often seasonal, nature, the fact that many women worked in a multi-occupational context, make it difficult to estimate the value of their contribution. But that it had value and made a significant contribution to the standard of living enjoyed there can be no doubt. Recently, two new contributors to the debate raised hopes by acknowledging that 'questions about work and earnings by women and children have always been lurking in the wings through- out the standard of living debate'. Such hopes were dashed by their conclusion that 'the relative earning power of women did not decline. It may have stayed the same, or it may have risen.'[17] There was no supporting evidence for such a conclusion. But then they started from the assumption that earnings are what the standard of living debate is all about, and even within such a narrow definition they considered the 'adult male employee' to be of central importance. They admit that between 1750 and 1850 there was a decline in the overall labour force participation of both women and children, but that such a trend was involuntary they dismiss as 'hard to sustain'.[18]

In the same way, any attempts at drawing up occupational tables for the eighteenth century which totally ignore women cannot be regarded as contributing satisfactorily to our understanding of the social history of the period. Attempts to deduce women's involve- ment in the eighteenth-century economy from nineteenth-century occupational census material are doomed to failure, for the assump- tions of the nineteenth century censuses about what constitutes work and gainful employment are of little or even no relevance to what we know of women's work throughout the eighteenth century.

[16] Eric Hobsbawm, 'The British standard of living, 1790–1850', *Economic History Review*, 2nd ser., 10/1 (1957), p. 46.
[17] Peter H. Lindert and Jeffrey G. Williamson, 'English workers' living standards during the Industrial Revolution: a new look', *Economic History Review*, 2nd ser., 36/1 (1983), p. 17.
[18] Ibid., p. 19.

For those of us who do not believe in keeping women's history separate from the rest of history, it is not a very encouraging scene. If we are conscious of the need to insert women into the main controversies and debates exercising social history today, we get little or no encouragement from methodologies that exclude women by the very nature of the source material, from historians of the eighteenth century who still regard any work done by women as somehow inferior and light-weight − 'a by-occupation to keep them out of mischief', as one has written, 'not intended to interfere with the more basic duties ... the quiet rests, of the women. ... Given such an essentially casual attitude to work, low average earnings were inevitable.'[19] There are still social historians who see society as made up of men.

Many historians of the Industrial Revolution have expressed their concern that Third World countries should look at the process of industrialization in this country as a model, and have emphasized the uniqueness and complexity of British experience. They have suggested it would be rash, if not dangerous, to see what happened in England as in any way representative of the process of industrialization. Very few have acknowledged that there might be something to learn by studying the way in which industrialization has occurred and is occurring in African, Latin American, and Asian countries. As I was writing this book I had the opportunity of comparing English experience with that of some of the Third World countries. The result was what appeared to be some fascinating parallels. To discover how English women in the eighteenth century were affected by industrialization means years of searching through a great variety of source material. But in many areas of Africa, Latin America, and India the process of industrialization is much more recent, and in many cases only now can its full effects on women be seen. Of course there is no one pattern to women's experience. There are often profound differences in the circumstances in which the process has occurred more recently relative to those of eighteenth-century England. But comparative studies do offer one way in which perhaps we can isolate what, if anything, was unique in the experience of eighteenth-century English women and look more closely at some of the interesting echoes of that experience among women in Third World countries today.

[19] Duncan Bythell, *The Handloom Weavers* (1969), p. 177.

Index

Aberdeenshire, 121
Abingdon, 99, 241
Acton, William, 173
Africa, 57, 267
Agriculture, 2, 3, 4–6, 10, 14, 16, 19–
20, 23, chs 3, 4, and 5 passim, 88,
154, 164, 236, 260, 261, 262;
Agrarian Revolution, 9–11, 194,
260–2; common rights, 23, 90, 236,
239, 253–4, 262, 265; enclosure, 11,
23, 236, 239, 254, 262; migrant
women workers in, 154, 164–8,
172, 237; seasonal unemployment in,
2, 154; sexual division of labour in,
3, 90–2; surveys of, 2; technology,
3, 260; women's employment in, 3,
5, 85, 90–1, 125, 151, 155, 192,
259, 262; wages, 255; see also
bondage system, dairymaids, fruit-
picking, gleaning, hoeing and
weeding, hop-picking, market-
gardening, mowing, reaping, service
in husbandry, vegetable-gatherers
Aikin, J., 41
Alexander, William, 176, 179
Anglesea, 184
apprentices and apprenticeship, 5, 7,
16, 22, 35, 42, 46, 51, 66, 69–71,
78, ch. 6 passim, 123, 125, 128, 145,
174, 180, 198, 227, 233, 236, 246–
8, 250, 260, 262; parish apprentices,
35, 66, 70, ch. 6 passim, 235

Archenholz, J. W. von, 105, 130, 172
Aries, Philip, 77
Arizpe, Lourdes, 150–1
Artificers, Statute of, 87
Ashford, Mary Ann, or Polly, 139,
142–3, 159, 177–8, 194, 236, 244
Ashton, T. S., 64
Astell, Mary, 186, 231
Austen, Jane, 231; Mansfield Park, 136
Australia, 265
Aylesbury, 72
Ayrshire, 39

Baird, Thomas, 166–7
Bamford, Samuel, 41, 112
Banbury, 171, 199
Banks, J. A., 161
banns, the calling of, 178, 203–4, 207,
209–10
Barker, Jane, 231–2
Basingstoke, 170
Bath, 160
Beattie, J. M., 139
Bedford, 66, 131
Bedford, Duke of, 129
Bedfordshire, 56, 65, 66, 67, 89, 90,
92, 93, 113, 200, 233, 256
Bell, John, 180
Bere, Nancy, 143
Berg, Maxine, 3
Berkshire, 54, 212
Berry, Mary, 129

Bettesworth, Lucy, 194
bigamy, 211, 213–16
Birmingham, 17, 96, 177, 224, 228, 254
Blackstone, Sir William, 72, 75, 196–8, 199, 207, 249, 251
Blundell, Nicholas, 121, 135, 138, 171–2, 253
bondage system, 58
Boserup, Esther, 57, 150, 151
Boulton, Matthew, 174
Bownas, Samuel (1676–1753), 176–7, 193
Boyson, Sir Rhodes, 264
Bradley, Richard, 37, 39, 164
Brassley, Paul, 58
'bridewains', or biddings, 189–90
Brodsky, Vivien, 236, 248, 249–50, 258 n. 71
Broughton, Thomas, 137
Brown, Elizabeth (1778–91), 113
Brown, Maria, 207, 209
Buckingham, 253
Buckinghamshire, 54, 66, 243
'bundling', 183–4
Burn, Richard, 213
Burrell, Timothy, 140
Burton, Robert, 229
Bury, 41
buttons, manufacture of, 3

Caernarvon, 209
Caernarvonshire, 184
Cambridgeshire, 54, 67, 81, 88, 165, 237–9
Campbell, R., 92, 95–6
Canada, letters from emigrants to, 265
Cardington, 26, 62–3, 131, 233–4
Carmarthenshire, 217
carpenters, women as, 246, 260
Carter, Elizabeth, 231
celibacy, 205, ch. 12 *passim*, 241; *see also* spinsters
Chancery, Court of, 200
Chapone, Hester, 219
Charke, Charlotte, 202
charring and charwomen, 140, 150, 155, 160–1, 172, 236, 254
chastity, premarital, 180–4, 207
Chaytor, Miranda, 21

Cheshire, 31, 74
Christian, Edward, 196
Clapham, 9, 12
Clare, John, 163, 185, 190
Clark, Alice, 2, 25, 39, 45, 51, 120, 128, 191
Cleveland, 67
Cobbett, William, 79
Cole, Revd William, 140, 161
Collier, Jane, 229, 231
Collier, Mary, 35, 42, 111, 158, 161, 236–7
Colquhoun, Patrick, 16, 19–20, 126, 149, 173
Corfe Castle, 233
Cornwall, 58, 162, 181, 212, 224
cottage industry, *see* domestic industry
courtship, 6–7, ch. 10 *passim*; *see also* pre-marital sex and pregnancy
Covent Garden, 95, 163, 165, 167, 169
Coventry, 86, 93, 245–6
Crabbe, George, 188–9
Crafts, N. F., 10–11
Cries of London, The, 160
Crompton, Samuel, and Betty, his mother, 41, 242
Cully, George, 58
Cumberland, 74, 189

dairymaids or -women, 28, 31–2, 39, 70, 72–3, 133, 187, 236
Dant, Joan, 171
Davidson, Caroline, 5, 111, 121, 128
Davies, David, 60, 67–8, 121, 212
Day, Thomas, 51
Defoe, Daniel, 41, 44, 51, 105, 124, 134, 184, 194, 199, 224, 245, 248; *Moll Flanders*, 124, 242; *Roxana*, 146, 231
Delamotte, Charles, and Elizabeth, his sister, 176
demography and demographers, 16–17, 20–2, 225–6
Denby, 244
Denman, R. D., 5, 85, 86, 90–1
Deptford, dockyards of, 166
Derby, 224–5
Derbyshire, 44, 65, 66, 194
desertion, 6, 201, 211–13, 239

Devon, 51, 58, 73, 90−1
divorce, law of, 6, 210−11, 215, 216,
218
domestic (or cottage) industry, 3, 6, 8,
11−12, 13−15, 53, 62−3, 65−7,
104, 149−50, 155, 165, 192, 236,
259, 261, 264; *see also* the 'dual
economy', glove manufacture, lace-
making, metal-workers, 'proto-
industrialization', straw-plaiting,
textile manufacture (hand and
framework knitting)
domestic service and servants, 2, 5, 6,
16, 18, 28, 31, 52, 69−71, 82, 83,
84, 98−100, 108, 117, 123−4, ch. 8
passim, 141−51, 155, 156−7, 160,
174, 177−9, 186−7, 188, 190, 201,
233, 235, 236, 242, 255, 258, 260;
see also hiring fairs or statutes,
service and servants in husbandry
Dorset, 90
dower, 203, 206, 248−50
dowries, or marriage portions, 97, 143,
168, 186−91, 203, 208, 222, 234,
249
'dual economy', the, 39−44, 62
Dublin, 217
Duck, Stephen, 34, 42
Dugaw, Dianne, 230
Dunbar, Janet, 226
Dunlop, O. J., 5, 85, 86, 90−1
Durham, 58, 160, 170, 252

East Anglia, 62, 88, 102
Eden, Sir F. M., 34, 38, 54, 55, 56, 60,
67, 75, 159, 167, 201−2, 232, 234−
5, 237, 257, 261
Edgeworth, Maria, 221, 231
Elliott, Vivien Brodsky, 236, 248, 249−
50, 258 n. 71; *see also* Brodsky,
Vivien
Ellis, William, 73, 140, 141, 162
Elstob, Elizabeth, 231
Employment of Women and Children
in Agriculture, Commission on, 90−
1, 100
Essex, 54, 67, 162, 237
Europe, 14, 77
Everitt, Alan, 36, 45
Exeter, 91

factory industry, 11, 14, 15, 25, 65−6,
149, 261−2
Fairchilds, Cissie, 6, 128, 145, 146, 147
family economy, the, 4−5, 6, 14, 22−
3, 26, 27, 36, 44−6, 77, 125, 129,
192, chs 3 and 4 *passim*, 59, 60, 62,
66, 68, 71, 119, 120, 123, 262,
264−5
Female Friendly Societies, 202,
feme covert, 196, 250
feme sole, 7, 221
fertility, 14, 17, 21, 23
Fielden, Abraham, 252
Fielden, John, and Mary, his wife, 251
Fielding, Henry, 175, 219
Fielding, Sir John, 128, 132, 134
Fielding, Sarah, 231
Fleet, market, 163; marriages, 204,
206−7, 213
Fleetwood, William, 77, 141
France and the French, 27, 45, 46, 113,
115−16, 120, 128, 145, 185, 187
fruit-picking, 35, 56, 154, 165−8
fuel-gathering, 45, 113−14
Furber, Thomas, 73−4

Gaskell, Peter, 181
Gawthern, Abigail, 133, 244
Gay, John, *The Beggars' Opera*, 240
General Description of All Trades, A,
95
gentility, aspirations to, 49−52, 78−
80, 104, 123−4, 126−9, 161, 245−
6, 248
Gentleman's Magazine, The, 232−3,
244, 246
George, Dorothy, 2, 85, 122
Gillis, John, 7, 137, 200
Gisborne, Thomas, 229
gleaning, 34, 37−8, 44,' 56
Glamorganshire, 189
Gloucester, 208
Gloucestershire, 31, 38, 56, 74
glove manufacture, 3, 66, 233, 261
Grey, Edwin, 109, 172
Grosley, P. J., 139

Hair, P. E. H., 181
Hale, Sir Matthew, 198
Halifax, 41

Hall, William (1748–1825), and Sukey, his wife, 163
Hammonds, the, 9, 12, 60–1, 85
Hampshire, 88, 107, 115–16, 215, 236
Hampson, E. M., 67, 238–9
'handfast' or betrothal ceremonies, 206, 218
Hanway, Jonas, 16, 126
Hardwicke's Marriage Act (1753), 185, 202, 206–7
Hardy, Mary, 28–30, 32, 110, 136, 157, 256
Hardy, Thomas, 194–5
Hardy, William, 28
Hasbach, W., 83
hawkers and pedlars, 151, 154, 168–72, 243
Hayes, Bonham, and Richard, his son, 251–2
Hayley, William, 230
Haywood, Eliza, 190–1
Hecht, Jean J., 5
Herefordshire, 80
Hertfordshire, 54, 66, 72, 109, 142, 172, 214, 237, 256
Hey, David, 43
Higgs, Edward, 150, 152
highwaywoman, 162
hiring fairs or statutes, 72, 82, 134, 135–6, 146, 219
History of Two Brothers' Misfortunes, at and after their Marriage, 190
Hobsbawm, Eric, 11, 265–6
hoeing and weeding, 33, 35, 54, 55, 70, 91, 143, 164, 166, 171, 228, 257, 260
Hogarth, William, 129–30
Hone, William, 134
hop-picking, 35, 39, 55, 161, 165
Hoskins, W. G., 265
Hostettler, Eve, 3, 57
housewifery or housewifry, 32, 45, 89, 92, 98, 99, 100, 102, 139, 162, 192, 227; *see also* housewives, housework
housewives, 44, 62, 73, 98, ch. 7 *passim*, 148, 151, 153, 155, 161, 162, 163; *see also* housewifery or housewifry, housework
housework, 5, 27, 34, 40, 51, 82, 98, 99, 100, ch. 7 *passim*, 127, 128, 150,

259, 260; *see also* fuel-gathering, housewifery or housewifry, housewives, ironing, washing
Howitt, William, 31, 33, 104, 161, 187
Hufton, Professor Olwen, 7, 24, 46, 185, 187, 225–6, 234, 243, 259
Hull, 57
Humphrey Clinker (Tobias Smollett) 169
Hunt, Margaret, 243
Hunt, William, 114, 200
Huntingdonshire, 54
Hutton, Catherine, 109, 163, 177, 209, 227–8
Hutton, William, 224

illegitimacy, 17, 174, 238–9
India, 152
Industrial Revolution, 1, 9–13, 18, 148, 261, 263, 264, 267
industrialization, 1, 5, 12–15, 19, 21, 22, 47, 49, 54, 125, 148–50, 161, 195, 261, 263, 265–6, 267
infanticide, 138
Ingram, Martin, 185, 206
innkeepers and licensed victuallers, 151, 159, 243, 244, 247
Ipswich Journal, 218
Ireland, 26, 47, 165–6, 169, 218
ironing, 112–13, 157, 161

Jackson's Oxford Journal, 219
Jeaffreson, John Cordy, 205
Jenyns, Soame, 126, 144
Johnson, Samuel, 180
jointures, 222, 249–51
Jones, Professor E., 18
Jones, Richard, 121
Jones, William, 110, 176
journeywomen, 86, 97, 102

Kalm, Pehr, 117, 122, 164, 166, 168
Kent, 39, 55, 74, 75, 166, 224, 251
Kent, Nathaniel, 59
King, Gregory, 16, 20, 149, 224–5
Knight, Charles, 108, 119, 171, 207
Kussmaul, Ann, 2, 70–1, 78

lace-making, 4, 14, 65, 66, 67, 96, 173, 233–4, 236, 261

Lackington, James, 153
Lady's Magazine, The, 124
Lanarkshire, 55
Lancashire, 13, 17, 30, 40, 65, 106, 112, 135, 139, 171, 235
Lardner, Revd Richard, 130
Laslett, Peter, 21, 120
Latin America, 150, 152, 267
law relating to wives and marriage, 6, ch. 11 *passim*
Leadbeater, Mary, 26, 107, 116, 118, 140, 144, 162, 188
Leapor, Molly, 109, 186
Leeds, 18
Leicestershire, 66, 165
Levellers, The, 192
Lichfield, 225, 233
Lincoln Inn Register of Marriage, 210
Lincolnshire, 54, 67, 74, 76, 106, 160, 165
Lindert, P. H., 155
Lipscomb, George, 162, 166
Liverpool, 18, 171−2
lodging-house keepers, 151, 158−9, 247, 254, 258
London, 16, 17, 19, 30, 39, 49, 50, 51, 69, 86, 93, 95, 105, 108−9, 111, 112, 117, 118, 122, 126, 129, 130, 135, 139, 141, 153, 155, 156, 159, 163, 164, 165, 166, 167, 168, 169, 170, 171, 172, 173, 181, 182, 199, 204, 216, 218, 225, 230, 232, 236, 244, 245, 249
London Chronicle, 128
Long Meg of Westminster, 139
Low Life, 157, 158
Lymington, 143
Lysons, Daniel, 164, 167

McBride, Theresa, 5−6, 117, 125, 128
Macdonald, John, 137
Macfarlane, Alan, 77
McKendrick, N., 4
Malcolmson, Professor R. W., 19, 23, 40, 48
Malcolmson, Patricia, 155, 161
Manchester, 17, 65, 144
market-gardening and market-gardens, 154, 164−8, 172
marriage, 6−7, 17, 73, 76, 81, 83, 97, 99, 132, 138, 143−4, 146, 160, 168, chs 10 and 11 *passim*, 221, 222, 223−4, 225, 238−9, 240, 241, 242, 263−4; Marriage Act of 1653, 203; Marriage Act, enumeration of 1694, 225; broomstick marriages, 206, 218; common law marriages, 205−6, 218, 250; irregular or clandestine marriages, 204, 206−7, 223; marriage age, 14, 17, 23, 223, 233, 238; marriage ceremony, 6, 184, 202−4, 208−9; smock marriages, 218; marriage settlements, 244−50; see also banns, bigamy, 'bridewains' or biddings, courtship, dowries, Fleet marriages, 'handfast' or betrothal ceremonies, Hardwicke's Marriage Act, jointures, law relating to wives and marriage, spousals, wives
Marriage Promoted (1690), 224
Marshall, Dorothy, 85
Marshall, William, 31, 37−8, 54−5, 58, 59, 72, 243
Martin, J. M., 261
Massie, Joseph, 20, 149
Mathias, Peter, 13
Mayhew, Henry, 168
Mayo, Richard, 69, 77, 131
Medick, Hans, 14, 15, 122
Menefee, Samuel Pyeatt, 7, 146, 217, 219
mercuries, 243
Merionethshire, 184
metal-workers, 43; nailers, 43; scissor-makers, 246, 247
Mexico City, 151
Middlesex, 88, 101, 166
Middleton, T., 79, 166
Midlands, 43, 54, 56, 88, 102
midwives, 256
Millenium Hall (Sarah Scott), 146
Milton, John, 210
Mingay, G. E., 49
Misson, Henri, 208−9
money-lenders, widows as, 244
Montagu, Elizabeth, 35, 52, 244
Montagu, Lady Mary Wortley, 231
Morning Chronicle, 219
Morpeth, 170
Morris, Claver, 138

mowing, 56–7
Myddle, 76–7, 130, 132, 138, 226
Myett, Joseph, 76

Nantwich, 74
Neeson, J. M., 61
Newark, 81
Newcastle, 247
Newgate market, 163
Newmarket, 208
Norfolk, 28, 54, 55, 110, 136, 157, 163, 205
Northamptonshire, 38, 54, 56, 61, 66
Northumberland, 57–8
Norwich, 32, 97, 208
Nottingham, 37, 74, 81, 133, 142, 244
Nottinghamshire, 66, 107, 165
Nugent, Robert, 209
nurses and nursing, 233, 256–7
occupational censuses, 16, 115, 122, 125–6, 148–56, 158, 160, 162, 168, 266
Old Bailey, 199, 213
Oxford, 98, 99, 210, 248
Oxford Magazine, The, 129
Oxfordshire, 66, 88, 104, 110, 241

Palmer, Charlotte, 124
patriarchal power, 6, 263
Pennington, Penelope, 135
Pennington, Lady Sarah, 175–6
Pennoyer, Lady Francis, 141–2
Phillips, Sir Richard, 167, 168
physicians, surgeons, and simplers, women as, 162–4, 172
Pinchbeck, Ivy; ch. 1 *passim*, 9–10, 11, 12, 16, 36, 52, 63, 83, 120, 148, 164, 235, 261, 263, 264
Piozzi, Hester, 135
Pitts, John, 47
Place, Francis, 105–6, 112, 118, 158, 179, 181–2, 184, 186, 188, 200, 211, 214, 255; Elizabeth, his wife, 105, 179, 186, 188, 200
Plymouth, 162, 214
Pococke, Richard, 225
Poll Tax of 1692, 69
polyandry and polygamy, 214
Poor Law, Poor Relief and Allowances, the, 49, 64, 67, 68, 79, 80, 81, 87, 88, 174, 212, 235, 237–8, 239, 253, 254, 256–7, 262
population, 14, 16–19, 20, 21, 23, 49, 55, 57, 65, 70, 71, 126, 149, 164, 207; population, censuses of, 16, 19, 23, 222
Portland, Isle of, 113, 182
Potter, Revd, 181
premarital sex and pregnancy, 81, 131, 136–8, 146, 180–4, 207–8, 238–9
Preston, 106, 171, 225
Pringle, A., 75
Prior, Mary, 8
printers, publishers, and book-sellers, 153, 172, 243, 247
prostitutes and prostitution, 8, 173, 231, 238
'proto-industrialization', 14–15, 122, 148
Purefoy, Elizabeth, 82, 133, 135, 137, 138, 139, 156–7, 253–4; Henry, her son, 253–4
putting-out system, 25, 43

Radcliffe, William, 62, 65, 235
Raffald, Elizabeth, 144
reaping, 3, 35, 37–8, 39, 56–8, 91, 260
Reeve, Clara, 231, 249, 250
Richards, Eric, 3, 66, 261
Richardson, Samuel, 132; *Pamela: Or Virtue Rewarded*, 137, 143, 147; *The History of Sir Charles Grandison*, 221
Roberts, Michael, 3, 56
Rochdale, 41
Rostow, W. W., 12
Rule, John, 181
Salmon, Thomas, 205, 206, 211, 214
Sanitary Conditions of the Labouring Population of Great British, Report of, 112
Scotland, 57, 109, 113, 119, 135, 165, 185, 206, 218
Scott, Joan, 4, 24
Segalen, Martine, 120
servants, 21, 23, 26, 27, 28, 29, 30, 31, 32, 40, 46, 51, 52, 69–71, 72–3, 75, 79, 81, 82, 98, 120, 124, 127, 129, 130, 156, 157, 161, 198, 219,

servants (*cont'd.*)
227, 229, 252
service and servants in husbandry, 2, 5,
21, 22, 27, 29, 30, 31, 50, ch. 5
passim, 86–7, 90–1, 98, 102, 123,
125, 128, 129, 133, 134, 150, 174,
182, 187, 190, 191, 262, 263, 265
Settlement, Laws of, 80, 81, 87, 238
sex ratio, the, 224–5, 241
sexual morality, 175
sexual division of labour, 15, 35, 38–9,
40, 55, 64, 84, 85, 94, 109, 113–15,
120–1, 127–8, 260, 261–2; *see
also* agriculture
sexual relations, 6–7, 46, 77, 146
Sheffield, 18, 246, 247
shopkeepers, 150, 151, 170, 172, 216,
243, 247, 254
Shorter, Edward, 115
Shrewsbury, 43–4, 166
Shropshire, 159, 165, 166, 167, 168,
218
Slough, 143
Smeaton, John, 182
Smith, Adam, 70
Smith, J. T., 157
Smith, K. J., 98
Smith, William (1790–1858), 107,
114, 116, 254
'Smithfield bargains', 219
smugglers, female, 162
Snell, K. D. M., 2, 5, 54, 55, 62, 84, 85,
98, 154, 194–5, 265
Society for Bettering the Condition and
Increasing the Comforts of the Poor,
68
Somerset, 66, 90
Sophia, 162
Southampton, 86, 98
Spencer, John, 132
spinsters, 7–8, 27, 63, 94, 96, 125,
146, 168, 173, 192, ch. 12 *passim*,
253, 255, 259, 263; *see also* celibacy
spousals, 205–6
Spufford, Margaret, 170
Staffordshire, 17, 99, 165, 166, 256
standard of living debate, 9, 23, 61, 68,
148, 265–6
Staves, Susan, 249
Sterne, Laurence, 95

Stoke, 233
Stone, Lawrence, 185, 191–2, 222,
241
Stout, William, 26, 32–3, 138, 156,
157, 187, 226–7, 242, 248, 252;
Elin, his sister, 138, 226–7, 232,
252; family of, 32–3, 226–7, 252;
mother of, 222, 242, 252
straw-plaiting, 3, 14, 66–7, 173, 236,
256, 259, 261
Sturt, George, 158, 194
Suffolk, 54, 210, 254
Sunderland, 108
Surrey, 55, 60, 89, 90, 93, 94, 141
Sussex, 89–90, 92–3, 96, 99, 232,
236, 242

Talbot, Catherine, 231
teachers and schoolmistresses, 151, 255
textile manufacture, 3, 6, 12, 40–1, 66,
149, 155, 260; cotton, 11, 12, 40–1,
62–3, 65, 148–9, 235, 261; hand
and framework knitting, 48, 62, 65–
6, 121, 236; linen, 34, 67, 149; silk,
149; spinning, 11, 31, 34, 38, 40,
41–2, 48, 51, 63–5, 67, 70, 75, 82,
83, 119, 121, 155, 160, 189, 191,
234–5, 237, 255, 260–1;
technology, 63–4, 261–2; wages,
63–5, 67, 234, 261; weaving, 11,
34, 38, 40–2, 63–5, 93, 155, 165,
261; wool, 34, 40–1, 42, 62–3, 67,
121, 149; *see also* lace-making
Third World, 14, 57, 152, 267
Thirsk, Joan, 14
Thompson, Edward, 44
Tilly, Louise, 4, 24
Todd, Barbara, 7, 241
towns, 16–18, 19, 38–9, 50, 54, 65,
67, 72, 86, 126, 129, 139, 150, 156,
163, 165, 172, 224, 232, 238
Turner, Thomas, 133, 137, 144, 159,
161, 178, 184, 192–3, 212, 242;
Molly Hicks, his second wife, 144,
178, 192–3, 242
Twamley, J., 31

United States, 14
unmarried mothers, 137–8
urbanization, 13, 18, 19

Vancouver, Charles, 91
Varley, Charles, 121, 165
vegetable-gatherers, 35, 154, 165, 166
Vicinus, Martha, 222
Vincent, David, 47

Wakefield, Priscilla, 228
Wales and the Welsh, 17, 20, 21, 35,
   47, 53, 55, 58, 109, 118, 121, 125–
   6, 139, 165, 166, 168, 177, 184,
   189, 206, 209
Wall, Richard, 7, 22, 233, 234
Warwick, 96
Warwickshire, 17, 36, 89–90, 94, 96,
   98, 134, 254, 261
washing, 28, 29, 82, 101, 105, 106,
   107–12, 115, 121, 127, 133, 139,
   154, 155, 156, 157, 158, 160, 161,
   236, 255
washerwomen and laundresses, 133,
   150, 155–61, 172, 236, 255
watchmakers, 92, 247
Watts, Isaac, 141
'wealing', 257
Welch, Saunders, 143
Wesley, John, 118, 176
Westmorland, 75, 235
White, Gilbert, 114–15, 164
Whitfield, George, 176
widowers, 144, 178, 192, 234, 242
widows, 7, 8, 27, 37, 41, 63, 86, 87,
   94, 96, 101, 102, 143, 146, 158,
   203, 206, 222, 225, 228, 230, 232,
   233–4, ch. 13 *passim*, 263; *see also*
   dower
wife-beating, 198–200, 216
wife sale, 6–7, 146, 211, 215–20
Wilson, Adrian, 120
Wiltshire, 15, 31, 34, 89–90, 94, 96,
   98, 114, 165, 167, 213, 261
Winchester Settlement Examinations,
   100, 255
wives, 7, 27, 34, 44–6, 49, 97, 99,
   124, 146, 152, 153, 155–6, 190,
   192, 193, 221, 229, 242, 249;
   agricultural labourers' wives, 29, 34,
   36, 38, 47, 53, 55, 60, 65, 119, 159,
   169, 191–2, 194; clothiers' wives,
   41–3, 48, 64, 247; colliers' wives,
   44, 194; farmers' wives, 28–33, 45,

47, 49–52, 78–9, 119, 153, 192;
   journeymen clothiers' wives, 41, 48;
   lead-miner's wife, 44, 194;
   smallholders' and cottagers' wives,
   23, 27, 33–4, 47, 52–3, 60, 61, 63,
   83–4, 90, 120, 151, 191–2;
   tradesmens' and artisans' wives, 51,
   93, 102, 126, 139, 155, 170, 191–2,
   243, 244, 245, 246, 248; *see also*
   housewives and housework, widows,
   wife-beating, wife sale
Wollstonecraft, Mary, 186, 229, 231;
   The Wrongs of Woman, 159, 198
women as child-bearers and rearers, 8,
   27, 34, 45, 104, 202, 259, 264;
   north–south divide in experience of,
   2–3, 52, 55–8, 64, 84; in towns, 8,
   18; 'women's trades', 85, 91–2, 93,
   94, 95–6, 102, 149, 173, 259–60;
   see also agriculture, domestic
   industry, housewives, spinsters,
   widows, wives
Wood, John, 118
Woodforde, Parson James, 134–5,
   136, 138, 159, 164;
Woodstock, 66
Woodward, George, 110, 131, 132,
   135, 136–7, 184; Albinia, his wife,
   162–3
Worcester, 66
Wright, Thomas (1736–99), 135, 140,
   179, 185, 193–4, 242, 245, 255
Wrightson, Keith, 21–2
Wrigley, E. A., 19
Wrigley E. A. and Schofield, R., 223,
   225, 238, 241
Wycherley, *The Plain Dealer*, 196

Yeovil, 66
York Dialogue, A, 178–9, 209–10
York, Vale of, 165
Yorkshire, 17, 30, 35, 37, 42, 43, 52,
   58, 67, 119, 189, 235, 245, 249; East
   Riding, 105, 165; West Riding, 15,
   17, 40, 41, 48, 62, 165
Young, Arthur, 35, 55, 57, 66, 67, 71,
   74, 75, 80, 243
*Young Coalman's Courtship to a
   Creelwife's Daughter, The*, 191